D1297413

DISCOURSES
ADDRESSED TO
MIXED CONGREGATIONS

THE WORKS OF
CARDINAL JOHN HENRY NEWMAN
BIRMINGHAM ORATORY
MILLENNIUM EDITION
VOLUME VI

SERIES EDITOR

JAMES TOLHURST DD

DISCOURSES
ADDRESSED TO
MIXED CONGREGATIONS

BY

JOHN HENRY CARDINAL NEWMAN

with an Introduction and Notes by

JAMES TOLHURST DD

Gracewing.

NOTRE DAME

First published in 1849
Published in the Birmingham Millennium Oratory Edition in 2002
jointly by

Gracewing	University of Notre Dame Press
2 Southern Avenue	310 Flanner Hall
Leominster	Notre Dame
Herefordshire HR6 0QF	IN 46556 USA

Library of Congress Cataloging-in-Publication Data
Newman, John Henry, 1801-1890.
　　Discourses addressed to mixed congregations/by John Henry Cardinal Newman; with an introduction and notes by James Tolhurst.
　　　p. cm. — (Birmingham Oratory millennium edition; v. 6)
　　Includes bibliographical references.
　　ISBN 0-268-02557-6 (cloth)
　　　1. Catholic Church—Sermons. 2. Sermons, English—19th century.
　I. Tolhurst, James. II. Title. III. Series.

BX1756.N5 D5 2003
252'.02—dc21　　　　　　　　　　　　　　　　　　　2002026638

UK ISBN 0 85244 455 9
US ISBN 0-268-02557-6

Additional typesetting by Action Publishing Technology Ltd,
Gloucester, GL1 5SR
Printed in England by MPG Books Ltd, Bodmin PL31 1EG

CONTENTS

NOTE ON THE TEXT
Discourses Addressed to Mixed Congregations
In this Millennium Edition, the text on pp. 1–376
follows the uniform Longmans Edition, published by
Longmans, Green & Co., London, 1891.

DEDICATION

To the pastor of Monrovia, Fr Charles Ramirez,
and his parishioners.

INTRODUCTION

Newman commented that his *Discourses* would be 'more rhetorical than my former sermons'.[1] In fact there is a natural sequence which leads from *Sermons on Subjects of the Day* to his *Sermons preached on Various Occasions*. The Anglican sermons were discourses that Newman, as the pastor, had with his congregation, which we are told he preached in a soft and conversational manner. But they did not lack their rhetorical aspects.

When he became a Catholic (and Catholics, he was told did not 'read' sermons) there was an inevitable adjustment. The very nature of Roman Catholicism imposes on the preacher a desire to be more dogmatic, because doctrine is of the essence of Catholic faith. This does not mean hectoring, but it does mean definite teaching, woven in to the scriptural presentation. For those who come to Roman Catholicism late in life (like Newman) the riches of the faith exert an almost magnetic fascination, with the consequent desire to display them in a way which will show them at their most attractive.

[1] *Letters and Diaries* XIII, p. 335.

It is perhaps necessary to explain the term *mixed congregation* which Newman uses on page 264 'I trust I need at present have none in insisting, before a congregation however mixed, on the mysteries or difficulties which attach to the doctrine of God's existence.' These discourses were aimed at an audience which comprised many Roman Catholics and also those who may have had a Christian affiliation to another Church or may have had no particular faith. According to Faber, the poor came to the early Masses, and 'shopkeepers' (among a congregation of 600) to late Benediction. Birmingham, as we shall mention later was a growing industrial city with its share of Unitarians, Plymouth Brethren and Agnostics. When Newman came to publish his *Sermons preached on Various Occasions*, he said they were 'polemic and hortatory after all, rather than dogmatic, and addressed to those who are external to the Church'.[2] The *Discourses* because they were not confined to that particular readership, were dogmatic, but did not lack their polemical side. We are fortunate in now being able to compare them with the sermons he preached between 1848 and 1849 (published as *Catholic Sermons* in 1957). If we look through the *Parochial and Plain Sermons*, however, there is that insistence on the need to attend to the faith and ritual of the Church of England, and to take it seriously because one's eternal destiny was at stake. In that sense, there is logic in Newman's words in the *Discourses* when he says 'He (=God) wishes to bring you further, He wishes to bestow on you the fullness

[2] *Sermons preached on Various Occasions (OS)*, p. vi.

of His blessing, and to make you Catholics'.[3] Hutton maintained that although the *Discourses* lacked for him 'the delicate charm of the reserve, and I might almost say the shy passion of his Oxford sermons, they represent the full-blown blossom of his genius, while the former show it only in bud'.[4]

The *Discourses* also occupy a place directly related to Newman's two novels. He had just completed *Loss and Gain* which was loosely based on the experience of a friend who had become a Roman Catholic, and drew on Newman's own experience. He had also begun *Callista*, which was part of the genre of historical fiction popular at the time (Wiseman's *Fabiola* would mine the same literary vein) and would be an argument for Catholicism, set against the background of North Africa in the time of Cyprian. It was begun in 1848 but would not be published until 1856.

Contemporary Background

Fr Stephen Dessain, the first editor of the *Letters and Diaries* maintains that the first sermon which Newman preached in Alcester Street formed the basis of the first *Discourse*.[5] This is all the more likely as we can also compare it with the series of sermons he preached at St Chad's in Birmingham between 30 January and 26 March 1848. Newman used the circumstances to prompt his work. He says in his foreword to *The Idea of a University* 'It has been the fortune of the author through life, that the Volumes which he has published

---

[3] *Discourses Addressed to Mixed Congregations (Discourses)*, p. 212.

[4] Richard H. Hutton, *Cardinal Newman*, London, Methuen, 1891, p. 197.

[5] Note on *Letters and Diaries* XIII, p. 22.

have grown for the most part out of the duties which lay upon him, or out of the circumstances of the moment. Rarely has he been master of his own studies.'[6]

For one thing, Newman's arrival in Birmingham was largely fortuitous. He wrote to Mrs Bowden in November 1849 'I am in Birmingham simply because Dr Wiseman (the bishop of the Midland district) put me here – nor had I the opportunity of changing the arrangement.'[7] The final part of the sentence is the interesting bit – implying that Newman might well have made an alteration, since he did not regard Birmingham as of any particular merit, in comparison, say with London, or with Oxford. However, since he was there, he intended to use the situation, which plainly needed a Catholic presence, due to the enormous influx of Irish immigrants drawn by the growing industrial might of the Midlands. He came to appreciate the advantages of the Midlands, because it enabled him to study and to write in a certain tranquility.

Those who have seen the present Oratory Church in Edgbaston (which was erected after Newman's death) should not think that the building in Alcester Street, Deritend (near the present Bus Station) resembles it even remotely. Newman says laconically that it was 'a gloomy gin distillery of which we have taken a lease.'[8] The house in Warwick Street where the fathers would live, needed work done to it, which

---

[6] *Advertisement* to *Idea* (November 1858).

[7] To Mrs Bowden, 9 November 1849, *Letters and Diaries* XIII, p. 286.

[8] To Henry Wilberforce, 9–25 December 1848, *Letters and Diaries* XII, p. 382. Newman has the pastoral context in mind and mentions the Scriptural quotation 'the harvest is great, but the labourers are few' (Matt. 9:37).

meant that from February to December they would have to contend with builders – which, as everyone knows – adds to the strain of any house moving. There is something rather touching about the actual arrival of furnishings at the new house (so very different from his lodgings in Oriel) on Friday 26 January 1849. He itemises 'a bag of books, a box of rattle traps loose, a large basket of vials and gallipols, a violin and case, a ditto belonging to F. Richard (Stanton), a box of relics, a large box containing the Spanish crucifix, a large glass case to go over the same, a plaister madonna, a plaister crucifix, a saucer of china shells, and the plaister decorated cross from the Guest Room.'[9]

The workload was immediately apparent: 'Our church is crowded to the very street – and we have been unable to shut the door – and so been obliged to give Benediction to the opposite pavement – but there seems no chance of our getting a larger one. There is hardly a rich Catholic in Birmingham.'[10] The evening service comprised English Compline, in spite of the translation of Psalm 91:5 which read 'the business which walketh in darkness' ... Coupled with the crowds, cholera broke out, and Newman and Ambrose St John went to Bilston, the source of the outbreak, until the epidemic peaked. The people wept at their going, and while they were in Deritend gave them monstrances, chalices and – in good Catholic tradition – bottles of Bass pale ale! Edward

---

[9] To Miss M. R. Giberne, 23 July 1849, *Letters and Diaries* XIII, p. 239.
[10] To Miss M. R. Giberne, 30 October 1849, *Letters and Diaries* XIII, p. 278. He writes to J. M. Capes, 14 February 1849, 'Boys and girls flow in for instructions as herrings in season.' *Letters and Diaries* XIII, p. 47.

Caswell, who was soon to join the Oratory, lost his wife to the disease (on 22 September). When he joined the community, his money was able to finance the move to Edgbaston.

But until that time, the community was in dire straits economically. Newman wrote to F. W. Faber in London 'I have got two groats† in my pocket. Also, we have summed up the accounts to Michaelmasday, and find that we are £60 minus.' He also noted that he could not afford new shoes or stockings or give anything to charity.[11] He would write later, rather pained at the London Oratory fathers' extravagance (knowing that their offertory collection amounted to £30 whereas Alcester Street could only manage £3) '£15 and ten shillings is the actual sum in hand. Tell me where to get any thing else from last year, and I will gladly do so.'[12] Newman strongly believed in good management (he had been bursar at Oriel). He was faced with the problem of serving a growing and poverty-stricken congregation and establishing a new religious house. The *Discourses* would be preached to the people *and* would help to pay for the upkeep of the new Oratory.

Anti-Catholicism in early Victorian England

It has been said, not without a certain amount of truth, that the residual religion of the English is anti-

†a groat = four pence

[11] To F. W. Faber, 17 November 1849, *Letters and Diaries* XIII, p. 294. Michaelmas is 29 September, a quarter day, used in financial audits.

[12] To Richard Stanton, 6 November 1849, *Letters and Diaries* XIII, p. 76. It is difficult to gauge the exact value of money but a male cloth presser in a Leeds factory earned £1.7s 0d a week in 1840 and Anthony Trollope, the future novelist, was paid an annual salary by the Post Office of £140 in 1841.

popery. There is a strange paradox that the average inhabitant of the British Isles in the early days of Queen Victoria's reign, considered himself tolerant and broad-minded in most matters but in the view of an impartial observer 'was fanatically opposed to Roman Catholicism'.[13]

In our days when religion has largely ceased to be a burning topic, and devotional practice is confined to a very small percentage, it is hard to realise that Catholics could provoke such feelings. But the Test Act of 1674, making subscription to the Thirty-Nine Articles of the Church of England a condition for civil office, public or military guaranteed 'that No Papist can possibly creep into any Employment'. In 1700 rightful Catholic heirs to an estate had to surrender their inheritance in favour of any Protestant claimant. In 1754 the celebration of Catholic marriages was made a criminal offence. A quarter of a century later, a violent riot started at St George's Fields in South London fuelled by proposals to relax anti-Catholic legislation, (to be dramatised by Dickens in *Barnaby Rudge*) which rampaged in search of chapels and their clergy. This resulted in the last declaration of martial law England has known. It showed the depth of English prejudice in a dramatic way.

If we had any doubt that this was still the case when Newman moved to Alcester Street, we have only to read *The Times* when Dr Wiseman was named the new Archbishop of Westminster in 1850, and issued his famous pastoral letter 'From out the Flaminian Gate'. The editorials on 'Papal Agression', blustering with

[13] Jaroslav Pelikan, *The Christian Tradition*, Volume 5, 'Christian Doctrine and Modern Culture', Chicago University Press, 1990, p. 11.

rage, commented that it was 'one of the grossest acts of folly and impertinence which the Court of Rome has ventured to commit since the Crown and People of England threw off its yoke'.[14] Dr Wiseman was quick to allay suspicions, but he was still burnt in effigy along with Guy Fawkes and the Pope on 5th November. Newman was under no illusions. Fr Bacchus, who was the first editor of *Sermon Notes* reminds us that 'from various causes the no-popery feeling (in Birmingham) was particularly strong'.[15] Newman himself had been warned by Wilberforce at the end of February that there were anti-Catholic lectures in the city.[16]

This explains Newman's comments that his *Discourses* 'were more rhetorical than his former sermons'. He had to get his audience questioning their prejudices, without arousing greater fears. The tack he employed was to draw attention to the widespread de facto ignorance of religion. He maintained to his congregation that the average Englishman 'has a secret antipathy to religious truths and religious doings, a disgust which *he is scarcely aware of* (my italics)'.[17] This vagueness in matters religious is then mixed with unconscious feelings about Catholicism: 'numbers, too, hear very little about Catholicism, or a great deal of abuse and calumny against it'.[18] There is an in-built bias in the English mind against the Catholic Church,

[14] *The Times* editorial of 14 October mentions 'the new-fangled Archbishop of Westminster'. It was followed by editorials on 19 and 22 October. See *Sermons preached on Various Occasions*, pp. 317–327 for documents.

[15] *Sermon Notes of Cardinal Newman*, p. v.

[16] 28 February 1849, *Letters and Diaries* XIII, p. 71.

[17] *Discourses*, p. 12.

[18] Ibid., p. 192.

he asserts. 'The truth is that the world, know(s) nothing of the blessings of the Catholic faith, and prophes(ies) nothing but ill concerning it'.[19] It is this mentality which leads to strange conjectures about what Catholics are and believe. This extends to miracles which are branded 'lying wonders'[20] and the whole structure which involves people 'pinning their faith upon Pope or Council'.[21] It is all priestcraft: 'to insist on this surrender of the reason, and superstition to make it'.[22] In a contemporary publication, William Taylor deprecatingly demands 'We do not ask what Romish priests are when surrounded by Protestantism but what (they are) where the system develops itself without restraint?'[23] Newman tells his congregation 'When it sees a Catholic priest, it looks hard at him, to make out how much there is of folly in his composition, and how much of hypocrisy'.[24] Newman will again confront this issue in *Present Position of Catholics* and his *Apologia*.

'A very sensible man. . .'

Since he was a stranger to Birmingham, Newman would not deliberately antagonise his congregation (nor would he seek to alienate the many Irish parishioners). He would appeal to their national pride, as

[19] Ibid., p. 221. Newman tells a congregation in St Chad's Church in Birmingham in 1848 'They go, not by their private judgement, but their private prejudice and by their private liking.' *Catholic Sermons of John Henry Newman*, C. S. Dessain (ed.), London, Burns & Oates, 1957, p. 61.

[20] Ibid., p. 205.

[21] *Discourses*, p. 202.

[22] Ibid., pp. 202–3.

[23] *Popery, Its Characteristics and Its Crimes*, London, 1847.

[24] Ibid., p. 222.

being the new power house for imperial expansion. Many of his listeners (and readers) would know, or work for these industrialists. They would agree that these were 'sensible, prudent and shrewd men'.[25] They would be flattered at Newman's delineation of the cultured Englishman 'So comprehensive a mind! Such a power of throwing light on a perplexed subject, and bringing conflicting ideas or facts into harmony! Such a speech it was that he made on such and such an occasion ... It was the saying of a very sensible man.'[26] They would be well aware of the accompaniments of upper class breeding: 'You have not learned the manners, nor caught the tone of good society; you have no share in the largeness of mind, the candour, the romantic sense of honour, the correctness of taste, the consideration for others, and the gentleness which the world puts forward as its highest type of excellence.'[27]

These characteristics, Newman would point out, were precisely those disseminated by the Established Church 'The national religion has many attractions; it leads to decency and order, propriety of conduct, justness of thought, beautiful domestic tastes'.[28] His hearers would be nodding their agreement at such an appreciation of the finer aspects of the English character which was responsible for governing an empire and ruling the waves. Newman knew all about English character. He had a great admiration for what constituted a gentleman – integrity, culture, good

[25] *Discourses*, p. 13.
[26] Ibid., p. 40.
[27] Ibid., p. 114.
[28] Ibid., p. 102.

taste and compassion – which explains his appreciation of Anthony Trollope, who makes his heroes espouse these qualities. At the same time Newman now belonged to that particular sub-culture which was so abhorrent to the English Church-going public.

Newman would point out that behind that suave veneer of good taste and engaging manners, there was an underlying irreligiousness. He would point out that many 'think it a mark both of reverence and good sense to be shocked, when they hear the Man [=Jesus] spoken of simply and plainly as God'.[29] There was a price to pay if you wedded religion to class, and Newman affirmed 'The established form itself is but the religion of a class'.[30] He would go so far as to say that one could admire 'the pure and beautiful English of its prayers, its literature, the piety found among its members ... its historical associations, its domestic character, the charm of a country life'[31] but underneath it all, 'Religion is simply a personal concern; there is no such thing really as a common or joint religion, that is, one in which a number of men, strictly speaking, partake; it is all a matter of private judgment.'[32] His congregation would be bound to agree that this was fair but they would not like to draw the conclusion that Newman drew for them 'Protestants, generally speaking, have not faith, in the primitive meaning of the word'.[33]

[29] Ibid., p. 346.

[30] Ibid., p. 252.

[31] Ibid., pp. 230–1. His friend John Keble had opted for a country parish after his years at Oriel.

[32] Ibid., p. 147.

[33] Ibid., p. 201 and also 'I mean to say that the great mass of men in this country have not this particular virtue called faith' (p. 194).

Priestcraft and mortification

Newman did not intend to be deliberately provoca-
tive, (although his remarks about Protestant Anglo-
Saxon views of Ireland[34] would seem to be a far from
subtle dig — and as such would have gone down well
with many of his parishioners) but rather to confront
them with their prejudices about Catholicism.

He introduced the word 'priestcraft' because it
was an insulting term. Dr George Hickes, an exact
contemporary says that there were those 'who called
the divine institution of priesthood by the spiteful
name of priestcraft'.[35] Newman wanted his readers
and the English in his congregation to face up to
their attitudes, which had been honed by years of
imperial pride and anti-Catholic propaganda. In spite
of being considered enlightened and broad-minded,
insofar as Rome was concerned, the English adopted
other criteria: 'How narrow-minded is this world at
bottom after all, in spite of its pretences and in spite
of appearances!'[36]

Newman could have further analysed the innate
jingoism present in his countrymen, but instead he
chose to identify what he saw as the underlying
reason for much of the animosity to Catholicism. He
returns again and again in the *Discourses* to the English
attitude to penance and mortification. It was something he had noticed in the press coverage of his stay
in Littlemore when the talk was of monasteries and

---

[34] *Discourses*, p. 252. 'He [=the Saracen] made as little impression upon
Spain as the Protestant Anglo-Saxon makes on Ireland.

[35] *Several Letters which passed between Dr George Hickes and a Popish Priest*,
London, 1705, p. 203.

[36] *Discourses*, p. 186.

the hint was of Catholic penances.[37] He would point out that 'voluntary humiliation they did not understand then, [i.e. in Jesus' time] nor do they now'.[38] On the one hand mortification was seen to be unnecessary, since salvation ultimately depends on God and we ought not to force his hand, therefore one should 'disregard all self-reproach, or deprecation, or penance, or mortification, and self-discipline, as affronting or derogatory to that mercy [of God]'.[39] But others resent talk of mortification because they are fond of indulgence. Newman would say frankly 'sinners wonder at those who mortify their passions'. At this point one can imagine some of his congregation beginning to squirm. This area of personal morality was considered sacrosanct ever since Queen Elizabeth had declared that she would not make windows of men's souls. Newman would argue that there were many who considered sensual inclinations, provided they did no harm, should be indulged not mortified – which, as a theory has a long ancestry – 'it sees that nature has a number of tendencies, inclinations, and passions; and because these are natural, it thinks that each of them may be indulged for its own sake, so far as it does no harm to others, or to a person's bodily, mental, and temporal

[37] Ibid., p. 7. Newman wrote to Miss Giberne on 16 September 1840 'The report is all about Warwickshire that a Nunnery is already set up at Littlemore.' *Letters and Diaries* VII, p. 392. He would write to his bishop 'No monastery is in process of erection, no "chapel", no "refectory",' on 14 April 1842.

[38] Ibid., p. 312. To a congregation at St. Chad's in 1848 Newman says 'fasting is only one branch of a large and momentous duty, the subdual of ourselves to Christ'. *Catholic Sermons*, p. 67.

[39] Ibid., p. 7.

well-being.'[40] In fact, in words which would hearten many today, he would say that for many sin is the very want of moderation – it was going to excess.[41] It was only a step to say therefore that sin and indulgence should be defended! 'If an impulse be allowable in itself, it must be always right in an individual, nay, that self-gratification is its own warrant, and that temptation is the voice of God.'[42] He would reduce the argument to its horrendous conclusion: 'It cannot be wrong to follow that nature which God has given us'.[43] But mortification is nothing if it is not animated by charity: 'Nothing but charity can enable you to live well or to die well'[44] and 'Those who are without love of God cannot really be pure.' But mindful of English sensibilities he doesn't harp on the theme, and in one place, changes the word 'purity' to 'sanctity'.[45]

It is this failure, however, to accept the real nature of sin which lay behind much of the venom directed at the structure of the Catholic Church. It was because Catholicism deliberately confronted sin, in its priests, its penances, its confessionals, that it made the English

---

[40] *Discourses*, p. 148. Tertulian (d. 230) denounced the theory that a member of the Church could become superior in holiness through self-indulgence (*De Jejunio* 17.4. CCSL 2:1276).

[41] Ibid., p. 148.

[42] Ibid., p. 12.

[43] Ibid., p. 23. See also 'Concupiscence it concludes, may be indulged because it is in its first element natural. (The world) sanctifies that very concupiscence which is the world's corruption' (pp. 149–50).

[44] Ibid., p. 80. Newman also reminds people that charity is the essence of perfect contrition, and says that 'nothing but a powerful act of charity which blots them out will be of avail to you'.

[45] Ibid., p. 95 and also (in the 1891 edition) 'the most dazzling purity is but as iciness and desolation unless it draws its life from fervent love'. See *Appendix* 2.

uncomfortable, who had previously liked either not to discuss such matters or to be free to commit sin in private. This, Newman argued, explained the attack on celibacy, the mockery of holy persons and holy things 'as far as they come across him'.[46] One should not be surprised that Newman would end his *Discourses* by putting before his audience the image of the Virgin Mother of God, and affirming that 'it is the boast of the Catholic Religion that it has the gift of making the young heart chaste'.[47] The answer to such subterfuge about sin and sensuality was to put the case for the triumph of chastity and purity and the power of God to overcome temptation in us, what Newman would call 'those awful doctrines of grace, which condemn the world, and which the world cannot endure'.[48]

The 'tone' of the Discourses

Newman considered that religion was a serious matter. He would no more have thought of starting with a joke than he would have used slang. He intended his words to provide food for thought, and when he became a Catholic he found simply that there was more material! He wrote to Richard Stanton of the London Oratory in November 1849 'I must have *matter* in what I deliver, if it is to be worth anything.'[49] Newman did not see any contradiction in his conversion to Catholicism because he had always

[46] Ibid., pp. 11–12.

[47] Ibid., p. 376. Also 'purity prepares the soul for love and love confirms the soul in purity' (p. 63, 1891 ed).

[48] Ibid., p. 148.

[49] To Richard Stanton, 30 December 1849, *Letters and Diaries* XIII, p. 352.

been concerned with doctrine, as he asserted in his
Apologia: 'from the age of fifteen, dogma has been the
fundamental principle of my religion: I know no other
religion; I cannot enter into the idea of any other sort
of religion.'[50]

For the first half of his life, John Henry Newman
sought to instil the very real concept of religion as a
life and death matter, he sought to make the Church
not a plaything, or merely an institution but the living
voice of God which commands our allegiance. At the
heart of that allegiance was the triumph of grace and
the drama of sin. We have already spoken of grace,
but Newman uses the same expression when he talks
of sin: 'Take His [=God's] word, or rather, His deed,
for the truth of this awful doctrine, – that a single
mortal sin is enough to cut you off from God for
ever'.[51] If these words are shocking today, it is largely
because we do not hear them spoken very often, but
they constitute a tract of theology known as 'The Last
Things': Death, Judgement, Hell and Heaven. It was
also part of Anglican belief, even if not presented in
such dogmatic form, that hell was a possibility for
sinners, just as certainly as was the mercy of God to
pardon us.

This leitmotif will recur throughout the *Discourses*.
Newman will emphasise the nature of divine grace
– God's mercy to us, his care and providence, the
light which he provides and the Church which
embodies that grace as well as the saints who manifest it. He will contrast that with the nature of sin,
the final end of our life, the impact of sin on the

[50] *Apologia Pro Vita Sua*, p. 2.
[51] *Discourses*, p. 34.

humanity of Jesus in his passion (which was shared by the Virgin Mary in her sorrows). Newman is uncompromising in his presentation of the reality of sin and eternal judgement: 'some have been cut off and sent to hell for their first sin.'[52] 'They are waking up into God's everlasting wrath.'[53] But he wants to make clear that there is an appalling ignorance which makes the drama so terrible: 'He forgets that all his sins are in God's hand and in one page of the book of judgment, and already added up against him.'[54] 'The gates of hell have yawned upon him, silently *and without his knowing it*' (my italics).[55] Newman is brought to contrast the successful and urbane businessman who keeps the engine of the British Empire fuelled, with the spiritual poverty that underlies it. He feels bound to make that amorality visible: 'Do you wish to have the judgment which I am led to form about you? It is, that probably you are not in the grace of God at all.'[56]

At the same time, people should realise the hold which sin has, and far from indulging it, should face up to it: 'We may securely prophesy of every man born into the world, that, if he comes to years of understanding, he will, in spite of God's general assistances, fall into mortal sin and lose his soul.'[57] But the cure for this malignancy is to be found in the Catholic

[52] Ibid., p. 32.
[53] Ibid., p. 41.
[54] Ibid., p. 26.
[55] Ibid., p. 10.
[56] Ibid., p. 163 and compare 'The only reason why we are not in certainty of mortal (sin) is that an extraordinary gift is given to those who supplicate for it' (p. 130).
[57] Ibid., p. 8.

Church, affirms Newman 'which alone has grace, which alone has power, which alone has Saints'.[58] Those who are prepared to dismiss Catholicism must reckon the cost. If sin is real and grace is real, then you need a Church which offers true pardon and abundant grace at the same time.

Newman's Catholicism

Immediately after his conversion, people began to say that Newman already regretted his action and was only waiting for an opportunity to return to the Established Church. He did his best to disillusion them.[59] At the root of their argument was the conviction that nobody of Newman's calibre and breeding could possibly envisage belonging to a Church that possessed such low class adherents.

The contemporary point of view varies slightly in its affirmation that Newman remains at heart a representative of the Church of England: 'how Anglican he

---

[58] *Discourses*, p. 61.

[59] Newman wrote to A. J. Hanmer on 11 December 1845: 'I am now so convinced of the truth and divinity of the Catholic Church that I am pained about persons who are external to it in a way in which I was not before' *Letters and Diaries* XI, p. 60 and in a letter to *The Globe* 28 June 1862 'Return to the Church of England! no; "the net is broken, and we are delivered". I should be a consummate fool (to use a mild term) if in my old age I left "the land flowing with milk and honey" for the city of confusion and the house of bondage' *Letters and Diaries* XX, p. 216. See also his statement in *The Apologia* 'I have been in perfect peace and contentment; I never have had one doubt. I was not conscious to myself, on my conversion of any change, intellectual or moral, wrought in my mind. I was not conscious of firmer faith in the fundamental truths of Revelation, or of more self-command; I had not more fervour; but it was like coming into port after a rough sea; and my happiness on that score remains to this day without interruption.' Also the passage in the *Apologia*: 'From the time that I became a Catholic . . . I have been in perfect peace and contentment' (p. 238).

still was in his manners and attitudes'.[60] A very brief perusal of *Discourses* gives quite another picture. In his second Discourse, he puts in the mouth of his character the politically incorrect phrase 'I am a Catholic; I am not an unregenerate Protestant.'[61] He goes on to remark that Catholicism is directly opposed to the faith of the Established Church: 'It will be found that either the Catholic Religion is verily and indeed the coming in of the unseen world into this, or that there is nothing positive, nothing dogmatic, nothing real, in any of our notions as to whence we come and whither we are going. Unlearn Catholicism, and you open the way to your becoming Protestant, Unitarian, Deist, Pantheist, Sceptic, in a dreadful, but inevitable succession.'[62] In Birmingham, a centre for Unitarianism, with the Martineau connection, his remarks would not have passed unnoticed. As if to hammer home the point he affirms roundly 'No man alive of fair abilities would put undoubting faith and reliance in the Church Established, except by doing violence to his reason.'[63] If people still demur and say that he is still holding on to a more purified *Via Media* Church, then what do they make of Newman's appeal? 'And you, my brethren, also, if such be present, who are not as yet Catholics, but who by your coming hither seem to show your interest in our teaching, and you wish to know more about it, you too remember, that though you may not yet have faith in the Church, still God

[60] Clifford Longley, *The Worlock Archives*, London, Geoffrey Chapman, 2000, p. 36.
[61] *Discourses*, p. 39.
[62] Ibid., p. 282.
[63] Ibid., p. 179.

has brought you into the way of obtaining it. You are under the influence of His grace; He has brought you a step on your journey; He wishes to bring you further, He wishes to bestow on you the fulness of His blessing, and to make you Catholics.'[64]

There is very little difference between Newman's sentiments and the words used by the Passionist priest, Fr Ignatius Spencer (an ancestor of Princess Diana) in his 1839 Crusade of Prayer for Christian Unity. 'I plainly declare to you that I believe you to be in error and that I most ardently desire to lead you to believe as I do.' Newman would say 'outside of that fold in which alone is salvation.'[65]

Major themes in the Discourses
Newman began to preach his sermons on 2 February and finished by 27 October (the dedication is dated 'S. Caroli = St Charles' whose feast day is 4 November). As can be seen from the distribution plan given on p. 425 the liturgical framework can be uncovered. It is likely for instance that *Neglect of Divine Calls and Warnings, God's Will the End of Life, Faith and Private Judgment* and *Faith and Doubt* would have been preached in the Lenten season. They also tie in with the first discourse *The Salvation of the Hearer, the Motive of the Preacher* and the second, *Neglect of Divine Calls and Warnings*. These may have been talks to novices or at Benediction. It is also reasonable to surmise that *Mental Sufferings of Our Lord in His Passion* would have been preached in what was then called Passiontide (the last two weeks of Lent) and that

[64] *Discourses*, p. 212.
[65] Ibid., p. 9.

The Mystery of Divine Condescension and *The Infinitude of the Divine Attributes* would either have been given as meditations or Holy Hours (reflections given at Benediction). The two discourses on Mary, *The Glories of Mary for the Sake of her Son* and *On the Fitness of the Glories of Mary* could well have been sermons during May, as it is the Oratory custom to honour Mary during this month with particular services. This leaves the discourses on Grace (Nos 8, 9 and 13). If we refer to *Sermon Notes* we find reference to a sermon on 1 July, *Purity and Love*. On 22 July there is a note against *Mysteries of Nature and Grace* which says 'not preached'. As Newman was accustomed to giving courses of sermons, it is likely that *Mysteries of Nature and of Grace, Illuminating Grace* and *Perseverance in Grace* can be put at this time. This leaves us with the fifth discourse: *Saintliness the Standard of Christian Principle* which could be 'the filler' prompted by the other discourses, to give cohesion to the collection, or it may have formed part of a meditation given to the community, or at Benediction (see comment above). This leaves *Prospects of the Catholic Missioner* which we can fix for evening Benediction at the opening of the London Oratory on 31 May 1849. Despite his dislike of 'formal occasional sermons' and the suffocating heat which caused Bishop Wiseman (now in the London district) to sweat 'through to his alb', Newman felt 'it went well'.[66] Those few words hint at the uneasy relationship between the two communities and their respective superiors.

[66] *Letters and Diaries* XIII, p. 167.

1. Faith

The thread which binds all the *Discourses* together is
Newman's conviction of his Catholicism, and his wish
to present it in as attractive and compelling a form as
he can. This can be seen from his conclusion of the
first discourse which states: 'It requires nothing great,
nothing heroic, nothing saint-like; it does but require
conviction, and that we have, that the Catholic
Religion [Newman uses the Anglican phrase] is given
from God for the salvation of mankind, and that all
other religions are but mockeries ...'[67] Against this
background we can locate Newman's comments on
faith, grace, the Church and the Incarnation.

Newman wants to point out that *faith* may have the
same expression but it has a different meaning for
Catholics which it does not possess for others. This is
not just a question of semantics. Newman tells his
hearers 'Now I mean to say that the great mass of men
in this country have not this particular virtue called
faith, have not this virtue at all.'[68]

Such a virtue is bound up with the concept of
authority – it is the acceptance of truths 'since God
says it is true, not with His own voice, but by the
voice of His messengers.'[69] The majority of English
people cannot 'submit their minds to living men,
who have not their own cultivation, or depth of
intellect.'[70] This same majority is quite prepared to
accept all of Scripture 'on faith' but this is something
purely mechanical 'nothing better than a prejudice or

[67] *Discourses*, p. 20.
[68] Ibid., p. 194.
[69] Ibid., p. 194.
[70] Ibid., p. 204.

inveterate feeling impressed on them when they were children'.[71] There is in fact a suspension of belief, which allows either of a constant state of doubt or gradually drifts into agnosticism. This explains the repugnance against so-called Catholic 'tyranny' of the will. There is a common misunderstanding that Catholics are forced to believe by the structure of the Church, which does not allow any freedom of choice. But this is to mistake the very essence of faith. It is not some transient emotion which allows of doubt: 'A person who says, "I believe just at this moment, but perhaps I am excited without knowing it, and I cannot answer for myself, that I shall believe tomorrow", does not believe now. A person who says, "Perhaps I am in a kind of delusion, which will one day pass away from me, and leave me as I was before"; or "I believe as far as I can tell, but there may be arguments in the background which will change my view", such a man has not faith at all.'[72] Catholics believe on the strength of God revealing, in fact by virtue of the Incarnation itself which commands the faith of those with whom the Son of God shared his humanity. There is no room for doubt once one has grasped that the Catholic Church is from God and speaks with his authority. This may seem to English people like an intellectual imprisonment (Newman speaks of 'a sort of tyranny') but the very nature of faith does not admit of any *caveats*: 'I cannot both really believe it now, and yet look forward to a time when perhaps I shall not believe it; to make provision for future doubt, is to doubt at present ... I may love

[71] Ibid., p. 205.
[72] Ibid., pp. 215–6.

by halves, I may obey by halves; I cannot believe by halves: either I have faith, or I have it not.'[73] Newman does not allow the argument to remain merely on the notional level. He poses the question of a close friendship which is betrayed: 'I should not say a friend trusted me, who listened to every idle story against me; and I should like his absence better than his company, if he gravely told me that it was a duty he owed to himself to encourage his misgivings of my honour.'[74] In the same way does the Catholic come to put absolute trust in the teachings of his Church because he sees them as part of his loving attachment to the God who 'spoke to us in these last days in his Son'. The Catholic is convinced of his faith (this *certainty* will form a major theme in *A Grammar of Assent*) 'faith is not a mere conviction in reason, it is a firm assent, it is a clear certainty greater than any other certainty; and this is wrought in the mind by the grace of God, and by it alone.'[75] In this sense it can be said that the Catholic is *bound* to the Church, yet, says Newman these are 'fetters of love … he is, with the Apostle, the slave of Christ, the Church's Lord'.[76] For many, this will have confirmed their worst suspicions about Catholics, but Newman is unrepentant. Does the Established Church, or indeed any other Christian community *dare* to impose itself on its adherents in such a manner? 'No other religious body has a right to demand such an exercise of faith in it, and a right

[73] *Discourses*, pp. 216–7.

[74] Ibid., p. 219. The source of such conviction is itself a gift: 'Grace gives certainty, reason is never decided.' p. 178. The reference to *The Grammar of Assent* can be found in the note to p. 178.

[75] Ibid., p. 224.

[76] Ibid., p. 221.

to forbid you further inquiry, but the Catholic Church ...'[77] There is in fact no difference between contemporary acts of faith and that demanded of Christians in apostolic times; both demand 'the sacrifice of their own liberty of thought' and those who withheld it 'would have died in their unbelief'.[78]

The extent of unbelief forms a large part of the first discourse, in which the English 'world' is set against the 'secret, hidden world' of the Catholic. Newman wants to confront the concept that Catholics are like the followers of the cult of Mithras in the early centuries, with their own arcane practices. Newman puts forward your average Englishman and tells his hearers to judge for themselves. He portrays a successful man, who would have been well known to Newman and to Birmingham: 'He is gradually educated for the world; he forms his own judgments; chooses his principles, and is moulded to a certain character.'[79] But there is a complete absence of any supernatural life. The intellect is well catered for, but not the soul and, lacking baptism 'reason and sin have gone together from the first'.[80] The advance of years and greater acquaintance with the ways of the world brings a hardening in sin like a callous so that 'by the measure of the world, he is come to an honourable and venerable old age'[81] but in reality a greater drama is being played out and Newman asks 'What about his

[77] Ibid., p. 229. Newman traces the path of those who have first believed 'They begin in self-will and disobedience and they end in apostasy' (p. 217).

[78] Ibid., p. 203.

[79] Ibid., p. 10.

[80] Ibid., p. 9.

[81] Ibid., p. 13.

soul?'[82] In reality the 'sensible man' has not bothered about it, but 'has cast off the thought of God, and set up self in His place'.[83]

There are others who have faith of a sort but it does not go very deep, they 'have no heart for religion'.[84] They allow the lure of their sinfulness to provide excuses for them to forgo the exercises of religion and then to justify their course of action. Newman has in mind those who have lapsed from their religious duties, especially fellow Catholics. He identifies one of the most common causes: despondency. 'Others say that it is no use trying to [serve God as they ought] that they have again and again gone to confession and tried to keep out of mortal sin, and cannot; and so they give up the attempt as hopeless.'[85]

It is also the case that faith demands perseverance if it is to be worthy of the name. Newman is not afraid to put before his fellow Catholics the possibility that even if they are not 'unregenerate Protestants' they can still merit damnation. There is no place in Catholic doctrine for predestination unto good. Newman commented to Faber on his discourse *Neglect of Divine Calls and Warnings* 'It is a saying of St Philip's that no one can hope for heaven, who has not feared hell and contemplated damnation – and in the said sermon I have but made easy-going Catholics in danger of hell'; .... This is behind his remark that a Catholic can be outwardly religious, going to Confession and Communion 'at regular intervals' but

[82] *Discourses*, p. 13.
[83] Ibid., p. 11.
[84] Ibid., p. 25.
[85] Ibid., pp. 22–3.

still be lost 'because he has never really turned his heart to God; or, if he had some poor measure of contrition for a while it did not last beyond his first or second confession'.[86] Newman thus neatly provides at the same time, a cautionary tale for Catholics and a correction for others who think that Catholicism is the home of cheap grace.

2. Grace and Sanctity

For Newman, this grace is no token, but a 'great gift from God' which has been given as something personal: 'lodged in the heart; it purifies the thoughts and motives, it raises the soul to God'.[87] Without such a gift we can never come to faith and love of God: 'We should have lived and died, every one of us, destitute of all saving knowledge and love of Him, but for a gift which we could not do anything ourselves to secure, had we lived ever so well – but for His grace.'[88] Newman is aware of the theological debate about the freedom of human will and the continual providence of God and puts the case with some skill: 'How man is able fully and entirely to do what he will, while God accomplishes His own supreme will also, is hidden from us, as it is hidden from us how God created out of nothing, or how He foresees the future, or how His attribute of justice is compatible with His attribute of love.'[89] It is also designed to work with us in our struggles so as to 'vanquish' nature[90] in

---

[86] Ibid., p. 37; *Letters and Diaries* XIII, p. 341.

[87] Ibid., p. 151.

[88] Ibid., p. 126.

[89] Ibid., p. 125. See Newman's changes for the 1891 edition in *Appendix* 2.

[90] Ibid., p. 49.

Newman's words, which means to uplift what is fallen
in humanity: 'The rebellion of the reason, the
waywardness of the feelings, the disorder of the
thoughts, the fever of passion, the treachery of the
senses.'[91] It is grace which is at the heart of sanctity.

As he is aware that many of his congregation are
imbued with the notion that saints are somehow
'foreign', thanks to centuries of anti-Catholic propaganda, Newman devotes several sections of the
Discourses to the subject. He wants to point out that
saints are neither an invention of Catholicism, nor
some pre-fabrication, which sets them apart from the
rest of humanity. A saint is not exempt from the daily
struggle against sin: 'temptation he has and he differs
from others not in being shielded from it, but in being
armed against it. Grace overcomes nature; it overcomes indeed in all who shall be saved'.[92] But that
does not mean that it is merely something undergone.
Saints must exhibit what is called 'heroic virtue':
'whatever was their special line of duty, they have
been heroes in it'.[93] This must involve a real degree of
fortitude in other words especially in the case of
martyrs: 'Saints overcome with a determination and a
vigour, a promptitude and a success, beyond any one
else.'[94]

For those who argue that certain aspects of sanctity
are not for them, Newman is very sympathetic. He
draws a comparison with the hyperbole of some of
Jesus' sayings: '[Saints] are not always our examples,

[91] *Discourses*, p. 66.
[92] Ibid., p. 98.
[93] Ibid., p. 101. See also note 45.
[94] Ibid., p. 98.

we are not always bound to follow them; not more than we are bound to obey literally some of our Lord's precepts, such as turning the cheek or giving away the coat.'[95] But people need saints as reminders of that call which we have all received to seek first the kingdom of God: 'they are always our standard of right and good; they are raised up to be monuments and lessons, they remind us of God, they introduce us into the unseen world, they teach us what Christ loves, they track out for us the way which leads heavenward'.[96] The fact that saints prove an encumbrance to the conscience of the members of the Established Church is, for Newman, bound up with that resignation in the face of the supernatural and a capitulation to the world: 'It has not power to lead the multitude upward, or to delineate for them the Heavenly City. It comes of mere nature, and its teaching is of nature. It uses religious words, of course, else it could not be called a religion; but it does not impress on the imagination, it does not engrave upon the heart, it does not inflict upon the conscience, the supernatural ...'[97]

But among the saints, Newman devotes particular attention to the Virgin Mary, both by reason of her exaltation by God and because of the peculiar difficulties which she represents for many – especially from Evangelical Protestantism. It has to be stated by Newman that there is no possibility of glorifying Mary at the expense of her Son: 'the glories of Mary are for the sake of Jesus ... we praise and bless her as the first of creatures, that we may duly confess Him as our sole

[95] Ibid., p. 101.
[96] Ibid., p. 102.
[97] Ibid., p. 102.

Creator'.[98] Mary, the unique handmaid of the Lord
shares with every individual member of humanity a
work entrusted to each by God. The difference is that
her work is nothing short of being the Mother of
God: 'She, as others, came into the world to do a
work, she had a mission to fulfil; her grace and her
glory are not for her own sake, but for her Maker's;
and to her is committed the custody of the
Incarnation.'[99] This can be seen in her life as portrayed
to us in the Gospels, thus we find her from her appearance at the marriage feast at Cana to her vigil by the
side of the Cross. Newman points out that Mary
remained always in the background, so that attention
was always focused on her Son: 'You know, when
first He went out to preach, she kept apart from Him;
she interfered not with His work; and, even when He
was gone up on high, yet she, a woman, went not out
to preach or teach, she seated not herself in the
Apostolic chair, she took no part in the priest's office;
she did but humbly seek her Son in the daily Mass of
those, who, though her ministers in heaven, were her
superiors in the Church on earth.'[100]

It is because she was chosen to be the Mother of
God that, Newman argues, Mary receives her other
prerogatives. The debate between Thomists and
Scotists divided over the reasons for the particular
grace of being immaculately conceived. Thomists
(followers of St Thomas Aquinas) considered that this
was a retrospective decree exempting Mary as an
exception to the rule. Scotists (followers of Blessed

[98] *Discourses*, p. 344.
[99] Ibid., pp. 348–9.
[100] Ibid., p. 356.

Duns Scotus, the Franciscan theologian) believed that when the Incarnation was decreed, this was before sin had entered the world, and therefore because of her role, it befitted her to be full of grace 'what ought she to be, what is it *becoming* that she should be, who was so favoured'.[101] In the same way, Newman points out that since it was fitting that she should be full of grace from the first moment of her existence, so it was equally fitting that she should not suffer the human consequences of sin, at the moment of her death. He says that the assumption into heaven was a logical conclusion of her surpassing holiness: 'If such as was her beginning, such was her end, her conception immaculate and her death an assumption.'[102] It is interesting that while he maintains that Mary should not be allowed to decay in the grave because Jesus had taken 'the elements of His human body' from her[103] he leaves open the question of actual death saying 'if she died, but revived, and is exalted on high'.[104] Because she was mortal and the term of her life was over she fulfils 'the debt of nature'[105] which unites her with the rest of humanity. It is no accident that the prayer which Catholics say most frequently, the *Hail Mary* asks for Mary's intercession now and *at the hour of our death*. The assumption of Mary into heaven at the end of her life, is only a logical consequence of her immaculate conception at the beginning of her life.

[101] Ibid., p. 362.
[102] Ibid., p. 374.
[103] Ibid., p. 371.
[104] Ibid., p. 374.
[105] Ibid., p. 372.

3. The Incarnation

Those of his audience who regarded themselves as intelligent and broad-minded harboured great reservations about Catholicism. Newman will maintain that these are somehow related to the fact of the Incarnation: 'they are shocked, and think it a mark both of reverence and good sense to be shocked, when they hear the Man [=Jesus] spoken of simply and plainly as God. They cannot bear to have it said, except as a figure or mode of speaking, that God had a human body, or that God suffered; they think that the "Atonement", and "Sanctification through the Spirit", as they speak, is the sum and substance of the Gospel, and they are shy of any dogmatic expression which goes beyond them.'[106] Needless to say they would not have heard St Irenaeus proclaim 'the Father is the invisible of the Son, the Son the visible of the Father.'[107] This is behind the belittling of Mary because it is easy to say that God somehow walked among his creation, but it is quite another to say God is the Son of the Virgin from Nazareth.

But just as it was fitting for Mary to be full of grace, so Newman argues it 'became Him who is higher than the highest, to act as if even humility, if this dare be said, was in the number of His attributes, by taking Adam's nature upon Himself, and manifesting Himself to men and Angels in it'.[108] Newman had been instructed in his

---

[106] *Discourses*, p. 346. Newman treats of this under 'the heresy of the Neologians' in *Arians of the Fourth century*, p. 88. See Archbishop Williams' note in the Millennium Edition and the reference to R. D. Hampden in note to p. 345 of this volume.

[107] *Adversus Haereses* IV, 6.6.

[108] *Discourses*, p. 299. Newman made clear in a revision to the 1849 text that he accepted Faber's comment 'by the very word "resolve" you exclude the Scotist', 8 December 1849, *Letters and Diaries* XIII, p. 335. See *Appendix* 2 for Textual Variations.

theology by Jesuits at the Collegio Romano, (principally, Frs. Perrone and Passaglia). Unlike the Dominicans, they would have introduced him to the sixteenth-century Jesuit, Francisco Suarez (Doctor Eximius), who incorporated Scotist insights into his theology and this would have reinforced Newman's view that the divine will to become incarnate preceded Adam's sin. Newman quotes the relevant passages from Cardinal de Lugo's tract *De Incarnatione* summarising the Scotist position. These taught that the Redemption was not the sole and adequate reason for the Incarnation but rather, the exaltation of human nature.[109]

The price paid however by the Incarnate Son was not somehow extrinsic – a debt to be settled, and the slate wiped clean. Newman draws attention to the humanity of the Son of God: 'You know, my brethren, that our Lord and Saviour, though he was God, was also perfect man; and hence He had not only a body, but a soul likewise, such as ours, though pure from all stain of evil.'[110] There is still some lingering trace of Apollinaris in most of us that thinks somehow of Jesus without a human soul – with his humanity as a veneer to his divinity. Newman however says that the sufferings which Jesus endured in his passion were that much more acute because he suffered not only in his body but in his soul. In fact he says that 'the agony, [in the garden] a pain of the soul, not of the body, was the first act of His tremendous sacrifice; "My soul is sorrowful even unto death"'.[111]

---

[109] See note on page 321. The Collegio Romano was founded in 1551, and is now known as the Gregorian University.

[110] *Discourses*, p. 324.

[111] Ibid., p. 325.

This human soul was in one sense different to others in that it was not subject to whims or passions but entirely centred on the will of the Father: 'His soul was subjected simply to His Eternal and Divine Personality. Nothing happened to His soul by chance, or on a sudden; He never was taken by surprise; nothing affected Him without His willing beforehand that it should affect Him.'[112] Far from lessening the suffering Jesus underwent in his passion, it is hard to comprehend the deliberate acceptance of the mental torment, with the awareness that behind that torment lay the whole tragedy of sin itself: 'You see how deliberately He acts; He comes to a certain spot; and then, giving the word of command, and withdrawing the support of the Godhead from his soul, distress, terror and dejection at once rush in upon it. Thus He walks forth into a mental agony with as definite an action as if it were some bodily torture, the fire or the wheel.'[113] In that sense his passion 'was an action'[114] confronting sin in its true nature of rebellion by a will that was innocent and uncontaminated: 'He is the One Victim for us all, the sole Satisfaction, the real Penitent, all but the real sinner'.[115] Newman returns to the point which was made clearly about the identity of Jesus – in Him was God made visible and therefore, it was God who suffered for us: '... pain is to be measured by the power of realising it. God was the sufferer; God suffered in His human nature'.[116]

---

[112] *Discourses*, p. 329.
[113] Ibid., p. 334.
[114] Ibid., p. 331.
[115] Ibid., p. 339.
[116] Ibid., p. 331.

4. The Sacraments

The sacraments are the means used to continue the saving work of the Incarnation. It strikes Newman as an unutterable tragedy that in the teeming cities of a highly industrialised nation there is an ignorance of the importance of baptism: '. . . a large town like this is a fearful sight. We walk the streets, and what number are there of those who meet us who have never been baptized at all!'[117] Success, power, reputation, influence count for nothing in the final analysis if there is such a neglect of the need of forgiveness.

It is only through the grace of God, and principally through the sacraments that our sins are forgiven. We tend to regard the whole matter of sin as something trivial and easily to be dismissed but there is a certain inevitability about sin, of which we need to be reminded: 'Though the aids which God gives us are sufficient to enable us to live without sin, yet our infirmity of will and of attention is a match for them, and we do not do in fact that which we might do.'[118] Above all we need to remember what it cost to redeem us. Newman does not embrace all the elements of St Alphonsus Liguori, (the founder of the Redemptorists who had died in 1787 and was famous for his moral theology.) He did however borrow some of his strictures about sin and the implications if we remain unrepentant: 'Go down to the grave with a single unrepented, unforgiven sin upon you, and you have enough to sink you down to hell; you have that, which to a certainty will be your ruin. It may be the

[117] Ibid., p. 9.
[118] Ibid., pp. 129–30.

hundredth sin, or it may be the first sin, no matter: one is enough to sink you; though the more you have, the deeper you will sink.'[119] But the remedy for this is available in the sacraments of forgiveness, Penance (Confession) and Anointing (Extreme Unction). Newman points out that mere routine reception of these sacraments is not sufficient: not for him, the idea of cheap grace. It was quite possible for Catholics to receive Confession regularly, but without any real repentance: 'He comes again and again to the Priest; he goes through his sins; the Priest is obliged to take his account of them, which is a very defective account, and sees no reason for not giving him absolution. He is absolved, as far as words can absolve him; he comes again to the Priest when the season comes round [=Lent]; again he confesses, and again he has the form [=absolution] pronounced over him. He falls sick, he receives the last Sacraments: he receives the last rites of the Church, and he is lost. He is lost, because he has never really turned his heart to God; or, if he had some poor measure of contrition for a while it did not last beyond his first or second confession.'[120] On the other hand, the power of the Sacrament is sufficient to forgive even the gravest of sins. God uses a sinful man – a priest – to be the means by which his compassion is brought to sinners. God in that sense makes use of sin to overcome sin: 'God in His mercy makes use of sin against itself, that He turns past sin into a present benefit, that, while He washes away its guilt and subdues its power, He leaves it in the penitent in such sense as enables him, from his

[119] *Discourses*, p. 34.
[120] Ibid., p. 37. See also Newman's comments on tepidity on p. 163.

knowledge of its devices, to assault it more vigorously, and strike at it more truly...'[121]

But it is the Eucharist which lies at the centre of the Church's worship, that Newman will describe as 'the Presence of the Word Incarnate'.[122] He laments that the world in general cannot comprehend 'the transforming power of the Most Holy Sacrament, the Bread of Angels'.[123] This transformation, or transubstantiation is not a problem for Catholics, for which they are anxious to apologise. Newman links the Eucharist with the Incarnation itself: 'Shocking indeed and most profane! a relief to rid ourselves of the doctrine that Jesus is on our Altars! as well say a relief to rid ourselves of the belief that Jesus is God, to rid ourselves of the belief that there is a God.'[124] It is indeed certainly a mystery: 'Catholics do not see that it is impossible at all, that our Lord should be in Heaven yet on the Altar; they do not indeed see *how* it can be both, but they do not see *why* it should not be; here are many things which exist, though we do not know *how*; do we know *how* anything exists? ... the Catholic doctrine concerning the Real Presence is not more mysterious than how Almighty God can exist, yet never have come into existence.'[125] But such is the central place of the Eucharist that Mary humbly sought her Son in the daily Mass provided by the Apostles.[126]

Newman contrasts the finest wheat and purest

[121] Ibid., p. 56.
[122] Ibid., p. 17.
[123] Ibid., p. 59.
[124] Ibid., p. 185.
[125] Ibid., p. 266.
[126] Ibid., p. 356.

wine, which are chosen for the Eucharist with the very human means that Jesus calls to the priesthood. He would presumably not have been surprised at all by modern publicity about clerical misdeeds because he notes God made 'sons of Adam, sons of your nature, the same by nature, differing only in grace – men like you, exposed to temptations, to the same temptations, to the same warfare within and without; with the same three deadly enemies – the world, the flesh, and the devil; with the same human, the same wayward heart: differing only as the power of God has changed and rules it. So it is; we are not Angels from Heaven that speak to you, but men, whom grace, and grace alone, has made to differ from you.'[127] The priest is seen as a minister therefore of reconciliation (especially through the sacrament of Penance) and intercession (through the Eucharist) because he has 'sins of his own to offer for'[128] and can identify with fellow sinners. Newman does not envisage a lofty and bureaucratic role for the clergy: 'Had Angels been your Priests, my brethren, they could not have condoled with you, sympathised with you, have had compassion on you, felt tenderly for you, and made allowances for you, as we can; they could not have been your patterns and guides, and have led you on from your old selves into a new life, as they can who come from the midst of you, who have been led on themselves as you are to be led, who know well your difficulties; who have had experience, at least of your temptations, who know the strength of the flesh

[127] *Discourses*, p. 45.
[128] Ibid., p. 47.

and the wiles of the devil, even though they have baffled them, who are already disposed to take your part, and be indulgent towards you, and can advise you most practically, and warn you most seasonably and prudently.'[129] This is how the ordinary people of Birmingham remembered Newman himself. Years after his death an old lady, dying in the Birmingham General Hospital, told the chaplain that her own grandmother had years before been in a similar state and had asked for a priest. She told her family when they came to visit her that a kind old gentleman had come from the Oratory and when they went over the list of all the Fathers to discover who it was she identified the eighty-year-old Cardinal: 'Yes, it was Fr Newman,' she confidently answered.[130]

5. The Church

For Newman, acceptance of the claims of Catholicism, now that he had himself made that step, followed on from revelation itself: 'The simple question to be decided is one of fact, has a revelation been given? ... a second remark, and I have done, is this – the teaching of the Church manifestly is that revelation.'[131] For those looking for any anticipation of modern ecumenical approaches Newman, like most Victorians, will prove a disappointment. Hindoos (sic) and gypsies are linked together, Islam is called the Arabian imposture 'of which Mahomet was the framer', and in a final insult, which time has not treated well 'Mahometanism has done little more than

[129] Ibid., pp. 47–8.
[130] Personal contribution to the author.
[131] *Discourses*, pp. 276, 278.

the Anglican communion is doing at present'.[132] Apart
from Christianity there is error (i.e. heathens, pagans
and infidels) and the full expression of Christianity is
in the Catholic Church. One of the functions of the
Church Newman saw from the time of his researches
into the history of the first Councils (which resulted in
The Arians of the Fourth Century) was its ability to
confront and to neutralise error which involved coun-
tering the ever-active mind of man to compound it.
Newman was convinced then, and remained
convinced that the Catholic Church 'can smite and
overthrow error ... She alone has had the Divine spell
of controlling the reason of man, and of eliciting faith
in her word from high and low, educated and ignorant, restless and dull-minded. [Was this a nudge to his
hearers?] Even those who are alien to her, and whom
she does not move to obedience, she moves to respect
and admiration.' He asked only that she be given – in
words which would later be echoed by a chastened
Archbishop Wiseman – 'an open field and freedom to
act'.[133]

The Church needs to be seen in Newman's
context as the living expression of the truth of revelation. This begins in the forum of the conscience
'which Nature begins, Revelation brings to perfection.'[134] It is then taken up by the prophets of the
old covenant – a theme which Newman developed

---

[132] Ibid., 250. Newman is at his most trenchant in this evening sermon
he preached at the opening of the London Oratory.

[133] Ibid., pp. 279 and 253. Archbishop Wiseman hastened to correct the
bad impressions created by 'Out of the Flaminian Gate' by saying that
he only wanted to evangelise the poor and needy of London and did
not intend any sinister ecclesiastical take-over.

[134] Ibid., p. 295.

frequently in his *Parochial and Plain Sermons* 'Revelation was ever in progress in the Jewish period, and pointed by its prophets to a day when it should be spread over the whole earth. Judaism then was local because it was imperfect; when it reached perfection within, it became universal without, and took the name of Catholic.'[135] Newman sees a development in the handing on of revelation which binds both covenants – after all, the Apostles were to sit on twelve thrones to judge the twelve tribes of Israel (Matt. 19:28). If one accepts that authority is needed in the handing on of revelation, we can demand the same faith in that authority. But it is precisely because the Catholic Church still claims such, that her believers do 'pin their faith upon Pope or Council'.[136] In fact Catholics do not put their faith in individuals, any more than they worship the Virgin Mary. They put their faith in the bearers of an office, in the context of revelation itself: 'They were nothing in themselves ... they were an infallible authority, as coming from God.'[137] If you accept the concept of revelation and the need for an authoritative means of propagation, then that, for Newman is the destruction of private judgement.[138] It may be considered a great English treasure, but if it is enshrined at the expense of

---

[135] Ibid., p. 247. For the context in Newman's *Essay on the Development of Christian Doctrine* see note on p. 197 and also the comment on p. 196 'The Church was their teacher'.

[136] Ibid., p. 202. Also 'No other body claims to be infallible, let alone the proof of such a claim', p. 229; the Church has the 'prerogative of infallibility', p. 27.

[137] Ibid., p. 197.

[138] Ibid., p. 197.

authoritiative revelation, then it has nothing to do with apostolic faith and can only lead to disbelief. Newman has made his position clear, but he will state it in unequivocal terms: 'On the long run it will be found that either the Catholic Religion is verily and indeed the coming in of the unseen world into this, of that there is nothing positive, nothing dogmatic, nothing real, in any of our notions as to whence we come and whither we are going.'[139] There is also the need not to be grateful for the small benefits which Catholic emancipation has given if they are at the expense of what is the unchanging faith of the Church. For it is undeniably true, in Newman's view, that we pay dearly for being fully accepted by society: 'is not this the case often ... that the world takes up your interests, because you share its sins?'[140] It is precisely in its attitude to sin that the Church to which Newman belongs shows its character: 'She is Catholic, because she brings a universal remedy for a universal disease.... If sin is a partial evil, let its remedy be partial; but if it be not local, not occasional, but universal, such must be the remedy.'[141]

The poetry of the Discourses

There have been numerous witnesses to the power of Newman's spoken delivery – its quiet and irresistible

---

[139] *Discourses*, p. 282.

[140] Ibid., p. 165.

[141] Ibid., p. 246. The freedom from national and political interference must be part of such universality, so Newman can say 'There is but one form of Christianity ... possessed of that real unity which is the primary form of independence' (p. 252).

force and the majesty of the expressive power of his inflection. Unfortunately there remain no records of his spoken words but becoming a Catholic in no way diminished his artistry and his mastery of the English language.

He displays at times a wonderful gift for conjuring up a scene. This passage, for instance in the sixth Discourse:

Go abroad into the streets of the populous city, contemplate the continuous outpouring there of human energy, and the countless varieties of human character, and be satisfied! The ways are thronged, carriage-way and pavement; multitudes are hurrying to and fro, each on his own errand, or are loitering about from listlessness, or from want of work, or have come forth into the public concourse, to see and to be seen, for amusement or for display, or on the excuse of business. The carriages of the wealthy mingle with the slow wains laden with provisions or merchandise, the productions of art or the demands of luxury. The streets are lined with shops, open and gay, inviting customers, and widen now and then into some spacious square or place, with lofty masses of brickwork or of stone, gleaming in the fitful sunbeam, and surrounded or fronted with what stimulates a garden's foliage. Follow them in another direction, and you find the whole groundstead covered with large buildings, planted thickly up and down, the homes of mechanical arts. The air is filled, below, with a ceaseless, importunate, monotonous din, which penetrates even to your most innermost chamber, and rings in your ears even when you are not conscious of it; and overhead, with a canopy of smoke, shrouding God's day from the realms of obstinate sullen toil. This is the end of man![142]

Or this description of the imagined entry of St Peter into Rome (Newman is already reviewing the scenario for his novel *Callista*):

He met throngs of the idle and the busy, of strangers and natives, who peopled the interminable suburb. He passed through the high gate, and wandered on marble palaces and columned temples; he met processions of heathen priests and ministers in honour of their idols; he met the wealthy lady, borne on her litter by her slaves; he met the stern legionaries who had been the 'massive iron hammers' of the whole earth; he met the anxious politician with his ready man of business at his side to prompt him on his canvass for popularity; he met the orator returning home from a successful pleading, with his young admirers and his grateful and hopeful clients.[143]

He can also rise to heights of great eloquence, as he talks of the impact of sin:

It is the long history of a world, and God alone can bear the load of it. Hopes blighted, vows broken,

---

[142] *Discourses*, pp. 105–6. See also *Notoriety* pp. 90–91 and *Wealth* p. 89. The 'homes of the mechanical arts' are the workshops and factories which are the trade mark of Birmingham.

[143] Ibid., p. 241.

lights quenched, warnings scorned, opportunities lost; the innocent betrayed, the young hardened, the penitent relapsing, the just overcome, the aged failing; the sophistry of misbelief, the wilfulness of passion, the obduracy of pride, the tyranny of habit, the canker of remorse, the wasting fever of care, the anguish of shame, the pining of disappointment, the sickness of despair; such cruel, such pitiable spectacles, such heart-rending, revolting, detestable, maddening scenes . . .[144]

Newman is also fond of painting in contrasting colours to make his point. So he can say 'He has cast off the thought of God and set up self in His place'[145] and 'They lived on here, to die eternally.'[146] He also adds 'Purity prepares the soul for love, and love confirms the soul in purity.'[147] Whereas it is the case for God 'He was from eternity ever in action, though ever at rest.'[148]

But he is also capable of the odd bit of purple prose – which contemporaries would term 'Italianate':

If the world has its fascinations, so surely has the Altar of the living God; if its pomps and vanities dazzle, so much more should the vision of Angels ascending and descending on the heavenly ladder; if sights of earth intoxicate, and its music is a spell

---

[144] Ibid., pp. 338–9. Compare Newman's lament on p. 122 'The world goes on from age to age, but the holy Angels and blessed Saints are always crying alas . . .'

[145] Ibid., p. 11.

[146] Ibid., p. 130.

[147] Ibid., p. 63.

[148] Ibid., p. 289.

upon the soul, behold Mary pleads with us, over against them, with her chaste eyes, and offers the Eternal Child for our caress, while sounds of cherubim are heard all round singing from out the fulness of the Divine Glory.[149]

Those who take all Newman's remarks at face value miss his sense of irony. Instead of wounding his former co-religionists, he prefers a more gentle treatment. He has the individual 'educated according to its principles' coming at last to his death where he is 'sincerely lamented, lamented by a large circle of friends'. And Newman continues 'Perhaps they add, "dying with a firm trust in the mercy of God"'[150] having made it clear that God was the last thing on the man's mind during his life. He mocks at the evident 'sensibleness' of another 'he is the perfect man who eats, and drinks, and sleeps and walks, and diverts himself, and studies, and writes, *and attends to religion, in moderation* [my italics].'[151]

When he describes the search for diversion (with London in mind – where news of ships' accidents and the money market is) he asks 'O this curious, restless, clamourous panting being, which we call life! – and is there to be no end to all this? Is there no object in it? It never has an end, it is forsooth its own object!'[152]

He does not spare the advocates of Scriptural Higher Criticism – undoubtedly recalling his conversations with Pusey about his time in Germany: 'I can

[149] *Discourses*, p. 70.
[150] Ibid., p. 15.
[151] Ibid., p. 148.
[152] Ibid., p. 107.

fancy a man magisterially expounding St. Paul's
Epistle to the Galatians or to the Ephesians, who
would be better content with the writer's absence
than his sudden re-appearance among us; lest the
Apostle should take his own meaning out his
commentator's hands and explain it for himself.'[153]

Use of Scripture

Those who are familiar with the *Parochial and Plain
Sermons* marvel at Newman's familiarity with the
books of the Old and New Testaments. When he
became a Catholic, he did not leave that memory
behind. Until the reform of the liturgy by Vatican II
Catholics in general did not have the abundance of
Scripture readings over the two- and three-year cycles
which they now possess. There was not that acquaintance with the Old Testament which characterises the
Protestant Churches to this day. But this gives his
writings a quality which we have largely lost. For
Newman the Scriptures were a ready source which he
could dive into for examples, illustrations, analogies
and everyday expressions.

   He is able to turn to Job and say: 'Thou hast sealed
up my sins as in a bag.'[154] When he thinks of perseverance he calls up the figure of Elisha.[155] The
commitment of faith evokes the figure of Ruth.[156]
Obstacles in the way and Newman retorts: 'Who art

[153] Ibid., pp. 200–1.

[154] Ibid., p. 27.

[155] Ibid., p. 141.

[156] Ibid., p. 208. 'Whithersoever thou shalt go, I will go! and where thou
     shalt dwell, I will dwell; thy people shall be my people, and thy God,
     my God' (Ruth 1:16).

thou, O great mountain, before Zorobabel? but a plain.'[157] Those who turn aside in their search are 'like a crooked bow'.[158] The end of life and Newman talks of the lofty palace crumbling, the busy city mute and the ships of Tarshish having sped away.[159] He has Ecclesiastes at hand when he talks of Jesus' earnest acceptance of his passion.[160] The heart of Jesus is broken like the foundations of the great deep at the creation.[161] Mary is compared with 'meek Moses'[162] and the honour due to her is put in the context of Ahasuerus' question to Haman.[163]

Use of words

Newman shows his familiarity with the classics, as was usual at the time, but still arouses a certain admiration, whether it is Herodotus, Plutarch or the works of Horace, Lucan and Ovid and the Argonautica of Apollonius Rhodius. But he is also fascinated by contemporary science – modern experiments and the discovery of Neptune, and the possible age of the solar system.

It is all woven together with great literary skill so that the words chime together harmoniously: 'Success is the measure of principle, and power is the exponent of right'[164] and 'Obedience is the consequence of

---

[157] *Discourses*, p. 213.

[158] Ibid., p. 142.

[159] Ibid., p. 123.

[160] Ibid., p. 330 'The wise man says *instanter*' (Eccli. 9:10).

[161] Ibid., p. 340.

[162] Ibid., p. 355.

[163] Ibid., p. 362 'What should be done to the man whom the king desireth to honour? (Esth. 6:6. Douai Version).

[164] Ibid., p. 239.

willing to obey, and faith is the consequence of willing to believe.'[165] He also provides pithy sayings: 'They praise what they do not imitate'[166] and 'No one is a Martyr for a conclusion, no one is a Martyr for an opinion; it is faith that makes Martyrs.'[167]

Newman is not averse to alliteration when it serves, so he remarks that some 'make a sort of science of their sensuality.'[168] He can also pile on the comparisons for dramatic effect, lamenting about the world: 'hopes without substance, promises without fulfilment, repentance without amendment, blossom without fruit, continuance and progress without perseverance'.[169] He can also sum up the Redemption succinctly: 'He died by it as well as for it.'[170]

'Such, then, is the truth . . .'
We should not compare the more vigorous *Lectures on the Present Position of Catholics* with the contents of this volume. Both were in effect, discourses, but most of these had a liturgical context. They are homilies which have been adapted for publication and may originally have contained more local colour which was not thought applicable for a wider market.

If we examine the *Discourses* carefully, we can see that they provide an almost complete exposition of the Catholic faith that Newman had embraced four years earlier. There is ample coverage of the articles of the Creed. It is noticeable that the office of the

[165] Ibid., p. 225.
[166] Ibid., p. 94.
[167] Ibid., p. 181.
[168] Ibid., p. 113.
[169] Ibid., pp. 142–3.
[170] Ibid., p. 41.

papacy receives a mention only in the context of the promise to Peter and in dealing with the 'prerogative of infallibility' – Newman anticipates modern theology in this. When he deals with the sacraments there is no mention of Confirmation and only indirect allusion to Holy Orders (insofar as there is a priestly office in the Church) and Marriage (this would not have been a Victorian subject for the pulpit).

For someone who has only just made contact with the Church, his grasp of the intricacies of theology would put many priests to shame. He neatly summarises the different positions on grace and takes an independent line on the Incarnation which would have been considered avant garde even in the 1950s. Those who are acquainted with his *Essay on the Development of Doctrine* will find the basis for his approach.

We can sense throughout the volume that earnest (one of Newman's favourite words) desire to win his hearers to a deeper commitment to the things of God. He continues to be aware of the struggle in which the Christian is engaged and the odds at stake. He is sympathetic to the attractions which lead to sin and paints them in technicolour because he wants his hearers and readers to recognise them for themselves. But he doesn't rant and rave, content to set the facts clearly and at times, vividly before the eyes. There is in all of this a *consistency* which – despite what critics allege – marks Newman's preaching from his days at St Mary's to his time in Dublin and Birmingham, which in its turn exemplifies his theory of development.

If we allow for the passage of a hundred and fifty years – the Victorian context and the Victorian prose

– we have in the *Discourses* a very good and surprisingly modern summary of Catholic faith and practice with little of the stodginess of later manuals and a real grasp of the circumstances of the English (and Irish) that crowded into the little chapel in the back streets of Birmingham. It explains why John Henry Newman was willing to move in to his converted gin distillery in the first place. The sale of the volume did help with the finances, and he would shortly move to the more congenial suburb of Edgbaston to continue his work.

Right Rev. NICHOLAS WISEMAN, D.D.,

My Dear Lord,

I present for your Lordship's kind acceptance and patronage the first work which I publish as a Father of the Oratory of St. Philip Neri. I have a sort of claim upon your permission to do so, as a token of my affection and gratitude toward your Lordship, since it is to you principally that I owe it, under God, that I am a client and subject, however unworthy, of so great a Saint.

When I found myself a Catholic, I also found myself in your Lordship's district; and, at your suggestion, I first moved into your immediate neighbourhood, and then, when your Lordship further desired it, I left you for Rome. There it was my blessedness to be allowed to offer myself, with the condescending approval of the Holy Father, to the service of St. Philip, of whom I had so often heard you speak before I left England, and whose bright and beautiful character had won my devotion, even when I was a Protestant.

You see then, my dear Lord, how much you have to do with my present position in the Church. But your concern with it is greater than I have yet stated; for I cannot forget that when, in the year 1839, a doubt first crossed my mind of the tenableness of the theological theory on which Anglicanism is based, it was caused in no slight degree by the perusal of a controversial paper, attributed to your Lordship, on the schism of the Donatists.

That the glorious intercession of St. Philip may be the reward of your faithful devotion to himself, and of your kindness to me, is,

My dear Lord,

while I ask your Lordship's blessing on me and mine,

the earnest prayer of

Your affectionate friend and servant,

JOHN HENRY NEWMAN,

OF THE ORATORY.

In Fest. S. Caroli,
1849.

DISCOURSE I.

THE SALVATION OF THE HEARER THE MOTIVE OF THE PREACHER.

WHEN a body of men come into a neighbourhood to them unknown, as we are doing, my brethren, strangers to strangers, and there set themselves down, and raise an altar, and open a school, and invite, or even exhort all men to attend them, it is natural that they who see them, and are drawn to think about them, should ask the question, What brings them hither? Who bids them come? What do they want? What do they preach? What is their warrant? What do they promise?—You have a right, my brethren, to ask the question.

Many, however, will not stop to ask it, as thinking they can answer it without difficulty for themselves. Many there are who would promptly and confidently answer it, according to their own habitual view of things, on their own principles, the principles of the world. The views, the principles, the aims of the world are very definite, are everywhere acknowledged, and are incessantly acted on. They supply an explanation of the conduct of individuals, whoever they be, ready at hand, and so sure to be true in the common run of cases, as to be probable and plausible in any case in particular. When we would account for effects which we see, we of course refer them to causes which we know of. To fancy causes of which we know nothing, is not to account for them at all. The world then naturally and necessarily judges of others by itself. Those who live the life of the world, and act from motives of the world, and live and act with those who do the like, as a matter of course ascribe the actions of others, however different they may be from their own, to one or other of the motives which weigh with themselves ; for some motive or other they must assign, and they can imagine none but those of which they have experience.

We know how the world goes on, especially in this country ; it is a laborious, energetic, indefatigable world. It takes up objects enthusiastically, and vigorously carries them through. Look into the world, as its course is faithfully traced day by day in those publications which are devoted to its service, and you will see at once the ends which stimulate it, and the views which govern it. You will read of great and persevering exertions, made for some temporal end, good or bad, but still temporal. Some temporal end it is, even if it be not a selfish one ;— generally, indeed, it is such as name, influence, power, wealth, station ; sometimes it is the relief of the ills of human life or society, of ignorance, sickness, poverty, or vice—still some temporal end it is, which is the exciting and animating principle of those exertions. And so pleasant is the excitement which those temporal objects create, that it is often its own reward ; insomuch that, forgetting the end for which they toil, men find a satisfaction in the toil itself, and are sufficiently repaid for their trouble *by* their trouble,—by the struggle for success, and the rivalry of party, and the trial of their skill, and the demand upon their resources, by the vicissitudes and hazards, and ever new emergencies, and varying requisitions of the contest which they carry on, though that contest never comes to an end.

Such is the way of the world ; and therefore, I say, it is not unnatural, that, when it sees any persons whatever anywhere begin to work with energy, and attempt to get others about them, and act in outward appearance like itself, though in a different direction and with a religious profession, it should unhesitatingly impute to them the motives which influence, or would influence, its own children. Often by way of blame, but sometimes not as blaming, but as merely stating a plain fact, which it thinks undeniable, it takes for granted that they are ambitious, or restless, or eager for distinction, or fond of power. It knows no better ; and it is vexed and annoyed if, as time goes on, one thing or another is seen in the conduct of those whom it criticises, which is inconsistent with the assumption on which, in the first instance, it so summarily settled their position and anticipated their course. It took a general view of them, looked them through, as it thought, and from some one action of theirs which came to its knowledge, assigned to them unhesitatingly some particular motive as their habitual actuating principle ; but presently it finds it is obliged to shift its ground, to take up some new hypothesis, and explain to itself their character and their conduct over again. O, my dear brethren, the world cannot help doing so, because it knows us not ; it ever will be impatient with us for not being of the world, because it *is* the world ; it is necessarily blind to the one strong motive which has influence with us, and, tired out at length with hunting through its catalogues and note-books for a description of us, it sits down in disgust, after its many conjectures, and flings us aside as inexplicable, or hates us as if mysterious and designing.

My brethren, we *have* secret views—secret, that is from men of this world ; secret from politicians, secret from the slaves of mammon, secret from all ambitious, covetous, selfish, and voluptuous men.   For religion itself, like its Divine Author and Teacher, is, as I have said, a hidden thing from them ; and not knowing it, they cannot use it as a key to interpret the conduct of those who are influenced by it.   They do not know the ideas and motives which religion sets before that mind which it has made its own.   They do not enter into them, or realise them, even when they are told them ; and they do not believe that a man can be influenced by them, even when he professes them.   They cannot put themselves into the position of a man simply striving, in what he does, to please God.   They are so narrow-minded, such is the meanness of their intellectual make, that, when a Catholic makes profession of this or that doctrine of the Church,—sin, judgment, heaven and hell, the blood of Christ, the power of Saints, the intercession of the Blessed Virgin, or the real presence in the Eucharist —and says that these are the objects which inspire his thoughts and direct his actions through the day, they cannot take in that he is in earnest ; for they think, forsooth, that these points ought to be his very difficulties, and are at most nothing more than trials to his faith, and that he gets over them by putting force on his reason, and thinks of them as little as he can ; and they do not dream that truths such as these have a hold upon his heart, and exert an influence on his life.   No wonder, then, that the sensual, and worldly-minded, and the unbelieving, are suspicious of one whom they cannot comprehend, and are so intricate and circuitous in their imputations, when they cannot bring themselves to accept an explanation which is straight before them.   So it has been from the beginning ; the Jews preferred to ascribe the conduct of our Lord and His forerunner to any motive but that of a desire to fulfil the will of God.   To the Jews they were, as He says, " like children sitting in the market-place, which cry to their companions, saying, We have piped to you, and you have not danced ; we have lamented to you, and you have not mourned."   And then He goes on to account for it : " I thank Thee, Father, Lord of heaven and earth, that Thou hast hid these things from the wise and prudent, and hast revealed them to little ones.   Yea, Father ; for so hath it been pleasing to Thy sight."

Let the world have its way, let it say what it will about us, my brethren; but that does not hinder our saying what we think, and what the eternal God thinks and says, about the world. We have as good a right to have our own judgment about the world, as the world to have its judgment about us: and we mean to exercise that right; for, while we know well it judges us amiss, we have God's testimony that we judge it truly. While, then, it is eager in ascribing our earnestness to one or other of its own motives, listen to me, while I show you, as it is not difficult to do, that it is our very fear and hatred of those motives and our compassion for the souls possessed by them, which makes us so busy and so troublesome, which prompts us to settle down in a district, so destitute of outward recommendations, but so overrun with religious error and so populous in souls.

O my brethren, little does the world, engrossed, as it is, with things of time and sense, little does it trouble itself about souls, about the state of souls in God's sight, about their past history, and about their prospects for the future. The world forms its views of things for itself, and in its own way, and lives in them. It never stops to consider whether they are sound and true; nor does it come into its thought to seek for any external standard, or channel of information, by which their truth can be ascertained. It is content to take things for granted according to their first appearance; it does not stop to think of God; it lives for the day, and (in a perverse sense) "is not solicitous for the morrow." What it sees, tastes, handles, is enough for it; this is the limit of its knowledge and of its aspirations; what tells, what works well, is alone respectable; efficiency is the measure of duty, and power is the rule of right, and success is the test of truth. It believes what it experiences, it disbelieves what it cannot demonstrate. And, in consequence, it teaches that a man has not much to do to be saved; that either he has committed no great sins, or that he will, as a matter of course, be pardoned for committing them; that he may securely trust in God's mercy for his prospects in eternity; and that he ought to discard all self-reproach, or deprecation, or penance, all mortification and self-discipline, as affronting or derogatory to that mercy. This is what the world teaches, by its many sects and philosophies, about our condition in this life, this and the like; but what, on the other hand, does the Catholic Church teach concerning it?

She teaches that man was originally made in God's image, was God's adopted son, was the heir of eternal glory, and, in foretaste of eternity, was partaker here on earth of great gifts and manifold graces; and she teaches that now he is a fallen being. He is under the curse of original sin; he is deprived of the grace of God; he is a child of wrath; he cannot attain to heaven, and he is in peril of sinking into hell. I do not mean he is fated to perdition by some necessary law; he cannot perish without his own real will and deed; and God gives him, even in his natural state, a multitude of inspirations and helps to lead him on to faith and obedience. There is no one born of Adam but might be saved, as far as divine assistances are concerned; yet, looking at the power of temptation, the force of the passions, the strength of self-love and self-will, the sovereignty of pride and sloth, in every one of his children, who will be bold enough to assert of any particular soul, that it will be able to maintain itself in obedience, without an abundance, a profusion of grace, not to be expected, as bearing no proportion, I do not say simply to the claims (for they are none), but to the bare needs of human nature? We may securely prophesy of every man born into the world, that, if he comes to years of understanding, he will, in spite of God's general assistances, fall into mortal sin and lose his soul. It is no light, no ordinary succour, by which man is taken out of his own hands and defended against himself. He requires an extraordinary remedy. Now what a thought is this! what a light does it cast upon man's present state! how different from the view which the world takes of it; how piercing, how overpowering in its influence on the hearts that admit it.

Contemplate, my brethren, more steadily the history of a soul born into the world, and educated according to its principles, and the idea, which I am putting before you, will grow on you. The poor infant passes through his two, or three, or five years of innocence, blessed in that he cannot yet sin; but at length (oh woeful day!) he begins to realise the distinction between right and wrong. Alas! sooner or later, for the age varies, but sooner or later the awful day has come; he has the power, the great, the dreadful, the awful power of discerning and pronouncing a thing to be wrong, and yet doing it. He has a distinct view that he shall grievously offend his Maker and his Judge by doing this or that; and while he is really able to keep from it, he is at liberty to choose it, and to commit it. He has the dreadful power of committing a mortal sin. Young as he is, he has as true an apprehension of that sin, and can give as real a consent, as did the evil spirit, when he fell. The day is come, and who shall say whether it will have closed, whether it will have run out many hours, before he will have exercised that power, and have perpetrated, in fact, what he ought not to do, what he need not do, what he can do? Who is there whom we ever knew, of whom we can assert that, had he remained in a state of nature, he would have used the powers given him,—that if he be in a state of nature, he has used the powers given him,—in such a way as to escape the guilt and penalty of offending Almighty God? No, my brethren, a large town like this is a fearful sight. We walk the streets, and what numbers are there of those who meet us who have never been baptized at all! And the remainder, what is it made up of, but for the most part of those who, though baptized, have sinned against the grace given them, and even from early youth have thrown themselves out of that fold in which alone is salvation! Reason and sin have gone together from the first. Poor child! he looks the same to his parents. They do not know what has been going on in him; or perhaps, did they know it, they would think very little of it, for they are in a state of mortal sin as well as he.

They too, long before they knew each other, had sinned, and mortally too, and were never reconciled to God; thus they lived for years, unmindful of their state. At length they married; it was a day of joy to them, but not to the Angels; they might be in high life or in low estate, they might be prosperous or not in their temporal course, but their union was not blessed by God. They gave birth to a child; he was not condemned to hell on his birth, but he had the omens of evil upon him, it seemed that he would go the way of all flesh: and now the time is come; the presage is justified; and he willingly departs from God. At length the forbidden fruit has been eaten; sin has been devoured with a pleased appetite; the gates of hell have yawned upon him, silently and without his knowing it; he has no eyes to see its flames, but its inhabitants are gazing upon him; his place in it is fixed beyond dispute;—unless his Maker interfere in some extraordinary way, he is doomed.

Yet his intellect does not stay its growth, because he is the slave of sin. It opens; time passes; he learns perhaps various things; he may have good abilities, and be taught to cultivate them. He may have engaging manners; anyhow he is light-hearted and merry, as boys are. He is gradually educated for the world; he forms his own judgments; chooses his principles, and is moulded to a certain character. That character may be more, or it may be less amiable; it may have much or little of natural virtue: it matters not—the mischief is within; it is done, and it spreads. The devil is unloosed and abroad in him. For a while

he used some sort of prayers, but he has left them off;
they were but a form, and he had no heart for them;
why should he continue them? and what was the use
of them? and what the obligation? So he has reasoned; and he has acted upon his reasoning, and
ceased to pray. Perhaps this was his first sin, that
original mortal sin, which threw him out of grace—
a disbelief in the power of prayer. As a child, he
refused to pray, and argued that he was too old to
pray, and that his parents did not pray. He gave
prayer up, and in came the devil, and took possession
of him, and made himself at home, and revelled in
his heart.

Poor child! Every day adds fresh and fresh mortal
sins to his account; the pleadings of grace have less
and less effect upon him; he breathes the breath of
evil, and day by day becomes more fatally corrupted.
He has cast off the thought of God, and set up self in
His place. He has rejected the traditions of religion
which float about him, and has chosen instead the
more congenial traditions of the world, to be the guide
of his life. He is confident in his own views, and
does not suspect that evil is before him, and in his
path. He learns to scoff at serious men and serious
things, catches at any story circulated against them,
and speaks positively when he has no means of
judging or knowing. The less he believes of revealed
doctrine, the wiser he thinks himself to be. Or, if
his natural temper keeps him from becoming hard-
hearted, still from easiness and from imitation he joins
in mockery of holy persons and holy things, as far as

they come across him. He is sharp and ready, and humorous, and employs these talents in the cause of Satan. He has a secret antipathy to religious truths and religious doings, a disgust which he is scarcely aware of, and could not explain, if he were. So was it with Cain, the eldest born of Adam, who went on to murder his brother, because his works were just. So was it with those poor boys at Bethel who mocked the great prophet Eliseus, crying out, Go up, thou bald head ! Anything serves the purpose of a scoff and taunt to the natural man, when irritated by the sight of religion.

O my brethren, I might go on to mention those other more loathsome and more hidden wickednesses which germinate and propagate within him, as time proceeds, and life opens on him. Alas ! who shall sound the depths of that evil whose wages is death? O what a dreadful sight to look on is this fallen world, specious and fair outside, plausible in its professions, ashamed of its own sins and hiding them, yet a mass of corruption under the surface ! Ashamed of its sins, yet not confessing to itself that they are sins, but defending them if conscience upbraids, and perhaps boldly saying, or at least implying, that, if an impulse be allowable in itself, it must be always right in an individual, nay, that self-gratification is its own warrant, and that temptation is the voice of God. Why should I attempt to analyze the intermingling influences, or to describe the combined power, of pride and lust,—lust exploring a way to evil, and pride fortifying the road,—till the first elementary truths of Revelation are looked upon as mere nursery tales? No, I have intended nothing more than to put wretched nature upon its course, as I may call it, and there to leave it, my brethren, to your reflections, to that individual comment which each of you may be able to put on this faint delineation, realising in your own mind and your own conscience what no words can duly set forth.

His secular course proceeds : the boy has become a man ; he has taken up a profession or a trade ; he has fair success in it ; he marries, as his father did before him. He plays his part in the scene of mortal life; his connexions extend as he gets older : whether in a higher or a lower sphere of society, he has his reputation and his influence : the reputation and the influence of, we will say, a sensible, prudent, and shrewd man. His children grow up around him ; middle age is over,—his sun declines in the heavens. In the balance and by the measure of the world, he is come to an honourable and venerable old age ; he has been a child of the world, and the world acknowledges and praises him. But what is he in the balance of heaven? What shall we say of God's judgment of him ? What about his soul?—about his *soul?* Ah, his soul; he had forgotten that ; he had forgotten he had a soul, but it remains from first to last in the sight of its Maker. *Posuisti sæculum nostrum in illuminatione vultûs Tui;* " Thou hast placed our life in the illumination of Thy countenance." Alas! alas! about his soul the world knows, the world cares, nought ; it does not recognise the soul ; it owns nothing in him but an intellect manifested in a mortal frame; it cares for the man while he is *here*, it loses sight of him when he is *there*. Still the time is coming when he is leaving *here*, and will find himself *there;* he is going out of sight, amid the shadows of that unseen world, about which the visible world is so sceptical; so, it concerns us who have a belief in that unseen world, to inquire, "How fares it all this while with his soul?" Alas! he has had pleasures and satisfactions in life, he has, I say, a good name among men; he sobered his views as life went on, and he began to think that order and religion were good things, that a certain deference was to be paid to the religion of his country, and a certain attendance to be given to its public worship; but he is still, in our Lord's words, nothing else but a whited sepulchre; he is foul within with the bones of the dead and all uncleanness. All the sins of his youth, never repented of, never really put away, his old profanenesses, his impurities, his animosities, his idolatries, are rotting with him; only covered over and hidden by successive layers of newer and later sins. His heart is the home of darkness, it has been handled, defiled, possessed by evil spirits; he is a being without faith, and without hope; if he holds anything for truth, it is only as an opinion, and if he has a sort of calmness and peace, it is the calmness, not of heaven, but of decay and dissolution. And now his old enemy has thrust aside his good Angel, and is sitting near him; rejoicing in his victory, and patiently waiting for his prey; not tempting him to fresh sins lest they should disturb his conscience, but simply letting well alone ; letting him amuse himself with shadows of faith, shadows of piety, shadows of worship ; aiding him readily in dressing himself up in some form of religion which may satisfy the weakness of his declining age, as knowing well that he cannot last long, that his death is a matter of time, and that he shall soon be able to carry him down with him to his fiery dwelling.

O how awful ! and at last the inevitable hour is come. He dies—he dies quietly—his friends are satisfied about him. They return thanks that God has taken him, has released him from the troubles of life and the pains of sickness ; " a good father," they say, " a good neighbour," " sincerely lamented," " lamented by a large circle of friends." Perhaps they add, " dying with a firm trust in the mercy of God ; "—nay, he has need of something beyond mercy, he has need of some attribute which is inconsistent with perfection, and which is not, cannot be, in the All-glorious, All-holy God ;—" with a trust," forsooth, " in the promises of the Gospel," which never were his, or were early forfeited. And then, as time travels on, every now and then is heard some passing remembrance of him, respectful or tender ; but he all the while (in spite of this false world, and though its children will not have it so, and exclaim, and protest, and are indignant when so solemn a truth is hinted at), he is lifting up his eyes, being in torment, and lies " buried in hell."

Such is the history of a man in a state of nature, or in a state of defection, to whom the Gospel has never been a reality, in whom the good seed has never taken root, on whom God's grace has been shed in vain, with whom it has never prevailed so far as to make him seek His face and to ask for those higher gifts which lead to heaven. Such is his dark record. But I have spoken of only one man : alas ! my dear brethren, it is the record of thousands; it is, in one shape or other, the record of all the children of the world. " As soon as they are born," the wise man says, " they forthwith have ceased to be, and they are powerless to show any sign of virtue, and are wasted away in their wickedness." They may be rich or poor, learned or ignorant, polished or rude, decent outwardly and self-disciplined, or scandalous in their lives,—but at bottom they are all one and the same ; they have not faith, they have not love ; they are impure, they are proud ; they all agree together very well, both in opinions and in conduct; they see that they agree ; and this agreement they take as a proof that their conduct is right and their opinions true. Such as is the tree, such is the fruit ; no wonder the fruit is the same in all when it comes of the same root of unregenerate, unrenewed nature ; but they consider it good and wholesome, because it is matured in so many ; and they chase away, as odious, unbearable, and horrible, the pure and heavenly doctrine of Revelation, because it is so severe upon themselves. No one likes bad news, no one welcomes what condemns him ; the world slanders the Truth in self-defence, because the Truth denounces the world.

My brethren, if these things be so, or rather (for

this is the point here), if we, Catholics, firmly believe
them to be so, so firmly believe them, that we feel it
would be happy for us to die rather than doubt them,
is it wonderful, does it require any abstruse explanation, that men minded as we are should come into the
midst of a population such as this, and into a neighbourhood where religious error has sway, and where
corruption of life prevails both as its cause and as its
consequence—a population, not worse indeed than
the rest of the world, but not better ; not better,
because it has not with it the gift of Catholic truth ;
not purer, because it has not within it that gift of
grace which alone can destroy impurity; a population,
sinful, I am certain, given to unlawful indulgences,
laden with guilt and exposed to eternal ruin, because
it is not blessed with that Presence of the Word
Incarnate, which diffuses sweetness, and tranquillity,
and chastity over the heart ; — is it a thing to be
marvelled at, that we begin to preach to such a
population as this, for which Christ died, and try to
convert it to Him and to His Church ? Is it necessary
to ask for reasons ? is it necessary to assign motives
of this world, for a proceeding which is so natural in
those who believe in the announcements and require-
ments of the other ? My dear brethren, if we are sure
that the Most Holy Redeemer has shed His blood
for all men, is it not a very plain and simple consequence that we, His servants, His brethren, His priests,
should be unwilling to see that blood shed in vain,—
wasted I may say, as regards you, and should wish
to make you partakers of those benefits which have

2

been vouchsafed to ourselves? Is it necessary for any by-stander to call us vain-glorious, or ambitious, or restless, greedy of authority, fond of power, resentful, party-spirited, or the like, when here is so much more powerful, more present, more influential a motive to which our eagerness and zeal may be ascribed? What is so powerful an incentive to preaching as the sure belief that it is the preaching of the truth? What so constrains to the conversion of souls, as the consciousness that they are at present in guilt and in peril? What so great a persuasive to bring men into the Church, as the conviction that it is the special means by which God effects the salvation of those whom the world trains in sin and unbelief? Only admit us to believe what we profess, and surely that is not asking a great deal (for what have we done that we should be distrusted?)—only admit us to believe what we profess, and you will understand without difficulty what we are doing. We come among you, because we believe there is but one way of salvation, marked out from the beginning, and that you are not walking along it; we come among you as ministers of that extraordinary grace of God, which you need; we come among you because we have received a great gift from God ourselves, and wish you to be partakers of our joy; because it is written, "Freely ye have received, freely give;" because we dare not hide in a napkin those mercies, and that grace of God, which have been given us, not for our own sake only, but for the benefit of others.

Such a zeal, poor and feeble though it be in us, has

been the very life of the Church, and the breath of her preachers and missionaries in all ages. It was a fire such as this which brought our Lord from heaven, and which He desired, which He travailed, to communicate to all around Him. "I am come to send fire on the earth," He says, "and what will I, but that it be kindled?" Such, too, was the feeling of the great Apostle to whom his Lord appeared in order to impart to him this fire. "I send thee to the Gentiles," He had said to him on his conversion, "to open their eyes, that they may be converted from darkness to light, and from the power of Satan unto God." And, accordingly, he at once began to preach to them, that they should do penance, and turn to God with worthy fruits of penance, "for," as he says, "the charity of Christ constrained him," and he was "made all things to all that he might save all," and he "bore all for the elect's sake, that they might obtain the salvation which is in Christ Jesus, with heavenly glory." Such, too, was the fire of zeal which burned within those preachers, to whom we English owe our Christianity. What brought them from Rome to this distant isle and to a barbarous people, amid many fears, and with much suffering, but the sovereign uncontrollable desire to save the perishing, and to knit the members and slaves of Satan into the body of Christ? This has been the secret of the propagation of the Church from the very first, and will be to the end; this is why the Church, under the grace of God, to the surprise of the world, converts the nations, and why no sect can do the like; this is why Catholic missionaries throw themselves so generously among the fiercest savages, and risk the most cruel torments, as knowing the worth of the soul, as realising the world to come, as loving their brethren dearly, though they never saw them, as shuddering at the thought of the eternal woe, and as desiring to increase the fruit of their Lord's passion, and the triumphs of His grace.

We, my brethren, are not worthy to be named in connexion with Evangelists, Saints, and Martyrs; we come to you in a peaceable time and in a well-ordered state of society, and recommended by that secret awe and reverence, which, say what they will, Englishmen for the most part, or in good part, feel for that Religion of their fathers, which has left in the land so many memorials of its former sway. It requires no great zeal in us, no great charity, to come to you at no risk, and entreat you to turn from the path of death, and be saved. It requires nothing great, nothing heroic, nothing saint-like; it does but require conviction, and that we have, that the Catholic Religion is given from God for the salvation of mankind, and that all other religions are but mockeries; it requires nothing more than faith, a single purpose, an honest heart, and a distinct utterance. We come to you in the name of God; we ask no more of you than that you would listen to us; we ask no more than that you would judge for yourselves whether or not we speak God's words; it shall rest with you whether we be God's priests and prophets or no. This is not much to ask, but it is more than most men will grant; they do not dare listen to us, they are

impatient through prejudice, or they dread conviction.
Yes! many a one there is, who has even good reason
to listen to us, nay, on whom we have a claim to be
heard, who ought to have a certain trust in us, who
yet shuts his ears, and turns away, and chooses to
hazard eternity without weighing what we have to
say. How frightful is this! but you are not, you
cannot be such; we ask not *your* confidence, my
brethren, for you have never known us: we are not
asking you to take for granted what we say, for we
are strangers to you; we do but simply bid you first
to consider that you have souls to be saved, and next
to judge for yourselves, whether, if God has revealed
a religion of His own whereby to save those souls,
that religion can be any other than the faith which
we preach.

DISCOURSE II.

N O one sins without making some excuse to himself for sinning.   He is obliged to do so : man is not like the brute beasts; he has a divine gift within him which we call reason, and which constrains him to account before its judgment-seat for what he does. He cannot act at random ; however he acts, he must act by some kind of rule, on some sort of principle, else he is vexed and dissatisfied with himself.   Not that he is very particular whether he finds a good reason or a bad, when he is very much straitened for a reason ; but a reason of some sort he must have. Hence you sometimes find those who give up religious duty altogether, attacking the conduct of religious men, whether their acquaintance, or the ministers or professors of religion, as a sort of excuse—a very bad one—for their neglect.   Others will make the excuse that they are so far from church, or so closely occupied at home, whether they will or not, that they cannot serve God as they ought.   Others say that it is no use trying to do so, that they have again and again gone to confession and tried to keep out of mortal sin, and

(22)

cannot ; and so they give up the attempt as hopeless. Others, when they fall into sin, excuse themselves on the plea that they are but following nature ; that the impulses of nature are so very strong, and that it cannot be wrong to follow that nature which God has given us. Others are bolder still, and they cast off religion altogether : they deny its truth ; they deny Church, Gospel, and Bible ; they go so far perhaps as even to deny God's governance of His creatures. They boldly deny that there is any life after death : and, this being the case, of course they would be fools indeed not to take their pleasure here, and to make as much of this poor life as they can.

And there are others, and to these I am going to address myself, who try to speak peace to themselves by cherishing the thought that something or other will happen after all to keep them from eternal ruin, though they now continue in their neglect of God ; that it is a long time yet to death ; that there are many chances in their favour ; that they shall repent in process of time when they get old, as a matter of course; that they mean to repent some day; that they mean, sooner or later, seriously to take their state into account, and to make their ground good ; and, if they are Catholics, they add, that they will take care to die with the last Sacraments, and that therefore they need not trouble themselves about the matter.

Now these persons, my brethren, tempt God ; they try Him, how far His goodness will go ; and, it may be, they will try Him too long, and will have experience, not of His gracious forgiveness, but of His

severity and His justice. In this spirit it was that
the Israelites in the desert conducted themselves towards Almighty God : instead of feeling awe of Him,
they were free with Him, treated Him familiarly, made
excuses, preferred complaints, upbraided Him ; as if
the Eternal God had been a weak man, as if He had
been their minister and servant ; in consequence, we
are told by the inspired historian, " The Lord sent
among the people fiery serpents ". To this St. Paul
refers when he says, " Neither let us tempt Christ, as
some of them tempted, and perished by the serpents;"
a warning to us now, that those who are forward and
bold with their Almighty Saviour, will gain, not the
pardon which they look for, but will find themselves
within the folds of the old serpent, will drink in his
poisonous breath, and at length will die under his
fangs. That seducing spirit appeared in person to
our Lord in the days of His flesh, and tried to entangle
Him, the Son of the Highest, in this very sin. He
placed Him on the pinnacle of the Temple, and said
to Him, "If Thou art the Son of God, cast Thyself
down, for it is written, He has given His Angels
charge of Thee, and in their hands they shall lift Thee,
lest perchance Thou strike Thy foot against a stone;"
but our Lord's answer was, " It is also written, Thou
shall not tempt the Lord thy God ". And so numbers are tempted now to cast themselves headlong
down the precipice of sin, assuring themselves the
while that they will never reach the hell which lies
at the bottom, never dash upon its sharp rocks, or be
plunged into its flames ; for Angels and Saints are

there, in their extremity, in their final need,—or at least, God's general mercies, or His particular promises,—to interpose and bear them away safely. Such is the sin of these men, my brethren, of which I am going to speak ; not the sin of unbelief, or of pride, or of despair, but of presumption.

I will state more distinctly the kind of thoughts which go through their minds, and which quiet and satisfy them in their course of irreligion. They say to themselves, " I cannot give up sin now ; I cannot give up this or that indulgence; I cannot break myself of this habit of intemperance ; I cannot do without these unlawful gains ; I cannot leave these employers or superiors, who keep me from following my conscience. It is impossible I should serve God now; and I have no leisure to look into myself; and I do not feel the wish to repent ; I have no heart for religion. But it will come easier by-and-by; it will be as natural then to repent and be religious, as it is now natural to sin. I shall then have fewer temptations, fewer difficulties. Old people are sometimes indeed reprobates, but, generally speaking, they are religious ; they are religious almost as a matter of course; they may curse and swear a little, and tell lies, and do such-like little things ; but still they are clear of mortal sin, and would be safe if they were suddenly taken off." And when some particular temptation comes on them, they think, " It is only one sin, and once in a way ; I never did the like before, and never will again while I live ;" or, " I have done as bad before now, and it is only one sin more, and I shall have to repent anyhow; and while I am about it, it will be as easy to repent of one sin more as of one less, for I shall have to repent of *all* sin;" or again, " If I perish, I shall not want company;—what will happen to this person or that? I am quite a Saint compared with such a one; and I have known men repent, who have done much worse things than I have done ".

Now, my dear brethren, those who make such excuses to themselves, know neither what sin is in its own nature, nor what their own sins are in particular; they understand neither the heinousness nor the multitude of their sins. It is necessary, then, to state distinctly one or two points of Catholic doctrine, which will serve to put this matter in a clearer view than men are accustomed to take of it. These truths are very simple and very obvious, but are quite forgotten by the persons of whom I have been speaking, or they would never be able to satisfy their reason and their conscience by such frivolous pleas and excuses, as those which I have been drawing out.

First then observe, that when a person says, " I have sinned as badly before now," or, " This is only one sin more," or, " I must repent anyhow, and then will repent once for all," and the like, he forgets that all his sins are in God's hand and in one page of the book of judgment, and already added up against him, according as each is committed, up to the last of them; that the sin he is now committing is not a mere single, isolated sin, but that it is one of a series, of a long catalogue; that though it be but one, it is not sin one, or sin two, or sin three in the list, but it is the thousandth, the ten thousandth, or the hundredth thousandth, in a long course of sinning. It is not the first of his sins, but the last, and perhaps the very last and finishing sin. He himself forgets, manages to forget, or tries to forget, wishes to forget, all his antecedent sins, or remembers them merely as instances of his having sinned with impunity before, and proofs that he may sin with impunity still. But every sin has a history: it is not an accident; it is the fruit of former sins in thought or in deed; it is the token of a habit deeply seated and widely spread; it is the aggravation of a virulent disease; and, as the last straw is said to break the horse's back, so our last sin, whatever it is, is that which destroys our hope, and forfeits our place in heaven. Therefore, my brethren, it is but the craft of the devil, which makes you take your sins one by one, while God views them as a whole. " *Signasti, quasi in sacculo, delicta mea,*" says holy Job, " Thou hast sealed up my sins as in a bag," and one day they will all be counted out. Separate sins are like the touches and strokes which the painter gives, first one and then another, to the picture on his canvas; or like the stones which the mason piles up and cements together for the house he is building. They are all connected together; they tend to a whole; they look towards an end, and they hasten on to their fulfilment.

Go, commit this sin, my brethren, to which you are tempted, which you persist in viewing in itself alone, look on it as Eve looked on the forbidden fruit, dwell upon its lightness and insignificance; and perhaps

you may find it after all to be just the coping-stone
of your high tower of rebellion, which comes into remembrance before God, and fills up the measure of
your iniquities. " Fill ye up," says our Lord to the
hypocritical Pharisees, "the measure of your fathers."
The wrath, which came on Jerusalem, was not simply
caused by the sins of that day, in which Christ came,
though in that day was committed the most awful
of all sins, viz., His rejection ; for that was but the
crowning sin of a long course of rebellion.   So again,
in an earlier age, the age of Abraham, ere the chosen
people had got possession of the land of promise,
there was already great and heinous sin among the
heathen who inhabited it, yet they were not put out
at once, and Abraham brought in ;—why ? because
God's mercies were not yet exhausted towards them.
He still bestowed His grace on the abandoned people,
and waited for their repentance.   But He foresaw
that He should wait in vain, and that the time of
vengeance would come; and this He implied when He
said, that He did not give the chosen seed the land at
once, "for as yet the iniquities of the Amorrhites were
not at the full ".   But they did come to the full some
hundred years afterwards, and then the Israelites were
brought in, with the command to destroy them utterly
with the sword.   And again, you know the history
of the impious Baltassar.   In his proud feast, when
he was now filled with wine, he sent for the gold and
silver vessels which belonged to the Temple at Jerusalem, and had been brought to Babylon on the
taking of the holy city,—he sent for these sacred

vessels, that out of them he might drink more wine, he, his nobles, his wives, and his concubines. In that hour, the fingers as of a man's hand were seen upon the wall of the banqueting-room, writing the doom of the king and of his kingdom. The words were these: "God hath numbered thy kingdom, and hath finished it: thou art weighed in the balance, and art found wanting". That wretched prince had kept no account of his sins; as a spendthrift keeps no account of his debts, so he went on day after day and year after year, revelling in pride, cruelty, and sensual indulgence, and insulting his Master, till at length he exhausted the Divine Mercy, and filled up the chalice of wrath. His hour came: one more sin he did, and the cup overflowed; vengeance overtook him on the instant, and he was cut off from the earth.

And that last sin need not be a great sin, need not be greater than those which have gone before it; perhaps it may be less. There was a rich man, mentioned by our Lord, who, when his crops were plentiful, said within himself, "What shall I do, for I have not where to bestow my fruits? I will pull down my barns, and build greater; and I will say to my soul, Soul, thou hast much goods laid up for many years; take thy rest, eat, drink, make good cheer." He was carried off that very night. This was not a very striking sin, and surely it was not his first great sin; it was the last instance of a long course of acts of self-sufficiency and forgetfulness of God, not greater in intensity than any before it, but completing their number. And so again, when the father of that impious king, whom I just now spoke of, when Nabuchodonosor had for a whole year neglected the warning of the prophet Daniel, calling him to turn from his pride and to repent, one day as he walked in the palace of Babylon, he said, " Is not this great Babylon, which I have built for the home of the kingdom, in the strength of my power and in the glory of my excellence?" and forthwith, while the word was yet in his mouth, judgment came upon him, and he was smitten with a new and strange disease, so that he was driven from men, and ate hay like the ox, and grew wild in his appearance, and lived in the open field. His consummating act of pride was not greater, perhaps, than any one of those which through the twelvemonth had preceded it.

No; you cannot decide, my brethren, whether you are outrunning God's mercy, merely because the sin you now commit seems to be a small one; it is not always the greatest sin that is the last. Moreover you cannot calculate, which is to be your last sin, by the particular number of those which have gone before it, even if you could count them, for the number varies in different persons. This is another very serious circumstance. You may have committed but one or two sins, and yet find that you are ruined beyond redemption, though others who have done more are not. Why we know not, but God, who shows mercy and gives grace to all, shows greater mercy and gives more abundant grace to one man than another. To all He gives grace sufficient for their salvation; to all He gives far more than they have any right to expect, and they can claim nothing; but to some He gives far more than to others. He tells us Himself, that, if the inhabitants of Tyre and Sidon had seen the miracles done in Chorazin, they would have done penance and turned to Him. That is, there was that which would have converted them, and it was not granted to them. Till we set this before ourselves, we have not a right view either of sin in itself, or of our own prospects if we live in it. As God determines for each the measure of his stature, and the complexion of his mind, and the number of his days, yet not the same for all; as one child of Adam is preordained to live one day, and another eighty years, so is it fixed that one should be reserved for his eightieth sin, another cut off after his first. Why this is, we know not; but it is parallel to what is done in human matters without exciting any surprise. Of two convicted offenders one is pardoned, one is left to suffer; and this might be done in a case where there was nothing to choose between the guilt of the one and of the other, and where the reasons which determine the difference of dealing towards the one and the other, whatever they are, are external to the individuals themselves. In like manner you have heard, I daresay, of decimating rebels, when they had been captured, that is, of executing every tenth and letting off the rest. So it is also with God's judgments, though we cannot sound the reasons of them. He is not bound to let off any; He has the power to condemn all: I only bring this to show how our rule of justice here below does not preclude a difference of dealing

with one man and with another. The Creator gives
one man time for repentance, He carries off another
by sudden death. He allows one man to die with the
last Sacraments ; another dies without a Priest to receive his imperfect contrition, and to absolve him ;
the one is pardoned, and will go to heaven; the other
goes to the place of eternal punishment. No one can
say how it will happen in his own case ; no one can
promise himself that he shall have time for repentance ; or, if he have time, that he shall have any
supernatural movement of the heart towards God ; or,
even then, that a Priest will be at hand to give him
absolution. We may have sinned less than our next-
door neighbour, yet that neighbour may be reserved
for repentance and may reign with Christ, while we
may be punished with the evil spirit.

Nay, some have been cut off and sent to hell for
their first sin. This was the case, as divines teach,
as regards the rebel Angels. For their first sin, and
that a sin of thought, a single perfected act of pride,
they lost their first estate, and became devils. And
Saints and holy people record instances of men, and
even children, who in like manner have uttered a first
blasphemy or other deliberate sin, and were cut off
without remedy. And a number of similar instances
occur in Scripture; I mean of the awful punishment
of a single sin, without respect to the virtue and
general excellence of the sinner. Adam, for a
single sin, small in appearance, the eating of the
forbidden fruit, lost Paradise, and implicated all his
posterity in his own ruin. The Bethsamites were

irreverent towards the ark of the Lord, and more than fifty thousand of them in consequence were smitten. Oza touched it with his hand, as if to save it from falling, and he was struck dead on the spot for his rashness. The man of God from Juda ate bread and drank water at Bethel, against the command of God, and he was forthwith killed by a lion on his return. Ananias and Sapphira told one lie, and fell down dead almost as the words left their mouth. Who are we, that God should wait for our repentance any longer, when He has not waited at all, before He cut off those who sinned less than we?

O my dear brethren, these presumptuous thoughts of ours arise from a defective notion of the malignity of sin viewed in itself. We are criminals, and we are no judges in our own case. We are fond of ourselves, and we take our own part, and we are familiar with sin, and, from pride, we do not like to confess ourselves lost. For all these reasons, we have no real idea what sin is, what its punishment is, and what grace is. We do not know what sin is, because we do not know what God is; we have no standard with which to compare it, till we know what God is. Only God's glories, His perfections, His holiness, His Majesty, His beauty, can teach us by the contrast how to think of sin; and since we do not see God here, till we see Him, we cannot form a just judgment what sin is; till we enter heaven, we must take what God tells us of sin, mainly on faith. Nay, even then, we shall be able to condemn sin, only so far as we are able to see and praise and glorify God; He alone can

3

duly judge of sin who can comprehend God; He only judged of sin according to the fulness of its evil, who, knowing the Father from eternity with a perfect knowledge, showed what He thought of sin by dying for it; He only, who was willing, though He was God, to suffer inconceivable pains of soul and body in order to make a satisfaction for it. Take His word, or rather, His deed, for the truth of this awful doctrine, —that a single mortal sin is enough to cut you off from God for ever. Go down to the grave with a single unrepented, unforgiven sin upon you, and you have enough to sink you down to hell; you have that, which to a certainty will be your ruin. It may be the hundredth sin, or it may be the first sin, no matter: one is enough to sink you; though the more you have, the deeper you will sink. You need not have your fill of sin in order to perish without remedy; there are those who lose both this world and the next; they choose rebellion, and receive, not its gains, but death.

Or grant, that God's anger delays its course, and you have time to add sin to sin, this is only to increase the punishment when it comes. God is terrible, when He speaks to the sinner; He is more terrible, when He refrains; He is more terrible, when He is silent and accumulates wrath. Alas! there are those who are allowed to spend a long life, and a happy life, in neglect of Him, and have nothing in the outward course of things to remind them of what is coming, till their irreversible sentence bursts upon them. As the stream flows smoothly before the cataract, so with these persons does life pass along swiftly and silently, serenely and joyously. "They are not in the labour of men, neither shall they be scourged like other men." "They are filled with hidden things ; they are full of children, and leave what remains of them to their little ones." "Their houses are secure and at peace, neither is the rod of God upon them. Their little ones go out like a flock, and their children dance and play. They take the timbrel and the harp, and rejoice at the sound of the organ. They spend their days in good, and in a moment they go down to hell." So was it with Jerusalem, when God had deserted it ; it seemed never so prosperous before. Herod the king had lately rebuilt the Temple ; and the marbles with which it was cased were wonderful for size and beauty, and it rose bright and glittering in the morning sun. The disciples called their Lord to look at it, but He did but see in it the whited sepulchre of a reprobate people, and foretold its overthrow. "See ye all these things?" He answered them, "Amen, I say to you, stone shall not be here left upon stone, which shall not be thrown down ". And "He beheld the city, and wept over it, saying, If thou hadst known, even thou, and in this thy day, the things that are for thy peace, but now they are hidden from thine eyes!" Hid, indeed, was her doom ; for millions crowded within the guilty city at her yearly festival, and her end seemed a long way off, and ruin to belong to a far future age, when it was at the door.

O the change, my brethren, the dismal change at

last when the sentence has gone forth, and life ends, and eternal death begins! The poor sinner has gone on so long in sin, that he has forgotten he has sin to repent of. He has learned to forget that he is living in a state of enmity to God. He no longer makes excuses, as he did at first. He lives in the world, and believes nothing about the Sacraments, nor puts any trust in a Priest if he falls in with one. Perhaps he has hardly ever heard the Catholic religion mentioned except for the purpose of abuse; and never has spoken of it, but to ridicule it. His thoughts are taken up with his family and with his occupation; and if he thinks of death, it is with repugnance, as what will separate him from this world, not with fear, as what will introduce him to another He has ever been strong and hale. He has never had an illness. His family is long-lived, and he reckons he has a long time before him. His friends die before him, and he feels rather contempt at their nothingness, than sorrow at their departure. He has just married a daughter, or established a son in life, and he thinks of retiring from his labours, except that he is at a loss to know how he shall employ himself when he is out of work. He cannot get himself to dwell upon the thought of what and where he will be, when life is over, or, if he begins to muse awhile over himself and his prospects, then he is sure of one thing, that the Creator is absolute and mere benevolence, and he is indignant and impatient when he hears eternal punishment spoken of. And so he fares, whether for a long time or a short; but whatever the period, it must have an end, and at last the end comes. Time has gone forward noiselessly, and comes upon him like a thief in the night; at length the hour of doom strikes, and he is taken away.

Perhaps, however, he was a Catholic, and then the very mercies of God have been perverted by him to his ruin. He has rested on the Sacraments, without caring to have the proper dispositions for attending them. At one time he had lived in neglect of religion altogether; but there was a date when he felt a wish to set himself right with his Maker; so he began, and has continued ever since, to go to Confession and Communion at convenient intervals. He comes again and again to the Priest; he goes through his sins; the Priest is obliged to take his account of them, which is a very defective account, and sees no reason for not giving him absolution. He is absolved, as far as words can absolve him; he comes again to the Priest when the season comes round; again he confesses, and again he has the form pronounced over him. He falls sick, he receives the last Sacraments: he receives the last rites of the Church, and he is lost. He is lost, because he has never really turned his heart to God; or, if he had some poor measure of contrition for a while it did not last beyond his first or second confession. He soon taught himself to come to the Sacraments without any contrition at all; he deceived himself, and left out his principal and most important sins. Somehow he deceived himself into the notion that they were not sins, or not mortal sins; for some reason or other he was silent, and his confession became as defective as his contrition. Yet this scanty show of religion was sufficient to soothe and stupefy his conscience : so he went on year after year, never making a good confession, communicating in mortal sin, till he fell ill ; and then, I say, the viaticum and holy oil were brought to him, and he committed sacrilege for his last time,—and so he went to his God.

O what a moment for the poor soul, when it comes to itself, and finds itself suddenly before the judgment-seat of Christ! O what a moment, when, breathless with the journey, and dizzy with the brightness, and overwhelmed with the strangeness of what is happening to him, and unable to realise where he is, the sinner hears the voice of the accusing spirit, bringing up all the sins of his past life, which he has forgotten, or which he has explained away, which he would not allow to be sins, though he suspected they were ; when he hears him detailing all the mercies of God which he has despised, all His warnings which he has set at nought, all His judgments which he has outlived ; when that evil one follows out into detail the growth and progress of a lost soul,—how it expanded and was confirmed in sin,—how it budded forth into leaves and flowers, grew into branches, and ripened into fruit, —till nothing was wanted for its full condemnation! And, oh! still more terrible, still more distracting, when the Judge speaks, and consigns it to the jailors, till it shall pay the endless debt which lies against it! "Impossible, I a lost soul! I separated from hope and from peace for ever! It is not I of whom the

Judge so spake! There is a mistake somewhere; Christ, Saviour, hold Thy hand,—one minute to explain it! My name is Demas: I am but Demas, not Judas, or Nicolas, or Alexander, or Philetus, or Diotrephes. What? hopeless pain! for me! impossible, it shall not be." And the poor soul struggles and wrestles in the grasp of the mighty demon which has hold of it, and whose very touch is torment. "Oh, atrocious!" it shrieks in agony, and in anger too, as if the very keenness of the affliction were a proof of its injustice. "A second! and a third! I can bear no more! stop, horrible fiend, give over; I am a man, and not such as thou! I am not food for thee, or sport for thee! I never was in hell as thou, I have not on me the smell of fire, nor the taint of the charnel-house! I know what human feelings are; I have been taught religion; I have had a conscience; I have a cultivated mind; I am well versed in science and art; I have been refined by literature; I have had an eye for the beauties of nature; I am a philosopher or a poet, or a shrewd observer of men, or a hero, or a statesman, or an orator, or a man of wit and humour. Nay,—I am a Catholic; I am not an unregenerate Protestant; I have received the grace of the Redeemer; I have attended the Sacraments for years; I have been a Catholic from a child; I am a son of the Martyrs; I died in communion with the Church: nothing, nothing which I have ever been, which I have ever seen, bears any resemblance to thee, and to the flame and stench which exhale from thee; so I defy thee, and abjure thee, O enemy of man!"

Alas! poor soul; and whilst it thus fights with that destiny which it has brought upon itself, and with those companions whom it has chosen, the man's name perhaps is solemnly chanted forth, and his memory decently cherished among his friends on earth. His readiness in speech, his fertility in thought, his sagacity, or his wisdom, are not forgotten. Men talk of him from time to time; they appeal to his authority; they quote his words; perhaps they even raise a monument to his name, or write his history. "So comprehensive a mind! such a power of throwing light on a perplexed subject, and bringing conflicting ideas or facts into harmony!" "Such a speech it was that he made on such and such an occasion; I happened to be present, and never shall forget it;" or, "It was the saying of a very sensible man;" or, "A great personage, whom some of us knew;" or, "It was a rule with a very worthy and excellent friend of mine, now no more;" or, "Never was his equal in society, so just in his remarks, so versatile, so unobtrusive;" or, "I was fortunate to see him once when I was a boy;" or, "So great a benefactor to his country and to his kind!" "His discoveries so great;" or, "His philosophy so profound". O vanity! vanity of vanities, all is vanity! What profiteth it? What profiteth it? His soul is in hell. O ye children of men, while thus ye speak, his soul is in the beginning of those torments in which his body will soon have part, and which will never die.

Vanity of vanities! misery of miseries! they will not attend to us, they will not believe us. We are

but a few in number, and they are many ; and the
many will not give credit to the few.   O misery of
miseries !   Thousands are dying daily ; they are
waking up into God's everlasting wrath ; they look
back on the days of the flesh, and call them few and
evil; they despise and scorn the very reasonings which
then they trusted, and which have been disproved by
the event ; they curse the recklessness which made
them put off repentance ; they have fallen under His
justice, whose mercy they presumed upon ;—and their
companions and friends are going on as they did, and
are soon to join them.   As the last generation presumed, so does the present.   The father would not
believe that God could punish, and now the son will
not believe ; the father was indignant when eternal
pain was spoken of, and the son gnashes his teeth
and smiles contemptuously.   The world spoke well of
itself thirty years ago, and so will it thirty years to
come.   And thus it is that this vast flood of life is
carried on from age to age ; myriads trifling with
God's love, tempting His justice, and like the herd
of swine, falling headlong down the steep! O mighty
God!   O God of love! it is too much! it broke the
heart of Thy sweet Son Jesus to see the misery of man
spread out before His eyes.   He died by it as well as
for it.   And we, too, in our measure, our eyes ache,
and our hearts sicken, and our heads reel, when we
but feebly contemplate it.   O most tender heart of
Jesus, why wilt Thou not end, when wilt Thou end,
this ever-growing load of sin and woe ?   When wilt
Thou chase away the devil into his own hell, and close

the pit's mouth, that Thy chosen may rejoice in Thee, quitting the thought of those who perish in their wilfulness? But, oh! by those five dear Wounds in Hands, and Feet, and Side—perpetual founts of mercy, from which the fulness of the Eternal Trinity flows ever fresh, ever powerful, ever bountiful to all who seek Thee—if the world must still endure, at least gather Thou a larger and a larger harvest, an ampler proportion of souls out of it into Thy garner, that these latter times may, in sanctity, and glory, and the triumphs of Thy grace, exceed the former.

"*Deus misereatur nostri, et benedicat nobis;*" "God, have mercy on us, and bless us; and cause His face to shine upon us, and have mercy on us; that we may know Thy way upon earth, Thy salvation among all the nations. Let the people praise Thee, O God; let all the people praise Thee. Let the nations be glad, and leap for joy; because Thou dost judge the people in equity, and dost direct the nations on the earth. God, even our God, bless us, may God bless us; and may all the ends of the earth fear Him."

DISCOURSE III.

WHEN Christ, the great Prophet, the great Preacher, the great Missionary, came into the world, He came in a way the most holy, the most august, the most glorious. Though He came in humiliation, though He came to suffer, though He was born in a stable, though He was laid in a manger, yet He issued from the womb of an Immaculate Mother, and His infant form shone with heavenly light. Sanctity marked every lineament of His character and every circumstance of His mission. Gabriel announced His incarnation ; a Virgin conceived, a Virgin bore, a Virgin suckled Him ; His foster-father was the pure and saintly Joseph ; Angels proclaimed His birth ; a luminous star spread the news among the heathen ; the austere Baptist went before His face ; and a crowd of shriven penitents, clad in white garments and radiant with grace, followed Him wherever He went. As the sun in heaven shines through the clouds, and is reflected in the landscape, so the eternal Sun of justice, when He rose upon the earth, turned

(43)

night into day, and in His brightness made all things
bright.

He came and He went ; and, seeing that He came
to introduce a new and final Dispensation into the
world, He left behind Him preachers, teachers, and
missionaries, in His stead.   Well then, my brethren,
you will say, since on His coming all about Him was
so glorious, such as He was, such must His servants
be, such His representatives, His ministers, in His
absence ; as He was without sin, they too must be
without sin ; as He was the Son of God, they must
surely be Angels.   Angels, you will say, must be
appointed to this high office , Angels alone are fit to
preach the birth, the sufferings, the death of God.
They might indeed have to hide their brightness, as
He before them, their Lord and Master, had put on
a disguise ; they might come, as they came under the
Old Covenant in the garb of men ; but still men they
could not be, if they were to be preachers of the everlasting Gospel, and dispensers of its divine mysteries.
If they were to sacrifice, as He had sacrificed ; to continue, repeat, apply, the very Sacrifice which He had
offered ; to take into their hands that very Victim
which was He Himself ; to bind and to loose, to bless
and to ban, to receive the confessions of His people,
and to give them absolution for their sins ; to teach
them the way of truth, and to guide them along the
way of peace ; who was sufficient for these things
but an inhabitant of those blessed realms of which
the Lord is the never-failing Light ?

And yet, my brethren, so it is, He has sent forth

for the ministry of reconciliation, not Angels, but
men; He has sent forth your brethren to you, not
beings of some unknown nature and some strange
blood, but of your own bone and your own flesh, to
preach to you. "Ye men of Galilee, why stand ye
gazing up into heaven?" Here is the royal style
and tone in which Angels speak to men, even though
these men be Apostles; it is the tone of those who,
having never sinned, speak from their lofty eminence
to those who have. But such is not the tone of those
whom Christ has sent; for it is your brethren whom
He has appointed, and none else,—sons of Adam,
sons of your nature, the same by nature, differing
only in grace,—men, like you, exposed to temptations, to the same temptations, to the same warfare
within and without; with the same three deadly
enemies—the world, the flesh, and the devil; with
the same human, the same wayward heart: differing
only as the power of God has changed and rules it.
So it is; we are not Angels from Heaven that speak
to you, but men, whom grace, and grace alone, has
made to differ from you. Listen to the Apostle:—
When the barbarous Lycaonians, seeing his miracle,
would have sacrificed to him and St. Barnabas, as to
gods, he rushed in among them, crying out, "O
men, why do ye this? we also are mortals, men like
unto you;" or, as the words run more forcibly in
the original Greek, "We are of like passions with
you". And again to the Corinthians he writes, "We
preach not ourselves, but Jesus Christ our Lord; and
ourselves your servants through Jesus. God, who

commanded the light to shine out of darkness, He hath shined in our hearts, to give the light of the knowledge of the glory of God in the face of Christ Jesus: *but* we hold this treasure *in earthen vessels*." And further, he says of himself most wonderfully, that, " lest he should be exalted by the greatness of the revelations," there was given him " an angel of Satan " in his flesh " to buffet him ". Such are your Ministers, your Preachers, your Priests, O my brethren ; not Angels, not Saints, not sinless, but those who would have lived and died in sin except for God's grace, and who, though through God's mercy they be in training for the fellowship of Saints here- after, yet at present are in the midst of infirmity and temptation, and have no hope, except from the un- merited grace of God, of persevering unto the end.

What a strange, what a striking anomaly is this! All is perfect, all is heavenly, all is glorious, in the Dispensation which Christ has vouchsafed us, except the persons of His Ministers. He dwells on our altars Himself, the Most Holy, the Most High, in light inaccessible, and Angels fall down before Him there ; and out of visible substances and forms He chooses what is choicest to represent and to hold Him. The finest wheat-flour, and the purest wine, are taken as His outward symbols ; the most sacred and majestic words minister to the sacrificial rite ; altar and sanctuary are adorned decently or splendidly, as our means allow ; and the Priests perform their office in befitting vestments, lifting up chaste hearts and holy hands ; yet those very Priests, so set apart, so consecrated, they, with their girdle of celibacy **and** their maniple of sorrow, are sons of Adam, sons of sinners, of a fallen nature, which they have not put off, though it be renewed through grace, so that it is almost the definition of a Priest that he has sins of his own to offer for. " Every high Priest," says the Apostle, " taken from among men, is appointed for men, in the things that appertain unto God, that he may offer gifts and sacrifices for sins ; who can condole with those who are in ignorance and error, because he also himself is compassed with infirmity. And therefore he ought, as for the people, so also for himself, to offer for sins." And hence in the Mass, when he offers up the Host before consecration, he says, *Suscipe, Sancte Pater, Omnipotens, æterne Deus,* "Accept, Holy Father, Almighty, Everlasting God, this immaculate Host, which I, Thine unworthy servant, offer to Thee, my Living and True God, for *mine* innumerable sins, offences, and negligences, *and* for all who stand around, and for all faithful Christians, living and dead ".

Most strange is this in itself, my brethren, but not strange, when you consider it is the appointment of an all-merciful God ; not strange in Him, because the Apostle gives the reason of it in the passage I have quoted. The priests of the New Law are men, in order that they may " condole with those who are in ignorance and error, because they too are compassed with infirmity ". Had Angels been your Priests, my brethren, they could not have condoled with you, sympathised with you, have had compassion on you, felt tenderly for you, and made allowances for you, as we can ; they could not have been your patterns and guides, and have led you on from your old selves into a new life, as they can who come from the midst of you, who have been led on themselves as you are to be led, who know well your difficulties, who have had experience, at least of your temptations, who know the strength of the flesh and the wiles of the devil, even though they have baffled them, who are already disposed to take your part, and be indulgent towards you, and can advise you most practically, and warn you most seasonably and prudently. Therefore did He send you men to be the ministers of reconciliation and intercession ; as He Himself, though He could not sin, yet even He, by becoming man, took on Him, as far as was possible to God, man's burden of infirmity and trial in His own person. He could not be a sinner, but He could be a man, and He took to Himself a man's heart that we might entrust our hearts to Him, and "was tempted in all things, like as we are, yet without sin".

Ponder this truth well, my brethren, and let it be your comfort. Among the Preachers, among the Priests of the Gospel, there have been Apostles, there have been Martyrs, there have been Doctors ;—Saints in plenty among them ; yet out of them all, high as has been their sanctity, varied their graces, awful their gifts, there has not been one who did not begin with the old Adam; not one of them who was not hewn out of the same rock as the most obdurate of reprobates ; not one of them who was not fashioned unto honour out of the same clay which has been the material of the most polluted and vile of sinners ; not one who was not by nature brother of those poor souls who have now commenced an eternal fellowship with the devil, and are lost in hell.   Grace has vanquished nature ; that is the whole history of the Saints.   Salutary thought for those who are tempted to pride themselves in what they do, and what they are ; wonderful news for those who sorrowfully recognise in their hearts the vast difference that exists between them and the Saints ; and joyful news, when men hate sin, and wish to escape from its miserable yoke, yet are tempted to think it impossible !

Come, my brethren, let us look at this truth more narrowly, and lay it to heart.   First consider, that, since Adam fell, none of his seed but has been conceived in sin ; none, save one.   One exception there has been,—who is that one ? not our Lord Jesus, for He was not conceived of man, but of the Holy Ghost ; not our Lord, but I mean His Virgin Mother, who, though conceived and born of human parents, as others, yet was rescued by anticipation from the common condition of mankind, and never was partaker in fact of Adam's transgression.   She was conceived in the way of nature, she was conceived as others are ; but grace interfered and was beforehand with sin ; grace filled her soul from the first moment of her existence, so that the evil one breathed not on her, nor stained the work of God.   *Tota pulchra es, Maria ; et macula originalis non est in te.*   " Thou art all fair, O Mary, and the stain original is not in thee."   But

4

putting aside the Most Blessed Mother of God,
every one else, the most glorious Saint, and the
most black and odious of sinners, I mean, the soul
which, in the event, became the most glorious, and
the soul which became the most devilish, were
both born in one and the same original sin, both
were children of wrath, both were unable to attain
heaven by their natural powers, both had the prospect of meriting for themselves hell.

They were both born in sin; they both lay in sin;
and the soul, which afterwards became a Saint, would
have continued in sin, would have sinned wilfully,
and would have been lost, but for the visitings of an
unmerited supernatural influence upon it, which did
for it what it could not do for itself. The poor infant,
destined to be an heir of glory, lay feeble, sickly,
fretful, wayward, and miserable; the child of sorrow;
without hope, and without heavenly aid. So it lay
for many a long and weary day ere it was born; and
when at length it opened its eyes and saw the light, it
shrank back, and wept aloud that it had seen it. But
God heard its cry from heaven in this valley of tears,
and He began that course of mercies towards it which
led it from earth to heaven. He sent His Priest to
administer to it the first sacrament, and to baptise it
with His grace. Then a great change took place in it,
for, instead of its being any more the thrall of Satan
it forthwith became a child of God; and had it died
that minute, and before it came to the age of reason,
it would have been carried to heaven without delay by
Angels, and been admitted into the presence of God.

But it did not die; it came to the age of reason, and, oh, shall we dare to say, though in some blessed cases it may be said, shall we dare to say, that it did not misuse the great talent which had been given to it, profane the grace which dwelt in it, and fall into mortal sin? In some instances, praised be God! we dare affirm it; such seems to have been the case with my own dear father, St. Philip, who surely kept his baptismal robe unsullied from the day he was clad in it, never lost his state of grace, from the day he was put into it, and proceeded from strength to strength, and from merit to merit, and from glory to glory, through the whole course of his long life, till at the age of eighty he was summoned to his account, and went joyfully to meet it, and was carried across purgatory, without any scorching of its flames, straight to heaven.

Such certainly have sometimes been the dealings of God's grace with the souls of His elect; but more commonly, as if more intimately to associate them with their brethren, and to make the fulness of His favours to them a ground of hope and an encouragement to the penitent sinner, those who have ended in being miracles of sanctity, and heroes in the Church, have passed a time in wilful disobedience, have thrown themselves out of the light of God's countenance, have been led captive by this or that sin, by this or that religious error, till at length they were in various ways recovered, slowly or suddenly, and regained the state of grace, or rather a much higher state, than that which they had forfeited. Such was the blessed Magdalen, who had lived a life of shame; so much so, that even to be touched by her was, according to the religious judgment of her day, a pollution. Happy in this world's goods, young and passionate, she had given her heart to the creature, before the grace of God prevailed with her. Then she cut off her long hair, and put aside her gay apparel, and became so utterly what she had not been, that, had you known her before and after, you had said it was two persons you had seen, not one; for there was no trace of the sinner in the penitent, except the affectionate heart, now set on heaven and Christ; no trace besides, no memory of that glittering and seductive apparition, in the modest form, the serene countenance, the composed gait, and the gentle voice of her who in the garden sought and found her Risen Saviour. Such, too, was he who from a publican became an Apostle and an Evangelist; one who for filthy lucre scrupled not to enter the service of the heathen Romans, and to oppress his own people. Nor were the rest of the Apostles made of better clay than the other sons of Adam; they were by nature animal, carnal, ignorant; left to themselves, they would, like the brutes, have grovelled on the earth, and gazed upon the earth, and fed on the earth, had not the grace of God taken possession of them, and set them on their feet, and raised their faces heavenward. And such was the learned Pharisee, who came to Jesus by night, well satisfied with his station, jealous of his reputation, confident in his reason; but the time at length came, when, even though disciples fled, he remained to anoint the abandoned corpse of Him, whom when living he had been ashamed to own. You see it was the grace of God that triumphed it Magdalen, in Matthew, and in Nicodemus; heavenly grace came down upon corrupt nature; it subdued impurity in the youthful woman, covetousness in the publican, fear of man in the Pharisee.

Let me speak of another celebrated conquest of God's grace in an after age, and you will see how it pleases Him to make a Confessor, a Saint and Doctor of His Church, out of sin and heresy both together. It was not enough that the Father of the Western Schools, the author of a thousand works, the triumphant controversialist, the especial champion of grace, should have been once a poor slave of the flesh, but he was the victim of a perverted intellect also. He, who of all others, was to extol the grace of God, was left more than others to experience the helplessness of nature. The great St. Augustine (I am not speaking of the holy missionary of the same name, who came to England and converted our pagan forefathers, and became the first Archbishop of Canterbury, but of the great African Bishop, two centuries before him) —Augustine, I say, not being in earnest about his soul, not asking himself the question, how was sin to be washed away, but rather being desirous, while youth and strength lasted, to enjoy the flesh and the world, ambitious and sensual, judged of truth and falsehood by his private judgment and his private fancy; despised the Catholic Church because it spoke so much of faith and subjection, thought to make his own reason the measure of all things, and accordingly joined a far-spread sect, which affected to be philosophical and enlightened, to take large views of things, and to correct the vulgar, that is the Catholic notions of God and Christ, of sin, and of the way to heaven. In this sect of his he remained for some years ; yet what he was taught there did not satisfy him. It pleased him for a time, and then he found he had been eating as if food what had no nourishment in it ; he became hungry and thirsty after something more substantial, he knew not what ; he despised himself for being a slave to the flesh, and he found his religion did not help him to overcome it ; thus he understood that he had not gained the truth, and he cried out, "O, who will tell me where to seek it, and who will bring me into it?"

Why did he not join the Catholic Church at once? I have told you why ; he saw that truth was nowhere else ; but he was not sure it was there. He thought there was something mean, narrow, irrational, in her system of doctrine ; he lacked the gift of faith. Then a great conflict began within him,—the conflict of nature with grace ; of nature and her children, the flesh and false reason, against conscience and the pleadings of the Divine Spirit, leading him to better things. Though he was still in a state of perdition, yet God was visiting him, and giving him the first fruits of those influences which were in the event to bring him out of it. Time went on ; and looking at him, as his Guardian Angel might look at him, you would have said that, in spite of much perverseness, and many a successful struggle against his Almighty

Adversary, in spite of his still being, as before, in a state of wrath, nevertheless grace was making way in his soul,—he was advancing towards the Church. He did not know it himself, he could not recognise it himself; but an eager interest in him, and then a joy, was springing up in heaven among the Angels of God. At last he came within the range of a great Saint in a foreign country; and, though he pretended not to acknowledge him, his attention was arrested by him, and he could not help coming to sacred places to look at him again and again. He began to watch him and speculate about him, and wondered with himself whether he was happy. He found himself frequently in Church, listening to the holy preacher, and he once asked his advice how to find what he was seeking. And now a final conflict came on him with the flesh: it was hard, very hard, to part with the indulgences of years, it was **hard to** part and never to meet again. O, sin was so sweet, how could he bid it farewell? how could he tear himself away from its embrace, and betake himself to that lonely and dreary way which led heavenwards? But God's grace was sweeter far, and it convinced him while it won him; it convinced his reason, and prevailed;—and he who without it would have lived and died a child of Satan, became, under its wonder-working power, an oracle of sanctity and truth.

And do you not think, my brethren, that he was better fitted than another to persuade his brethren as he had been persuaded, and to preach the holy doctrine which he had despised? Not that sin is better than obedience, or the sinner than the just; but that God in His mercy makes use of sin against itself, that He turns past sin into a present benefit, that, while He washes away its guilt and subdues its power, He leaves it in the penitent in such sense as enables him, from his knowledge of its devices, to assault it more vigorously, and strike at it more truly, when it meets him in other men; that, while our Lord, by His omnipotent grace, can make the soul as clean as if it had never been unclean, He leaves it in possession of a tenderness and compassion for other sinners, an experience how to deal with them, greater than if it had never sinned; and again that, in those rare and special instances, of one of which I have been speaking, He holds up to us, for our instruction and our comfort, what He can do, even for the most guilty, if they sincerely come to Him for a pardon and a cure. There is no limit to be put to the bounty and power of God's grace; and that we feel sorrow for our sins, and supplicate His mercy, is a sort of present pledge to us in our hearts, that He will grant us the good gifts we are seeking. He can do what He will with the soul of man. He is infinitely more powerful than the foul spirit to whom the sinner has sold himself, and can cast him out.

O my dear brethren, though your conscience witnesses against you, He can disburden it; whether you have sinned less or whether you have sinned more, He can make you as clean in His sight and as acceptable to Him as if you had never gone from Him. Gradually will He destroy your sinful habits, and at once will He restore you to His favour. Such is the power of the

Sacrament of Penance, that, be your load of guilt heavier or be it lighter, it removes it, whatever it is. It is as easy to Him to wash out the many sins as the few. Do you recollect in the Old Testament the history of the cure of Naaman the Syrian, by the prophet Eliseus? He had that dreadful, incurable disease called the leprosy, which was a white crust upon the skin, making the whole person hideous, and typifying the hideousness of sin. The prophet bade him bathe in the river Jordan, and the disease disappeared; "his flesh," says the inspired writer, was "restored to him as the flesh of a little child". Here, then, we have a representation not only of what sin is, but of what God's grace is. It can undo the past, it can realise the hopeless. No sinner, ever so odious, but may become a Saint; no Saint, ever so exalted, but has been, or might have been, a sinner. Grace overcomes nature, and grace only overcomes it. Take that holy child, the blessed St. Agnes, who, at the age of thirteen, resolved to die rather than deny the faith, and stood enveloped in an atmosphere of purity, and diffused around her a heavenly influence, in the very home of evil spirits into which the heathen brought her; or consider the angelical Aloysius, of whom it hardly is left upon record that he committed even a venial sin; or St. Agatha, St. Juliana, St. Rose, St. Casimir, or St. Stanislas, to whom the very notion of any unbecoming imagination had been as death; well, there is not one of these seraphic souls but might have been a degraded, loathsome leper, except for God's grace, an outcast from his kind; not one but might, or rather would, have lived the life of a brute creature, and died the death of a reprobate, and lain down in hell eternally in the devil's arms, had not God put a new heart and a new spirit within him, and made him what he could not make himself.

All good men are not Saints, my brethren—all converted souls do not become Saints. I will not promise, that, if you turn to God, you will reach that height of sanctity which the Saints have reached:—true; still, I am showing you that even the Saints are by nature no better than you; and so (much more) that the Priests, who have the charge of the faithful, whatever be their sanctity, are by nature no better than those whom they have to convert, whom they have to reform. It is God's special mercy towards you that we by nature are no other than you; it is His consideration and compassion for you that He has made us, who are your brethren, His legates and ministers of reconciliation.

This is what the world cannot understand; not that it does not apprehend clearly enough that we are by nature of like passions with itself; but what it is so blind, so narrow-minded as not to comprehend, is, that, being so like itself by nature, we may be made so different by grace. Men of the world, my brethren, know the power of nature; they know not, experience not, believe not, the power of God's grace; and since they are not themselves acquainted with any power that can overcome nature, they think that none exists, and therefore, consistently, they believe that every one, Priest or not, remains to the end such as nature made him, and they will not believe it possible that any one can lead a supernatural life. Now, not Priest only, but every one who is in the grace of God, leads a supernatural life, more or less supernatural, according to his calling, and the measure of the gifts given him, and his faithfulness to them. This they know not, and admit not; and when they hear of the life which a Priest must lead by his profession from youth to age, they will not credit that he is what he professes to be. They know nothing of the presence of God, the merits of Christ, the intercession of the Blessed Virgin; the virtue of recurring prayers, of frequent confession, of daily Masses; they are strangers to the transforming power of the Most Holy Sacrament, the Bread of Angels; they do not contemplate the efficacy of salutary rules, of holy companions, of long-enduring habit, of ready spontaneous vigilance, of abhorrence of sin and indignation at the tempter, to secure the soul from evil. They only know that when the tempter once has actually penetrated into the heart, he is irresistible; they only know that when the soul has exposed and surrendered itself to his malice, there is (so to speak) a necessity of sinning. They only know that when God has abandoned it, and good Angels are withdrawn, and all safeguards, and protections, and preventives are neglected, that then (which is their own case), when the victory is all but gained already, it is sure to be gained altogether. They themselves have ever, in their best estate, been all but beaten by the Evil One before they began to fight; this is the only state they have experienced: they know this, and they know nothing else. They have never stood on vantage ground; they have never been within the walls of the strong city, about which the enemy prowls in vain, into which he cannot penetrate, and outside of which the faithful soul will be too wise to venture. They judge, I say, by their experience, and will not believe what they never knew.

If there be those here present, my dear brethren, who will not believe that grace is effectual within the Church, because it does little outside of it, to them I do not speak : I speak to those who do not narrow their belief to their experience; I speak to those who admit that grace can make human nature what it is not ; and such persons, I think, will feel it, not a cause of jealousy and suspicion but a great gain, a great mercy, that those are sent to preach to them, to receive their confessions, and to advise them, who can sympathise with their sins, even though they have not known them. Not a temptation, my brethren, can befall you, but what befalls all those who share your nature, though you may have yielded to it, and they may not have yielded. They can understand you, they can anticipate you, they can interpret you, though they have not kept pace with you in your course. They will be tender to you, they will " instruct you in the spirit of meekness," as the Apostle says, "considering themselves lest they also be tempted ". Come then unto us, all ye that labour and are heavy laden, and ye shall find rest to your souls ; come unto us, who now stand to you in Christ's stead, and who speak in Christ's name ; for we too, like you, have been saved by Christ's all-saving blood. We too, like you, should be lost sinners, unless Christ had had mercy on us, unless His grace had cleansed us, unless His Church had received us, unless His saints had interceded for us. Be ye saved, as we have been saved; "come, listen, all ye that fear God, and we will tell you what He hath done for our souls". Listen to our testimony; behold our joy of heart, and increase it by partaking in it yourselves. Choose that good part which we have chosen; join ye yourselves to our company; it will never repent you, take our word for it, who have a right to speak, it will never repent you to have sought pardon and peace from the Catholic Church, which alone has grace, which alone has power, which alone has Saints; it will never repent you, though you go through trouble, though you have to give up much for her sake. It will never repent you, to have passed from the shadows of sense and time, and the deceptions of human feeling and false reason, to the glorious liberty of the sons of God.

And O, my brethren, when you have taken the great step, and stand in your blessed lot, as sinners reconciled to the Father you have offended (for I will anticipate, what I surely trust will be fulfilled as regards many of you), O then forget not those who have been the ministers of your reconciliation; and as they now pray you to make your peace with God, so do you, when reconciled, pray for them, that they may gain the great gift of perseverance, that they may continue to stand in the grace in which they trust they stand now, even till the hour of death, lest, perchance, after they have preached to others, they themselves become reprobate.

DISCOURSE IV.

PURITY AND LOVE.

WE find two especial manifestations of divine grace
in the human heart, whether we turn to Scripture for instances of it, or to the history of the Church;
whether we trace it in the case of Saints, or in persons
of holy and religious life; and the two are even found
among our Lord's Apostles, being represented by the
two foremost of that favoured company, St. Peter and
St. John. St. John is the Saint of purity, and St. Peter
is the Saint of love. Not that love and purity can
ever be separated; not as if a Saint had not all virtues
in him at once; not as if St. Peter were not pure as
well as loving, and St. John loving, for all he was so
pure. The graces of the Spirit cannot be separated
from each other; one implies the rest; what is love
but a delight in God, a devotion to Him, a surrender
of the whole self to Him? what is impurity, on the
other hand, but the turning to something of this
world, something sinful, as the object of our affections
instead of God? What is it but a deliberate abandonment of the Creator for the creature, and seeking
pleasure in the shadow of death, not in the all-blissful

Presence of light and holiness? The impure then cannot love God; and those who are without love of God cannot really be pure. Purity prepares the soul for love, and love confirms the soul in purity. The flame of love will not be bright unless the substance which feeds it be pure and unadulterate; and the most dazzling purity is but as iciness and desolation unless it draws its life from fervent love.

Yet, certain as this is, it is certain also that the spiritual works of God show differently from each other to our eyes, and that they display, in their character and their history, some of them this virtue more than other virtues, and some that. In other words, it pleases the Giver of grace to endue His Saints specially with certain gifts, for His glory, which light up and beautify one particular portion or department of their souls, so as to cast their other excellences into the shade. And then this special gift of grace becomes their characteristic, and we put it first in our thoughts of them, and consider what they have besides as included in it, or dependent upon it, and speak of them as if they had not the rest, though we know they really have them; and we give them some title or description taken from that particular grace which is so emphatically theirs. And in this way we may speak, as I intend to do in what I am going to say, of two chief classes of Saints, whose emblems are the lily and the rose, who are bright with angelic purity or who burn with divine love.

The two St. Johns are the great instances of the Angelic life. Whom, my brethren, can we conceive to have such majestic and severe sanctity as the Holy Baptist? He had a privilege which reached near upon the prerogative of the Most Blessed Mother of God; for, if she was conceived without sin, at least without sin he was born. She was all-pure, all-holy, and sin had no part in her: but St. John was in the beginning of his existence a partaker of Adam's curse; he lay under God's wrath, deprived of that grace which Adam had received, and which is the life and strength of human nature. Yet, as soon as Christ, his Lord and Saviour, came to him, and Mary saluted his own mother, Elizabeth, forthwith the grace of God was given to him, and the original guilt was wiped away from his soul. And therefore it is that we celebrate the nativity of St. John; nothing unholy does the Church celebrate; not St. Peter's birth, nor St. Paul's, nor St. Augustine's, nor St. Gregory's, nor St. Bernard's, nor St. Aloysius's, nor the nativity of any other Saint, however glorious, because they were all born in sin. She celebrates their conversions, their prerogatives, their martyrdoms, their deaths, their translations, but not their birth, because in no case was it holy. Three nativities alone does she commemorate, our Lord's, His Mother's, and lastly, St. John's. What a special gift was this, my brethren, separating the Baptist off, and distinguishing him from all prophets and preachers, who ever lived, however holy, except perhaps the prophet Jeremias! And such as was his commencement, was the course of his life. He was carried away by the Spirit into the desert, and there he lived on the simplest fare, in the rudest clothing, in the caves of wild beasts, apart from men, for thirty years, leading a life of mortification and of prayer, till he was called to preach penance, to proclaim the Christ, and to baptise Him ; and then having done his work, and having left no act of sin on record, he was laid aside as an instrument which had lost its use, and languished in prison, till he was suddenly cut off by the sword of the executioner. Sanctity is the one idea of him impressed upon us from first to last; a most marvellous Saint, a hermit from his childhood, then a preacher to a fallen people, and then a Martyr. Surely such a life fulfils that expectation concerning him what follows on Mary's salutation of his mother before his birth.

Yet still more beautiful, and almost as majestic, is the image of his namesake, that great Apostle, Evangelist, and Prophet of the Church, who came so early into our Lord's chosen company, and lived so long after all his fellows. We can contemplate him in his youth and in his venerable age; and on his whole life, from first to last, as his special gift, is marked purity. He is the virgin Apostle, who on that account was so dear to his Lord, "the disciple whom Jesus loved," who lay on His Bosom, who received His Mother from Him when upon the Cross, who had the vision of all the wonders which were to come to pass in the world to the end of time. "Greatly to be honoured," says the Church, "is blessed John, who on the Lord's Breast lay at supper, to whom, a virgin, did Christ on the Cross commit his Virgin Mother. He was chosen a virgin by the Lord, and was more beloved than the rest. The special prerogative of chastity had made him meet for his Lord's larger love, because, being chosen by Him a virgin, a virgin he remained unto the end." He it was who in his youth professed his readiness to drink Christ's chalice with Him ; who wore away a long life as a desolate stranger in a foreign land ; who was at length carried to Rome and plunged into the hot oil, and then was banished to a far island, till his days drew near their close.

O how impossible it is worthily to conceive of the sanctity of these two great servants of God, so different is their whole history, in their lives and in their deaths, yet agreeing together in their seclusion from the world, in their tranquillity, and in their all but sinlessness ! Mortal sin had never touched them, and we may well believe that even from deliberate venial sin they were ever exempt; nay, that at particular seasons or on certain occasions they did not sin at all. The rebellion of the reason, the waywardness of the feelings, the disorder of the thoughts, the fever of passion, the treachery of the senses, these evils did the all-powerful grace of God subdue in them. They lived in a world of their own, uniform, serene, abiding; in visions of peace, in communion with heaven, in anticipation of glory ; and, if they spoke to the world without, as preachers or as confessors, they spoke as from some sacred shrine, not mixing with men while they addressed them, as " a voice crying in the wilderness " or " in the Spirit on the Lord's Day ". And therefore it is we speak of them rather as patterns of sanctity than of love, because love regards an external object, runs towards it and labours for it, whereas such Saints came so close to the Object of their love, they were granted so to receive Him into their breasts, and so to make themselves one with Him, that their hearts did not so much love heaven as were themselves a heaven, did not so much see light as were light ; and they lived among men as those Angels in the old time, who came to the patriarchs and spake as though they were God, for God was in them, and spake by them. Thus these two were almost absorbed in the Godhead, living an angelical life, as far as man could lead one, so calm, so still, so raised above sorrow and fear, disappointment and regret, desire and aversion, as to be the most perfect images that earth has seen of the peace and immutability of God. Such too are the many virgin Saints whom history records for our veneration, St. Joseph, the great St. Antony, St. Cecilia who was waited on by Angels, St. Nicolas of Bari, St. Peter Celestine, St. Rose of Viterbo, St. Catharine of Sienna, and a host of others, and above all, the Virgin of Virgins, and Queen of Virgins, the Blessed Mary, who, though replete and overflowing with the grace of love, yet for the very reason that she was the " seat of wisdom," and the " ark of the covenant," is more commonly represented under the emblem of the lily than of the rose.

But now, my brethren, let us turn to the other class of Saints. I have been speaking of those who in a wonderful, sometimes in a miraculous way, have been defended from sin, and conducted from strength to strength, from youth till death ; but now suppose it has been the will of God to shed the light and

power of His Spirit upon those who have misused the
talents, and quenched the grace already given them,
and who therefore have a host of evils within them of
which they are to be dispossessed ; who are under the
dominion of obstinate habits, indulged passions, false
opinions ; who have served Satan, not as infants
before their baptism, but with their will, with their
reason, with their faculties responsible, and their hearts
alive and conscious. Is He to draw these elect souls
to Him without themselves, or by means of themselves ? Is He to change them at His word, as He
created them, as He will make them die, as He will
raise them from the grave, or is He to enter into their
souls, to address Himself to them, to persuade them,
and so to win them ? Doubtless He might have been
urgent with them, and masterful ; He might by a
blessed violence have come upon them, and so turned
them into Saints ; He might have superseded any
process of conversion, and out of the very stones have
raised up children to Abraham. But He has willed
otherwise ; else, why did He manifest Himself on
earth ? Why did He surround Himself on His coming with so much that was touching and attractive
and subduing ? Why did He bid His angels proclaim
that He was to be seen as a little infant, in a manger
and in a Virgin's bosom, at Bethlehem ? Why did
He go about doing good ? Why did He die in public,
before the world, with His mother and His beloved
disciple by Him? Why does He now tell us how He
is exalted in Heaven with a host of glorified Saints,
who are our intercessors, about His throne ? Why

does He give us His own Mother Mary for our mother, the most perfect image after Himself of what is beautiful and tender, and gentle and soothing, in human nature? Why does He manifest Himself by an ineffable condescension on our Altars, still humbling Himself, though He reigns on high? What does all this show, but that, when souls wander away from Him, He reclaims them by means of themselves, "by cords of Adam," or of human nature, as the prophet speaks,—conquering us indeed at His will, saving us in spite of ourselves,—and yet by ourselves, so that the very reason and affections of the old Adam, which have been made "the instruments of iniquity unto sin," should, under the power of His grace, become "the instruments of justice unto God"?

Yes, doubtless He draws us "by cords of Adam," and what are those cords, but, as the prophet speaks in the same verse, "the cords," or "the twine of love"? It is the manifestation of the glory of God in the Face of Jesus Christ; it is that view of the attributes and perfections of Almighty God; it is the beauty of His sanctity, the sweetness of His mercy, the brightness of His heaven, the majesty of His law, the harmony of His providences, the thrilling music of His voice, which is the antagonist of the flesh, and the soul's champion against the world and the devil. "Thou hast seduced me, O Lord," says the prophet, "and I was seduced; Thou art stronger than I, and hast prevailed;" Thou hast thrown Thy net skilfully, and its subtle threads are entwined round each affection of my heart, and its meshes have been a power of God, "bring

ing into captivity the whole intellect to the service of Christ ". If the world has its fascinations, so surely has the Altar of the living God; if its pomps and vanities dazzle, so much more should the vision of Angels ascending and descending on the heavenly ladder; if sights of earth intoxicate, and its music is a spell upon the soul, behold Mary pleads with us, over against them, with her chaste eyes, and offers the Eternal Child for our caress, while sounds of cherubim are heard all round singing from out the fulness of the Divine Glory. Has divine hope no emotion? Has divine charity no transport? "How dear are Thy tabernacles, O Lord of hosts!" says the prophet; "my soul doth lust, and doth faint for the courts of the Lord; my heart and my flesh have rejoiced in the living God. Better is one day in Thy courts above a thousand: I have chosen to be an abject in the house of my God, rather than to dwell in the tabernacles of sinners."

So is it, as a great Doctor and penitent has said, St. Augustine; " It is not enough to be drawn by the will; thou art also drawn by the sense of pleasure. What is to be drawn by pleasure? 'Delight thou in the Lord, and He will give thee the petitions of thy heart.' There is a certain pleasure of heart, when that heavenly Bread is sweet to a man. Moreover, if the poet saith, 'Every one is drawn by his own pleasure,' not by necessity, but by pleasure; not by obligation, but by delight; how much more boldly ought we to say, that man is drawn to Christ, when he is delighted with truth, delighted with bliss, delighted with justice, delighted with eternal life, all which is Christ? Have the bodily senses their pleasures, and is the mind without its own? If so, whence is it said, 'The sons of men shall hope under the covering of Thy wings; they shall be intoxicate with the richness of Thy house, and with the torrent of Thy pleasure shalt Thou give them to drink: for with Thee is the well of life, and in Thy light we shall see light'? 'He, whom the Father draweth, cometh to Me'?" he continues; "Whom hath the Father drawn? him who said, 'Thou art Christ, the Son of the living God'. You present a green branch to the sheep, and you draw it forward; fruits are offered to the child, and he is drawn; in that he runs, he is drawn, he is drawn by loving, drawn without bodily hurt, drawn by the bond of the heart. If then it be true that the sight of earthly delight draws on the lover, doth not Christ too draw us when revealed by the Father? For what doth the soul desire more strongly than truth?"

Such are the means which God has provided for the creation of the Saint out of the sinner; He takes him as he is, and uses him against himself: He turns his affections into another channel, and extinguishes a carnal love by infusing a heavenly charity. Not as if He used him as a mere irrational creature, who is impelled by instincts and governed by external incitements without any will of his own, and to whom one pleasure is the same as another, the same in kind, though different in degree. I have already said, it is the very triumph of His grace, that He enters into the heart of man, and persuades it, and prevails with it, while He changes it. He violates in nothing that

original constitution of mind which He gave to man :
He treats him as man ; He leaves him the liberty of
acting this way or that ; He appeals to all his powers
and faculties, to his reason, to his prudence, to his
moral sense, to his conscience: He rouses his fears
as well as his love; He instructs him in the depravity
of sin, as well as in the mercy of God ; but still,
on the whole, the animating principle of the new
life, by which it is both kindled and sustained, is the
flame of charity. This only is strong enough to
destroy the old Adam, to dissolve the tyranny of
habit, to quench the fires of concupiscence, and to
burn up the strongholds of pride.

And hence it is that love is presented to us as the
distinguishing grace of those who were sinners before
they were Saints ; not that love is not the life of all
Saints, of those who have never needed a conversion,
of the Most Blessed Virgin, of the two St. John's, and
of those others, many in number, who are "first-fruits
unto God and the Lamb;" but that, while in those who
have never sinned gravely love is so contemplative as
almost to resolve itself into the sanctity of God Himself; in those, on the contrary, in whom it dwells as
a principle of recovery, it is so full of devotion, of zeal,
of activity, and good works, that it gives a visible
character to their history, and is ever associating
itself with our thoughts of them.

Such was the great Apostle, on whom the Church
is built, and whom I contrasted, when I began, with
his fellow-Apostle St. John: whether we contemplate
him after his first calling, or on his repentance, he who

denied his Lord, out of all the Apostles, is the most conspicuous for his love of Him. It was for this love of Christ, flowing on, as it did, from its impetuosity and exuberance, into love of the brethren, that he was chosen to be the chief Pastor of the fold. "Simon, son of John, lovest thou Me more than these?" was the trial put on him by his Lord; and the reward was, "Feed My lambs, feed My sheep". Wonderful to say, the Apostle whom Jesus loved, was yet surpassed in love for Jesus by a brother Apostle, not virginal as he; for it is not John of whom our Lord asked this question, and who was rewarded with this commission, but Peter.

Look back at an earlier passage of the same narrative; there, too, the two Apostles are similarly contrasted in their respective characters; for when they were in the boat, and their Lord spoke to them from the shore, and "they knew not that it was Jesus," first "that disciple, whom Jesus loved, said to Peter, It is the Lord," for "the clean of heart shall see God;" and then at once "Simon Peter," in the impetuosity of his love, "girt his tunic about him, and cast himself into the sea," to reach Him the quicker. St. John beholds and St. Peter acts.

Thus the very presence of Jesus enkindled Peter's heart, and at once drew him unto Him; also at a former time, when he saw his Lord walking on the sea, his very first impulse was, as in the passage to which I have been referring, to leave the vessel and hasten to His side: "Lord, if it be Thou, bid me come to Thee upon the waters". And when he had been

betrayed into his great sin, the very Eye of Jesus
brought him to himself: "And the Lord turned and
looked upon Peter; and Peter remembered the word
of the Lord, and he went out and wept bitterly".
Hence, on another occasion, when many of the disciples fell away, and "Jesus said to the twelve, Do
you too wish to go away?" St. Peter answered,
"Lord, to whom shall we go? Thou hast the words
of eternal life; and we have believed and have known
that Thou art Christ, the Son of God."

Such, too, was that other great Apostle, who, in so
many ways, is associated with St. Peter—the Doctor
of the Gentiles. He indeed was converted miraculously, by our Lord's appearing to him, when he
was on his way to carry death to the Christians of
Damascus: but how does he speak? "Whether we
are beside ourselves," he says, "it is to God; or
whether we be sober, it is for you: for the charity of
Christ constraineth us. If, therefore, any be a new
creature in Christ, old things have passed away,
behold all things are made new." And so again:
"With Christ am I nailed to the cross; but I live,
yet no longer I, but Christ liveth in me; and the life
I now live in the flesh, I live by the faith of the Son of
God, who loved me, and gave Himself for me". And
again: "I am the least of the Apostles, who am not
worthy to be called an Apostle, because I persecuted
the Church of God. But by the grace of God I am
what I am; and His grace in me hath not been void,
but I laboured more abundantly than they all, yet not
I, but the grace of God with me." And once more:

"Whether we live, unto the Lord we live ; whether we die, unto the Lord we die ; whether we live or whether we die, we are the Lord's ". You see, my brethren, the character of St. Paul's love ; it was a love fervent, eager, energetic, active, full of great works, "strong as death," as the inspired Word says, a flame which "many waters could not quench, nor the streams drown," which lasted to the end, when he could say, " I have fought the good fight, I have finished the course, I have kept the faith ; henceforth is laid up for me the crown of justice, which the Lord will render to me at that day, the just Judge".

And there is a third, my brethren, there is an illustrious third in Scripture, whom we must associate with these two great Apostles, when we speak of the saints of penance and love. Who is it but the loving Magdalen ? Who is it so fully instances what I am showing, as "the woman who was a sinner," who watered the Lord's feet with her tears, and dried them with her hair, and anointed them with precious ointment ? What a time for such an act ! She, who had come into the room, as if for a festive purpose, to go about an act of penance ! It was a formal banquet, given by a rich Pharisee, to honour, yet to try, our Lord. Magdalen came, young and beautiful, and "rejoicing in her youth," "walking in the ways of her heart and the gaze of her eyes : " she came as if to honour that feast, as women were wont to honour such festive doings, with her sweet odours and cool unguents for the forehead and hair of the guests. And he, the proud Pharisee, suffered her to come, so that she touched not him ; let her come as we might suffer inferior animals to enter our apartments, without caring for them ; perhaps suffered her as a necessary embellishment of the entertainment, yet as having no soul, or as destined to perdition, but anyhow as nothing to him. He, proud being, and his brethren like him, might "compass sea and land to make one proselyte ;" but, as to looking into that proselyte's heart, pitying its sin, and trying to heal it, this did not enter into the circuit of his thoughts. No, he thought only of the necessities of his banquet, and he let her come to do her part, such as it was, careless what her life was, so that she did that part well, and confined herself to it. But, lo, a wondrous sight ! was it a sudden inspiration, or a mature resolve? was it an act of the moment, or the result of a long conflict ?—but behold, that poor, many-coloured child of guilt approaches to crown with her sweet ointment the head of Him to whom the feast was given ; and see, she has stayed her hand. She has looked, and she discerns the Immaculate, the Virgin's Son, "the brightness of the Eternal Light, and the spotless mirror of God's majesty". She looks, and she recognises the Ancient of Days, the Lord of life and death, her Judge ; and again she looks, and she sees in His face and in His mien a beauty, and a sweetness, awful, serene, majestic, more than that of the sons of men, which paled all the splendour of that festive room. Again she looks, timidly yet eagerly, and she discerns in His eye, and in His smile, the loving-kindness, the tenderness, the compassion, the mercy of the Saviour of man. She looks at herself, and oh! how vile, how hideous is she, who but now was so vain of her attractions!—how withered is that comeliness, of which the praises ran through the mouths of her admirers!—how loathsome has become the breath, which hitherto she thought so fragrant, savouring only of those seven bad spirits which dwell within her! And there she would have stayed, there she would have sunk on the earth, wrapped in her confusion and in her despair, had she not cast one glance again on that all-loving, all-forgiving Countenance. He is looking at her: it is the Shepherd looking at the lost sheep, and the lost sheep surrenders herself to Him. He speaks not, but He eyes her; and she draws nearer to Him. Rejoice, ye Angels, she draws near, seeing nothing but Him, and caring neither for the scorn of the proud, nor the jests of the profligate. She draws near, not knowing whether she shall be saved or not, not knowing whether she shall be received, or what will become of her; this only knowing that He is the Fount of holiness and truth, as of mercy, and to whom should she go, but to Him who hath the words of eternal life? "Destruction is thine own, O Israel; in Me only is thy help. Return unto Me, and I will not turn away My face from thee: for I am holy, and will not be angry for ever." "Behold we come unto thee; for Thou art the Lord our God. Truly the hills are false, and the multitude of the mountains: Truly the Lord our God is the salvation of Israel." Wonderful meeting between what was most base and what is

most pure! Those wanton hands, those polluted lips,
have touched, have kissed the feet of the Eternal, and
He shrank not from the homage.   And as she hung
over them, and as she moistened them from her full
eyes, how did her love for One so great, yet so gentle,
wax vehement within her, lighting up a flame which
never was to die from that moment even for ever!
and what excess did it reach, when He recorded before all men her forgiveness, and the cause of it!
" Many sins are forgiven her, for she loved much; but
to whom less is forgiven, the same loveth less.   And
He said unto her, Thy sins are forgiven thee; thy
faith hath made thee safe, go in peace."

Henceforth, my brethren, love was to her, as to
St. Augustine and to St. Ignatius Loyola afterwards
(great penitents in their own time), as a wound in the
soul, so full of desire as to become anguish.   She
could not live out of the presence of Him in whom
her joy lay: her spirit languished after Him, when
she saw Him not; and waited on Him silently,
reverently, wistfully, when she was in His blissful
Presence.   We read of her (if it was she), on one occasion, sitting at His feet to hear His words, and of His
testifying that she had chosen that best part which
should not be taken away from her.   And, after His
resurrection, she, by her perseverance, merited to see
Him even before the Apostles.   She would not leave
the sepulchre, when Peter and John retired, but stood
without, weeping; and when the Lord appeared to her,
and held her eyes that she should not know Him, she
said piteously to the supposed keeper of the garden,

" Tell me where thou hast laid Him, and I will take Him away ". And when at length He made Himself known to her, she turned herself, and rushed impetuously to embrace His feet, as at the beginning, but He, as if to prove the dutifulness of her love, forbade her : " Touch Me not," He said, " for I have not yet ascended to My Father ; but go to my brethren and say to them, I ascend to my Father and your Father, to my God and your God ". And so she was left to long for the time when she should see Him, and hear His voice, and enjoy His smile, and be allowed to minister to Him, for ever in heaven.

Such then is the second great class of Saints, as viewed in contrast with the first. Love is the life of both : but while the love of the innocent is calm and serene, the love of the penitent is ardent and impetuous, commonly engaged in contest with the world, and active in good works. And this is the love which you, my brethren, must have in your measure, if you would have a good hope of salvation. For you were once sinners ; either by open and avowed contempt of religion, or by secret transgression, or by carelessness and coldness, or by some indulged bad habit, or by setting your heart on some object of this world, and doing your own will instead of God's, I think I may say you have needed, or now need, a reconciliation to Him. You have needed, or you need, to be brought near to Him, and to have your sins washed away in His blood, and your pardon recorded in Heaven. And what will do this for you, but contrition ? and what is contrition without love ? I do not say that you must have the love which Saints have, in order to your for giveness, the love of St. Peter or of St. Mary Magdalen ; but still without your portion of that same heavenly grace, how can you be forgiven at all ? If you would do works meet for penance, they must proceed from a living flame of charity. If you would secure perse- verance to the end, you must gain it by continual loving prayer to the Author and Finisher of faith and obedi- ence. If you would have a good prospect of His acceptance of you in your last moments, still it is love alone which secures His love, and blots out sin. My brethren, at that awful hour you may be unable to obtain the last Sacraments ; death may come on you suddenly, or you may be at a distance from a Priest. You may be thrown on yourselves, simply on your own compunction of heart, your own repentance, your own resolutions of amendment. You may have been weeks and weeks at a distance from spiritual aid ; you may have to meet your God without the safeguard, the compensation, the mediation of any holy rite ; and oh ! what will save you at such disadvantage, but the exercise of divine love " poured over your hearts by the Holy Ghost who is given to you "? At that hour nothing but a firm habit of charity, which has kept you from mortal sins, or a powerful act of charity which blots them out, will be of any avail to you. Nothing but charity can enable you to live well or to die well. How can you bear to lie down at night, how can you bear to go a journey, how can you bear the presence of pestilence, or the attack of ever so slight an indisposition, if you are ill provided in yourselves

with divine love against that change, which will come
on you some day, yet when and how you know not?
Alas! how will you present yourselves before the
judgment-seat of Christ, with the imperfect mixed
feelings which now satisfy you, with a certain amount
of faith, and trust, and fear of God's judgments, but
with nothing of that real delight in Him, in His
attributes, in His will, in His commandments, in His
service, which Saints possess in such fulness, and
which alone can give the soul a comfortable title to
the merits of His death and passion?

How different is the feeling with which the loving
soul, on its separation from the body, approaches the
judgment-seat of its Redeemer! It knows how great
a debt of punishment remains upon it, though it has
for many years been reconciled to Him; it knows that
purgatory lies before it, and that the best it can
reasonably hope for is to be sent there. But to see
His face, though for a moment! to hear His voice, to
hear Him speak, though it be to punish! O Saviour of
men, it says, I come to Thee, though it be in order to
be at once remanded from Thee; I come to Thee who
art my Life and my All; I come to Thee on the thought
of whom I have lived all my life long. To Thee I
gave myself when first I had to take a part in the
world; I sought Thee for my chief good early, for
early didst Thou teach me, that good elsewhere there
was none. Whom have I in heaven but Thee? whom
have I desired on earth, whom have I had on earth,
but Thee? whom shall I have amid the sharp flame
but Thee? Yea, though I be now descending thither,

into "a land desert, pathless and without water," I will fear no ill, for Thou art with me. I have seen Thee this day face to face, and it sufficeth; I have seen Thee, and that glance of Thine is sufficient for a century of sorrow, in the nether prison. I will live on that look of Thine, though I see Thee not, till I see Thee again, never to part from Thee. That eye of Thine shall be sunshine and comfort to my weary, longing soul; that voice of Thine shall be everlasting music in my ears. Nothing can harm me, nothing shall discompose me: I will bear the appointed years, till the end comes, bravely and sweetly. I will raise my voice, and chant a perpetual *Confiteor* to Thee and to Thy Saints in that dreary valley;—" to God Omnipotent, and to the Blessed Mary Ever-Virgin," (Thy Mother and mine, immaculate in her conception), "and to blessed Michael Archangel," (created in his purity by the very hand of God), and "to Blessed John Baptist," (sanctified even in his mother's womb); and after these three, "to the Holy Apostles Peter and Paul," (penitents, who compassionate the sinner from their experience of sin); "to all Saints," (whether they have lived in contemplation or in toil, during the days of their pilgrimage), to all Saints will I address my supplication, that they may "remember me, since it is well with them, and do mercy by me, and make mention of me unto the King that He bring me out of prison". And then at length "God shall wipe away every tear from my eyes, and death shall be no longer, nor mourning, nor crying, nor pain any more, for the former things are passed away".

DISCOURSE V.

SAINTLINESS THE STANDARD OF CHRISTIAN PRINCIPLE.

YOU know very well, my brethren, and there are few persons anywhere who deny it, that in the breast of every one there dwells a feeling or perception, which tells him the difference between right and wrong, and is the standard by which to measure thoughts and actions. It is called conscience; and even though it be not at all times powerful enough to rule us, still it is distinct and decisive enough to influence our views and form our judgments in the various matters which come before us. Yet even this office it cannot perform adequately without external assistance; it needs to be regulated and sustained. Left to itself, though it tells truly at first, it soon becomes wavering, ambiguous, and false; it needs good teachers and good examples to keep it up to the mark and line of duty; and the misery is, that these external helps, teachers, and examples are in many instances wanting.

Nay, to the great multitude of men they are so far wanting, that conscience loses its way and guides the soul in its journey heavenward but indirectly and circuitously. Even in countries called Christian, the natural inward light grows dim, because the Light, which lightens every one born into the world, is removed out of sight. I say, it is a most miserable and frightful thought. that, in this country, among this people which boasts that it is so Christian and so enlightened, the sun in the heavens is so eclipsed that the mirror of conscience can catch and reflect few rays, and serves but poorly and scantily to preserve the foot from error. That inward light, given as it is by God, is powerless to illuminate the horizon, to mark out for us our direction, and to comfort us with the certainty that we are making for our Eternal Home. That light was intended to set up within us a standard of right and of truth ; to tell us our duty on every emergency, to instruct us in detail what sin is, to judge between all things which come before us, to discriminate the precious from the vile, to hinder us from being seduced by what is pleasant and agreeable, and to dissipate the sophisms of our reason. But alas ! what ideas of truth, what ideas of holiness, what ideas of heroism, what ideas of the good and great, have the multitude of men ? I am not asking whether they act up to any ideas, or are swayed by any ideas, of these high objects; that is a further point ; I only ask, have they any ideas of them at all ? or, if they cannot altogether blot out from their souls their ideas of greatness and goodness, I ask still, whether their mode of conceiving of them, and the things and persons in which they embody them, be not such, that we may truly say of the bulk of mankind, that "the light that is in them is darkness".

Attend to me, my dear brethren, I am saying nothing very abstruse, nothing very difficult to understand, nothing unimportant ; but something intelligible, undeniable, and of very general concern. You know there are persons who never see the light of day ; they live in pits and mines, and there they work, there they take their pleasure, and there perhaps they die. Do you think they have any right idea, though they have eyes, of the sun's radiance, of the sun's warmth ? any idea of the beautiful arching heavens, the blue sky, the soft clouds, and the moon and stars by night ? any idea of the high mountain, and the green smiling earth ? O what an hour it is for him who is suddenly brought from such a pit or cave, from the dull red glow and the flickering glare of torches, and that monotony of an artificial twilight, in which day and night are lost,—is suddenly, I say, brought thence, and for the first time sees the bright sun moving majestically from East to West, and witnesses the gradual graceful changes of the air and sky from morn till fragrant evening ! And oh ! what a sight for one born blind to begin to see,—a sense altogether foreign to all his previous conceptions ! What a marvellous new state of being, which, though he ever had the senses of hearing and of touch, never had he been able, by the words of others, or any means of information he possessed, to bring home to himself in the faintest measure ! Would he not find himself, as it is said, in a "new world" ? What a revolution would take place in his modes of thought, in his habits, in his ways, and in his doings hour by hour! He would no longer direct himself with his hands and his hearing, he would no longer grope about; he would see ;—he would at a glance take in ten thousand objects, and, what is more, their relations and their positions the one towards the other. He would know what was great and what was little, what was near, what was distant, what things converged together and what things were ever separate— in a word, he would see all things as a whole, and in subjection to himself as a centre.

But further, he would gain knowledge of something closer to himself and more personal than all these various objects ; of something very different from the forms and groups in which light dwelt as in a tabernacle, and which excited his admiration and love. He would discover lying upon him, spreading over him, penetrating him, the festering seeds of unhealthiness and disease in their primary and minutest forms. The air around us is charged with a subtle powder or dust, which falls down softly on everything, silently sheds itself on everything, soils and stains everything, and, if suffered to remain undisturbed, induces sickness and engenders pestilence. It is like those ashes of the furnace which Moses was instructed to take up and scatter in the face of heaven, that they might become ulcers and blisters upon the flesh of the Egyptians. This subtle plague is felt in its ultimate consequences by all, the blind as well as those who see ; but it is by the eyesight that we discern it in its origin and in its progress ; it is by the sun's light that we discern our own defilement, and the need we have of continual cleansing to rid ourselves of it.

Now what is this dust and dirt, my brethren, but a figure of sin? so subtle in its approach, so multitudinous in its array, so incessant in its solicitations, so insignificant in its appearance, so odious, so poisonous in its effects. It falls on the soul gently and imperceptibly ; but it gradually breeds wounds and sores, and ends in everlasting death. And as we cannot see the atoms of dust that have settled on us without the light, and as that same light, which enables us to see them, teaches us withal, by their very contrast with itself, their unseemliness and dishonour, so the light of the invisible world, the teachings and examples of revealed truth, bring home to us both the existence and also the deformity of sin, of which we should be unmindful or forgetful without them. And as there are men who live in caverns and mines, and never see the face of day, and do their work as best they can by torch-light, so there are multitudes, nay, whole races of men, who, though possessed of eyes by nature, cannot use them duly, because they live in the spiritual pit, in the region of darkness, "in the land of wretchedness and gloom, where there is the shadow of death, and where order is not".

There they are born, there they live, there they die ; and instead of the bright, broad, and all-revealing luminousness of the sun, they grope their way from place to place with torches, as best they may, or fix up lamps at certain points, and " walk in the light of their fire, and in the flames which they have kindled ; " because they have nothing clearer, nothing purer, to serve the needs of the day and the year. Light of some kind they must secure, and, when they can do no better, they make it for themselves. Man, a being endued with reason, cannot on that very account live altogether at random ; he is obliged in some sense to live on principle, to live by rule, to profess a view of life, to have an aim, to set up a standard, and to take to him such examples as seem to him to fulfil it. His reason does not make him independent (as men sometimes speak) ; it forces on him a dependency on definite principles and laws, in order to satisfy its own demands. He must, by the necessity of his nature, look up to something ; and he creates, if he cannot discover, an object for his veneration. He teaches himself, or is taught by his neighbour, falsehoods, if he is not taught truth from above ; he makes to himself idols, if he knows not of the Eternal God and His Saints. Now, of which of the two, think you, my brethren, are our own countrymen in possession ? have they possession of the true Object of worship, or have they a false one? have they created what is not, or discovered what is ? do they walk by the luminaries of heaven, or are they as those who are born and live in caverns, and who strike their light as best they may, by means of the stones and metals of the earth ?

Look around, my brethren, and answer for yourselves. Contemplate the objects of this people's praise, survey their standards, ponder their ideas and judgments, and then tell me whether it is not most evident, from their very notion of the desirable and the excellent, that greatness, and goodness, and sanctity, and sublimity, and truth are unknown to them ; and that they not only do not pursue, but do not even admire, those high attributes of the Divine Nature. *This* is what I am insisting on, not what they actually do or what they are, but what they revere, what they adore, what their gods are. Their god is mammon ; I do not mean to say that all seek to be wealthy, but that all bow down before wealth. Wealth is that to which the multitude of men pay an instinctive homage. They measure happiness by wealth ; and by wealth they measure respectability. Numbers, I say, there are who never dream that they shall ever be rich themselves, but who still at the sight of wealth feel an involuntary reverence and awe, just as if a rich man must be a good man. They like to be noticed by some particular rich man ; they like on some occasion to have spoken with him ; they like to know those who know him, to be intimate with his dependants, to have entered his house, nay, to know him by sight. Not, I repeat, that it ever comes into their mind that the like wealth will one day be theirs ; not that they *see* the wealth, for the man who has it may dress, and live, and look like other men ; not that they expect to gain some benefit from it : no, theirs is a disinterested homage, it is a homage resulting from an honest, genuine, hearty admiration of wealth for its own sake, such as that pure love which holy men feel for the

Maker of all; it is a homage resulting from a profound faith in wealth, from the intimate sentiment of their hearts, that, however a man may look,—poor, mean, starved, decrepit, vulgar; or again, though he may be ignorant, or diseased, or feeble-minded, though he have the character of being a tyrant or a profligate, yet, if he be rich, he differs from all others; if he be rich, he has a gift, a spell, an omnipotence; —that with wealth he may do all things.

Wealth is one idol of the day, and notoriety is a second. I am not speaking, I repeat, of what men actually pursue, but of what they look up to, what they revere. Men may not have the opportunity of pursuing what they admire still. Never could notoriety exist as it does now, in any former age of the world; now that the news of the hour from all parts of the world, private news as well as public, is brought day by day to every individual, as I may say, of the community, to the poorest artisan and the most secluded peasant, by processes so uniform, so unvarying, so spontaneous, that they almost bear the semblance of a natural law. And hence notoriety, or the making a noise in the world, has come to be considered a great good in itself, and a ground of veneration. Time was when men could only make a display by means of expenditure; and the world used to gaze with wonder on those who had large establishments, many servants, many horses, richly-furnished houses, gardens, and parks: it does so still, that is, when it has the opportunity of doing so: for such magnificence is the fortune of the few, and comparatively few are its witnesses.

Notoriety, or, as it may be called, newspaper fame, is to the many what style and fashion, to use the language of the world, are to those who are within or belong to the higher circles ; it becomes to them a sort of idol, worshipped for its own sake, and without any reference to the shape in which it comes before them. It may be an evil fame or a good fame ; it may be the notoriety of a great statesman, or of a great preacher, or of a great speculator, or of a great experimentalist, or of a great criminal ; of one who has laboured in the improvement of our schools, or hospitals, or prisons, or workhouses, or of one who has robbed his neighbour of his wife. It matters not ; so that a man is talked much of, and read much of, he is thought much of ; nay, let him even have died justly under the hands of the law, still he will be made a sort of martyr of. His clothes, his handwriting, the circumstances of his guilt, the instruments of his deed of blood, will be shown about, gazed on, treasured up as so many relics ; for the question with men is, not whether he is great, or good, or wise, or holy ; not whether he is base, and vile, and odious, but whether he is in the mouths of men, whether he has centred on himself the attention of many, whether he has done something out of the way, whether he has been (as it were) canonised in the publications of the hour. All men cannot be notorious : the multitudes who thus honour notoriety, do not seek it themselves ; nor am I speaking of what men do, but how they judge ; yet instances do occur from time to time of wretched men, so smitten with passion for notoriety, as even to dare in fact some detestable and

wanton act, not from love of it, not from liking or
dislike of the person against whom it is directed, but
simply in order thereby to gratify this impure desire
of being talked about, and gazed upon. " These are
thy gods, O Israel!" Alas! alas! this great and
noble people, born to aspire, born for reverence, behold
them walking to and fro by the torch-light of the
cavern, or pursuing the wild-fires of the marsh, not
understanding themselves, their destinies, their defile-
ments, their needs, because they have not the glorious
luminaries of heaven to see, to consult, and to admire!

But oh! what a change, my brethren, when the
good hand of God brings them by some marvellous
providence to the pit's mouth, and then out into the
blessed light of day! what a change for them when
they first begin to see with the eyes of the soul, with
the intuition which grace gives, Jesus, the Sun of
Justice ; and the heaven of Angels and Archangels in
which He dwells ; and the bright Morning Star, which
is His Blessed Mother; and the continual floods of light
falling and striking against the earth, and transformed,
as they fall, into an infinity of hues, which are His
Saints ; and the boundless sea, which is the image of
His divine immensity ; and then again the calm, placid
Moon by night, which images His Church ; and the
silent stars, like good and holy men, travelling on in
lonely pilgrimage to their eternal rest ! Such was the
surprise, such the transport, which came upon the
favoured disciples, whom on one occasion our Lord
took up with Him to the mountain's top. He left the
sick world, the tormented, restless multitude, at its

foot, and He took them up, and was transfigured
before them. " His face did shine as the sun, and
His raiment was white as the light ; " and they lifted
their eyes, and saw on either side of Him a bright
form ;—these were two Saints of the elder covenant,
Moses and Elias, who were conversing with Him.
How truly was this a glimpse of Heaven ! the holy
Apostles were introduced into a new range of ideas,
into a new sphere of contemplation, till St. Peter,
overcome by the vision, cried out, " Lord, it is good
to be here ; and let us make three tabernacles ".   He
would fain have kept those heavenly glories always
with him ; everything on earth, the brightest, the
fairest, the noblest, paled and dwindled away, and
turned to corruption before them ; its most substantial good was vanity, its richest gain was dross, its
keenest joy a weariness, and its sin a loathsomeness
and abomination.   And such as this in its measure
is the contrast, to which the awakened soul is witness,
between the objects of its admiration and pursuit in
its natural state, and those which burst upon it when
it has entered into communion with the Church Invisible, when it has come " to Mount Sion, and to the
city of the Living God, the heavenly Jerusalem, and
to a company of many thousand Angels, and to the
Church of the first-born, who are enrolled in heaven,
and to God the Judge of all, and to the spirits of the
just now perfected, and to Jesus the Mediator of the
New Testament ".   From that day it has begun a new
life : I am not speaking of any moral conversion which
takes place in it ; whether or not it is moved (as surely

we believe it will be) to act upon the sights which it
sees, still consider only what a change there will be in
its views and estimation of things, as soon as it has
heard and has faith in the word of God, as soon as it
understands that wealth, and notoriety, and influence,
and high place, are not the first of blessings and the
real standard of good ; but that saintliness and all its
attendants,—saintly purity, saintly poverty, heroic
fortitude and patience, self-sacrifice for the sake of
others, renouncement of the world, the favour of
Heaven, the protection of Angels, the smile of the
Blessed Virgin, the gifts of grace, the interpositions
of miracle, the intercommunion of merits,—that these
are the high and precious things, the things to be
looked up to, the things to be reverently spoken of.
Hence worldly-minded men, however rich, if they are
Catholics, cannot, till they utterly lose their faith, be
the same as those who are external to the Church ;
they have an instinctive veneration for those who have
the traces of heaven upon them, and they praise what
they do not imitate.

Such men have an idea before them which a Protestant nation has not ; they have the idea of a Saint ;
they believe, they realise the existence of those rare
servants of God, who rise up from time to time in the
Catholic Church like Angels in disguise, and shed
around them a light, as they walk on their way heavenward.   Such Catholics may not in practice do what is
right and good, but they know what is true ; they know
what to think and how to judge.   They have a standard
for their principles of conduct, and it is the image of

Saints which forms it for them. A Saint is born like another man ; by nature a child of wrath, and needing God's grace to regenerate him. He is baptised like another, he lies helpless and senseless like another, and like another child he comes to years of reason. But soon his parents and their neighbours begin to say, " This is a strange child, he is unlike any other child ; " his brothers and his playmates feel an awe of him, they do not know why ; they both like him and dislike him, perhaps love him much in spite of his strangeness, perhaps respect him more than they love him. But if there were any holy Priest there, or others who had long served God in prayer and obedience, these would say, " This truly is a wonderful child ; this child bids fair to be a Saint ". And so he grows up, whether at first he is duly prized by his parents or not ; for so it is with all greatness, that, because it is great, it cannot be comprehended by ordinary minds at once ; but time, and distance, and contemplation are necessary for its being recognised by beholders, and, therefore, this special heir of glory of whom I am speaking, for a time at least excites no very definite observation, unless indeed (as sometimes happens) any thing of miracle occurs from time to time to mark him out. He has come to the age of reason, and, wonderful to say, he has never fallen away into sin. Other children begin to use the gift of reason by abusing it ; they understand what is right, only to go counter to it ; it is otherwise with him,—not that he may not sin in many things, when we place him in the awful ray of divine Sanctity, but that he does not sin wilfully and grievously,—he is preserved from mortal sin, he is never separated from God by sin, nay, perhaps, he is betrayed only at intervals, or never at all, into any deliberate sin, be it ever so slight, and he is ever avoiding the occasions of sin and resisting temptation. He ever lives in the presence of God, and is thereby preserved from evil, for "the wicked one toucheth him not". Nor, again, as if in other and ordinary matters he necessarily differed from other boys; he may be ignorant, thoughtless, improvident of the future, rash, impetuous; he is a child, and has the infirmities, failings, fears, and hopes of a child. He may be moved to anger, he may say a harsh word, he may offend his parents, he may be volatile and capricious, he may have no fixed view of things, such as a man has. This is not much to allow ; such things are accidents, and are compatible with the presence of a determinate influence of grace, uniting his heart to God. O that the multitude of men were as religious in their best seasons, as the Saints are in their worst! though there have been Saints who seem to have been preserved even from the imperfections I have been mentioning. There have been Saints whose reason the all-powerful grace of God seems wonderfully to have opened from the very time of their baptism, so that they have offered to their Lord and Saviour, "a living, holy, acceptable sacrifice," "a rational service," even while they have been infants. And, anyhow, whatever are the acts of infirmity and sin in the child I am imagining, still they are the exception in his day's course ; the course of each day is religious : while other children are light-minded, and cannot fix their thoughts in prayer, prayer and praise and meditation are his meat and drink. He frequents the Churches, and places himself before the Blessed Sacrament : or he is found before some holy image ; or he sees visions of the Blessed Virgin, or of the Saints to whom he is devoted. He lives in intimate converse with his guardian Angel, and he shrinks from the very shadow of profaneness or impurity. And thus he is a special witness of the world unseen, and he fulfils the vague ideas and the dreams of the supernatural, which one reads of in poems or romances, with which young people are so much taken, and after which they cannot help sighing, before the world corrupts them.

He grows up, and he has just the same temptations as others, perhaps more violent ones. Men of this world, carnal men, unbelieving men, do not believe that the temptations which they themselves experience and to which they yield, can be overcome. They reason themselves into the notion that to sin is their very nature, and, therefore, is no fault of theirs ; that is, they deny the existence of sin. And accordingly, when they read about the Saints or about holy men generally, they conclude either that these have not had the temptations which they experienced themselves, or that they have not overcome them. They either consider such an one to be a hypocrite, who practises in private the sins which he denounces in public; or, if they have decency enough to abstain from these calumnies, then they consider that he never felt the temptation, and they regard him as a cold and simple person, who has never outgrown his childhood, who has a contracted mind, who does not know the world and life, who is despicable while he is without influence, and dangerous and detestable from his very ignorance when he is in power. But no, my brethren; read the lives of the Saints, you will see how false and narrow a view this is; these men, who think, forsooth, they know the world so well, and the nature of man so deeply, they know nothing of one great far-spreading phenomenon in man,—and that is, his nature under the operation of grace; they know nothing of the second nature, of the supernatural gift, induced by the Almighty Spirit upon our first and fallen nature; they have never met, they have never read of, and they have formed no conception of, a Saint.

He has, I say, the same temptations as another; perhaps greater, because he is to be tried as in a furnace, because he is to become rich in merits, because there is a bright crown reserved for him in Heaven; still temptation he has, and he differs from others, not in being shielded from it, but in being armed against it. Grace overcomes nature; it overcomes indeed in all who shall be saved: none will see God's face hereafter who do not, while here, put away from them mortal sin of every kind; but the Saints overcome with a determination and a vigour, a promptitude and a success, beyond any one else. You read, my brethren, in the lives of Saints, the wonderful account of their conflicts, and their triumphs over the enemy. They are, as I was saying, like heroes of romance, so gracefully, so nobly, so royally do they bear themselves. Their actions are as beautiful as fiction, yet as real as fact. There was St. Benedict, who, when a boy, left Rome, and betook himself to the Apennines in the neighbourhood. Three years did he live in prayer, fasting, and solitude, while the Evil One assaulted him with temptation. One day, when it grew so fierce that he feared for his perseverance, he suddenly flung himself, in his scanty hermit's garb, among the thorns and nettles near him, thus turning the current of his thoughts, and chastising the waywardness of the flesh, by sensible stings and smarts. There was St. Thomas, too, the Angelical Doctor, as he is called, as holy as he was profound, or rather the more profound in theological science, because he was so holy. " Even from a youth " he had " sought wisdom, he had stretched out his hands on high, and directed his soul to her, and possessed his heart with her from the beginning ;" and so, when the minister of Satan came into his very room, and no other defence was at hand, he seized a burning brand from the hearth, and drove that wicked one, scared and baffled, out of his presence. And there was that poor youth in the early persecutions, whom the impious heathen bound down with cords, and then brought in upon him a vision of evil ; and he in his agony bit off his tongue, and spit it out into the face of the temptress, that so the intenseness of the pain might preserve him from the seduction.

Such acts as these, my brethren, are an opening of the heavens, a sudden gleam of supernatural brightness across a dark sky. They enlarge the mind with ideas it had not before, and they show to the multitude

what God can do, and what man can be. Not that
all Saints have been such in youth : for there are
those on the contrary, who, not till after a youth
of sin, have been brought by the sovereign grace
of God to repentance, still, when once converted,
they differed in nothing from those who had ever
served Him,—not in supernatural gifts, not in accept-
ableness, not in detachment from the world, nor in
union with Christ, nor in exactness of obedience,—in
nought save in the severity of their penance. Others
have been called, not from vice and ungodliness, but
from a life of mere ordinary blamelessness, or from a
state of lukewarmness, or from thoughtlessness, to
heroical greatness ; and these have often given up
lands, and property, and honours, and station, and
repute, for Christ's sake. Kings have descended
from their thrones, bishops have given up their rank
and influence, the learned have given up their pride
of intellect, to become poor monks, to live on coarse
fare, to be clad in humble weeds, to rise and pray
while others slept, to mortify the tongue with silence
and the limbs with toil, and to avow an unconditional
obedience to another. In early times were the Martyrs,
many of them girls and even children, who bore the
most cruel, the most prolonged, the most diversified
tortures, rather than deny the faith of Christ. Then
came the Missionaries among the heathen, who, for
the love of souls, threw themselves into the midst of
savages, risking and perhaps losing their lives in the
attempt to extend the empire of their Lord and
Saviour, and who, whether living or dying, have by

their lives or by their deaths succeeded in bringing over whole nations into the Church. Others have devoted themselves in the time of war or captivity, to the redemption of Christian slaves from pagan or Mahometan masters or conquerors; others to the care of the sick in pestilences, or in hospitals; others to the instruction of the poor; others to the education of children; others to incessant preaching and the duties of the confessional; others to devout study and meditation; others to a life of intercession and prayer. Very various are the Saints, their very variety is a token of God's workmanship; but however various, and whatever was their special line of duty, they have been heroes in it; they have attained such noble self-command, they have so crucified the flesh, they have so renounced the world; they are so meek, so gentle, so tender-hearted, so merciful, so sweet, so cheerful, so full of prayer, so diligent, so forgetful of injuries; they have sustained such great and continued pains, they have persevered in such vast labours, they have made such valiant confessions, they have wrought such abundant miracles, they have been blessed with such strange successes, that they have been the means of setting up a standard before us of truth, of magnanimity, of holiness, of love. They are not always our examples, we are not always bound to follow them; not more than we are bound to obey literally some of our Lord's precepts, such as turning the cheek or giving away the coat; not more than we can follow the course of the sun, moon, or stars in the heavens; but, though not always our examples, they are always our standard of right and good ; they are raised up to be monuments and lessons, they remind us of God, they introduce us into the unseen world, they teach us what Christ loves, they track out for us the way which leads heavenward. They are to us who see them, what wealth, notoriety, rank, and name are to the multitude of men who live in darkness,—objects of our veneration and of our homage.

O who can doubt between the two ? The national religion has many attractions; it leads to decency and order, propriety of conduct, justness of thought, beautiful domestic tastes; but it has not power to lead the multitude upward, or to delineate for them the Heavenly City. It comes of mere nature, and its teaching is of nature. It uses religious words, of course, else it could not be called a religion ; but it does not impress on the imagination, it does not engrave upon the heart, it does not inflict upon the conscience, the supernatural; it does not introduce into the popular mind any great ideas, such as are to be recognised by one and all, as common property, and first principles or dogmas from which to start, to be taken for granted on all hands, and handed down as forms and specimens of eternal truth from age to age. It in no true sense inculcates the Unseen ; and by consequence, sights of this world, material tangible objects, become the idols and the ruin of its children, of souls which were made for God and Heaven. It is powerless to resist the world and the world's teaching : it cannot supplant error by truth; it follows when it should lead. There is but one real Antagonist of the world, and that is the faith of Catholics;— Christ set that faith up, and it will do its work on earth, as it ever has done, till He comes again.

DISCOURSE VI.

GOD'S WILL THE END OF LIFE.

I AM going to ask you a question, my dear brethren, so trite, and therefore so uninteresting at first sight, that you may wonder why I put it, and may object that it will be difficult to fix the mind on it, and may anticipate that nothing profitable can be made of it. It is this:—"Why were you sent into the world?" Yet, after all, it is perhaps a thought more obvious than it is common, more easy than it is familiar; I mean it ought to come into your minds, but it does not, and you never had more than a distant acquaintance with it, though that sort of acquaintance with it you have had for many years. Nay, once or twice, perhaps you have been thrown across the thought somewhat intimately, for a short season, but this was an accident which did not last. There are those who recollect the first time, as it would seem, when it came home to them. They were but little children, and they were by themselves, and they spontaneously asked themselves, or rather God spake in them, "Why am I here? how came I here? who brought me here? What am I to do here?" Perhaps it was

(104)

the first act of reason, the beginning of their real responsibility, the commencement of their trial ; perhaps from that day they may date their capacity, their awful power, of choosing between good and evil, and of committing mortal sin. And so, as life goes on, the thought comes vividly, from time to time, for a short season across their conscience ; whether in illness, or in some anxiety, or at some season of solitude, or on hearing some preacher, or reading some religious work. A vivid feeling comes over them of the vanity and unprofitableness of the world, and then the question recurs, " Why then am I sent into it ? "

And a great contrast indeed does this vain, unprofitable, yet overbearing world present with such a question as that. It seems out of place to ask such a question in so magnificent, so imposing a presence, as that of the great Babylon. The world professes to supply all that we need, as if we were sent into it for the sake of being sent here, and for nothing beyond the sending. It is a great favour to have an introduction to this august world. This is to be our exposition, forsooth, of the mystery of life. Every man is doing his own will here, seeking his own pleasure, pursuing his own ends, and that is why he was brought into existence. Go abroad into the streets of the populous city, contemplate the continuous outpouring there of human energy, and the countless varieties of human character, and be satisfied ! The ways are thronged, carriage-way and pavement ; multitudes are hurrying to and fro, each on his own errand, or are loitering about from listlessness, or from want of work, or have come forth into the public concourse, to see and to be seen, for amusement or for display, or on the excuse of business. The carriages of the wealthy mingle with the slow wains laden with provisions or merchandise, the productions of art or the demands of luxury. The streets are lined with shops, open and gay, inviting customers, and widen now and then into some spacious square or place, with lofty masses of brickwork or of stone, gleaming in the fitful sunbeam, and surrounded or fronted with what simulates a garden's foliage. Follow them in another direction, and you find the whole groundstead covered with large buildings, planted thickly up and down, the homes of the mechanical arts. The air is filled, below, with a ceaseless, importunate, monotonous din, which penetrates even to your most innermost chamber, and rings in your ears even when you are not conscious of it ; and overhead, with a canopy of smoke, shrouding God's day from the realms of obstinate sullen toil. This is the end of man !

Or stay at home, and take up one of those daily prints, which are so true a picture of the world ; look down the columns of advertisements, and you will see the catalogue of pursuits, projects, aims, anxieties, amusements, indulgences which occupy the mind of man. He plays many parts : here he has goods to sell, there he wants employment ; there again he seeks to borrow money, here he offers you houses, great seats or small tenements ; he has food for the million, and luxuries for the wealthy, and sovereign medicines for the credulous, and books, new and cheap, for the inquisitive. Pass on to the news of the day, and you will learn what great men are doing at home and abroad: you will read of wars and rumours of wars; of debates in the Legislature; of rising men, and old statesmen going off the scene; of political contests in this city or that county; of the collision of rival interests. You will read of the money market, and the provision market, and the market for metals; of the state of trade, the call for manufactures, news of ships arrived in port, of accidents at sea, of exports and imports, of gains and losses, of frauds and their detection. Go forward, and you arrive at discoveries in art and science, discoveries (so-called) in religion, the court and royalty, the entertainments of the great, places of amusement, strange trials, offences, accidents, escapes, exploits, experiments, contests, ventures. O this curious, restless, clamorous, panting being, which we call life!—and is there to be no end to all this? Is there no object in it? It never has an end, it is forsooth its own object!

And now, once more, my brethren, put aside what you see and what you read of the world, and try to penetrate into the hearts, and to reach the ideas and the feelings of those who constitute it; look into them as closely as you can; enter into their houses and private rooms; strike at random through the streets and lanes: take as they come, palace and hovel, office or factory, and what will you find? Listen to their words, witness, alas! their works; you will find in the main the same lawless thoughts, the same unrestrained desires, the same ungoverned passions, the same earthly opinions, the same wilful deeds, in high and low, learned and unlearned ; you will find them all to be living for the sake of living; they one and all seem to tell you, " We are our own centre, our own end ". Why are they toiling ? why are they scheming? for what are they living? " We live to please ourselves ; life is worthless except we have our own way ; we are not *sent* here at all, but we find ourselves here, and we are but slaves unless we can think what we will, believe what we will, love what we will, hate what we will, do what we will. We detest interference on the part of God or man. We do not bargain to be rich or to be great ; but we do bargain, whether rich or poor, high or low, to live for ourselves, to live for the lust of the moment, or, according to the doctrine of the hour, thinking of the future and the unseen just as much or as little as we please."

O my brethren, is it not a shocking thought, but who can deny its truth ? The multitude of men are living without any aim beyond this visible scene ; they may from time to time use religious words, or they may profess a communion or a worship, as a matter of course, or of expedience, or of duty, but, if there was any sincerity in such profession, the course of the world could not run as it does. What a contrast is all this to the end of life, as it is set before us in our most holy Faith ! If there was one among the sons of men, who might allowably have taken His pleasure, and have done His own will here below, surely it was He who came down on earth from the bosom of the Father, and who was so pure and spotless in that human nature which He put on Him, that He could have no human purpose or aim inconsistent with the will of His Father. Yet He, the Son of God, the Eternal Word, came, not to do His own will, but His who sent Him, as you know very well is told us again and again in Scripture. Thus the Prophet in the Psalter, speaking in His person, says, "Lo, I come to do Thy will, O God". And He says in the Prophet Isaias, "The Lord God hath opened Mine ear, and I do not resist; I have not gone back". And in the Gospel, when He had come on earth, "My food is to do the will of Him that sent Me, and to finish His work". Hence, too, in His agony, He cried out, "Not My will, but Thine, be done;" and St. Paul, in like manner, says, that "Christ pleased not Himself;" and elsewhere, that, "though He was God's Son, yet learned He obedience by the things which He suffered". Surely so it was; as being indeed the Eternal Co-equal Son, His will was one and the same with the Father's will, and He had no submission of will to make; but He chose to take on Him man's nature, and the will of that nature; He chose to take on Him affections, feelings, and inclinations proper to man, a will innocent indeed and good, but still a man's will, distinct from God's will; a will, which, had it acted simply according to what was pleasing to its nature, would, when pain and toil were to be endured, have held back from an active co-operation with the will of God. But, though He took on Himself the nature of man, He took not on Him that selfishness, with which fallen man wraps himself round, but in all things He devoted Himself as a ready sacrifice to His Father. He came on earth, not to take His pleasure, not to follow His taste, not for the mere exercise of human affection, but simply to glorify His Father and to do His will. He came charged with a mission, deputed for a work ; He looked not to the right nor to the left, He thought not of Himself, He offered Himself up to God.

Hence it is that He was carried in the womb of a poor woman, who, before His birth, had two journeys to make, of love and of obedience, to the mountains and to Bethlehem. He was born in a stable, and laid in a manger. He was hurried off to Egypt to sojourn there ; then He lived till He was thirty years of age in a poor way, by a rough trade, in a small house, in a despised town. Then, when He went out to preach, He had not where to lay His head ; He wandered up and down the country, as a stranger upon earth. He was driven out into the wilderness, and dwelt among the wild beasts. He endured heat and cold, hunger and weariness, reproach and calumny. His food was coarse bread, and fish from the lake, or depended on the hospitality of strangers. And as He had already left His Father's greatness on high, and had chosen an earthly home ; so again, at that Father's bidding, He gave up the sole solace given Him in this world, and denied Himself His Mother's presence. He parted with her who bore Him ; He endured to be

strange to her; He endured to call her coldly
" woman," who was His own undefiled one, all
beautiful, all gracious, the best creature of His hands,
and the sweet nurse of His infancy. He put her
aside, as Levi, His type, merited the sacred ministry,
by saying to His parents and kinsmen, " I know you
not". He exemplified in His own person the severe
maxim, which He gave to His disciples, " He that
loveth mother more than Me is not worthy of Me ".
In all these many ways He sacrificed every wish of
His own ; that we might understand, that, if He, the
Creator, came into His own world, not for His own
pleasure, but to do His Father's will, we too have
most surely some work to do, and have seriously to
bethink ourselves what that work is.

Yes, so it is ; realise it, my brethren ;—every one
who breathes, high and low, educated and ignorant,
young and old, man and woman, has a mission, has
a work. We are not sent into this world for nothing ;
we are not born at random ; we are not here, that we
may go to bed at night, and get up in the morning,
toil for our bread, eat and drink, laugh and joke, sin
when we have a mind, and reform when we are tired
of sinning, rear a family and die. God sees every one
of us ; He creates every soul, He lodges it in the body,
one by one, for a purpose. He needs, He deigns to
need, every one of us. He has an end for each of us ;
we are all equal in His sight, and we are placed in
our different ranks and stations, not to get what we
can out of them for ourselves, but to labour in them
for Him. As Christ has His work, we too have ours ;

as He rejoiced to do His work, we must rejoice in ours also.

St. Paul on one occasion speaks of the world as a scene in a theatre. Consider what is meant by this. You know, actors on a stage are on an equality with each other really, but for the occasion they assume a difference of character ; some are high, some are low, some are merry, and some sad. Well, would it not be a simple absurdity in any actor to pride himself on his mock diadem, or his edgeless sword, instead of attending to his part? what, if he did but gaze at himself and his dress? what, if he secreted, or turned to his own use, what was valuable in it? Is it not his business, and nothing else, to act his part well? common sense tells us so. Now we are all but actors in this world ; we are one and all equal, we shall be judged as equals as soon as life is over ; yet, equal and similar in ourselves, each has his special part at present, each has his work, each has his mission,—not to indulge his passions, not to make money, not to get a name in the world, not to save himself trouble, not to follow his bent, not to be selfish and self-willed, but to do what God puts on him to do.

Look at that poor profligate in the Gospel, look at Dives; do you think he understood that his wealth was to be spent, not on himself, but for the glory of God?—yet for forgetting this, he was lost for ever and ever. I will tell you what he thought, and how he viewed things:—he was a young man, and had succeeded to a good estate, and he determined to enjoy himself. It did not strike him that his wealth had any other use than that of enabling him to take his pleasure. Lazarus lay at his gate; he might have relieved Lazarus; *that* was God's will; but he managed to put conscience aside, and he persuaded himself he should be a fool, if he did not make the most of this world, while he had the means. So he resolved to have his fill of pleasure; and feasting was to his mind a principal part of it. "He fared sumptuously every day;" everything belonging to him was in the best style, as men speak; his house, his furniture, his plate of silver and gold, his attendants, his establishments. Everything was for enjoyment, and for show too; to attract the eyes of the world, and to gain the applause and admiration of his equals, who were the companions of his sins. These companions were doubtless such as became a person of such pretensions; they were fashionable men; a collection of refined, high-bred, haughty men, eating, not gluttonously, but what was rare and costly; delicate, exact, fastidious in their taste, from their very habits of indulgence; not eating for the mere sake of eating, or drinking for the mere sake of drinking, but making a sort of science of their sensuality; sensual, carnal, as flesh and blood can be, with eyes, ears, tongue steeped in impurity, every thought, look, and sense, witnessing or ministering to the evil one who ruled them; yet, with exquisite correctness of idea and judgment, laying down rules for sinning;—heartless and selfish, high, punctilious, and disdainful in their outward deportment, and shrinking from Lazarus,

8

who lay at the gate, as an eye-sore, who ought for the sake of decency to be put out of the way. Dives was one of such, and so he lived his short span, thinking of nothing, loving nothing, but himself, till one day he got into a fatal quarrel with one of his godless associates, or he caught some bad illness ; and then he lay helpless on his bed of pain, cursing fortune and his physician, that he was no better, and impatient that he was thus kept from enjoying his youth, trying to fancy himself mending when he was getting worse, and disgusted at those who would not throw him some word of comfort in his suspense, and turning more resolutely from his Creator in proportion to his suffering ;—and then at last his day came, and he died, and (oh! miserable!) "was buried in hell". And so ended he and his mission.

This was the fate of your pattern and idol, O ye, if any of you be present, young men, who, though not possessed of wealth and rank, yet affect the fashions of those who have them. You, my brethren, have not been born splendidly or nobly ; you have not been brought up in the seats of liberal education ; you have no high connexions ; you have not learned the manners nor caught the tone of good society ; you have no share of the largeness of mind, the candour, the romantic sense of honour, the correctness of taste, the consideration for others, and the gentleness which the world puts forth as its highest type of excellence ; you have not come near the courts or the mansions of the great ; yet you ape the sin of Dives, while you are strangers to his refinement. You think it the sign of

a gentleman to set yourselves above religion, to criticise the religious and professors of religion, to look
at Catholic and Methodist with impartial contempt,
to gain a smattering of knowledge on a number of
subjects, to dip into a number of frivolous publications, if they are popular, to have read the latest
novel, to have heard the singer and seen the actor of
the day, to be well up with the news, to know the names
and, if so be, the persons of public men, to be able to
bow to them, to walk up and down the street with
your heads on high, and to stare at whatever meets
you; and to say and do worse things, of which these
outward extravagances are but the symbol.   And this
is what you conceive you have come upon earth for!
The Creator made you, it seems, O my children, for
this work and office, to be a bad imitation of polished
ungodliness, to be a piece of tawdry and faded finery,
or a scent which has lost its freshness, and does but
offend the sense!   O! that you could see how absurd
and base are such pretences in the eyes of any but
yourselves!   No calling of life but is honourable; no
one is ridiculous who acts suitably to his calling and
estate; no one, who has good sense and humility, but
may, in any station of life, be truly well-bred and
refined; but ostentation, affectation, and ambitious
efforts are, in every station of life, high or low,
nothing but vulgarities.   Put them aside, despise
them yourselves, O my very dear sons, whom I love,
and whom I would fain serve;—oh! that you could feel
that you have souls! oh, that you would have mercy
on your souls! oh, that, before it is too late, you

would betake yourselves to Him who is the Source of all that is truly high and magnificent and beautiful, all that is bright and pleasant, and secure what you ignorantly seek, in Him whom you so wilfully, so awfully despise!

He alone, the Son of God, "the brightness of the Eternal Light, and the spotless mirror of His Majesty," is the source of all good and all happiness to rich and poor, high and low. If you were ever so high, you would need Him; if you were ever so low, you could offend Him. The poor can offend Him; the poor man can neglect his divinely appointed mission as well as the rich. Do not suppose, my brethren, that what I have said against the upper or the middle class, will not, if you happen to be poor, also lie against you. Though a man were as poor as Lazarus, he could be as guilty as Dives. If you are resolved to degrade yourselves to the brutes of the field, who have no reason and no conscience, you need not wealth or rank to enable you to do so. Brutes have no wealth; they have no pride of life; they have no purple and fine linen, no splendid table, no retinue of servants, and yet they are brutes. They are brutes by the law of their nature: they are the poorest among the poor; there is not a vagrant and outcast who is so poor as they; they differ from him, not in their possessions, but in their want of a soul, in that he has a mission and they have not, he can sin and they can not. O my brethren, it stands to reason, a man may intoxicate himself with a cheap draught, as well as with a costly one; he may steal another's money for his appetites, though he does not waste his own upon them ; he may break through the natural and social laws which encircle him, and profane the sanctity of family duties, though he be, not a child of nobles, but a peasant or artisan,—nay, and perhaps he does so more frequently than they. This is not the poor's blessedness, that he has less temptations to self-indulgence, for he has as many, but that from his circumstances he receives the penances and corrections of self-indulgence. Poverty is the mother of many pains and sorrows in their season, and these are God's messengers to lead the soul to repentance ; but, alas ! if the poor man indulges his passions, thinks little of religion, puts off repentance, refuses to make an effort, and dies without conversion, it matters nothing that he was poor in this world, it matters nothing that he was less daring than the rich, it matters not that he promised himself God's favour, that he sent for the Priest when death came, and received the last Sacraments ; Lazarus too, in that case, shall be buried with Dives in hell, and shall have had his consolation neither in this world nor in the world to come.

My brethren, the simple question is, whatever a man's rank in life may be, does he in that rank perform the work which God has given him to do ? Now then, let me turn to others, of a very different description, and let me hear what they will say, when the question is asked them ;—why, they will parry it thus : —" You give us no alternative," they will say to me, " except that of being sinners or Saints. You put

before us our Lord's pattern, and you spread before us
the guilt and the ruin of the deliberate transgressor;
whereas we have no intention of going so far one way
or the other; we do not aim at being Saints, but we
have no desire at all to be sinners. We neither intend
to disobey God's will, nor to give up our own. Surely
there is a middle way, and a safe one, in which God's
will and our will may both be satisfied. We mean to
enjoy both this world and the next. We will guard
against mortal sin; we are not obliged to guard
against venial; indeed it would be endless to attempt
it. None but Saints do so; it is the work of a life;
we need have nothing else to do. We are not monks,
we are in the world, we are in business, we are parents,
we have families; we must live for the day. It is a
consolation to keep from mortal sin; that we do, and
it is enough for salvation. It is a great thing to keep
in God's favour; what indeed can we desire more?
We come at due time to the Sacraments; this is our
comfort and our stay; did we die, we should die in
grace, and escape the doom of the wicked. But if we
once attempted to go further, where should we stop?
how will you draw the line for us? the line between
mortal and venial sin is very distinct; we understand
that; but do you not see that, if we attended to our
venial sins, there would be just as much reason to
attend to one as to another? If we began to repress
our anger, why not also repress vainglory? why not
also guard against niggardliness? why not also keep
from falsehood? from gossiping, from idling, from
excess in eating? And, after all, without venial sin we

never can be, unless indeed we have the prerogative of the Mother of God, which it would be almost heresy to ascribe to any one but her. You are not asking us to be converted ; that we understand ; we *are* converted, we were converted a long time ago. You bid us aim at an indefinite vague something, which is less than perfection, yet more than obedience, and which, without resulting in any tangible advantage, debars us from the pleasures and embarrasses us in the duties of this world."

This is what you will say ; but your premises, my brethren, are better than your reasoning, and your conclusions will not stand. You have a right view why God has sent you into the world, viz., in order that you may get to heaven ; it is quite true also that you would fare well indeed if you found yourselves there, you could desire nothing better ; nor, it is true, can you live any time without venial sin. It is true also that you are not obliged to aim at being Saints ; it is no sin not to aim at perfection. So much is true and to the purpose ; but it does not follow from it that you, with such views and feelings as you have expressed, are using sufficient exertions even for attaining to purgatory. Has your religion any difficulty in it, or is it in all respects easy to you ? Are you simply taking your own pleasure in your mode of living, or do you find your pleasure in submitting yourself to God's pleasure ? In a word, is your religion a work ? for if it be not, it is not religion at all. Here at once, before going into your argument, is a proof that it is an unsound one, because it brings you to the conclusion that, whereas Christ came to do a work, and all Saints, nay, nay, and sinners do a work too, you, on the contrary, have no work to do, because, forsooth, you are neither sinners nor Saints ; or, if you once had a work, at least that you have despatched it already, and you have nothing upon your hands. You have attained your salvation, it seems, before your time, and have nothing to occupy you, and are detained on earth too long. The work days are over, and your perpetual holiday is begun. Did then God send you, above all other men, into the world to be idle in spiritual matters ? Is it your mission only to find pleasure in this world, in which you are but as pilgrims and sojourners ? Are you more than sons of Adam, who, by the sweat of their brow, are to eat bread till they return to the earth out of which they are taken ? Unless you have some work in hand, unless you are struggling, unless you are fighting with yourselves, you are no followers of those who "through many tribulations entered into the kingdom of God ". A fight is the very token of a Christian. He is a soldier of Christ ; high or low, he is this and nothing else. If you have triumphed over all mortal sin, as you seem to think, then you must attack your venial sins ; there is no help for it ; there is nothing else to do, if you would be soldiers of Jesus Christ. But, O simple souls ! to think you have gained any triumph at all ! No : you cannot safely be at peace with any, even the least malignant, of the foes of God ; if you are at peace with venial sins, be certain that in their company and under their shadow mortal sins are lurking.

Mortal sins are the children of venial, which, though they be not deadly themselves, yet are prolific of death. You may think that you have killed the giants who had possession of your hearts, and that you have nothing to fear, but may sit at rest under your vine and under your fig-tree; but the giants will live again, they will rise from the dust, and, before you know where you are, you will be taken captive and slaughtered by the fierce, powerful, and eternal enemies of God.

The end of a thing is the test. It was our Lord's rejoicing in His last solemn hour, that He had done the work for which He was sent. " I have glorified Thee on earth," He says in His prayer, " I have finished the work which Thou gavest Me to do; I have manifested Thy name to the men whom Thou hast given Me out of the world." It was St. Paul's consolation also; " I have fought the good fight, I have finished the course, I have kept the faith; henceforth there is laid up for me a crown of justice, which the Lord shall render to me in that day, the just Judge". Alas! alas! how different will be our view of things when we come to die, or when we have passed into eternity, from the dreams and pretences with which we beguile ourselves now! What will Babel do for us then? Will it rescue our souls from the purgatory or the hell to which it sends them? If we were created, it was that we might serve God; if we have His gifts, it is that we may glorify Him; if we have a conscience, it is that we may obey it; if we have the prospect of heaven, it is that we may keep it before us; if we have light, that we may follow it; if we have grace, that we may save ourselves by means of it. Alas! alas! for those who die without fulfilling their mission! who were called to be holy, and lived in sin; who were called to worship Christ, and who plunged into this giddy and unbelieving world; who were called to fight, and who remained idle; who were called to be Catholics, and who did but remain in the religion of their birth! Alas for those who have had gifts and talent, and have not used, or have misused, or abused them; who have had wealth, and have spent it on themselves; who have had abilities, and have advocated what was sinful, or ridiculed what was true, or scattered doubts against what was sacred; who have had leisure, and have wasted it on wicked companions, or evil books, or foolish amusements! Alas! for those, of whom the best that can be said is, that they are harmless and naturally blameless, while they never have attempted to cleanse their hearts or to live in God's sight!

The world goes on from age to age, but the holy Angels and blessed Saints are always crying alas, alas! and woe, woe! over the loss of vocations, and the disappointment of hopes, and the scorn of God's love, and the ruin of souls. One generation succeeds another, and whenever they look down upon earth from their golden thrones, they see scarcely anything but a multitude of guardian spirits, downcast and sad, each following his own charge, in anxiety, or in terror, or in despair, vainly endeavouring to shield him from the enemy, and failing because he will not be shielded.

Times come and go, and man will not believe, that that is to be which is not yet, or that what now is only continues for a season, and is not eternity. The end is the trial; the world passes; it is but a pageant and a scene; the lofty palace crumbles, the busy city is mute, the ships of Tarshish have sped away. On heart and flesh death is coming; the veil is breaking. Departing soul, how hast thou used thy talents, thy opportunities, the light poured around thee, the warnings given thee, the grace inspired into thee? O my Lord and Saviour, support me in that hour in the strong arms of Thy Sacraments, and by the fresh fragrance of Thy consolations. Let the absolving words be said over me, and the holy oil sign and seal me, and Thy own Body be my food, and Thy Blood my sprinkling; and let my sweet Mother Mary breathe on me, and my Angel whisper peace to me, and my glorious Saints, and my own dear Father, Philip, smile on me; that in them all, and through them all, I may receive the gift of perseverance, and die, as I desire to live, in Thy faith, in Thy Church, in Thy service, and in Thy love.

DISCOURSE VII.

THERE is no truth, my brethren, which Holy Church is more earnest in impressing upon us than that our salvation from first to last is the gift of God. It is true indeed that we merit eternal life by our works of obedience ; but that those works are meritorious of such a reward, this takes place, not from their intrinsic worth, but from the free appointment and bountiful promise of God ; and that we are able to do them at all, is the simple result of His grace. That we are justified is of His grace ; that we have the dispositions for justification is of His grace ; that we are able to do good works when justified is of His grace ; and that we persevere in those good works is of His grace. Not only do we actually depend on His power from first to last, but our destinies depend on His sovereign pleasure and inscrutable counsel. He holds the arbitration of our future in His hands ; without an act of His will, independent of ours, we should not have been brought into the grace of the Catholic Church ; and without a further act of His will, though we are now members of it, we shall not

(124)

be brought on to the glory of the kingdom of Heaven. Though a soul justified can merit eternal life, yet neither can it merit to be justified, nor can it merit to remain justified to the end ; not only is a state of grace the condition and the life of all merit, but grace brings us into that state of grace, and grace continues us in it ; and thus, as I began by saying, our salvation from first to last is the gift of God.

Precise and absolute as is the teaching of Holy Church concerning the sovereign grace of God, she is as clear and as earnest in teaching also that we are really free and responsible. Every one upon earth might, without any verbal evasion, be saved, as far as God's assistances are concerned. Every man born of Adam's seed, simply and truly, might save himself, if he would, and every man might will to save himself ; for grace is given to every one for this end. How it is, however, that in spite of this real freedom of man's will, our salvation still depends so absolutely on God's good pleasure, is unrevealed ; divines have devised various modes of reconciling two truths which at first sight seem so contrary to each other ; and these explanations have severally been received by some theologians, and not received by others, and do not concern us now. How man is able fully and entirely to do what he will, while God accomplishes His own supreme will also, is hidden from us, as it is hidden from us how God created out of nothing, or how He foresees the future, or how His attribute of justice is compatible with His attribute of love. It is one of those " hidden things which belong unto

the Lord our God ; " but " what are revealed," as the
inspired writer goes on to say, " are for us and our
children even for everlasting ". And this is what is
revealed, viz. :—on the one hand, that our salvation
depends on ourselves, and on the other, that it depends on God. Did we not depend on ourselves, we
should become careless and reckless, nothing we did
or did not do having any bearing on our salvation ;
did we not depend on God, we should be presumptuous and self-sufficient.   I began by telling you,
my brethren, and I shall proceed in what is to come
more distinctly to tell you, that you depend upon
God ; but such admonitions necessarily imply your
dependence upon yourselves also ; for, did not your
salvation in some sufficient sense depend on yourselves, what would be the use of appealing to you not
to *forget* your dependence on God ?   It is because
you have so great a share in your own salvation, that
it avails, that it is pertinent, to speak to you of God's
part in it.

He is the Alpha and Omega, the beginning and the
ending, as of all things, so of our salvation.   We
should have lived and died, every one of us, destitute
of all saving knowledge and love of Him, but for a
gift which we could not do anything ourselves to
secure, had we lived ever so well,—but for His grace
and now that we have known Him, and have been
cleansed from our sins by Him, it is quite certain
that we cannot do anything, even with the help of
grace, to purchase for ourselves perseverance in justice
and sanctity, though we live ever so well.   His grace

begins the work, His grace also finishes it ; and now I am going to speak to you of His finishing it ; I mean of the necessity under which we lie of His finishing it ; else it will never be finished, or rather will be reversed ; I am going to speak to you of the gift of perseverance in grace, of its extreme preciousness, and of our utter hopelessness, in spite of all that we are, without it.

It is this gift which our Lord speaks of, when He prays His Father for His disciples, before He departs from them : " Holy Father, *keep* in Thy name those whom Thou hast given Me ; . . . I ask not that Thou take them out of the world, but that Thou preserve them from evil ". And St. Paul intends it when he declares to the Philippians that " He who had begun a good work " in His disciples, " would perfect it unto the day of Christ Jesus ". St. Peter, too, when he says in like manner, that " God, who had called His brethren into His eternal glory, would perfect, confirm, and establish them ". And so the Prophet in the Psalms prays that God would " perfect his walking in His paths, that his steps might not be moved ; " and the Prophet Jeremias declares in God's name, " I will put My fear in their hearts, that they draw not back from Me ". In these and many other passages of Scripture the blessing spoken of is the gift of final perseverance, and I will tell you how and why it is necessary.

This is what we find to be the case, not only in matters of religion, but of this world, viz., that, let a person do a thing ever so well, the chance is that he will not be able to do it a number of times running without a mistake. Let a person be ever so good an accountant, he will add up a sum wrongly now and then, though you could not guess beforehand when or why he was to fail. Let him get by heart a number of lines ever so perfectly, and say them accurately over, yet it does not follow that he will say them a dozen times and be accurate throughout. So it is with our religious duties ; we may be able to keep from every sin in particular as the particular temptation comes, but this does not hinder its being certain that we shall not in fact keep from all sins, though that " all " is made up of those particular sins. This is how the greatest Saints come to commit venial or lesser sins, though grace they have sufficient to keep them from any sin whatever. It is the result of human frailty ; nothing could keep the Saints from such falls, light as they may be, but a special prerogative, and this, the Church teaches, has been granted to the Blessed Virgin, and apparently to her alone. Now these lesser or venial sins do not separate the soul from God, or forfeit its perseverance in grace ; and they are permitted by the Giver of all grace for a good purpose, to humble us, and to give us an incentive to works of penance. No exemption then from these is given us, because it is not necessary in order to our perseverance that we should be exempted ; on the other hand, what *is* most necessary is, that we should be preserved from mortal sins, yet here too that very difficulty besets us in our warfare with them which meets us in the case of venial. Here too, though a man may have grace sufficient to keep him clear of all mortal sins whatever, taken one by one, still we may prophesy surely, that the hour will come, sooner or later, when he will neglect and baffle that grace, unless he has some further gift bestowed on him to guard him against himself. He needs grace to use grace; he needs something over and above to secure his being faithful to what he has already. And he needs it imperatively; for, since even one mortal sin separates from God, he is in immediate risk of his salvation, if he has it not. This additional gift is called the gift of perseverance; and it consists in an ever-watchful superintendence of us, on the part of our All-merciful Lord, removing temptations which He sees will be fatal to us, succouring us at those times when we are in particular peril, whether from our negligence or other cause, and ordering the course of our life so, that we may die at a time when He sees that we are in a state of grace. And, since it is so simply necessary for us, God grants it to us; nay, did He not, no one could be saved. He grants it to us, though He does not grant even to Saints the prerogative of avoiding every venial sin; He grants it, out of His bounty, to our prayers, though we cannot merit it by anything we do for Him or say to Him, even with the aid of His grace.

What a lesson of humility and watchfulness have we in this doctrine as now explained! It is one ground of humiliation, that, do what we will, strive as we will, we cannot escape from lesser sins while we are on earth. Though the aids which God gives us are sufficient to enable us to live without sin, yet our

9

infirmity of will and of attention is a match for them, and we do not do in fact that which we might do. And again, what is not only humbling, but even frightful and appalling, we are in danger of mortal sin as well as in certainty of venial ; and the only reason why we are not in certainty of mortal is, that an extraordinary gift is given to those who supplicate for it, to secure them from mortal, though no such extraordinary gift is given to secure them from venial. In spite of the presence of grace in our souls, in spite of the actual assistances given us, we owe any hope we have of heaven, not to that inward grace simply, nor to those aids, but, I repeat, to a supplementary mercy which protects us against ourselves, rescues us from occasions of sin, strengthens us in our hour of danger, and ends our days at that very time, perhaps cuts short our life in order to secure a time, when no mortal sin has separated us from God.   Nothing we are, nothing we do, is any guarantee to us that this supplementary mercy has been accorded to us ; we cannot know till the end ; all we know is, that God has helped us hitherto, and we trust He will help us still.   But yet the experience of what He has already done is no proof that He will do more ; our present religiousness need not be the consequence of the gift of perseverance as bestowed upon us; it may have been intended merely to prompt and enable us to pray earnestly and continually for that gift.   There are men who, had they died at a particular time, would have died the death of Saints, and who lived to fall. They lived on here to die eternally.   O dreadful thought! Never be you offended, my brethren, or overwhelmed, when you find that the good and gentle, or the zealous and useful, is cut down and taken off in the midst of his course; it is hard to bear, but who knows that he is not taken away *à facie malitiæ*, "from the presence of evil," from the evil to come? "He was taken away," as the Wise Man says, "lest wickedness should alter his understanding, or deceit beguile his soul. For the bewitching of vanity obscureth good things, and the wandering of concupiscence overturneth the innocent mind. Being made perfect in a short space, he fulfilled a long time. For his soul pleased God; and therefore He hastened to bring him out of the midst of iniquities. But the people see this and understand not, nor lay such things in their hearts: that the grace of God and His mercy is with His Saints, and that He hath respect unto His chosen."

Bad is it to bear, when such a one is taken away; cruel to his friends, sad even to strangers, and a surprise to the world; but O, how much better, how happy so to die, instead of being reserved to sin! You may wonder how sin was possible in him, my brethren; he had so many graces, he had lived and matured in them so long; he had overcome so many temptations. He had struck his roots deeply, and spread abroad his branches on high. One grace grew out of another; and all things in him were double one against another. He seemed from the very completeness of his sanctity, which encircled him on every side, to defy assault and to be proof against injury. He, if any one, could have said with the proud Church in the Apocalypse, " I am wealthy and enriched, and have need of nothing ; " that he had started well, seemed a reason why he should go on well ; strength would lead to strength, and merit to merit ; as a flame increases and sweeps along and round about, as soon as, and for the very reason that, it is once kindled, so he had on him the presage of greater and greater triumphs as time proceeded. He was fit to scale Heaven by an inherent power, which, though at first of grace, yet, when once given, became not so much grace as a claim for more grace—as by the action of a law and the process of a series, in which grace and merit alternated, man meriting and meriting, and the God of grace being forced to give and give again, if He would be true to His promise. Thus we might look at him, and think we had already in our hands all the data of a great and glorious and infallible conclusion, and might deny that a reverse or a fall was possible. My brethren, there was once an Eastern king, in his day the richest of men ; and a Grecian sage came to visit him, and, having seen all his glory and his majesty, was pressed by this poor child of vanity to say whether he was not the happiest of men. To whom the wise man did but reply, that he should wait till he saw the end. So it is as regards spiritual wealth ; because Almighty God, in spite of His ample promises, and His faithful performance of them, has not put out of His own hands the issues of life and death, and the end comes from Him as well as the beginning. When He has once given grace, He has not therefore simply made over to the creature his own salvation. The creature can merit much; but as he could not merit the grace of conversion, neither can he merit the gift of perseverance. From first to last he is dependent on Him who made him; he cannot be extortionate with Him, he cannot turn His bounty to the prejudice of the Bountiful; he may not exalt himself, he dare not presume, but "if he thinketh he standeth, let him take heed lest he fall". He must watch and pray, he must fear and tremble, he must "chastise his body and bring it into subjection, lest, after he has preached to others, he himself should be reprobate ".

But I need not go to heathen history for an instance in point; Scripture furnishes one a thousand times more apposite and more impressive. Who was so variously gifted, so inwardly endowed, so laden with external blessings, as Solomon? on whom are lavished, as on him, the titles and the glories of the Eternal Son, God and man? The only aspect of Christ's adorable Person, which his history does not represent, does but bring out to us the peculiarity of his privileges. He does not symbolise Christ's sufferings; he was neither a priest, nor, like David his father, had he been a man of strife and toil and blood Everything which betokens mortality, everything which savours of the fall, is excluded from our idea of Solomon. He is as if an ideal of perfection; the king of peace, the builder of the temple, the father of a happy people, the heir of an empire, the wonder of all nations; a prince, yet a sage; palace-bred, yet taught in the schools ; a student, yet a man of the world ; deeply read in human nature, yet learned too in animals and plants.   He has the crown without the cross, peace without war, experience without suffering ; and all this is not in the mere way of men, or from the general providence of God, but vouchsafed to him from the very hands of his Creator, by a particular designation, and as the result of inspiration.   He obtained it when young ; and where shall we find anything so touching in the whole of Scripture as the circumstances of his obtaining ? who shall accuse him of want of religious fear and true love, whose dawning is so beautiful ?   When the Almighty appeared to him in a dream on his coming to the throne and said, " Ask what I shall give thee ; " " O Lord God," he made answer, " Thou hast made Thy servant king instead of David my father ; and I am but a child, and know not how to go out and come in.   And Thy servant is in the midst of the people which Thou hast chosen, an immense people, which cannot be numbered nor counted for multitude."   Accordingly, he asked for nothing else but the gift of wisdom to enable him to govern his people well ; and as his reward for so excellent a petition, he received, not only the wisdom for which he had asked, but those other gifts for which he had not asked : " And the Lord said unto Solomon, Because thou hast asked this thing, and hast not asked for thyself long life, nor riches, nor the lives of thine enemies, but hast asked for thyself wisdom to discern judgment, behold I have done to thee according to thy words, and I have given to thee a wise and understanding heart, so that none has been like thee before thee, nor shall rise after thee. Yea, and the things also, which thou didst not ask, I have given to thee, to wit, riches and glory, so that none has been like to thee among the kings in all days heretofore."

Rare inauguration to his greatness! the most splendid of monarchs owes nothing to injustice, or to cruelty, or to violence, or to treachery, nothing to human art or to human arm, that he is so powerful, so famous, and so wise; it is a divine gift which endued him within, which clothed him without. What was wanting to his blessedness? seeking God in his youth, growing up year after year in sanctity, fortifying his faith by wisdom, and his obedience by experience, and his aspirations by habit, what shall he not be in the next world, who is so glorious in this? He is a Saint ready made; he is in his youth what others are in their age; he is fit for heaven ere others begin the way heavenward: why should he delay? what lacks he yet? why tarry the wheels of his chariot? why does he remain longer on earth, when he has already won his crown, and may be carried away in a happy youth, and be securely taken into God's keeping, not with the common throng of holy souls, but, like Enoch and Elias, passing his long mysterious ages up on high, in some fit secret paradise till the day of redemption? Alas! he remains on earth to show us that there might be one thing lacking amidst that multitude of graces; to show that though there be in a man all faith, all hope, all love, all wisdom, though there be an exuberance of merits, it is all but a vanity, it is only a woe in the event, if one gift be wanting,—the gift of perseverance! He was in his youth, what others hardly are in age; well were it, had he been in his end, what the feeblest of God's servants is in his beginning!

His great father, whose sanctity had been wrought into him by many a fight with Satan, and who knew how difficult it was to persevere, when his death drew near, as if in prophecy rather than in prayer, had spoken thus of and to his son and his people: " God said to me, Thou shalt not build a house to My name, because thou art a man of war, and hast shed blood ; Solomon, thy son, shall build My house and My courts ; for I have chosen him to Me for a son, and I will be to him a father ; and I will establish his kingdom even for ever, if he shall *persevere* to do My precepts and judgments, as at this day. And thou, Solomon, my son, know the God of thy father, and serve Him with a perfect heart and a willing mind, for if thou shalt forsake Him, He will cast thee off for ever." And then, when he had collected together the precious materials for that house which he himself was not to build, and was resigning the kingdom to his son, " I know," he said, " O my God, that Thou provest hearts, and lovest simplicity, wherefore, have I in the simplicity of my heart and with joy offered to Thee all these things ; and Thy people too, which are present here, have I seen with great joy to offer to Thee their gifts. O Lord God of Abraham, and Isaac, and Israel, our fathers, keep for ever this will of our hearts, and let this mind remain always for the worship of Thee. And to Solomon also, my son, give a perfect heart, that he may keep Thy commandments, and Thy testimonies, and Thy ceremonies, and do all things, and build the building for the which I have provided the charges."

Such had been the dim foreboding of the father, fearing perhaps for his son from the very abundance of that son's prosperity. And in truth, it is not good for a man to live in so cloudless a splendour, and under so unchequered a heaven. There is a moral in the history, that he who prefigured the coming Saviour in all His offices but that of suffering, should fall ; that the King and the Prophet, who was neither Priest nor Warrior, should come short ;—thereby to show that penance is the only sure mother of love. " They who sow in tears shall reap in exultation ; " but Solomon, like the flowers of the field which are so beautiful, yet are cast into the oven, so he too, with all his glory, retained not his comeliness, but withered in his place. He who was wisest became as the most brutish ; he who was the most devout was lifted up and fell ; he who wrote the Song of Songs became the slave and the prey of vile affections. " King Solomon loved many strange women, unto them he clave with the most burning love. And when he was now old, his heart was depraved by women, to follow other gods, Astarte, goddess of the Sidonians, and Moloch the idol of the Ammonites ; and so did he for all his strange wives, whc did burn incense and sacrifice unto their gods." O, what a contrast between that grey-headed apostate, laden with years and with sins, bowing down to women and to idols, and the bright and youthful form standing, on the day of Dedication, in the Temple he had built, as a mediator between God and his people, when he acknowledged so simply, so fervently, God's mercies and God's faithfulness, and prayed that He would "incline their hearts unto Himself, that they might walk in all His ways, and keep His commandments, and His ceremonies, and His judgments, whatever He had commanded to their fathers!"

Well were it for us, my dear brethren, were it only kings and prophets and sages, and other rare creations of God's grace, to whom this warning applied; but it applies to all of us. It is indeed most true that the holier a man is, and the higher in the kingdom of heaven, so much the greater need has he to look carefully to his footing, lest he stumble and be lost; and a deep conviction of this necessity has been the sole preservation of the Saints. Had they not feared, they never would have persevered. Hence, like St. Paul, they are always full of their sin and their peril. You would think them the most polluted of sinners, and the most unstable of penitents. Such was the blessed Martyr Ignatius, who, when on his way to his death, said, " Now I begin to be Christ's disciple ". Such was the great Basil, who was ever ascribing the calamities of the Church and of his country to the wrath of Heaven upon his own sins. Such was St. Gregory, who submitted to his elevation to the Popedom, as if it were his spiritual death. Such too was my own dear Father St. Philip, who was ever showing, in the midst of the gifts he received from God, the anxiety and jealousy with which he regarded himself and his prospects. " Every day," says his biographer, " he used to make a protest to God with the Blessed Sacrament in his hands, saying, ' Lord, beware of me to-day, lest I should betray Thee, and do Thee all the mischief in the world'." At other times he would say, " The wound in Christ's side is large, but, if God did not guard me, I should make it larger ". In his last illness, " Lord, if I recover, so far as I am concerned, I shall do more evil than ever, because I have promised so many times before to change my life, and have not kept my word, so that I despair of myself". He would shed abundance of tears and say, " I have never done one good action". When he saw young persons, he began considering how much time they had before them to do good in, and said, " O, happy you ! O, happy you ! " He often said, " I am past hope," and, when urged, he added, " but I trust in God ". When a penitent of his called him a Saint, he turned to her with a face full of anger, and said, " Begone with you, I am a devil, not a Saint". When another said to him, " Father, a temptation has come to me to think you are not what the world takes you for," he answered, " Be sure of this, that I am a man like my neighbours, and nothing more ".

What a reflection on ordinary Christians is the language of Saints about themselves ! Multitudes indeed live in mortal sin, and have no concern at all about present, past, or future. But even those who go so far as to come to the Sacraments, never trouble themselves with the thought of perseverance. They seem to take it as a matter of course that, if they are in a good state of mind at present, it will continue. Perhaps they have been converted from a sinful life, and are very different from what they have been. They feel the comfort of the change, they feel the peace and satisfaction of a cleansed conscience, but they are so taken up with that comfort and peace, that they rest in it and become secure. They do not guard against temptation, or pray for support under it ; it does not occur to them that, as they have changed from sin to religion, so they may, if so be, change back again from religion to sin. They do not realise enough their continual dependence on God ; some temptation comes on them, or some vicissitude of life, they are surprised, they fall, and perhaps they never recover.

What a scene is this life, a scene of almost universal disappointment ! of springs blighted, — of harvests beaten down by the storm, when they should have been gathered into the storehouses ! of tardy and imperfect repentances, when there is nothing else left to be done, of unsatisfactory resolves and poor efforts, when the end of life is come ! O my dear children, how subdued our rejoicing in you is, even when you are walking well and hopefully ! how anxious are we for you, even when you are cheerful from the lightness of your conscience and the sincerity of your hearts ! how we sigh when we give thanks for you,

and tremble even while we rejoice in hearing your confessions and absolving you ! And why ? because we
know how great and high is the gift of perseverance.
When Hazael came with his presents to the prophet
Eliseus, the man of God stood over against him, in
silence and in bitter thought, till at last the blood
mounted up into his countenance, and he wept. He
wept, to Hazael's surprise, at the prospect of the
dreadful butcheries which the soldier before him, little
as he himself expected it, was to perpetrate when he
succeeded to the throne of Syria. We, O honest and
cheerful hearts, are not prophets as Eliseus, nor are
you destined to high estate and extraordinary temptation as Hazael ; but still the tears which the man of
God shed, what if some Angel should be shedding the
like over any of you, what time you are receiving pardon and grace from the voice and hand of the Priests
of Christ ! O, how many are there who pass well
and hopefully through what seem to be their most
critical years, and fall just when one might consider
them beyond danger ! How many are good youths,
yet careless men ; blameless from fifteen to twenty, yet
captives to habits of sin between twenty and thirty !
How many persevere till they marry, and then perhaps
get inextricably entangled in the cares or pleasures
of this world, and give up attendance on the Sacraments, and other holy practices, which they have
hitherto observed ! how many pass through their
married life well, but lapse into sin on the death of
wife or husband ! How many are there who by mere
change of place lose their religious habits, and be-

come first careless and then shameless! How many upon the commission of one sin fall into remorse, disgust of themselves, and recklessness, avoid the Confessional from shame and despair, and live on year after year, burdened with the custody of some miserable secret! How many fall into trouble, lose their spirit and heart, shut themselves up in themselves, and feel a sort of aversion to religion, when religion would be all in all to them! How many come to some great prosperity, and, carried away by it, "wax fat and kick, and leave God their Maker, and recede from God their Saviour"! How many fall into lukewarmness almost like death, after their first fervour! How many lose the graces begun in them by self-confidence and arrogant impetuosity! How many, not yet Catholics, who under God's guidance were making right for the Catholic Church, suddenly turn short and miss, "like a crooked bow"! How many, when led forward by God's unmerited grace, are influenced by the persuasions of relatives or the inducements of station or of wealth, and become in the event sceptics or infidels when they might have almost died in the odour of sanctity! How many, whose contrition once gained for them even the grace of justification, yet afterwards, by refusing to go forward, have gone backwards, though they maintain a semblance of what they once were, by means of the mere natural habits which supernatural grace has formed within them! What a miserable wreck is the world, hopes without substance, promises without fulfilment, repentance without amendment, blossom without fruit, continuance and progress without perseverance!

O my dearest children, let me not depress you; it is your duty, your privilege to rejoice; I would not frighten you more than it is good for you to be frightened. Some of you will take it too much to heart, and will fret yourselves unduly, as I fear. I do not wish to sadden you, but to make you cautious; doubt not you will be led on, fear not to fall, provided you do but fear a fall. Fearing will secure you from what you fear. Only "be sober, be vigilant," as St. Peter says, beware of taking satisfaction in what you are, understand that the only way to avoid falling back is to press forward. Dread all occasions of sin, get a habit of shrinking from the beginnings of temptation. Never speak confidently about yourselves, nor contemptuously of the religiousness of others, nor lightly of sacred things; guard your eyes, guard the first springs of thought, be jealous of yourselves when alone, neglect not your daily prayers; above all, pray specially and continually for the gift of perseverance. Come to Mass as often as you can, visit the Blessed Sacrament, make frequent acts of faith and love, and try to live in the Presence of God.

And further still, interest your dear Mother, the Mother of God, in your success; pray to her earnestly for it; she can do more for you than any one else. Pray her by the pain she suffered, when the sharp sword went through her, pray her, by her own perseverance, which was in her the gift of the same God of whom you ask it for yourselves. God will not refuse you, He will not refuse her, if you have recourse to her succour. It will be a blessed thing, in your last hour, when flesh and heart are failing, in the midst of the pain, the weariness, the restlessness, the prostration of strength, and the exhaustion of spirits, which then will be your portion, it will be blessed indeed to have her at your side, more tender than an earthly mother, to nurse you and to whisper peace. It will be most blessed, when the evil one is making his last effort, when he is coming on you in his might to pluck you away from your Father's hand, if he can—it will be blessed indeed if Jesus, if Mary and Joseph are then with you, waiting to shield you from his assaults and to receive your soul. If they are there, all are there ; Angels are there, Saints are there, heaven is there, heaven is begun in you, and the devil has no part in you. That dread day may be sooner or later, you may be taken away young, you may live to fourscore, you may die in your bed, you may die in the open field, but if Mary intercedes for you, that day will find you watching and ready. All things will be fixed to secure your salvation ; all dangers will be foreseen, all obstacles removed, all aids provided. The hour will come, and in a moment you will be translated beyond fear and risk, you will be translated into a new state where sin is not, nor ignorance of the future, but perfect faith and serene joy, and assurance and love everlasting.

DISCOURSE VIII.

NATURE AND GRACE.

IN the Parable of the Good Shepherd our Lord sets before us a dispensation or state of things, which is very strange in the eyes of the world. He speaks of mankind as consisting of two bodies, distinct from each other, divided by as real a line of demarcation as the fence which encloses the sheepfold. " I am the Door," He says, "by Me if any man shall have entered in, he shall be saved : and he shall go in and go out, and shall find pastures. My sheep hear My voice, and I know them, and they follow Me and I give them life everlasting ; and they shall not perish for ever, and no man shall snatch them out of My Hand." And in His last prayer for His disciples to His Eternal Father, He says, " I have manifested Thy Name to the men whom Thou hast given Me out of the world. Thine they were, and Thou hast given them to Me, and they have kept Thy word. I pray for them, I pray not for the world, but for those whom Thou hast given Me, for they are Thine. Holy Father, keep them in Thy Name whom Thou hast given Me, that they may be one, as We also."

Nor are these passages solitary or singular ; " Fear not, little flock," He says by another Evangelist, "for it hath pleased your Father to give you the kingdom". And again, "I thank Thee, Father, Lord of heaven and earth, that Thou hast hid these things from the wise and prudent, and hast revealed them unto little ones ; " and again, " How narrow is the gate, and strait the way which leadeth to life, and few there are who find it !" St. Paul repeats and insists on this doctrine of his Lord, " Ye were once darkness, but now are light in the Lord ; " " He hath delivered us from the power of darkness, and hath translated us into the kingdom of the Son of His love". And St. John, " Greater is He that is in you than he that is in the world. They are of the world, we are of God." Thus there are two parties on this earth, and two only, if we view men in their religious aspect ; those, the few, who hear Christ's words and follow Him, who are in the light, and walk in the narrow way, and have the promise of heaven ; and those, on the other hand, who are many, for whom Christ prays not, though He has died for them, who are wise and prudent in their own eyes, who are possessed by the Evil One, and are subject to his rule.

And such is the view taken of mankind, as by their Maker and Redeemer, so also by the small company in whom He lives and is glorified ; but far differently does the larger body, the world itself, look upon mankind at large, upon its own vast multitudes, and upon those whom God has taken out of it for His own special inheritance. It considers that all men are pretty much on a level, or that, differ though they may, they differ by such fine shades from each other, that it is impossible, because forsooth it would be untrue and unjust, to divide them into two bodies, or to divide them at all. " Each man is like himself and no one else ; each man has his own opinions, his own rule of faith and conduct, his own worship ; if a number join together in a religious form, this is an accident, for the sake of convenience ; for each is complete in himself ; religion is simply a personal concern ; there is no such thing really as a common or joint religion, that is, one in which a number of men, strictly speaking, partake; it is all matter of private judgment. Hence, as they sometimes proceed even to avow, there is no such thing as a true religion or a false ; that is true to each, which each sincerely believes to be true ; and what is true to one, is not true to his neighbour. There are no special doctrines, necessary to be believed in order to salvation ; it is not very difficult to be saved ; and most men may take it for granted that they shall be saved. All men are in God's favour, except so far as, and while, they commit acts of sin ; but when the sin is over, they get back into His favour again, naturally and as a thing of course, no one knows how, owing to God's infinite indulgence, unless indeed they persevere and die in a course of sin, and perhaps even then. There is no such place as hell, or at least punishment is not eternal. Predestination, election, grace, perseverance, faith, sanctity, unbelief, and reprobation are strange ideas, and, as they think, very false ones." This is the cast of opinion of men in general, in proportion as they exercise their minds on the subject of religion, and think for themselves; and if in any respect they depart from the easy, cheerful, and tranquil temper of mind which it expresses, it is when they are led to think of those who presume to take the contrary view, that is, who take the view set forth by Christ and His Apostles. On these they are commonly severe, that is, on the very persons whom God acknowledges as His, and is training heavenward,— on Catholics, who are the witnesses and preachers of those awful doctrines of grace, which condemn the world, and which the world cannot endure.

In truth the world does not know of the existence of grace; nor is it wonderful, for it is ever contented with itself, and has never turned to account the super-natural aids bestowed upon it. Its highest idea of man lies in the order of nature; its pattern man is the natural man; it thinks it wrong to be anything else than a natural man. It sees that nature has a number of tendencies, inclinations, and passions; and because these are natural, it thinks that each of them may be indulged for its own sake, so far as it does no harm to others, or to a person's bodily, mental, and temporal well-being. It considers that want of mode-ration, or excess, is the very definition of sin, if it goes so far as to recognise that word. It thinks that he is the perfect man who eats, and drinks, and sleeps, and walks, and diverts himself, and studies, and writes, and attends to religion, in moderation. The devotional feeling and the intellect, and the flesh, have each its claim upon us, and each must have play, if the Creator is to be duly honoured. It does not understand, it will not admit, that impulses and propensities, which are found in our nature, as God created it, may nevertheless, if indulged, become sins, on the ground that He has subjected them to higher principles, whether these principles be in our nature, or be superadded to our nature. Hence it is very slow to believe that evil thoughts are really displeasing to God, and incur punishment. Works, indeed, tangible actions, which are seen and which have influence, it will allow to be wrong ; but it will not believe even that deeds are sinful, or that they are more than reprehensible, if they are private or personal ; and it is blind utterly to the malice of thoughts, of imaginations, of wishes, and of words. Because the wild emotions of anger, lust, greediness, craft, cruelty, are no sin in the brute creation, which has neither the means nor the command to repress them, therefore they are no sins in a being who has a diviner sense and a controlling power. Concupiscence, it considers, may be indulged, because it is in its first elements natural.

Behold here the true origin and fountain-head of the warfare between the Church and the world ; here they join issue, and diverge from each other. The Church is built upon the doctrine that impurity is hateful to God, and that concupiscence is its root ; with the Prince of the Apostles, her visible Head, she denounces " the corruption of concupiscence which is in the world," or, that corruption in the world which comes of concupiscence; whereas the corrupt world defends, nay, I may even say, sanctifies that very concupiscence which is the world's corruption. Just as its bolder teachers, as you know, my brethren, hold that the laws of this physical creation are so supreme, as to allow of their utterly disbelieving in the existence of miracles, so, in like manner, it deifies and worships human nature and its impulses, and denies the power and the grant of grace. This is the source of the hatred which the world bears to the Church; it finds a whole catalogue of sins brought into light and denounced, which it would fain believe to be no sins at all; it finds itself, to its indignation and impatience, surrounded with sin, morning, noon, and night; it finds that a stern law lies against it in matters where it believed it was its own master and need not think of God; it finds guilt accumulating upon it hourly, which nothing can prevent, nothing remove, but a higher power, the grace of God. It finds itself in danger of being humbled to the earth as a rebel, instead of being allowed to indulge its self-dependence and self-complacency. Hence it takes its stand on nature, and denies or rejects divine grace. Like the proud spirit in the beginning, it wishes to find its supreme good in its own itself, and nothing above it; it undertakes to be sufficient for its own happiness; it has no desire for the supernatural, and therefore does not believe in it. And because nature cannot rise above nature, it will not believe that the narrow way is possible; it hates those who enter upon it as if pretenders and hypocrites, or laughs at their

aspirations as romance and fanaticism ; lest it should
have to believe in the existence of grace.

Now you may think, my brethren, from the way in
which I have been contrasting nature and grace, that
they cannot possibly be mistaken for each other ; but
I wish to show you, in the next place, how grace
may be mistaken for nature, and nature mistaken for
grace. And in explaining this very grave matter, I
wish, lest I should be misunderstood, first to say
distinctly, that I am merely comparing and contrasting nature and grace one with another in their several
characters, and by no means presuming to apply
what I shall say of them to actual individuals, or to
judge what persons, living or dead, are specimens
of the one or of the other. This then being my
object, I repeat that, contrary to what might be
thought, they may easily be mistaken for each other,
because, as it is plain from what I have said, the difference is in a great measure an inward, and therefore
a secret one. Grace is lodged in the heart ; it purifies the thoughts and motives, it raises the soul to God,
it sanctifies the body, it corrects and exalts human
nature in regard to those sins of which men are
ashamed, and do not make a public display. Accordingly, in outward show, in single actions, in word, in
profession, in teaching, in the social and political
virtues, in striking and heroical exploits, on the public
transitory scene of things, nature may counterfeit
grace, nay even to the deception of the man himself
in whom the counterfeit occurs. Recollect that it is
by nature, not by grace, that man has the gifts of

reason and conscience ; and mere reason and conscience will lead him to discover, and in a measure pursue, objects which are, properly speaking, supernatural and divine. From the things which are seen, from the voice of tradition, from the existence of the soul, and from the necessity of the case, the natural reason can infer the existence of God. The natural heart can burst forth by fits and starts into emotions of love towards Him ; the natural imagination can depict the beauty and glory of His attributes ; the natural conscience may ascertain and put in order the truths of the great moral law, nay even to the condemnation of that concupiscence, which it is too weak to subdue, and is therefore persuaded to tolerate. The natural will can do many things really good and praiseworthy ; nay, in particular cases, or at particular seasons, when temptation is away, it may seem to have a strength which it has not, and to be imitating the austerity and purity of a Saint. One man has no temptation to this sin, nor another to that ; hence human nature may often show to great advantage ; and, as seen in its happier specimens, it may become quite a trial to faith, seeing that in its best estate it has really no relationship to the family of Christ, and no claim whatever to a heavenly reward,—though it can talk of Christ and heaven too, read Scripture, and "do many things willingly" in consequence of reading it, and can exercise a certain sort of belief, however different from that faith which is imparted to us by grace.

For instance, it is a most mournful, often quite a piercing thought, to contemplate the conduct and the

character of those who have never received the elementary grace of God in the Sacrament of Baptism.*
They may be in fact, so benevolent, so active and
untiring in their benevolence ; they may be so wise
and so considerate ; they may have so much in them to
engage the affections of those who see them ! Well,
let us leave them to God; His grace is over all the
earth ; if that grace comes to good effect and bears
fruit in the hearts of the unbaptised, He will reward
it; but, where grace is not, there doubtless what
looks so fair has its reward in this world, such good
as is in it having no better claim on a heavenly reward than skill in any art or science, than eloquence
or wit. And moreover, it often happens, that, where
there is much that is specious and amiable, there is
also much that is sinful, and frightfully so. Men show
their best face in the world ; but for the greater part
of their time, the many hours of the day and the night,
they are shut up in their own thoughts. They are their
own witnesses, none see them besides, save God and
His Angels ; therefore in such cases we can only judge
of what we actually see, and can only admire what is
in itself good, without having any means of determining the real moral condition of those who display
it. Just as children are caught by the mere good-
nature and familiarity with which they are treated by
some grown man, and have no means or thought of
forming a judgment about him in other respects, and
may be surprised, when they grow up, to find how
unworthy he is of their respect or affection ; as the

* *Vid.* Sermons on Subjects of the Day, pp. 68-70.

uneducated, who have seen very little of the world, have no faculties for distinguishing between one rank of men and another, and consider all persons on a level who are respectably dressed, whatever be their accent, their carriage, or their countenance ; so all of us, not children only or the uncultivated, are but novices, or less than novices, in the business of deciding what is the real state in God's sight of this or that man, who is external to the Church, yet in character or conduct resembles her true sons.

Not entering then upon this point, which is beyond us, so much we even can see and are sure of, that human nature is, in a degree beyond all words, inconsistent, and that we must not take for granted that it can do anything at all more than it actually does, or that those, in whom it shows most plausibly, are a whit better than they look. We see the best, and (as far as moral excellence goes) the whole of them. We cannot argue from what we see in favour of what we do not see ; we cannot take what we see as a specimen of what they really are. Sad, then, as the spectacle of such a man is to a Catholic, he is no difficulty to him. He may have many virtues, yet he may have nothing of a special Christian cast about him, humility, purity, or devotion. He may like his own way intensely, have a great opinion of his own powers, scoff at faith and religious fear, and seldom or never have said a prayer in his life. Nay, even outward gravity of deportment is no warrant that there is not within an habitual indulgence of evil thoughts, and secret offences odious to Almighty God. We admire, for instance, whatever is excellent in the ancient heathen ; we acknowledge without jealousy whatever they have done virtuous and praiseworthy, but we understand as little of the character or destiny of the being in whom that goodness is found, as we understand the nature of the material substances which present themselves to us under the outward garb of shape and colour. They are to us as unknown causes which have influenced or disturbed the world, and which manifest themselves in certain great effects, political, social, or ethical ; they are to us as pictures, which appeal to the eye, but not to the touch. We do not know that they would prove to be more real than a painting, if we could touch them. Thus much we know, that, if they have attained to heaven, it has been by the grace of God and their co-operation with it ; if they have lived without using that grace which is given to all, they have no hope of life ; and, if they have lived and died in mortal sin, they are in the state of bad Catholics, and have the prospect of never-ending death.

Yet, if we allow ourselves to take the mere outward appearance of things, and the happier, though partial and occasional, efforts of human nature, how great it is, how amiable, how brilliant,—that is, if we may pretend to the power of viewing it distinct from the super-natural influences which have ever haunted it ! How great are the old Greek lawgivers and statesmen, whose histories and works are known to some of us, and whose names to many more ! How great are those stern Roman heroes, who conquered the world, and pre-pared the way for Christ ! How wise, how profound, are those ancient teachers and sages! what power of imagination, what a semblance of prophecy, is manifest in their poets! The present world is in many respects not so great as in that old time, but even now there is enough in it to show both the strength of human nature in this respect, and its weakness. Consider the solidity of our own political fabric at home, and the expansion of our empire abroad, and you will have matter enough spread out before you to occupy many a long day in admiration of the genius, the virtues, and the resources of human nature. Take a second meditation upon it ; alas! you will find nothing of faith there, but mainly expedience as the measure of right and wrong, and temporal well-being as the end of action.

Again, many are the tales and poems written now-a-days, expressing high and beautiful sentiments ; I dare say some of you, my brethren, have fallen in with them, and perhaps you have thought to yourselves, that he must be a man of deep religious feeling and high religious profession who could write so well. Is it so in fact, my brethren? it is not so ; why? because after all it is *but* poetry, not religion ; it is human nature exerting the powers of imagination and reason, which it has, till it seems also to have powers which it has not. There are, you know, in the animal world various creatures, which are able to imitate the voice of man ; nature in like manner is often a mockery of grace. The truth is, the natural man sees this or that principle to be good or true from the light of conscience ; and then, since he has the power of reasoning, he knows that, if this be true, many other things are true likewise; and then, having the power of imagination, he pictures to himself those other things as true, though he does not really understand them. And then he brings to his aid what he has read and gained from others who *have* had grace, and thus he completes his sketch; and then he throws his feelings and his heart into it, meditates on it, and kindles in himself a sort of enthusiasm, and thus he is able to write beautifully and touchingly about what to others indeed may be a reality, but to him is nothing more than a fiction. Thus some can write about the early Martyrs, and others describe some great Saint of the Middle Ages, not exactly as a Catholic would, but as if they had a piety and a seriousness to which really they are strangers. So, too, actors on a stage can excite themselves till they think they are the persons they represent; and, as you know, prejudiced persons, who wish to quarrel with another, impute something to him, which at first they scarcely believe themselves; but they wish to believe it and act as if it were true, and raise and cherish anger at the thought of it, till at last they come simply to believe it. So it is, I say, in the case of many an author in verse and prose; readers are deceived by his fine writing; they not only praise this or that sentiment, or argument, or description, in what they read, which happens to be true, but they put faith in the writer himself; and they believe sentiments or statements which are false on the credit of the truth. Thus it is that people are led away into false religions and false philosophies; a preacher or speaker, who is in a state of nature, or has fallen from grace, is able to say many things to touch the heart of a sinner or to strike his conscience, whether from his natural powers, or from what he has read in books ; and the latter forthwith takes him for his prophet and guide, on the warrant of these accidental truths which it required no supernatural gifts to discover and enforce.

Scripture provides us an instance of such a prophet (nay, of one far more favoured and honoured than any false teacher is now), who nevertheless was the enemy of God ; I mean the prophet Balaam.   He went forth to curse the chosen people in spite of an express prohibition from heaven, and that for money ; and at length he died fighting against them in battle.   Such was he in his life and in his death ; such were his deeds ; but what were his words ? most religious, most conscientious, most instructive.   " If Balac," he says, "shall give me his house full of silver and gold, I cannot alter the word of the Lord my God."   Again, " Let my soul die the death of the just, and let my end be like to theirs ! "   And again, " I will show thee, O man, what is good, and what the Lord requireth of thee ; to do judgment and to love mercy, and to walk heedfully with thy God ".   Here is a man, who is not in a state of grace, speaking so religiously, that at first sight you might have thought he was to be followed in whatever he said, and that your soul would have been safe with his.

And thus it often happens, that those who seem so amiable and good, and so trustworthy, when we only know them from their writings, disappoint us so painfully, if at length we come to have a personal acquaintance with them. We do not recognise in the living being the eloquence or the wisdom which so much enchanted us. He is rude, perhaps, and unfeeling ; he is selfish, he is dictatorial, he is sensual, he is empty-minded and frivolous ; while we in our simplicity had antecedently thought him the very embodiment of purity and tenderness, or an oracle of heavenly truth.

Now, my dear brethren, I have been engaged in bringing before you what human nature can do, and what it can appear, without being reconciled to God, without any hope of heaven, without any security against sin, without any pardon of the original curse, nay, in the midst of mortal sin ; but it is a state which has never existed in fact, without great modifications. No one has ever been deprived of the assistance of grace, both for illumination and con-version ; even the heathen world as a whole had to a certain extent its darkness relieved by these fitful and recurrent gleams of light ; but I have thought it useful to get you to contemplate what human nature is, viewed in itself, for various reasons. It explains how it is that men look so like each other as they do,— grace being imitated, and, as it were, rivalled by nature, both in society at large, and in the hearts of particular persons. Hence the world will not believe the separa-tion really existing between it and the Church, and the smallness of the flock of Christ. And hence too it is, that numbers who have heard the Name of Christ, and profess to believe in the Gospel, will not be persuaded as regards themselves that they are exterior to the Church, and do not enjoy her privileges ; merely because they do their duty in some general way, or because they are conscious to themselves of being benevolent or upright. And this is a point which concerns Catholics too, as I now proceed to show you.

Make yourselves quite sure then, my brethren, of the matter of fact, before you go away with the belief, that you are not confusing, in your own case, nature and grace, and taking credit to yourselves for supernatural works, which merit heaven, when you are but doing the works of a heathen, are unforgiven, and lie under an eternal sentence. O, it is a dreadful thought, that a man may deceive himself with the notion that he is secure, merely because he is a Catholic, and because he has some kind of love and fear of God, whereas he may be no better than many a Protestant round about him, who either never was baptised, or threw himself once for all out of grace on coming to years of understanding. This idea is entirely conceivable ; it is well if it be not true in matter of fact. You know, it is one opinion entertained among divines and holy men, that the number of Catholics that are to be saved will on the whole be small. Multitudes of those who never knew the Gospel will rise up in the judgment against the children of the Church, and will be shown to have done more with scantier opportunities. Our Lord speaks of His people as a small flock, as I cited His words when I began : He says, " Many are called, few are chosen". St. Paul, speaking in the first instance of the Jews, says that but " a remnant is saved according to the election of grace ". He speaks even of the possibility of his own reprobation. What a thought in an Apostle ! yet it is one with which Saints are familiar; they fear both for themselves and for others. It is related in the history of my own dear Patron, St. Philip Neri, that some time after his death he appeared to a holy religious, and bade him take a message of consolation to his children, the Fathers of the Oratory. The consolation was this, that, by the grace of God, up to that day not one of the Congregation had been lost. " None of them lost ! " a man may cry out ; " well, had his consolation for his children been, that they were all in paradise, having escaped the dark lake of purgatory, that would have been something worth telling ; but all he had to say was, that none of them were in hell ! Strange if they were ! Here was a succession of men, who had given up the world for a religious life, who had given up self for God and their neighbour, who had passed their days in prayer and good works, who had died happily with the last Sacraments, and it is revealed about them, as a great consolation, that not even one of them was lost ! " Still such after all is our holy Father's consolation ; and, that it should be such, only proves that salvation is not so easy a matter, or so cheap a possession, as we are apt to suppose. It is not obtained by the mere wishing. And, if it was a gift so to be coveted by men, who had made sacrifices for Christ, and were living in sanctity, how much more rare and arduous of attainment is it in those who have confessedly loved the world more than God, and have never dreamed of doing any duty to which the Church did not oblige them !

Tell me, what is the state of your souls and the rule of your lives? You come to Confession, once a year;—four times a year;—at the Indulgences;—you communicate as often; do you not miss Mass on days of obligation; you are not conscious of any great sin.—There you come to an end; you have nothing more to say. What? do you not take God's name in vain? only when you are angry; that is, I suppose, you are subject to fits of violent passion, in which you use every shocking word which the devil puts into your mouth, and abuse and curse, and perhaps strike the objects of your anger?—Only now and then, you say, when you are in liquor. Then it seems you are given to intoxication?—you answer, you never drink so much as not to know what you are doing. Do you really mean that for an excuse! Well, have you improved in these respects in the course of several years past? You cannot say you have, but such sins are not mortal at the most. Then, I suppose, you have not lately fallen into mortal sin at all? You pause, and then you are obliged to confess that you have, and that once and again; and the more I question you, perhaps the longer becomes the catalogue of offences which have separated you from God. But this is not all; your sole idea of sin is, the sinning in act and in deed; sins of habit, which cling so close to you that they are difficult to detect, and manifest themselves in slight but continual influences on your thoughts, words, and works, do not engage your attention at all. You are selfish, and obstinate, and worldly, and self-indulgent; you neglect your children;

you are fond of idle amusements ; you scarcely ever think of God from day to day, for I cannot call your hurried prayers morning and night any thinking of Him at all. You are friends with the world, and live a good deal among those who have no sense of religion.

Now what have you to tell me which will set against this? what good have you done? in what is your hope of heaven ? whence do you gain it ? You perhaps answer me, that the Sacrament of Penance reconciles you from time to time to God ; that you live in the world ; that you are not called to the religious state ; that it is true you love the world more than God, but that you love God sufficiently for salvation, and that you rely in the hour of death upon the powerful intercession of the Blessed Mother of God. Then besides, you have a number of good points, which you go through, and which are to you signs that you *are* in the grace of God ; you conceive that your state at worst is one of tepidity. Tepidity ! I tell you, you have no marks of tepidity; do you wish to know what a tepid person is ? one who has begun to lead almost the life of a Saint, and has fallen from his fervour ; one who retains his good practices, but does them without devotion ; one who does so much, that we only blame him for not doing more. No, you need not confess tepidity, my brother ;—do you wish to have the judgment which I am led to form about you ? it is, that probably you are not in the grace of God at all. The probability is, that for a long while past you have gone to Confession without the proper dispositions, without real grief, and without sincere purpose of amendment for your sins. You are probably such, that were you to die this night, you would be lost for ever. What do you do more than nature does? You do certain good things; " what reward have ye? do not even the publicans so? what do ye more than others? do not even the heathen so?" You have the ordinary virtues of human nature, or some of them; you are what nature made you, and care not to be better. You may be naturally kind-hearted, and then you do charitable actions to others; you have a natural strength of character,—if so, you are able to bring your passions under the power of reason; you have a natural energy, and you labour for your family; you are naturally mild, and so you do not quarrel; you have a dislike of intemperance, and therefore you are sober. You have the virtues of your Protestant neighbours, and their faults too; what are you better than they?

Here is another grave matter against you, that you are so well with the Protestants about you; I do not mean to say that you are not bound to cultivate peace with all men, and to do them all the offices of charity in your power. Of course you are, and if they respect, esteem, and love you, it redounds to your praise and will gain you a reward; but I mean more than this; I mean they do *not* respect you, but they like you, because they think of you as of themselves, they see no difference between themselves and you. This is the very reason why they so often take your part, and assert or defend your political rights. Here again, there is a sense, of course, in which our civil rights may be advocated by Protestants without any reflection on us, and with honour to them. We are like others in this, that we are men; that we are members of the same state with them, subjects, contented subjects, of the same Sovereign, that we have a dependence on them, and have them dependent on us; that, like them, we feel pain when ill-used, and are grateful when well-treated. We need not be ashamed of a fellowship like this, and those who recognise it in us are generous in doing so. But we have much cause to be ashamed, and much cause to be anxious what God thinks of us, if we gain their support by giving them a false impression in our persons of what the Catholic Church is and what Catholics are bound to be, what bound to believe, and to do; and is not this the case often, my brethren, that the world takes up your interests, because you share its sins?

Nature is one with nature, grace with grace; the world then witnesses against you by being good friends with you; you could not have got on with the world so well, without surrendering something which was precious and sacred. The world likes you, all but your professed creed; distinguishes you from your creed in its judgment of you, and would fain separate you from it in fact. Men say, "These persons are better than their Church; we have not a word to say for their Church; but Catholics are not what they were, they are very much like other men now. Their Creed certainly is bigoted and cruel, but what would you have of them? You cannot expect them to confess this; let them change quietly, no one changes in public,—be satisfied that they are changed. They are as fond of the world as we are ; they take up political objects as warmly; they like their own way just as well ; they do not like strictness a whit better ; they hate spiritual thraldom, and they are half ashamed of the Pope and his Councils. They hardly believe any miracles now, and are annoyed when their own brethren confess that there are such ; they never speak of purgatory ; they are sore about images ; they avoid the subject of Indulgences; and they will not commit themselves to the doctrine of exclusive salvation. The Catholic doctrines are now mere badges of party. Catholics think for themselves and judge for themselves, just as we do ; they are kept in their Church by a point of honour, and a reluctance at seeming to abandon a fallen cause."

Such is the judgment of the world, and you, my brethren, are shocked to hear it ;—but may it not be, that the world knows more about you than you know about yourselves ? " If ye had been of the world," says Christ, " the world would love its own ; but because ye are not of the world, but I have chosen you out of the world, therefore the world hateth you." So speaks Christ of His Apostles. How run His words when applied to you ? " If ye be of the world, the world will love its own ; therefore ye *are* of the world, and I have *not* chosen you out of the world, because the world *doth* love you." Do not complain of the world's imputing to you more than is true ; those who live as the world lives give countenance to those who think them of the world, and seem to form but one party with them. In proportion as you put off the yoke

of Christ, so does the world by a sort of instinct recognise you, and think well of you accordingly. Its
highest compliment is to tell you that you disbelieve.
O my brethren, there is an eternal enmity between
the world and the Church. The Church declares by
the mouth of an Apostle, "Whoso will be a friend of
the world, becomes an enemy of God ;" and the world
retorts, and calls the Church apostate, sorceress,
Beelzebub, and Antichrist. She is the image and the
mother of the predestinate, and, if you would be found
among her children when you die, you must have part
in her reproach while you live. Does not the world
scoff at all that is glorious, all that is majestic, in our
holy religion ? Does it not speak against the special
creations of God's grace ? Does it not disbelieve the
possibility of purity and chastity ? Does it not slander
the profession of celibacy ? Does it not deny the
virginity of Mary ? Does it not cast out her very
name as evil ? Does it not scorn her as "a dead
woman," whom you know to be the Mother of all
the living, and the great Intercessor of the faithful ?
Does it not ridicule the Saints ? Does it not make
light of their relics ? Does it not despise the Sacraments ? Does it not blaspheme the awful Presence
which dwells upon our altars, and mock bitterly and
fiercely at our believing that what it calls bread and
wine is that very same Body and Blood of the Lamb,
which lay in Mary's womb and hung on the Cross ?
What are we, that we should be better treated than
our Lord, and His Mother, and His servants, and His
works ? Nay, what are we, if we *be* better treated,

but friends of those who thus treat us well, and who ill-treat Him?

O my dear brethren, be children of grace, not of nature; be not seduced by this world's sophistries and assumptions; it pretends to be the work of God, but in reality it comes of Satan. "I know My sheep," says our Lord, "and Mine know Me, and they follow Me." "Show me, O Thou whom my soul loveth," says the Bride in the Canticle, "where Thou feedest, where Thou restest at noon:" and He answers her, "Go forth, and follow after the steps of the flocks, and feed thy kids beside the shepherds' tents". Let us follow the Saints, as they follow Christ; so that, when He comes in judgment, and the wretched world sinks to perdition, "on us sinners, His servants, hoping in the multitude of His mercies, He may vouchsafe to bestow some portion and fellowship with His Holy Apostles and Martyrs, with John, Stephen, Matthias, Barnabas, Ignatius, Alexander, Marcelline, Peter, Felicity, Perpetua, Agatha, Lucy, Agnes, Cicely, Anastasia, and all His Saints, not for the value of our merit, but according to the bounty of His pardon, through the same Christ our Lord".

DISCOURSE IX.

ILLUMINATING GRACE.

WHEN man was created, he was endowed withal with gifts above his own nature, by means of which that nature was perfected. As some potent stimulant which is not nourishment, a scent or a draught, rouses, invigorates, concentrates our animal powers, gives keenness to our perceptions, and intensity to our efforts, so, or rather in some far higher sense, and in more diversified ways, did the supernatural grace of God give a meaning, and an aim, and a sufficiency, and a consistency, and a certainty, to the many faculties of that compound of soul and body, which constitutes man. And when man fell, he lost this divine, unmerited gift, and, instead of soaring heavenwards, fell down feeble to the earth, in a state of exhaustion and collapse. And, again, when God, for Christ's sake, is about to restore any one to His favour, His first act of mercy is to impart to him a portion of this grace; the first-fruits of that sovereign, energetic power, which forms and harmonises his whole nature, and enables it to fulfil its own end, while it fulfils one higher than its own.

Now, one of the defects which man incurred on the fall was ignorance, or spiritual blindness; and one of the gifts received on his restoration is a perception of things spiritual; so that, before he is brought under the grace of Christ, he can but inquire, reason, argue, and conclude, about religious truth; but afterwards he sees it. "Blessed art Thou, Simon, Son of Jona," said our Lord to St. Peter, when he confessed the Incarnation, "for flesh and blood hath not revealed it to thee, but My Father, which is in heaven." Again: "I thank Thee, O Father, Lord of heaven and earth, because Thou hast hid these things from the wise and prudent, and hath revealed them unto little ones. . . . No one knoweth the Father, save the Son, and no one knoweth the Son but the Father, and he to whom it shall please the Son to reveal Him." In like manner St. Paul says, "The animal" or natural "man perceiveth not the things of the Spirit of God;" and elsewhere, "No one can say the Lord Jesus, but in the Holy Ghost". And St. John, "Ye have an unction from the Holy One, and ye know all things". The Prophets had promised the same gift before Christ came;—"I will make all thy sons taught of the Lord," says Isaias, "and the multitude of peace upon thy sons;" "No more," says Jeremias, "shall man teach his neighbour, and man his brother, saying, Know the Lord, for all shall know Me from the least of them even to the greatest of them ".

Now here you may say, my brethren, "What is the meaning of this? are we men, or are we not? have we lost part of our nature by the fall, or have we not? is not the Reason a part of man's nature? does not the Reason see, as the eye does? cannot we, by the natural power of our Reason, understand all kinds of truths, about this earth, about human society, about the realms of space, about matter, about the soul? why should religion be an exception? Why, then, cannot we understand by our natural reason about Almighty God and heaven?—if we can inquire into one thing, we can inquire into another; if we can imagine one thing, we can imagine another; how then is it that we cannot arrive at the truths of religion without the supernatural aid of grace?" This is a question which may give rise to some profitable reflections, and I shall now attempt to answer it.

You ask, what it is you need, besides eyes, in order to see the truths of revelation : I will tell you at once; you need light. Not the keenest eyes can see in the dark. Now, though your mind be the eye, the grace of God is the light; and you will as easily exercise your eyes in this sensible world without the sun, as you will be able to exercise your mind in the spiritual world without a parallel gift from without. Now, you are born under a privation of this blessed spiritual light; and, while it remains, you will not, cannot, really see God. I do not say you will have no thought at all about God, nor be able to talk about Him. True, but you will not be able to do more than reason about Him. Your thoughts and your words will not get beyond a mere reasoning. I grant then what you claim ; you claim to be able by your mental powers to reason about God; doubtless you can, but to infer a thing is not to see it in respect to the physical world, nor is it in the spiritual.

Consider the case of a man without eyes talking about forms and colours, and you will understand what I mean. A blind man may pick up a good deal of information of various kinds, and be very conversant with the objects of sight, though he does not see. He may be able to talk about them fluently, and may be fond of doing so; he may even talk of seeing as if he really saw, till he almost seems to pretend to the faculty of sight. He speaks of heights and distances, and directions, and the dispositions of places, and shapes, and appearances, as naturally as other men; and he is not duly aware of his own extreme privation; and, if you ask how this comes about, it is partly because he hears what other men say about these things, and he is able to imitate them, and partly because he cannot help reasoning upon the things he hears, and drawing conclusions from them; and thus he comes to think he knows what he does not know at all.

He hears men converse; he may have books read to him; he gains vague ideas of objects of sight, and when he begins to speak, his words are tolerably correct, and do not at once betray how little he knows what he is talking about. He infers one thing from another, and thus is able to speak of many things which he does not see, but only perceives must be so, granting other things are so. For instance, if he knows that blue and yellow make green, he may pronounce, without a chance of mistake, that green is more like blue than yellow is; if he happens to know that one man is under six feet in height, and another is full six feet, he may, when they are both before him, boldly declare, as if he saw, that the latter is the taller of the two. It is not that he judges by sight, but that reason takes the place of it. There was much talk in the world some little time since of a man of science, who was said to have found out a new planet ; how did he do it ? Did he watch night after night, wearily and perseveringly, in the chill air, through the tedious course of the starry heavens, for what he might possibly find there, till at length, by means of some powerful glass, he discovered in the dim distance this unexpected addition to our planetary system ? Far from it ; it is said that he sat at his ease in his library, and made calculations on paper in the daytime, and thus, without looking once up at the sky, he determined, from what was already known of the sun and the planets, of their number, their positions, their motions, and their influences, that, in addition to them all, there must be some other body in that very place where he said it would be found, if astronomers did but turn their instruments upon it. Here was a man reading the heavens, not with eyes, but by reason. Reason, then, is a sort of substitute for sight ; and so in many respects are the other senses, as is obvious. You know how quick the blind are often found to be in discovering the presence of friends, and the feelings of strangers, by the voice, and the tone, and the tread ; so that they seem to understand looks, and gestures, and dumb show, as if they saw, to the surprise of those who wish to keep their meaning secret from them.

Now this will explain the way in which the natural man is able partly to understand, and still more to speak upon, supernatural subjects. There is a large floating body of Catholic truth in the world ; it comes down by tradition from age to age ; it is carried forward by preaching and profession from one generation to another, and is poured about into all quarters of the world. It is found in fulness and purity in the Church alone, but portions of it, larger or smaller, escape far and wide, and penetrate into places which have never been blest with her presence and ministration. Now men may take up and profess these scattered truths, merely because they fall in with them ; these fragments of Revelation, such as the doctrine of the Holy Trinity, or the Atonement, are the religion which they have been taught in their childhood ; and therefore they may retain them, and profess them, and repeat them, without really seeing them, as the Catholic sees them, but as receiving them merely by word of mouth, from imitation of others. And in this way it often happens that a man external to the Catholic Church writes sermons and instructions, draws up and arranges devotions, or composes hymns, which are faultless, or nearly so ; which are the fruit, not of his own illuminated mind, but of his careful study, sometimes of his accurate translation, of Catholic originals. Then, again, Catholic truths and rites are so beautiful, so great, so consolatory, that they draw one on to love and admire them with a natural love, as a prospect might attract us, or a skilful piece of mechanism. Hence men of lively imagination may profess this doctrine or that, or adopt this or that ceremony or usage, for its very beauty sake, not asking themselves whether it be true, and having no real perception or mental hold of it. Thus, too, they will decorate their churches, stretch and strain their ritual, introduce candles, vestments, flowers, incense, and processions, not from faith, but from poetical feeling. And, moreover, the Catholic Creed, as coming from God, is so harmonious, so consistent with itself, holds together so perfectly, so corresponds part to part, that an acute mind, knowing one portion of it, would often infer another portion, merely as a matter of just reasoning. Thus a correct thinker might be sure, that if God is infinite and man finite, there must be mysteries in religion. It is not that he really feels the mysteriousness of religion, but he infers it; he is led to it as a matter of necessity, and from mere clearness of mind and love of consistency, he maintains it. Again, a man may say, "Since this or that doctrine has so much historical evidence in its favour, I must accept it;" he has no real sight or direct perception of it, but he takes up the profession of it, because he feels it would be absurd, under the conditions with which he starts, to do otherwise. He does no more than load himself with a form of words instead of contemplating, with the eye of the soul, God Himself, the source of all truth, and this doctrine as proceeding from His mouth. A keen, sagacious intellect will carry a man a great way in anticipating doctrines which he has never been told;—thus, before it knew what Scripture said on the subject, it might argue; "Sin is an offence against God beyond conception great, and involving vast evils on the sinner, for, if it were not so, why should Christ have suffered?" that is, he sees that it is necessary for the Christian system of doctrine that sin should be a great evil, without necessarily feeling in his conscience that it is so. Nay, I can fancy a man conjecturing that our bodies would rise again, as arguing it out from the fact that the Eternal God has so honoured our mortal flesh as to take it upon Him as part of Himself. Thus he would be receiving the resurrection, nay, eternal punishment, merely as truths which follow from what he knew already. And in like manner learned men, outside the Church, may compose most useful works on the Evidences of religion, or in defence of particular doctrines, or in explanation of the whole scheme of Catholicity ; in these cases reason becomes the handmaid of faith : still it is not faith ; it does not rise above an intellectual view or notion ; it affirms, not as grasping the truth, not as seeing, but as "being of opinion," as "judging," as "coming to a conclusion".

Here, then, you see what the natural man can do; he can feel, he can imagine, he can admire, he can reason, he can infer; in all these ways he may proceed to receive the whole or part of Catholic truth ; but he cannot see, he cannot love. Yet he will perplex religious persons who do not understand the secret by which he is able to make so imposing a display; for they will be at a loss to understand how it is that he is able to speak so well, except he speak, though he be out of the Church, by the Spirit of God. Thus it is with the writing of some of the ancient heretics, who wrote upon the Incarnation; so it is with heretics of modern times who have written on the doctrine of grace; they write sometimes with such beauty and depth, that one cannot help admiring what they say on those very subjects, as to which we know withal that at the bottom they are unsound. But, my brethren, the sentiments may be right and good in themselves, but not in those men; these are the solitary truths which they have happened to infer in a range of matters about which they see and know nothing, and their heresy on other points, which are close upon the acceptance of these truths, is a proof that they do not see what they speak of. A blind man, discoursing upon form and colour, might say some things truly, and some things falsely; but even one mistake which he happened to make, though only one, would be enough to betray that he had no real possession of the truths which he enunciated, though they were many; for, had he had eyes, he not only would have been correct in many, but would have been mistaken in none. For instance, supposing that he knew that two buildings were the same in height, he might perhaps be led boldly to pronounce that their appearance was the same when he looked at them, not knowing that the greater distance of the one of them from us might reduce it to the eye to half or a fourth of the other. And thus men who are not in the Church and who have no practical experience of Catholic devotion to the Blessed Mother of God, when they read our prayers and litanies, and observe the strength of their language, and the length to which they go, confidently assert that she is, in every sense and way, the object of our worship, to the exclusion, or in rivalry, of the Supreme God ; not understanding that He " in whom we live, and move and are," who new-creates us with His grace, and who feeds us with His own Body and Blood, is closer to us and more intimately with us than any creature ; that Saints and Angels, and the Blessed Virgin herself, are necessarily at a distance from us, compared with Him, and, that whatever language we use towards them, though it be the same as that which we use to our Maker, it only carries with it a sense which is due and proportionate to the object we address. And thus these objectors are detected, as Catholics feel, by their objection itself, as really knowing and seeing nothing of what they dispute about.

And now I have explained sufficiently what is meant by saying that the natural man holds divine truths merely as an opinion, and not as a point of faith ; grace believes, reason does but opine ; grace gives certainty, reason is never decided. Now it is remarkable that this characteristic of reason is so clearly understood by the persons themselves of whom I am speaking, that, in spite of the confidence which they have in their own opinions, whatever that be, still, conscious that they have no grounds for real and fixed conviction about revealed truth, they boldly face the difficulty, and consider it a fault to be certain about revealed truth, and a merit to doubt. For instance, " the Holy Catholic Church " is a point of faith, as being one of the articles of the Apostles' Creed ; yet they think it an impatience to be dissatisfied with uncertainty as to where the Catholic Church is, and what she says. They are well aware that no man alive of fair abilities would put undoubting faith and reliance in the Church Established, except by doing violence to his reason ; they know that the great mass of its members in no sense believe in it, and that of the remainder no one could say more than that it indirectly comes from God, and that it is safest to remain in it. There is, in these persons, no faith, only a mere opinion, about this article of the Creed. Accordingly they are obliged to say, in mere defence of their own position, that faith is not necessary, and a state of doubt is sufficient, and all that is expected of us. In consequence they attribute it to mere restlessness, when one of their own members seeks to exercise faith in the Holy Catholic Church as a revealed truth, as they themselves profess to exercise it in the Holy Trinity or our Lord's resurrection, and when in consequence he hunts about, and asks on all sides, how he is to do so. Nay, they go so far as to impute it to a Catholic as a fault, when he manifests a simple trust in the Church and her teaching. It sometimes happens that those who join the Catholic Church from some Protestant communion, are observed to change the uncertainty and hesitation of mind on religious subjects, which they showed before their conversion, into a clear and fearless confidence ; they doubted about their old communion, they have no doubt about their new. They have no fears, no

anxieties, no difficulties, no scruples.   They speak,
accordingly, as they feel ; and the world, not understanding that this is the effect of the grace which (as
we may humbly trust) these happy souls have received,
—not understanding that, though it has full experience
of the region of the shadow of death in which it lies,
it has none at all of that city, whereof the Lord God
and the Lamb is the light,—measuring what Catholics
have by what itself has not, the world, I say, cries
out, " How forward, how unnatural, how excited, how
extravagant" ; and it considers that such a change is
a change for the worse, and is proved to be a mistake
and a fault, because it produces precisely that effect,
which it would produce were it a change for the
better.

It tells us that certainty, and confidence, and bold-
ness in speech are unchristian ; is this pleading a
cause, or a judgment from facts ?   Was it confidence
or doubt, was it zeal or coldness, was it keenness or
irresolution in action, which distinguished the Martyrs
in the first ages of the Church ?   Was the religion of
Christ propagated by the vehemence of faith and love,
or by a philosophical balance of arguments ?   Look
back at the early Martyrs, my brethren, what were
they ? why, they were very commonly youths and
maidens, soldiers and slaves ;—a set of hot-headed
young men, who would have lived to be wise, had
they not been obstinately set on dying first ; who tore
down imperial manifestoes, broke the peace, challenged
the judges to dispute, would not rest till they got into
the same den with a lion, and who, if chased out of

one city, began preaching in another! So said the blind world about those who saw the Unseen. Yes! it was the spiritual sight of God which made them what they were. No one is a Martyr for a conclusion, no one is a Martyr for an opinion; it is faith that makes Martyrs. He who knows and loves the things of God has no power to deny them; he may have a natural shrinking from torture and death, but such terror is incommensurate with faith, and as little acts upon it as dust and mire touch the sun's light, or scents or voices could stop a wheel in motion. The Martyrs saw, and how could they but speak what they had seen? They might shudder at the pain, but they had not the power not to see; if threats could undo the heavenly truths, then might pain silence their confession of them. O my brethren, the world is inquiring, and large-minded, and knows many things; it talks well and profoundly; but is there one among its Babel of religious opinions which it would be a Martyr for? Some of them may be true, and some false; let it choose any one of them to die for. Its children talk loudly, they declaim angrily against the doctrine that God is an avenger; would they die rather than confess it? They talk eloquently of the infinite indulgence of God; would they die rather than deny it? If not, they have not even enthusiasm, they have not even obstinacy, they have not even bigotry, they have not even party spirit to sustain them,—much less have they grace; they speak upon opinion only, and by an inference. Again, there are those who call on men to trust the Established Communion, as considering it to be a branch of the Catholic Church; they may urge that this opinion can be cogently defended, but an opinion it is; for say, O ye who hold it, how many of you would die rather than admit a doubt about it? Do you now hold it sinful to doubt it? or rather, as I have said, do you not think it allowable, natural, necessary, becoming, humble-minded and sober-minded to doubt it? do you not almost think better of a man for doubting it, provided he does not follow his doubts out, and end in disbelieving it?

Hence these very same persons, who speak so severely of any one who leaves the communion in which he was born, doubting of it themselves, are in consequence led to view his act as an affront done to their body, rather than as an evil to himself. They consider it as a personal affront to a party and an injury to a cause, and the affront is greater or less according to the mischief which it does them in the particular case. It is not his loss but their inconvenience, which is the real measure of his sin. If a person is in any way important or useful to them, they will protest against his act; if he is troublesome to them, if he goes (as they say) too far, if he is a scandal, or a centre of perverse influence, or in any way disturbs the order and welfare of their body, they are easily reconciled to his leaving them; the more courteous of them congratulate him on his honesty, and the more bitter congratulate themselves on being rid of him. Is such the feeling of a mother and of kinsmen towards a son and a brother? "can a woman forget her babe, that she should not have compassion

on the son of her womb?" Did a man leave the
Catholic Church, our first feeling, my brethren, as
you know so well, would be one of compassion and
fear; we should consider that, though we were even
losing one who was a scandal to us, still that our
gain would be nothing in comparison of his loss. We
know that a man cannot desert the Church without
quenching an inestimable gift of grace; that he has
already received a definite influence and effect upon
his soul, such, that he cannot dispossess himself of it
without the gravest sin; that, though he may have
had many temptations to disbelieve, they are only like
temptations to sensuality, harmless without his willing co-operation. This is why the Church cannot
sanction him in his reconsidering the question of her
own Divine mission; she holds that such inquiries,
though the appointed means of entering her pale, are
superseded on his entrance by the gift of a spiritual
sight, a gift which consumes doubt so utterly, in any
proper sense of the word, that henceforth it is not that
he must not, but that he cannot entertain it; cannot
entertain it except by his own great culpability; and
therefore must not, because he cannot. This is what
we hold and are conscious of, my brethren; and, as
holding it, we never could feel satisfaction and relief,
on first hearing of the defection of a brother, be he
ever so unworthy, ever so scandalous; our first feeling
would be sorrow. We are, in fact, often obliged to
bear with scandalous members against our will from
charity to them; but those, whose highest belief is
but an inference, who are obliged to go over in their

minds from time to time the reasons and the ground of their creed, lest they should suddenly find themselves left without their conclusion, these persons not having faith, have no opportunity for charity, and think that when a man leaves them who has given them any trouble, it is a double gain—to him, that he is where he is better fitted to be ; to themselves, that they are at peace.

What I have been saying will account for another thing, which otherwise will surprise us.   The world cannot believe that Catholics really hold what they profess to hold; and supposes that, if they are educated men, they are kept up to their profession by external influence, by superstitious fear, by pride, by interest, or other bad or unworthy motive.   Men of the world have never believed in their whole life, never have had simple faith in things unseen, never have had more than an opinion about them, that they might be true and might be false, but probably were true, or doubtless were true ; and in consequence they think an absolute, unhesitating faith in anything unseen to be simply an extravagance, and especially when it is exercised on objects which they do not believe themselves, or even reject with scorn or abhorrence.   And hence they prophesy that the Catholic Church must lose, in proportion as men are directed to the sober examination of their own thoughts and feelings, and to the separation of what is real and true from what is a matter of words and pretence.   They cannot understand how our faith in the Blessed Sacrament is a genuine, living portion of our minds ; they think it a mere profession which we embrace with no inward assent, but only because we are told that we should be lost unless we profess it; or because, the Catholic Church having in dark ages committed herself to it, we cannot help ourselves, though we would if we could, and therefore receive it by constraint, from a sense of duty towards our cause, or in a spirit of party. They will not believe that we would not gladly get rid of the doctrine of transubstantiation, as a heavy stone about our necks, if we could. What shocking words to use! It would be wrong to use them, were they not necessary to make you understand, my brethren, the privilege which you have, and the world has not. Shocking indeed and most profane! a relief to rid ourselves of the doctrine that Jesus is on our Altars! as well say a relief to rid ourselves of the belief that Jesus is God, to rid ourselves of the belief that there is a God. Yes, that I suppose is the true relief, to believe nothing at all, or, at least, not to be bound to believe anything; to believe first one thing, then another; to believe what we please for as long as we please; that is, not really to believe, but to have an opinion about everything, and let nothing sit close upon us, to commit ourselves to nothing, to keep the unseen world altogether at a distance. But if we are to believe anything at all, if we are to make any one heavenly doctrine our own, if we are to take some dogmas as true, why, in that case, it should be a burden to believe what is so gracious and what so concerns us, rather than what is less intimate and less winning,—why we must not believe that God is among us, if God there is, why we may not believe that God dwells on our Altars as well as that He dwells in the sky, certainly is not so self-evident, but that we have a claim to ask the reasons for it of those, who profess to be so rational and so natural in all their determinations. O my brethren, how narrow-minded is this world at bottom after all, in spite of its pretences and in spite of appearances! Here you see, it cannot by a stretch of imagination conceive that anything exists, of which it has not cognisance in its own heart; it will not admit into its imagination the mere idea that we have faith, because it does not know what faith is from experience, and it will not admit that there is anything in the mind of man which it does not experience itself, for that would be all one with admitting after all that there is such a thing as a mystery. It must know, it must be the measure of all things; and so in self-defence it considers us hypocritical, as professing what we cannot believe, lest it should be forced to confess itself blind. "Behold what manner of love the Father had bestowed on us, that we should be named, and should be, the sons of God; therefore the world knoweth not us, because it knoweth not Him!"

It is for the same reason that inquirers, who are approaching the Church, find it difficult to persuade themselves that their doubts will not continue after they have entered it. This is the reason they assign for not becoming Catholics; for what is to become of them, they ask, if their present doubts continue after their conversion? they will have nothing to fall back upon.

They do not reflect that their present difficulties are moral ones, not intellectual ;—I mean, that it is not that they really doubt whether the conclusion at which they have arrived, that the Catholic Church comes from God, is true ; this they do not doubt in their reason at all, but that they cannot rule their mind to grasp and keep hold of this truth. They recognise it dimly, though certainly, as the sun through mists and clouds, and they forget that it is the office of grace to clear up gloom and haziness, to steady that fitful vision, to perfect reason by faith, and to convert a logical conclusion into an object of intellectual sight. And thus they will not credit it as possible, when we assure them of what we have seen in so many instances, that all their trouble will go, when once they have entered the communion of Saints and the atmosphere of grace and light, and that they will be so full of peace and joy as not to know how to thank God enough, and from the very force of their feelings and the necessity of relieving them, they will set about converting others with a sudden zeal which contrasts strangely with their late vacillation.

Two remarks I must add in conclusion, in explanation of what I have been saying.

First, do not suppose I have been speaking in disparagement of human reason : it is the way to faith ; its conclusions are often the very objects of faith. It precedes faith, when souls are converted to the Catholic Church ; and it is the instrument which the Church herself is guided to make use of, when she is called upon to put forth those definitions of doctrine, in which, according to the promise and power of her Lord and Saviour, she is infallible; but still reason is one thing and faith is another, and reason can as little be made a substitute for faith, as faith can be made a substitute for reason.

Again, I have been speaking as if a state of nature were utterly destitute of the influences of grace, and as if those who are external to the Church acted simply from nature. Recollect, I have so spoken for the sake of distinctness, that grace and nature might clearly be contrasted with each other; but it is not the fact. God gives His grace to all men, and to those who profit by it He gives more grace, and even those who quench it still have the offer. Hence some men act simply from nature; some act from nature in some respects, not in others; others are yielding themselves to the guidance of the assistances given them; others, who have faithfully availed themselves of that guidance and are sincerely in search of the Church and her gifts, may even already be in a state of justification. Hence it is impossible to apply what has been said above to individuals, whose hearts are a secret with God. Many, I repeat, are under the influence partly of reason and partly of faith, believe some things firmly, and have but an opinion on others. Many are in conflict with themselves, and are advancing to a crisis, after which they embrace or recede from the truth. Many are using the assistances of grace so well, that they are in the way to receive its permanent indwelling in their hearts. Many, we may trust, are enjoying that permanent light, and are coming steadily and securely into the Church; some, alas! may have received it, and, as not advancing towards the Holy House in which it is stored, are losing it, and, though they know it not, are living only by the recollections of what was once present within them. These are secret things with God; but the great and general truths remain, that nature cannot see God, and that grace is the sole means of seeing Him; and that, while grace enables us to do so, it also brings us into His Church, and is never given us for our illumination, without being also given to make us Catholics.

O my dear brethren, what joy and what thankfulness should be ours, that God has brought us into the Church of His Son! What gift is equal to it in the whole world in its preciousness and in its rarity? In this country in particular, where heresy ranges far and wide, where uncultivated nature has so undisputed a field all her own, where grace is given to great numbers only to be profaned and quenched, where baptisms only remain in their impress and character, and faith is ridiculed for its very firmness, for us to find ourselves here in the region of light, in the home of peace, in the presence of Saints, to find ourselves where we can use every faculty of the mind and affection of the heart in its perfection, because in its appointed place and office, to find ourselves in the possession of certainty, consistency, stability, on the highest and holiest subjects of human thought, to have hope here and heaven hereafter, to be on the Mount with Christ, while the poor world is guessing and quarrelling at its foot, who among us shall not

wonder at his own blessedness? who shall not be awe-
struck at the inscrutable grace of God, which has
brought himself, not others, where he stands? As
the Apostle says, "Through our Lord Jesus Christ
let us have by faith access into this grace wherein we
stand, and glory in the hope of the glory of the sons
of God. And hope confoundeth not; because the
love of God is poured out into our hearts by the
Holy Ghost who is given to us." And, as St. John
says, still more exactly to our purpose, "Ye have an
unction from the Holy One";—your eyes are anointed
by Him who put clay on the eyes of the blind man;
"from Him have you an unction, and ye know," not
conjecture, or suppose, or opine, but "know," see, "all
things". "So let the unction which you have received
of Him abide in you. Nor need ye that any one teach
you, but as His unction teaches you of all things, and
is true and no lie, and hath taught you, so abide in
Him." You can abide in nothing else; opinions
change, conclusions are feeble, inquiries run their
course, reason stops short, but faith alone reaches to
the end, faith only endures. Faith and prayer alone
will endure in that last dark hour, when Satan urges
all his powers and resources against the sinking soul.
What will it avail* us then, to have devised some

* Te maris et terræ, numeroque carentis are ·æ
    Mensorem cohibent, Archyta,
  Pulveris exigui prope littus parva Matinum
    Munera ; nec quicquam tibi prodest
  Aerios tentasse domos, animoque rotundum
    Percurrisse polum, morituro !

subtle argument, or to have led some brilliant attack, or to have mapped out the field of history, or to have numbered and sorted the weapons of controversy, and to have the homage of friends and the respect of the world for our successes,—what will it avail to have had a position, to have followed out a work, to have re-animated an idea, to have made a cause to triumph, if after all we have not the light of faith to guide us on from this world to the next? Oh, how fain shall we be in that day to exchange our place with the humblest, and dullest, and most ignorant of the sons of men, rather than to stand before the judgment-seat in the lot of him who has received great gifts from God, and used them for self and for man, who has shut his eyes, who has trifled with truth, who has repressed his misgivings, who has been led on by God's grace, but stopped short of its scope, who has neared the land of promise, yet not gone forward to take possession of it !

DISCOURSE X.

FAITH AND PRIVATE JUDGMENT.

WHEN we consider the beauty, the majesty, the completeness, the resources, the consolations, of the Catholic Religion, it may strike us with wonder, my brethren, that it does not convert the multitude of those who come in its way. Perhaps you have felt this surprise yourselves; especially those of you who have been recently converted, and can compare it, from experience, with those religions which the millions of this country choose instead of it. You know from experience how barren, unmeaning, and baseless those religions are; what poor attractions they have, and how little they have to say for themselves. Multitudes, indeed, are of no religion at all; and you may not be surprised that those who cannot even bear the thought of God, should not feel drawn to His Church; numbers, too, hear very little about Catholicism, or a great deal of abuse and calumny against it, and you may not be surprised that they do not all at once become Catholics; but what may fairly surprise those who enjoy the fulness of Catholic blessings is, that those who see the Church ever so distantly, who see even gleams or the faint lustre of her

(192)

majesty, nevertheless should not be so far attracted by what they see as to seek to see more,—should not at least put themselves in the way to be led on to the Truth, which of course is not ordinarily recognised in its Divine authority except by degrees. Moses, when he saw the burning bush, turned aside to see "that great sight"; Nathaniel, though he thought no good could come out of Nazareth, at least followed Philip to Christ, when Philip said to him, "Come and see"; but the multitudes about us see and hear, in some measure, surely,—many in ample measure,—and yet are not persuaded thereby to see and hear more, are not moved to act upon their knowledge. Seeing they see not, and hearing they hear not; they are contented to remain as they are; they are not drawn to inquire, or at least not drawn on to embrace.

Many explanations may be given of this difficulty; I will proceed to suggest to you one, which will sound like a truism, but yet has a meaning in it. Men do not become Catholics, because they have not faith. Now you may ask me, how this is saying more than that men do not believe the Catholic Church *because* they do not believe it; which is saying nothing at all. Our Lord, for instance, says, "He who cometh to Me shall not hunger, and he who believeth in Me shall never thirst";—to believe then and to come are the same thing. If they had faith, of course they would join the Church, for the very meaning, the very exercise of faith, is joining the Church. But I mean something more than this: faith is a state of mind, it is a particular mode of thinking and acting, which is

13

exercised, always indeed towards God, but in very various ways. Now I mean to say, that the multitude of men in this country have not this habit or character of mind. We could conceive, for instance, their believing in their own religions, even if they did not believe in the Church ; this would be faith, though a faith improperly directed ; but they do not believe even their own religions ; they do not believe in anything at all. It is a definite defect in their minds : as we might say that a person had not the virtue of meekness, or of liberality, or of prudence, quite independently of this or that exercise of the virtue, so there is such a religious virtue as faith, and there is such a defect as the absence of it. Now I mean to say that the great mass of men in this country have not this particular virtue called faith, have not this virtue at all. As a man might be without eyes or without hands, so they are without faith ; it is a distinct want or fault in their soul ; and what I say is, that *since* they have not this faculty of religious belief, no wonder they do not embrace that, which cannot really be embraced without it. They do not believe any teaching at all in any true sense ; and therefore they do not believe the Church in particular.

Now, in the first place, what is faith ? it is assenting to a doctrine as true, which we do not see, which we cannot prove, because God says it is true, who cannot lie. And further than this, since God says it is true, not with His own voice, but by the voice of His messengers, it is assenting to what man says, not simply viewed as a man, but to what he is commissioned to declare, as a messenger, prophet, or ambassador from God. In the ordinary course of this world we account things true either because we see them, or because we can perceive that they follow and are deducible from what we do see ; that is, we gain truth by sight or by reason, not by faith. You will say indeed, that we accept a number of things which we cannot prove or see, on the word of others ; certainly, but then we accept what they say only as the word of man ; and we have not commonly that absolute and unreserved confidence in them, which nothing can shake. We know that man is open to mistake, and we are always glad to find some confirmation of what he says, from other quarters, in any important matter ; or we receive his information with negligence and unconcern, as something of little consequence, as a matter of opinion ; or, if we act upon it, it is as a matter of prudence, thinking it best and safest to do so. We take his word for what it is worth, and we use it either according to our necessity, or its probability. We keep the decision in our own hands, and reserve to ourselves the right of re-opening the question whenever we please. This is very different from Divine faith ; he who believes that God is true, and that this is His word, which He has committed to man, has no doubt at all. He is as certain that the doctrine taught is true, as that God is true ; and he is certain, *because* God is true, *because* God has spoken, not because he sees its truth or can prove its truth. That is, faith has two peculiarities ;—it is most certain, decided, positive, immovable in its assent, and it gives this assent not because it sees with eye, or sees with the reason, but because it receives the tidings from one who comes from God.

This is what faith was in the time of the Apostles, as no one can deny ; and what it was then, it must be now, else it ceases to be the same thing. I say, it certainly was this in the Apostles' time, for you know they preached to the world that Christ was the Son of God, that He was born of a Virgin, that He had ascended on high, that He would come again to judge all, the living and the dead. Could the world see all this ? could it prove it ? how then were men to receive it ? why did so many embrace it ? on the word of the Apostles, who were, as their powers showed, messengers from God. Men were told to submit their reason to a living authority. Moreover, whatever an Apostle said, his converts were bound to believe ; when they entered the Church, they entered it in order to learn. The Church was their teacher ; they did not come to argue, to examine, to pick and choose, but to accept whatever was put before them. No one doubts, no one can doubt this, of those primitive times. A Christian was bound to take without doubting all that the Apostles declared to be revealed ; if the Apostles spoke, he had to yield an internal assent of his mind ; it would not be enough to keep silence, it would not be enough not to oppose : it was not allowable to credit in a measure ; it was not allowable to doubt. No ; if a convert had his own private thoughts of what was said, and only kept them to himself, if he made some secret opposition to the teaching, if he waited for further proof before he believed it, this would be a proof that he did not think the Apostles were sent from God to reveal His will ; it would be a proof that he did not in any true sense believe at all. Immediate, implicit submission of the mind was, in the lifetime of the Apostles, the only, the necessary token of faith ; then there was no room whatever for what is now called private judgment. No one could say : " I will choose my religion for myself, I will believe this, I will not believe that ; I will pledge myself to nothing ; I will believe just as long as I please, and no longer ; what I believe to-day I will reject to-morrow, if I choose. I will believe what the Apostles have as yet said, but I will not believe what they shall say in time to come." No ; either the Apostles were from God, or they were not; if they were, everything that they preached was to be believed by their hearers ; if they were not, there was nothing for their hearers to believe. To believe a little, to believe more or less, was impossible ; it contradicted the very notion of believing : if one part was to be believed, every part was to be believed ; it was an absurdity to believe one thing and not another ; for the word of the Apostles, which made the one true, made the other true too ; they were nothing in themselves, they were all things, they were an infallible authority, as coming from God. The world had either to become Christian, or to let it alone ; there was no room for private tastes and fancies, no room for private judgment.

Now surely this is quite clear from the nature of the case ; but is also clear from the words of Scripture. " We give thanks to God," says St. Paul, " without ceasing, because when ye had received from us the word of hearing, which is of God, ye received it, not as the word of men, but (as it is indeed) the Word of God." Here you see St. Paul expresses what I have said above ; that the Word comes from God, that it is spoken by men, that it must be received, not as man's word, but as God's word. So in another place he says : " He who despiseth these things, despiseth not man, but God, who hath also given in us His Holy Spirit ". Our Saviour had made a like declaration already : " He that heareth you, heareth Me ; and he that despiseth you, despiseth Me ; and he that despiseth Me, despiseth Him that sent Me ". Accordingly, St. Peter on the day of Pentecost said : " Men of Israel, *hear* these words, God hath raised up this Jesus, whereof *we* are *witnesses.* Let all the house of Israel *know most certainly* that God hath made this Jesus, whom you have crucified, both Lord and Christ." At another time he said : " We ought to obey God, rather than man ; we are *witnesses* of these things, and so *is the Holy Ghost*, whom God has given to all who obey Him ". And again : " He commanded us to preach to the people, and to testify that it is He (Jesus) who hath been appointed by God to be the Judge of the living and of the dead ". And you know that the persistent declaration of the first preachers was : " Believe and thou shalt be saved " : they do not say, " prove our doctrine by your own reason,"

nor " wait till you see before you believe " ; but,
" believe without seeing and without proving, because
our word is not our own, but God's word ". Men
might indeed use their reason in inquiring into the
pretensions of the Apostles ; they might inquire
whether or not they did miracles ; they might inquire
whether they were predicted in the Old Testament as
coming from God ; but when they had ascertained
this fairly in whatever way, they were to take all the
Apostles said for granted without proof ; they were to
exercise their faith, they were to be saved by hearing.
Hence, as you perhaps observed, St. Paul significantly
calls the revealed doctrine " the word of hearing," in
the passage I quoted ; men came to hear, to accept,
to obey, not to criticise what was said ; and in accordance with this he asks elsewhere : " How shall they
believe Him, whom they have not heard ? and how
shall they hear without a preacher ? Faith cometh
by hearing, and hearing by the word of Christ."

Now, my dear brethren, consider, are not these two
states or acts of mind quite distinct from each other ;
—to believe simply what a living authority tells you,
and to take a book, such as Scripture, and to use it
as you please, to master it, that is, to make yourself
the master of it, to interpret it for yourself, and to
admit just what you choose to see in it, and nothing
more ? Are not these two procedures distinct in
this, that in the former you submit, in the latter you
judge ? At this moment I am not asking you which
is the better, I am not asking whether this or that is
practicable now, but are they not two ways of taking

up a doctrine, and not one? is not submission quite contrary to judging? Now, is it not certain that faith in the time of the Apostles consisted in submitting? and is it not certain that it did not consist in judging for one's self. It is in vain to say that the man who judges from the Apostles' writings, does submit to those writings in the first instance, and therefore has faith in them; else why should he refer to them at all? There is, I repeat, an essential difference between the act of submitting to a living oracle, and to his written words; in the former case there is no appeal from the speaker, in the latter the final decision remains with the reader. Consider how different is the confidence with which you report another's words in his presence and in his absence. If he be absent, you boldly say that he holds so and so, or said so and so; but let him come into the room in the midst of the conversation, and your tone is immediately changed. It is then, " I *think* I have heard you say something *like* this, or what I *took* to be this"; or you modify considerably the statement or the fact to which you originally pledged him, dropping one-half of it for safety sake, or retrenching the most startling portions of it; and then after all you wait with some anxiety to see whether he will accept any portion of it at all. The same sort of process takes place in the case of the written document of a person now dead. I can fancy a man magisterially expounding St. Paul's Epistle to the Galatians or to the Ephesians, who would be better content with the writer's absence than his sudden re-appearance among us;

lest the Apostle should take his own meaning out of his commentator's hands and explain it for himself. In a word, though he says he has faith in St. Paul's writings, he confessedly has no faith in St. Paul; and though he may speak much about truth as found in Scripture, he has no wish at all to be like one of these Christians whose names and deeds occur in it.

I think I may assume that this virtue, which was exercised by the first Christians, is not known at all among Protestants now; or at least if there are instances of it, it is exercised towards those, I mean their own teachers and divines, who expressly disclaim that they are fit objects of it, and who exhort their people to judge for themselves. Protestants, generally speaking, have not faith, in the primitive meaning of that word; this is clear from what I have been saying, and here is a confirmation of it. If men believed now as they did in the times of the Apostles, they could not doubt nor change. No one can doubt whether a word spoken by God is to be believed; of course it is; whereas any one, who is modest and humble, may easily be brought to doubt of his own inferences and deductions. Since men now-a-days deduce from Scripture, instead of believing a teacher, you may expect to see them waver about; they will feel the force of their own deductions more strongly at one time than at another, they will change their minds about them, or perhaps deny them altogether; whereas this cannot be, while a man has faith, that is, belief that what a preacher says to him comes from God. This is what St. Paul especially insists on, telling us that

Apostles, prophets, evangelists, pastors, and teachers, are given us that "we may all attain to unity of faith," and, on the contrary, in order "that we be *not* as children tossed to and fro, and carried about by every gale of doctrine". Now, in matter of fact, do not men in this day change about in their religious opinions without any limit? Is not this, then, a proof that they have not that faith which the Apostles demanded of their converts? If they had faith, they would not change. Once believe that God has spoken, and you are sure He cannot unsay what He has already said; He cannot deceive; He cannot change; you have received it once for all; you will believe it ever.

Such is the only rational, consistent account of faith; but so far are Protestants from professing it, that they laugh at the very notion of it. They laugh at the notion itself of men pinning their faith (as they express themselves) upon Pope or Council; they think it simply superstitious and narrow-minded, to profess to believe just what the Church believes, and to assent to whatever she will say in time to come on matters of doctrine. That is, they laugh at the bare notion of doing what Christians undeniably did in the time of the Apostles. Observe, they do not merely ask whether the Catholic Church has a claim to teach, has authority, has the gifts;—this is a reasonable question; —no, they think that the very state of mind which such a claim involves in those who admit it, namely, the disposition to accept without reserve or question, that *this* is slavish. They call it priestcraft to insist on this surrender of the reason, and superstition to make it. That is, they quarrel with the very state of mind which all Christians had in the age of the Apostles ; nor is there any doubt (who will deny it ?) that those who thus boast of not being led blindfold, of judging for themselves, of believing just as much and just as little as they please, of hating dictation, and so forth, would have found it an extreme difficulty to hang on the lips of the Apostles, had they lived at their date, or rather would have simply resisted the sacrifice of their own liberty of thought, would have thought life eternal too dearly purchased at such a price, and would have died in their unbelief. And they would have defended themselves on the plea that it was absurd and childish to ask them to believe without proof, to bid them give up their education, and their intelligence, and their science, and in spite of all those difficulties which reason and sense find in the Christian doctrine, in spite of its mysteriousness, its obscurity, its strangeness, its unacceptableness, its severity, to require them to surrender themselves to the teaching of a few unlettered Galilæans, or a learned indeed but fanatical Pharisee. This is what they would have said then ; and if so, is it wonderful they do not become Catholics now ? The simple account of their remaining as they are, is, that they lack one thing,—they have not faith ; it is a state of mind, it is a virtue, which they do not recognise to be praiseworthy, which they do not aim at possessing.

What they feel now, my brethren, is just what both Jew and Greek felt before them in the time of the Apostles, and what the natural man has felt ever since.

The great and wise men of the day looked down upon faith, then as now, as if it were unworthy the dignity of human nature: " See your vocation, brethren, that there are not," among you, " many wise according to the flesh, not many mighty, not many noble ; but the foolish things of the world hath God chosen to confound the strong, and the mean things of the world, and the things that are contemptible, hath God chosen, and things that are not, that He might destroy the things that are, that no flesh might glory in His sight ". Hence the same Apostle speaks of " the foolishness of preaching ". Similar to this is what our Lord had said in His prayer to the Father : " I thank Thee, Father, Lord of heaven and earth, because thou hast hid these things from the wise and prudent, and hast revealed them unto little ones ". Now, is it not plain that men of this day have just inherited the feelings and traditions of these falsely wise and fatally prudent persons in our Lord's day ? They have the same obstruction in their hearts to entering the Catholic Church, which Pharisees and Sophists had before them ; it goes against them to believe her doctrine, not so much for want of evidence that she is from God, as because, if so, they shall have to submit their minds to living men, who have not their own cultivation or depth of intellect, and because they must receive a number of doctrines, whether they will or no, which are strange to their imagination and difficult to their reason. The very characteristic of the Catholic teaching and of the Catholic teacher is to them a preliminary objection to their becoming

Catholics, so great, as to throw into the shade any argument however strong, which is producible in behalf of the mission of those teachers and the origin of that teaching. In short, they have not faith.

They have not in them the principle of faith ; and I repeat, it is nothing to the purpose to urge that at least they firmly believe Scripture to be the Word of God. In truth, it is much to be feared that their acceptance of Scripture itself is nothing better than a prejudice or inveterate feeling impressed on them when they were children. A proof of it is this ; that, while they profess to be so shocked at Catholic miracles, and are not slow to call them "lying wonders," they have no difficulty at all about Scripture narratives, which are quite as difficult to the reason as any miracles recorded in the history of the Saints. I have heard on the contrary of Catholics who have been startled at first reading in Scripture the narratives of the ark in the deluge, of the tower of Babel, of Balaam and Balac, of the Israelites' flight from Egypt and entrance into the promised land, and of Esau's and Saul's rejection ; which the bulk of Protestants receive without any effort of mind. How, then, do these Catholics accept them ? by faith. They say, " God is true, and every man a liar ". How come Protestants so easily to receive them ? by faith ? Nay, I conceive that in most cases there is no submission of the reason at all ; simply they are so familiar with the passages in question, that the narrative presents no difficulties to their imagination ; they have nothing to overcome. If, however, they *are* led to contemplate these passages

in themselves, and to try them in the balance of probability, and to begin to question about them, as will
happen when their intellect is cultivated, then there
is nothing to bring them back to their former habitual
or mechanical belief; they know nothing of submitting to authority, that is, they know nothing of faith;
for they have no authority to submit to. They either
remain in a state of doubt without any great trouble
of mind, or they go on to ripen into utter disbelief on
the subjects in question, though they may say nothing about it. Neither before they doubt, nor when
they doubt, is there any token of the presence in them
of a power subjecting reason to the Word of God. No;
what looks like faith, is a mere hereditary persuasion,
not a personal principle; it is a habit which they
have learned in the nursery, which has never changed
into anything higher, and which is scattered and dis-
appears, like a mist, before the light, such as it is, of
reason. If, however, there are Protestants, who are
not in one or other of these two states, either of
credulity or of doubt, but who firmly believe in spite
of all difficulties, they certainly have some claim to
be considered under the influence of faith; but there
is nothing to show that such persons, where they are
found, are not in the way to become Catholics, and
perhaps they are already called so by their friends,
showing in their own examples the logical, indispu-
table connexion which exists between possessing faith
and joining the Church.

If, then, faith be now the same faculty of mind, the
ame sort of habit or act, which it was in the days of

the Apostles, I have made good what I set about showing. But it must be the same; it cannot mean two
things; the Word cannot have changed its meaning.
Either say that faith is not necessary now at all, or
take it to be what the Apostles meant by it, but do
not say that you have it, and then show me something
quite different, which you have put in the place of it.
In the Apostles' days the peculiarity of faith was submission to a living authority; this is what made it so
distinctive; this is what made it an act of submission
at all; this is what destroyed private judgment in matters of religion. If you will not look out for a living
authority, and will bargain for private judgment, then
say at once that you have not Apostolic faith And in
fact you have it not; the bulk of this nation has it
not; confess you have it not; and then confess that
this is the reason why you are not Catholics. You are
not Catholics because you have not faith. Why do not
blind men see the sun? because they have no eyes;
in like manner it is vain to discourse upon the beauty,
the sanctity, the sublimity of the Catholic doctrine
and worship, where men have no faith to accept it
as Divine. They may confess its beauty, sublimity,
and sanctity, without believing it; they may acknowledge that the Catholic religion is noble and
majestic; they may be struck with its wisdom, they
may admire its adaptation to human nature, they may
be penetrated by its tender and winning bearing, they
may be awed by its consistency. But to commit themselves to it, that is another matter; to choose it for
their portion, to say with the favoured Moabitess,

" Whithersoever thou shalt go, I will go! and where thou shalt dwell, I will dwell; thy people shall be my people, and thy God my God," this is the language of faith. A man may revere, a man may extol, who has no tendency whatever to obey, no notion whatever of professing. And this often happens in fact: men are respectful to the Catholic religion; they acknowledge its services to mankind, they encourage it and its professors; they like to know them, they are interested in hearing of their movements, but they are not, and never will be Catholics. They will die as they have lived, out of the Church, because they have not possessed themselves of that faculty by which the Church is to be approached. Catholics who have not studied them or human nature, will wonder they remain where they are; nay, they themselves, alas for them! will sometimes lament they cannot become Catholics. They will feel so intimately the blessedness of being a Catholic, that they will cry out, "Oh, what would I give to be a Catholic! Oh, that I could believe what I admire! but I do not, and I can no more believe merely because I wish to do so, than I can leap over a mountain. I should be much happier were I a Catholic; but I am not; it is no use deceiving myself; I am what I am; I revere, I cannot accept."

Oh, deplorable state! deplorable because it is utterly and absolutely their own fault, and because such great stress is laid in Scripture, as they know, on the necessity of faith for salvation. Faith is there made the foundation and commencement of all acceptable obedience. It is described as the " argument " or " proof of things not seen "; by faith men have understood that God is, that He made the world, that He is a rewarder of those who seek Him, that the flood was coming, that their Saviour was to be born. "Without faith it is impossible to please God "; "by faith we stand " ; " by faith we walk " ; " by faith we overcome the world ". When our Lord gave to the Apostles their commission to preach all over the world, He continued, "He that believeth and is baptised, shall be saved; but he that believeth not, shall be condemned ". And He declared to Nicodemus, " He that believeth in the Son, is not judged ; but he that doth not believe is already judged, because he believeth not in the Name of the Only-begotten Son of God ". He said to the Pharisees, " If you believe not that I am He, ye shall die in your sins ". To the Jews, "Ye believe not, because ye are not of My sheep ". And you may recollect that before His miracles, He commonly demands faith of the supplicant : " All things are possible," He says, "to him that believeth"; and we find in one place, "He could not do any miracle," on account of the unbelief of the inhabitants.

Has faith changed its meaning, or is it less necessary now ? Is it not still what it was in the Apostles' day, the very characteristic of Christianity, the special instrument of renovation, the first disposition for justification, one out of the three theological virtues ? God might have renewed us by other means, by sight, by reason, by love, but He has chosen to " purify our hearts by faith "; it has been His will to select an instrument which the world despises, but which is of

14

immense power. He preferred it, in His infinite
wisdom, to every other; and if men have it not, they
have not the very element and rudiment, out of which
are formed, on which are built, the Saints and Servants of God.   And they have it not; they are living,
they are dying, without the hopes, without the aids
of the Gospel, because, in spite of so much that is
good in them, in spite of their sense of duty, their
tenderness of conscience on many points, their benevolence, their uprightness, their generosity, they are
under the dominion (I must say it) of a proud fiend;
they have this stout spirit within them, they determine
to be their own masters in matters of thought, about
which they know so little; they consider their own
reason better than any one's else; they will not admit
that any one comes from God who contradicts their
own view of truth.   What! is none their equal in
wisdom anywhere? is there none other whose word is
to be taken on religion? is there none to wrest from
them their ultimate appeal to themselves? Have they
in no possible way the occasion or opportunity of faith?
Is it a virtue, which, in consequence of their transcendent
sagacity, their prerogative of omniscience, they must
give up hope of exercising?   If the pretensions of the
Catholic Church do not satisfy them, let them go
somewhere else, if they can.   If they are so fastidious
that they cannot trust her as the oracle of God, let
them find another more certainly from Him than the
House of His own institution, which has ever been
called by His name, has ever maintained the same
claims, has ever taught one substance of doctrine,

and has triumphed over those who preached any other. Since Apostolic faith was in the beginning reliance on man's word, as being God's word, since what faith was then such it is now, since faith is necessary for salvation, let them attempt to exercise it towards another, if they will not accept the Bride of the Lamb. Let them, if they can, put faith in some of those religions which have lasted a whole two or three centuries in a corner of the earth. Let them stake their eternal prospects on kings and nobles and parliaments and soldiery, let them take some mere fiction of the law, or abortion of the schools, or idol of a populace, or upstart of a crisis, or oracle of lecture-rooms, as the prophet of God. Alas! they are hardly bestead if they must possess a virtue, which they have no means of exercising,—if they must make an act of faith, they know not on whom, and know not why!

What thanks ought we to render to Almighty God, my dear brethren, that He has made us what we are! It is a matter of grace. There are, to be sure, many cogent arguments to lead one to join the Catholic Church, but they do not force the will. We may know them, and not be moved to act upon them. We may be convinced without being persuaded. The two things are quite distinct from each other, seeing you ought to believe, and believing; reason, if left to itself, will bring you to the conclusion that you have sufficient grounds for believing, but belief is the gift of grace. You are then what you are, not from any excellence or merit of your own, but by the grace of God who has chosen you to believe. You might have been as the barbarian of Africa, or the freethinker of Europe, with grace sufficient to condemn you, because it had not furthered your salvation.   You might have had strong inspirations of grace and have resisted them, and then additional grace might not have been given to overcome your resistance.   God gives not the same measure of grace to all.   Has He not visited you with over-abundant grace? and was it not necessary for your hard hearts to receive more than other people? Praise and bless Him continually for the benefit ; do not forget, as time goes on, that it is of grace ; do not pride yourselves upon it ; pray ever not to lose it ; and do your best to make others partakers of it.

And you, my brethren, also, if such be present, who are not as yet Catholics, but who by your coming hither seem to show your interest in our teaching, and you wish to know more about it, you too remember, that though you may not yet have faith in the Church, still God has brought you into the way of obtaining it.   You are under the influence of His grace ; He has brought you a step on your journey ; He wishes to bring you further, He wishes to bestow on you the fulness of His blessings, and to make you Catholics. You are still in your sins ; probably you are laden with the guilt of many years, the accumulated guilt of many a deep, mortal offence, which no contrition has washed away, and to which no Sacrament has been applied.   You at present are troubled with an uneasy conscience, a dissatisfied reason, an unclean heart, and a divided will ; you need to be converted.   Yet now the first suggestions of grace are working in your souls, and are to issue in pardon for the past and sanctity for the future. God is moving you to acts of faith, hope, love, hatred of sin, repentance; do not disappoint Him, do not thwart Him, concur with Him, obey Him. You look up, and you see, as it were, a great mountain to be scaled; you say, "How can I possibly find a path over these giant obstacles, which I find in the way of my becoming Catholic? I do not comprehend this doctrine, and I am pained at that; a third seems impossible; I never can be familiar with one practice, I am afraid of another; it is one maze and discomfort to me, and I am led to sink down in despair." Say not so, my dear brethren, look up in hope, trust in Him who calls you forward. "Who art thou, O great mountain, before Zorobabel? but a plain." He will lead you forward step by step, as He has led forward many a one before you. He will make the crooked straight and the rough plain. He will turn the streams, and dry up the rivers, which lie in your path. "He shall strengthen your feet like harts' feet, and set you up on high places. He shall widen your steps under you, and your tread shall not be weakened." "There is no God like the God of the righteous; He that mounts the heaven is thy Helper; by His mighty working the clouds disperse. His dwelling is above, and underneath are the everlasting arms; He shall cast out the enemy from before thee, and shall say, Crumble away." "The young shall faint, and youths shall fall; but they that hope in the Lord shall be new-fledged in strength, they shall take feathers like eagles, they shall run and not labour, they shall walk and not faint."

DISCOURSE XI.

FAITH AND DOUBT.

THOSE who are drawn by curiosity or a better motive to inquire into the Catholic Religion, sometimes put to us a strange question,—whether, if they took up the profession of it, they would be at liberty, when they felt inclined, to reconsider the question of its Divine authority; meaning, by "reconsideration," an inquiry springing from doubt of it, and possibly ending in a denial. The same question, in the form of an objection, is often asked by those who have no thoughts at all of becoming Catholics, and who enlarge upon it, as something terrible, that whoever once enters the pale of the Church, on him the door of egress is shut for ever ; that, once a Catholic, he never, never can doubt again ; that, whatever his misgivings may be, he must stifle them, nay must start from them as the suggestions of the evil spirit; in short, that he must give up altogether the search after truth, and do a violence to his mind, which is nothing short of immoral. This is what is said, my brethren, by certain objectors, and their own view is, or ought to be, if they are consistent, this,—that it is a fault ever to make up our mind once for all on any religious subject whatever ; and that, however sacred a doctrine may be, and however evident to us,—let us say, for instance, the divinity of our Lord, or the existence of God,—we ought always to reserve to ourselves the liberty of doubting about it. I cannot help thinking that so extravagant a position, as this is, confutes itself; however, I will consider the contrary (that is, the Catholic) view of the subject, on its own merits, though without admitting the language in which it was just now stated by its opponents.

It is, then, perfectly true, that the Church does not allow her children to entertain any doubt of her teaching ; and that, first of all, simply for this reason, because they are Catholics only while they have faith, and faith is incompatible with doubt. No one can be a Catholic without a simple faith, that what the Church declares in God's name, is God's word, and therefore true. A man must simply believe that the Church is the oracle of God ; he must be as certain of her mission, as he is of the mission of the Apostles. Now, would any one ever call him certain that the Apostles came from God, if, after professing his certainty, he added, that perhaps he might have reason to doubt one day about their mission ? Such an anticipation would be a real, though latent, doubt, betraying that he was not certain of it at present. A person who says, " I believe just at this moment, but perhaps I am excited without knowing it, and I cannot answer for myself, that I shall believe to-morrow," does not believe now. A man who says, " Perhaps I am in a kind of delusion,

which will one day pass away from me, and leave me
as I was before "; or " I believe as far as I can tell,
but there may be arguments in the background which
will change my view," such a man has not faith at
all. When, then, Protestants quarrel with us for
saying that those who join us must give up all ideas
of ever doubting the Church in time to come, they do
nothing else but quarrel with us for insisting on the
necessity of faith in her. Let them speak plainly ;
our offence is that of demanding faith in the Holy
Catholic Church ; it is this, and nothing else. I must
insist upon this : faith implies a confidence in a man's
mind, that the thing believed is really true ; but, if it
is once true, it never can be false. If it is true that God
became man, what is the meaning of my anticipating
a time when perhaps I shall not believe that God became man ? this is nothing short of anticipating a time
when I shall disbelieve a truth. And if I bargain to
be allowed in time to come not to believe, or to doubt,
that God became man, I am but asking to be allowed
to doubt or disbelieve what I hold to be an eternal truth.
I do not see the privilege of such a permission at all,
or the meaning of wishing to secure it :—if at present I
have no doubt whatever about it, then I am but asking
leave to fall into error ; if at present I have doubts
about it, then I do not believe it at present, that is, I
have not faith. But I cannot both really believe it now,
and yet look forward to a time when perhaps I shall
not believe it ; to make provision for future doubt, is
to doubt at present. It proves I am not in a fit state
to become a Catholic now. I may love by halves, I

may obey by halves; I cannot believe by halves: either I have faith, or I have it not.

And so again, when a man has become a Catholic, were he to set about following a doubt which has occurred to him, he has already disbelieved. *I* have not to warn him against losing his faith, he is not merely in danger of losing it, he has lost it; from the nature of the case he has already lost it; he fell from grace at the moment when he deliberately entertained and pursued his doubt. No one can determine to doubt what he is already sure of; but if he is not sure that the Church is from God, he does not believe it. It is not I who forbid him to doubt; he has taken the matter into his own hands when he determined on asking for leave; he has begun, not ended, in unbelief; his very wish, his purpose, is his sin. I do not make it so, it is such from the very state of the case. You sometimes hear, for example, of Catholics falling away, who will tell you it arose from reading the Scriptures, which opened their eyes to the " unscripturalness," so they speak, of the Church of the Living God. No; Scripture did not make them disbelieve (impossible!); they disbelieved *when* they opened the Bible; they opened it in an unbelieving spirit, and for an unbelieving purpose; they would not have opened it, had they not anticipated—I might say, hoped—that they should find things there inconsistent with Catholic teaching. They begin in self-will and disobedience, and they end in apostasy. This, then, is the direct and obvious reason why the Church cannot allow her children the liberty of doubting the truth of her word.

He who really believes in it now, cannot imagine the future discovery of reasons to shake his faith; if he imagines it, he has not faith; and that so many Protestants think it a sort of tyranny in the Church to forbid any children of hers to doubt about her teaching, only shows they do not know what faith is —which is the case; it is a strange idea to them. Let a man cease to inquire, or cease to call himself her child.

This is my first remark, and now I go on to a second. You may easily conceive, my brethren, that they who are entering the Church, or at least those who have entered it, have more than faith; that they have some portion of Divine love also. They have heard in the Church of the charity of Him who died for them, and who has given them His Sacraments as the means of conveying the merits of His death to their souls, and they have felt more or less in those poor souls of theirs the beginnings of a responsive charity drawing them to Him. Now, does it stand with a loving trust, better than with faith, for a man to anticipate the possibility of doubting or denying the great mercies in which he is rejoicing? Take an instance; what would you think of a friend whom you loved, who could bargain that, in spite of his present trust in you, he might be allowed some day to doubt you? who, when a thought came into his mind, that you were playing a game with him, or that you were a knave, or a profligate, did not drive it from him with indignation, or laugh it away for its absurdity, but considered that he had an evident right to indulge it, nay, should be wanting in duty to himself, unless he did? Would you think that your friend trifled with truth, that he was unjust to his reason, that he was wanting in manliness, that he was hurting his mind if he shrank from the thought? or would you not call him cruel and miserable if he did not? For me, my brethren, if he took the latter course, may I never be intimate with so unpleasant a person; suspicious, jealous minds, minds that keep at a distance from me, that insist on their rights, fall back on their own centre, are ever fancying offences, and are cold, censorious, wayward, and uncertain, these are often to be borne as a cross; but give me for my friend one who will unite heart and hand with me, who will throw himself into my cause and interest, who will take my part when I am attacked, who will be sure beforehand that I am in the right, and, if he is critical, as he may have cause to be towards a being of sin and imperfection, will be so from very love and loyalty, from an anxiety that I should always show to advantage, and a wish that others should love me as heartily as he does. I should not say a friend trusted me, who listened to every idle story against me; and I should like his absence better than his company, if he gravely told me that it was a duty he owed to himself to encourage his misgivings of my honour.

Well, pass on to a higher subject;—could a man be said to trust in God, and to love God, who was familiar with doubts whether there was a God at all, or who bargained that, just as often as he pleased, he might be at liberty to doubt whether God was good, or just or mighty ; and who maintained that, unless he did this, he was but a poor slave, that his mind was in bondage, and could render no free acceptable service to his Maker ; that the very worship which God approved was one attended with a *caveat*, on the worshipper's part, that he did not promise to render it to-morrow ; that he would not answer for himself that some argument might not come to light, which he had never heard before, which would make it a grave, moral duty in him to suspend his judgment and his devotion ? Why, I should say, my brethren, that that man was worshipping his own mind, his own dear self and not God ; that his idea of God was a mere accidental form which his thoughts took at this time or that,—for a long period or a short one, as the case might be,—not an image of the great Eternal Object, but a passing sentiment or imagination which meant nothing at all. I should say, and most men would agree with me, did they choose to give attention to the matter, that the person in question was a very self-conceited, self-wise man, and had neither love, nor faith, nor fear, nor anything super-natural about him ; that his pride must be broken, and his heart new made, before he was capable of any religious act at all. The argument is the same, in its degree, when applied to the Church ; she speaks to us as a messenger from God,—how can a man who feels this, who comes to her, who falls at her feet as such, make a reserve, that he may be allowed to doubt her at some future day ? Let the world cry out, if it will, that his reason is in fetters ; let it pronounce that he is a bigot, unless he reserves his right of doubting; but he knows full well himself that he would be an ingrate and a fool, if he did. Fetters, indeed! yes, "the cords of Adam," the fetters of love, these are what bind him to the Holy Church; he is, with the Apostle, the slave of Christ, the Church's Lord; united (never to part, as he trusts, while life lasts), to her Sacraments, to her Sacrifices, to her Saints, to the Blessed Mary her advocate, to Jesus, to God.

The truth is, that the world, knowing nothing of the blessings of the Catholic faith, and prophesying nothing but ill concerning it, fancies that a convert, after the first fervour is over, feels nothing but disappointment, weariness, and offence in his new religion, and is secretly desirous of retracing his steps. This is at the root of the alarm and irritation which it manifests at hearing that doubts are incompatible with a Catholic's profession, because it is sure that doubts will come upon him, and then how pitiable will be his state! That there can be peace, and joy, and knowledge, and freedom, and spiritual strength in the Church, is a thought far beyond the world's imagination; for it regards her simply as a frightful conspiracy against the happiness of man, seducing her victims by specious professions, and, when they are once hers, caring nothing for the misery which breaks upon them, so that by any means she may detain them in bondage. Accordingly, it conceives we are in perpetual warfare with our own reason, fierce objections ever rising within us, and we forcibly repressing them. It believes that, after the likeness of a vessel which has met with some accident at sea, we are ever baling out the water which rushes in upon us, and have hard work to keep afloat; we just manage to linger on, either by an unnatural strain on our minds, or by turning them away from the subject of religion. The world disbelieves our doctrines itself, and cannot understand our own believing them. It considers them so strange, that it is quite sure, though we will not confess it, that we are haunted day and night with doubts, and tormented with the apprehension of yielding to them. I really do think it is the world's judgment, that one principal part of a confessor's work is the putting down such misgivings in his penitents. It fancies that the reason is ever rebelling, like the flesh; that doubt, like concupiscence, is elicited by every sight and sound, and that temptation insinuates itself in every page of letter-press, and through the very voice of a Protestant polemic. When it sees a Catholic Priest, it looks hard at him, to make out how much there is of folly in his composition, and how much of hypocrisy.

But, my dear brethren, if these are your thoughts, you are simply in error. Trust me, rather than the world, when I tell you, that it is no difficult thing for a Catholic to believe; and that unless he grievously mismanages himself, the difficult thing is for him to doubt. He has received a gift which makes faith easy: it is not without an effort, a miserable effort, that any one who has received that gift, unlearns to believe. He does violence to his mind, not in exercising, but in withholding his faith. When objections occur to him, which they may easily do if he lives in the world, they are as odious and unwelcome to him as impure thoughts are to the virtuous. He does certainly shrink from them, he flings them away from him, but why? not in the first instance, because they are dangerous, but because they are cruel and base. His loving Lord has done everything for him, and has He deserved such a return? *Popule meus, quid feci tibi?* "O My people, what have I done to thee, or in what have I afflicted thee? answer thou Me. I brought thee out of the land of Egypt, and delivered thee out of the house of slaves; and I sent before thy face Moses, and Aaron, and Mary; I fenced thee in, and planted thee with the choicest vines; and what is there that I ought to do more to My vineyard that I have not done to it?" He has poured on us His grace, He has been with us in our perplexities, He has led us on from one truth to another, He has forgiven us our sins, He has satisfied our reason, He has made faith easy, He has given us His Saints, He shows before us day by day His own Passion; why should I leave Him? What has He ever done to me but good? Why must I re-examine what I have examined once for all? Why must I listen to every idle word which flits past me against Him, on pain of being called a bigot and a slave, when, if I did, I should be behaving to the Most High, as you yourselves, who so call me, would not behave towards a human friend or benefactor? If I am convinced in my reason, and persuaded in my heart, why may I not be allowed to remain unmolested in my worship?

I have said enough on this subject; still there is a

third point of view in which it may be useful to consider it.   Personal prudence is not the first or second
ground for refusing to hear objections to the Church,
but a motive it is, and that from the peculiar nature
of Divine faith, which cannot be treated as an ordinary
conviction of belief.   Faith is the gift of God, and
not a mere act of our own, which we are free to exert
when we will.   It is quite distinct from an exercise
of reason, though it follows upon it.   I may feel the
force of the argument for the Divine origin of the
Church ; I may see that I ought to believe ; and yet
I may be unable to believe.   This is no imaginary
case; there is many a man who has ground enough
to believe, who wishes to believe, but who cannot
believe.   It is always indeed his own fault, for God
gives grace to all who ask for it, and use it, but still
such is the fact, that conviction is not faith.   Take
the parallel case of obedience ; many a man knows
he ought to obey God, and does not and cannot—
through his own fault, indeed—but still he cannot ;
for through grace only can he obey.   Now, faith is
not a mere conviction in reason, it is a firm assent, it
is a clear certainty greater than any other certainty ;
and this is wrought in the mind by the grace of God,
and by it alone.   As then men may be convinced,
and not act according to their conviction, so may they
be convinced, and not believe according to their conviction.   They may confess that the argument is against
them, that they have nothing to say for themselves,
and that to believe is to be happy ; and yet, after all,
they avow they cannot believe, they do not know why,

but they cannot ; they acquiesce in unbelief, and they turn away from God and His Church. Their reason is convinced, and their doubts are moral ones, arising in their root from a fault of the will. In a word, the arguments for religion do not compel any one to believe, just as arguments for good conduct do not compel any one to obey. Obedience is the consequence of willing to obey, and faith is the consequence of willing to believe ; we may see what is right, whether in matters of faith or obedience, of ourselves, but we cannot will what is right without the grace of God. Here is the difference between other exercises of reason, and arguments for the truth of religion. It requires no act of faith to assent to the truth that two and two make four ; we cannot help assenting to it ; and hence there is no merit in assenting to it ; but there is merit in believing that the Church is from God ; for though there are abundant reasons to prove it to us, yet we can, without an absurdity, quarrel with the conclusion ; we may complain that it is not clearer, we may suspend our assent, we may doubt about it, if we will, and grace alone can turn a bad will into a good one.

And now you see why a Catholic dare not in prudence attend to such objections as are brought against his faith ; he has no fear of their proving that the Church does not come from God, but he is afraid, if he listened to them without reason, lest God should punish him by the loss of his supernatural faith. This is one cause of that miserable state of mind, to which I have already alluded, in which men would fain be

Catholics, and are not. They have trifled with conviction, they have listened to arguments against what
they knew to be true, and a deadness of mind has
fallen on them ; faith has failed them, and, as time
goes on, they betray in their words and their actions,
the Divine judgment, with which they are visited.
They become careless and unconcerned, or restless and
unhappy, or impatient of contradiction ; ever asking
advice and quarrelling with it when given ; not attempting to answer the arguments urged against them,
but simply not believing. This is the whole of their
case, they do not believe. And then it is quite an
accident what becomes of them ; perhaps they continue on in this perplexed and comfortless state,
lingering about the Church, yet not of her ; not knowing what they believe and what they do not, like
blind men, or men deranged, who are deprived of the
eye, whether of body or mind, and cannot guide themselves in consequence ; ever exciting hopes of a return,
and ever disappointing them ;—or, if they are men of
more vigorous minds, they launch forward in a course
of infidelity, not really believing less, as they proceed,
for from the first they believed nothing, but taking
up, as time goes on, more and more consistent forms
of error, till sometimes, if a free field is given them,
they even develop into atheism. Such is the end of
those who, under the pretence of inquiring after truth,
trifle with conviction.

Here then are some of the reasons why the Catholic
Church cannot consistently allow her children to doubt
the divinity and the truth of her words. Mere investiga-

tion indeed into the grounds of our faith is not to doubt ;
nor is it doubting to consider the arguments urged
against it, when there is good reason for doing so ; but
I am speaking of a real doubt, or a wanton entertainment of objections. Such a procedure the Church
denounces, and not only for the reasons which I have
assigned, but because it would be a plain abandonment
of her office and character to act otherwise. How can
she, who has the prerogative of infallibility, allow her
children to doubt of her gift ? It would be a simple
inconsistency in her, who is the sure oracle of truth
and messenger of heaven, to look with indifference on
rebels to her authority. She simply does what the
Apostles did before her, whom she has succeeded.
" He that despiseth," says St. Paul, " despiseth not
man, but God, who hath also given in us His Holy
Spirit." And St. John : " We are of God ; he that
knoweth God, heareth us . he that is not of God,
heareth us not ; by this we know the spirit of truth and
the spirit of error ". Take, again, an instance from
the Old Testament : When Elias was taken up into
heaven, Eliseus was the only witness of the miracle ;
on his coming back then to the sons of the Prophets,
they doubted what had become of his master, and
wished to search for him ; and, though they acknowledged Eliseus as his successor, they in this instance
refused to take his word on the subject. Eliseus had
struck the waters of Jordan, they had divided, and he
had passed over ; here, surely, was ground enough for
faith, and accordingly " the sons of the prophets at
Jericho, who were over against him, seeing it, said,

The spirit of Elias hath rested upon Eliseus ; and they came to meet him, and worshipped him, falling to the ground ". What could they require more ? they confessed that Eliseus had the spirit of his great master, and, in confessing it, they implied that that master was taken away ; yet, they proceed, from infirmity of mind, to make a request indicative of doubt : " Behold, there are with thy servants fifty strong men, that can go and search for thy master, lest perhaps the Spirit of the Lord hath taken him up, and cast him upon some mountain or into some valley ". Now here was a request to follow up a doubt into an inquiry ; did Eliseus allow it ? he knew perfectly well that the inquiry would but end, as it really did end, in confirmation of the truth, but it was indulging a wrong spirit to engage in it, and he would not allow it. These religious men were, as he would feel, strangely inconsistent : they were doubting his word whom they had just now worshipped as a prophet, and, not only so, but they were doubting his supreme authority, for they implied that Elias was still among them. Accordingly he forbade their request ; " he said : Send not ". This is what the world would call stifling an inquiry ; it was, forsooth, tyrannical and oppressive to oblige them to take on his word what they might ascertain for themselves ; yet he could not do otherwise without being unfaithful to his Divine mission, and sanctioning them in a fault. It is true when " they pressed him, he consented, and said, Send " ; but we must not suppose this to be more than a condescension to their weakness, or a concession in displeasure, like that which Almighty

God gave to Balaam, who pressed his request in a similar way. When Balaam asked to go with the ancients of Moab, God said : " Thou shalt not go with them " ; when Balaam asked Him " once more," " God said to him, Arise and go with them " ; then it is added: " Balaam went with them, and God was angry". Here in like manner, the prophet said, Send ; " and they sent fifty men, and they sought three days, but found him not," yet though the inquiry did but prove that Elias was removed, Eliseus showed no satisfaction at it, even when it had confirmed his authority : but " he said to them, Said I not to you, Send not ? " It is thus that the Church ever forbids inquiry in those who already acknowledge her authority ; but if they will inquire, she cannot hinder it ; but they are not justified in doing so.

And now I think you see, my brethren, why inquiry precedes faith, and does not follow it. You inquired before you joined the Church ; you were satisfied, and God rewarded you with the grace of faith ; were you now determined to inquire further, you would lead us to think you had lost it again, for inquiry and faith are in their very nature incompatible. I will add, what is very evident, that no other religious body has a right to demand such an exercise of faith in it, and a right to forbid you further inquiry, but the Catholic Church ; and for this simple reason, that no other body even claims to be infallible, let alone the proof of such a claim. Here is the defect at first starting, which disqualifies them, one and all, from ever competing with the Church of God. The sects about us, so far from demanding your faith, actually call on you to inquire and to doubt freely about their own merits ; they protest that they are but voluntary associations, and would be sorry to be taken for anything else ; they beg and pray you not to mistake their preachers for anything more than mere sinful men, and they invite you to take the Bible with you to their sermons, and to judge for yourselves whether their doctrine is in accordance with it. Then, as to the Established Religion, grant that there are those in it who forbid inquiry into its claims ; yet still, dare they maintain that it is infallible? If they do not (and no one does), how can they forbid inquiry about it, or claim for it the absolute faith of any of its members? Faith under these circumstances is not really faith, but obstinacy. Nor do they commonly venture to demand it ; they will say, negatively : "Do not inquire" ; but they cannot say positively : "Have faith" ; for in whom are their members to have faith? of whom can they say, whether individual or collection of men, "He or they are gifted with infallibility, and cannot mislead us"? Therefore, when pressed to explain themselves, they ground their duty of continuance in their communion, not on faith in it, but on attachment to it, which is a very different thing ; utterly different, for there are very many reasons why they should feel a very great liking for the religion in which they have been brought up. Its portions of Catholic teaching, its "decency and order," the pure and beautiful English of its prayers, its literature, the piety found among its members, the influence of superiors and friends, its historical associations, its domestic character, the charm of a country life, the remembrance of past years,—there is all this and much more to attach the mind to the national worship. But attachment is not trust, nor is to obey the same as to look up to, and to rely upon ; nor do I think that any thoughtful or educated man can simply believe or confide in the *word* of the Established Church. I never met any such person who did, or said he did, and I do not think that such a person is possible. Its defenders would believe if they could ; but their highest confidence is qualified by a misgiving. They obey, they are silent before the voice of their superiors, but they do not profess to believe. Nothing is clearer than this, that if faith in God's word is required of us for salvation, the Catholic Church is the only medium by which we can exercise it.

And now, my brethren, who are not Catholics, perhaps you will tell me, that, if all inquiry is to cease when you become Catholics, you ought to be very sure that the Church is from God before you join it. You speak truly ; no one should enter the Church without a firm purpose of taking her word in all matters of doctrine and morals, and that, on the ground of her coming directly from the God of Truth. You must look the matter in the face, and count the cost. If you do not come in this spirit, you may as well not come at all ; high and low, learned and ignorant, must come to learn. If you are right as far as this, you cannot go very wrong; you have the foundation ; but, if you come in any other temper, you had better wait till you have got rid of it. You must come, I say, to the Church to learn ; you must come, not to bring your own notions to her, but with the intention of ever being a learner ; you must come with the intention of taking her for your portion, and of never leaving her. Do not come as an experiment ; do not come as you would take sittings in a chapel, or tickets for a lecture-room ; come to her as to your home, to the school of your souls, to the Mother of Saints, and to the vestibule of heaven. On the other hand, do not distress yourselves with thoughts whether, when you have joined her, your faith will last ; this is a suggestion of your enemy to hold you back. He who has begun a good work in you, will perfect it ; He who has chosen you, will be faithful to you ; put your cause into His hand, wait upon Him, and you will surely persevere. What good work will you ever begin, if you bargain first to see the end of it ? If you wish to do all at once, you will do nothing ; he has done half the work, who has begun it well ; you will not gain your Lord's praise at the final reckoning by hiding His talent. No ; when He brings you from error to truth, He will have done the more difficult work (if aught is difficult to Him), and surely He will preserve you from returning from truth to error. Take the experience of those who have gone before you in the same course ; they had many fears that their faith would fail them, before taking the great step, but those fears vanished on their taking it ; they had fears, before they received the grace of faith, lest, after receiving it, they should lose it again, but no fears (except on the ground of their general frailness) after it was actually given them.

Be convinced in your reason that the Catholic Church is a teacher sent to you from God, and it is enough. I do not wish you to join her, till you are. If you are half convinced, pray for a full conviction, and wait till you have it. It is better indeed to come quickly, but better slowly than carelessly; and some times, as the proverb goes, the more haste, the worse speed. Only make yourselves sure that the delay is not from any fault of yours, which you can remedy. God deals with us very differently; conviction comes slowly to some men, quickly to others; in some it is the result of much thought and many reasonings, in others of a sudden illumination. One man is con-vinced at once, as in the instance described by St. Paul: "If all prophesy," he says, speaking of expo-sition of doctrine, "and there come in one that be-lieveth not, or one unlearned, he is convinced of all, he is judged of all. The secrets of his heart are made manifest; and so, falling down on his face, he will worship God, and say that God is among you of a truth." The case is the same now; some men are converted merely by entering a Catholic Church; others are converted by reading one book; others by one doctrine. They feel the weight of their sins, and they see that that religion must come from God which alone has the means of forgiving them. Or they are touched and overcome by the evident sanctity, beauty, and (as I may say) fragrance of the Catholic Religion.

Or they long for a guide amid the strife of tongues; and the very doctrine of the Church about faith, which is so hard to many, is conviction to them. Others, again, hear many objections to the Church, and follow out the whole subject far and wide; conviction can scarcely come to them except as at the end of a long inquiry. As in a court of justice, one man's innocence may be proved at once, another's is the result of a careful investigation; one has nothing in his conduct or character to explain, against another there are many unfavourable presumptions at first sight; so Holy Church presents herself very differently to different minds who are contemplating her from without. God deals with them differently; but, if they are faithful to their light, at last, in their own time, though it may be a different time to each, He brings them to that one and the same state of mind, very definite and not to be mistaken, which we call *conviction*. They will have no doubt, whatever difficulties may still attach to the subject, that the Church is from God; they may not be able to answer this objection or that, but they will be certain in spite of it.

This is a point which should ever be kept in view: conviction is a state of mind, and it is something beyond and distinct from the mere arguments of which it is the result; it does not vary with their strength or their number. Arguments lead to a conclusion, and when the arguments are stronger, the conclusion is clearer; but conviction may be felt as strongly in consequence of a clear conclusion, as of one which is clearer. A man may be so sure upon six reasons, that he does not need.a seventh, nor would feel surer if he had it. And so as regards the Catholic Church : men are convinced in very various ways,—what convinces one, does not convince another ; but this is an accident ; the time comes anyhow, sooner or later, when a man ought to be convinced, and is convinced, and then he is bound not to wait for any more arguments, though more arguments be producible. He will find himself in a condition when he may even refuse to hear more arguments in behalf of the Church ; he does not wish to read or think more on the subject ; his mind is quite made up. In such a case it is his duty to join the Church at once; he must not delay ; let him be cautious in counsel, but prompt in execution. This it is that makes Catholics so anxious about him : it is not that they wish him to be precipitate ; but, knowing the temptations which the evil one ever throws in our way, they are lovingly anxious for his soul, lest he has come to the point of conviction, and is passing it, and is losing his chance of conversion. If so, it may never return ; God has not chosen every one to salvation : it is a rare gift to be a Catholic ; it may be offered to us once in our lives and never again ; and, if we have not seized on the "accepted time," nor know "in our day the things which are for our peace," oh, the misery for us ! What shall we be able to say when death comes, and we are not converted, and it is directly and immediately our own doing that we are not ?

" Wisdom preacheth abroad, she uttereth her voice in the streets : How long, ye little ones, love ye childishness, and fools covet what is hurtful to them, and the unwise hate knowledge? Turn ye at My reproof; behold, I will bring forth to you My Spirit, and I will show My words unto you. Because I have called, and ye refused, I stretched out My hand, and there was none who regarded, and ye despised all My counsel and neglected My chidings; I also will laugh in your destruction, and will mock when that shall come to you which you feared; when a sudden storm shall rush on you, and destruction shall thicken as a tempest, when tribulation and straitness shall come upon you. Then shall they call on Me, and I will not hear; they shall rise betimes, but they shall not find Me; for that they hated discipline, and took not on them the fear of the Lord, nor acquiesced in My counsel, but made light of My reproof, therefore shall they eat the fruit of their own way, and be filled with their own devices."

Oh, the misery for us, as many of us as shall be in that number! Oh, the awful thought for all eternity! Oh, the remorseful sting, " I was called, I might have answered, and I did not!" And oh, the blessedness, if we can look back on the time of trial, when friends implored and enemies scoffed, and say : The misery for me, which would have been, had I not followed on, had I hung back, when Christ called! Oh, the utter confusion of mind, the wreck of faith and opinion, the blackness and void, the dreary scepticism, the hopelessness, which would have been my lot, the pledge of the outer darkness to come, had I been afraid to follow Him! I have lost friends, I have lost the world, but I have gained Him, who gives in Himself houses and brethren and sisters and mothers and children and lands a hundred-fold ; I have lost the perishable, and gained the Infinite ; I have lost time, and I have gained eternity ; " O Lord, my God, I am Thy servant, and the son of Thine handmaid ; Thou hast broken my bonds. I will sacrifice to Thee the sacrifice of praise, and I will call on the Name of the Lord

DISCOURSE XII.

PROSPECTS OF THE CATHOLIC MISSIONER.

A STRANGE time this may seem to some of you, my brethren, and a strange place, to commence an enterprise such as that, which relying on God's mercy, we are undertaking this day.* In this huge city, amid a population of human beings, so vast that each is solitary, so various that each is independent, which, like the ocean, yields before and closes over every attempt made to influence and impress it,—in this mere aggregate of individuals, which admits of neither change nor reform, because it has no internal order, or disposition of parts, or mutual dependence, because it has nothing to change from and nothing to change to, where no one knows his next-door neighbour, where in every place are found a thousand worlds, each pursuing its own functions unimpeded by the rest—how can we, how can a handful of men, do any service worthy of the Lord who has called us, and the objects to which our lives are dedicated ? " Cry aloud, spare not ! " says the prophet; well may he say it ! no room for sparing ; what cry is loud enough, except the last trumpet of God, to pierce the omni-

* This discourse was delivered, in substance, at the first opening of the London Oratory, in 1849.

present din of turmoil and of effort, which rises, like an exhalation from the very earth, along the public thoroughfares, and to reach the dense multitudes on each side of them in the maze of lanes and alleys known only to those who live in them? It is but a fool's work to essay the impossible; keep to your own place, and you are respectable; tend your sheep in the wilderness, and you are intelligible; build upon the old foundations, and you are safe; but begin nothing new, make no experiments, quicken not the action, nor strain the powers, nor complicate the responsibilities of your Mother, lest in her old age you bring her to shame, and the idlers laugh at her who once bare many children, but now is waxed feeble.

And here is another thing, the time; the time of your coming hither! Now, when you rest on no immovable centre, as of old, when you are not what you were lately, when your life is in jeopardy, your future in suspense, your Master in exile; look at home, you have enough to do at home. Look to the rock whence ye were hewn, and to the quarry whence ye were dug out! Where is Peter now? *Magni nominis umbra,* as the heathen author says: an antiquated cause, noble in its time, but of a past day; nay, true and Divine in its time, as far as anything can be such, but false now, and of the earth now, because it is feeble now, bent with the weight of eighteen hundred years, tottering to its fall; for with Englishmen, you should know, success is the measure of principle, and power is the exponent of right. Do you not understand our rule of action? we take up men and lay them down, we praise or we blame, we feel respect or contempt, according as they succeed or are defeated. You are wrong, because you are in misfortune ; power is truth. Wealth is power, intellect is power, good name is power, knowledge is power ; we venerate wealth, intellect, name, knowledge. Intellect we know, and wealth we know, but who are ye ? what have we to do with the ghosts of an old world, and the types of a former organisation ?

It is true, my brethren, this is a strange time, a strange place, for beginning our work. A strange place for Saints and Angels to pitch their tabernacles in, this metropolis ; strange—I will not say for thee, my Mother Mary, to be found in ; for no part of the Catholic inheritance is foreign to thee, and thou art everywhere, where the Church is found, *Porta manes et Stella maris*, the constant object of her devotion, and the universal advocate of her children,—not strange to thee, but strange enough to him, my own Saint and Master, Philip Neri. Yes, dear Father, it is strange for thee, to pass from the bright, calm cities of the South to this scene of godless toil and self-trusting adventure ; strange for thee to be seen hurrying to and fro across our crowded streets, in thy grave, black cassock, and thy white collar, instead of moving at thy own pace amid the open ways or vacant spaces of the great City, in which, according to God's guidance of thee in thy youth, thou didst for life and death fix thy habitation. Yes, it is all very strange to the world ; but no new thing to her, the Bride of the Lamb, whose very being and primary gifts are stranger in the eyes of unbelief, than any details, as to place of abode and method of proceeding, in which they are manifested. It is no new thing in her, who came in the beginning as a wanderer upon earth, whose condition is a perpetual warfare, and whose empire is an incessant conquest.

In such a time as this did the prince of the Apostles, the first Pope, advance towards the heathen city, where, under a Divine guidance, he was to fix his seat. He toiled along the stately road which led him straight onwards to the capital of the world. He met throngs of the idle and the busy, of strangers and natives, who peopled the interminable suburb. He passed under the high gate, and wandered on amid marble palaces and columned temples ; he met processions of heathen priests and ministers in honour of their idols ; he met the wealthy lady, borne on her litter by her slaves ; he met the stern legionaries who had been the "massive iron hammers" of the whole earth ; he met the anxious politician with his ready man of business at his side to prompt him on his canvass for popularity ; he met the orator returning home from a successful pleading, with his young admirers and his grateful and hopeful clients. He saw about him nothing but tokens of a vigorous power, grown up into a definite establishment, formed and matured in its religion, its laws, its civil traditions, its imperial extension, through the history of many centuries ; and what was he but a poor, feeble, aged stranger, in nothing different from the multitude of men—an Egyptian or a Chaldean, or perhaps a Jew, some Eastern or other—as passers-by would

16

guess according to their knowledge of human kind, carelessly looking at him (as we might turn our eyes upon Hindoo or gipsy, as they met us), without the shadow of a thought that such a one was destined then to commence an age of religious sovereignty, in which they might spend their own heathen times twice over, and not see its end!

In such a time as this, did the great Doctor, St. Gregory Nazianzen, he too an old man, a timid man, a retiring man, fond of solitude and books, and un-practised in the struggles of the world, suddenly appear in the Arian city of Constantinople; and, in despite of a fanatical populace, and an heretical clergy, preach the truth, and prevail—to his own wonder, and to the glory of that grace which is strong in weakness, and is ever nearest to its triumph when it is most despised.

In such a time did another St. Gregory, the first Pope of the name, when all things were now failing, when barbarians had occupied the earth, and fresh and more savage multitudes were pouring down, when pestilence, famine, and heresy ravaged far and near—oppressed, as he was, with continual sickness, his bed his Pontifical Throne—in such a time did he rule, direct, and consolidate the Church, in what he augured were the last moments of the world; subdu-ing Arians in Spain, Donatists in Africa, a third heresy in Egypt, a fourth in Gaul, humbling the pride of the East, reconciling the Goths to the Church, bringing our own pagan ancestors within her pale, and completing her order and beautifying her ritual, while he strengthened the foundations of her power.

And in such a time did the six Jesuit Fathers, Ignatius and his companions, while the world was exulting in the Church's fall, and men "made merry, and sent their gifts one to another," because the prophets were dead who "tormented them that dwelt upon earth," make their vow in the small Church of Montmartre; and, attracting others to them by the sympathetic force of zeal, and the eloquence of sanctity, went forward calmly and silently into India in the East, and into America in the West, and, while they added whole nations to the Church abroad, restored and reanimated the Catholic populations at home.

It is no new thing then with the Church, in a time of confusion or of anxiety, when offences abound, and the enemy is at her gates, that her children, far from being dismayed, or rather glorying in the danger, as vigorous men exult in trials of their strength—it is no new thing, I say, that they should go forth to do her work, as though she were in the most palmy days of her prosperity. Old Rome, in her greatest distress, sent her legions to foreign destinations by one gate, while the Carthaginian conqueror was at the other. In truth, as has been said of our own countrymen, we, Catholics, do not know when we are beaten; we advance, when by all the rules of war we ought to fall back; we dream but of triumphs, and mistake (as the world judges) defeat for victory. For we have upon us the omens of success in the recollections of the

past ; we read upon our banners the names of many
an old field of battle and of glory ; we are strong in
the strength of our fathers, and we mean to do, in our
humble measure, what Saints have done before us. It
is nothing great or wonderful in us to be thus minded;
only Saints indeed do exploits, and carry contests
through, but ordinary men, the serving men and
privates of the Church, are equal to attempting them.

It needs no heroism in us, my brethren, to face
such a time as this, and to make light of it ; for we
are Catholics. We have the experience of eighteen
hundred years. The great philosopher of antiquity tells
us, that mere experience is courage, not indeed of the
highest kind, but sufficient to succeed upon. It is
not one or two or a dozen defeats, if we had them,
which will reverse the majesty of the Catholic Name.
We are willing to take this generation on its own
standard of truth, and to make our intenseness of purpose the very voucher for our divinity. We are confident, zealous, and unyielding, because we are the
heirs of St. Peter, St. Gregory Nazianzen, St. Gregory
Pope, and all other holy and faithful men, who, in
their day, by word, deed, or prayer, have furthered the
Catholic cause. We share in their merits and inter-
cessions, and we speak with their voice. Hence we
do that without heroism, which others, who are not
Catholics, do only with it. It would be heroism in
others, certainly, to set about our work. Did Jews
aim at bringing over this vast population to the rites
of the Law, or did Unitarians address themselves to
the conversion of the Holy Roman Church, or did the

Society of Friends attempt the great French nation, this might rightly be called heroism ; not a true religious heroism, but it would be a something extraordinary and startling. It would be a peculiar, special, original, audacious idea ; it would be making a great venture on a great uncertainty. But there is nothing of special courage, nothing of personal magnanimity, in a Catholic's making light of the world, and beginning to preach to it, though it turn its face from him. He knows the nature and habits of the world ; and it is his immemorial way of dealing with it ; he does but act according to his vocation ; he would not be a Catholic, did he act otherwise. He knows whose vessel he has entered ; it is the bark of Peter When the greatest of the Romans was in an open boat on the Adriatic, and the sea rose, he said to the terrified boatman, *Cæsarem vehis et fortunam Cæsaris—* " Cæsar is your freight and Cæsar's fortune " What he said in presumption, we, my dear brethren, can repeat in faith, of that boat, in which Christ once sat and preached. We have not chosen it to have fear about it ; we have not entered it to escape out of it ; no, but to go forth in it upon the flood of sin and unbelief, which would sink any other craft. We began our work at the first with Peter for our guide, on the very Feast of his Chair, and at the very Shrine of his relics ; so, when any of you marvel that we should choose this place and this time for our missionary labours, let him know that we are of those who measure the present by the past, and poise the world upon a distant centre. We act according to our name; Catholics are at home in every time and place, in every state of society, in every class of the community, in every stage of cultivation. No state of things comes amiss to a Catholic priest ; he has always a work to do, and a harvest to reap.

Were it otherwise, had he not confidence in the darkest day, and the most hostile district, he would be relinquishing a principal note, as it is called, of the Church. She is Catholic, because she brings a universal remedy for a universal disease. The disease is sin ; all men have sinned ; all men need a recovery in Christ ; to all must that recovery be preached and dispensed. If then there be a preacher and dispenser of recovery, sent from God, that messenger must speak, not to one, but to all ; he must be suited to all, he must have a mission to the whole race of Adam, and be cognisable by every individual of it. I do not mean that he must persuade all, and prevail with all— for that depends upon the will of each ; but he must show his capabilities for converting all by actually converting some of every time, and every place, and every rank, and every age of life, and every character of mind. If sin is a partial evil, let its remedy be partial ; but, if it be not local, not occasional, but universal, such must be the remedy. A local religion is not from God. The true religion must indeed begin, and may linger, in one place ; nay, for centuries remain there, provided it is expanding and maturing in its internal character, and professes the while that it is not yet perfect. There may be deep reasons in God's counsels, why the proper revelation of His will to man should have been slowly elaborated and gradually completed in the elementary form of Judaism ; but that Revelation was ever in progress in the Jewish period, and pointed by its prophets to a day when it should be spread over the whole earth. Judaism then was local because it was imperfect ; when it reached perfection within, it became universal without, and took the name of Catholic.

Look around, my brethren, at the forms of religion now in the world, and you will find that one, and one only, has this note of a Divine origin. The Catholic Church has accompanied human society through one revolution of its great year ; and is now beginning a second. She has passed through the full cycle of changes, in order to show us that she is independent of them all. She has had trial of East and West, of monarchy and democracy, of peace and war, of imperial and of feudal tyranny, of times of darkness and times of philosophy, of barbarousness and luxury, of slaves and freemen, of cities and nations, of marts of commerce and seats of manufacture, of old countries and young, of metropolis and colonies. She arose in the most happy age which perhaps the world has ever known ; for two or three hundred years she had to fight against the authority of law, establish forms of religion, military power, an ably cemented empire, and prosperous, contented population. And in the course of that period, this poor, feeble, despised Association was able to defeat its imperial oppressor, in spite of his violent efforts, again and again exerted, to rid himself of so despicable an assailant. In spite of calumny, in spite of popular outbreaks, in spite of cruel torments, the lords of the world were forced, as their sole chance of maintaining their empire, to come to terms with that body, of which the present Church is in name, in line, in doctrine, in principles, in manner of being, in moral characteristics, the descendant and representative. They were forced to humble themselves to her, and to enter her pale, and to exalt her, and to depress her enemies. She triumphed as never any other triumphed before or since. But this was not all ; scarcely had she secured her triumph, or rather set about securing it, when it was all reversed; for the Roman Power, her captive, which with so much blood and patience she had subjugated, suddenly came to nought. It broke and perished ; and against her rushed millions of wild savages from the North and East, who had neither God nor conscience, nor even natural compassion. She had to begin again ; for centuries they came down, one horde after another, like roaring waves, and dashed against her base. They came again and again, like the armed bands sent by the King of Israel against the prophet ; and, as he brought fire down from heaven which devoured them as they came, so in her more gracious way did Holy Church, burning with zeal and love, devour her enemies, multitude after multitude, with the flame which her Lord had kindled, "heaping coals of fire upon their heads," and "overcoming evil with good ". Thus out of those fierce strangers were made her truest and most loyal children ;—and, then, when from among them there arose a strong military power, more artificially constructed than the old Roman, with traditions and precedents which lasted on for centuries, at first the Church's champion and then her rival, here too she had to undergo a new conflict, and to gain a new triumph. And so I might proceed, going to and fro, and telling of her political successes since, and of her intellectual victories from the beginning, and of her social improvements, and of her encounters with those other circumstances of human nature or combinations of human kind, which I just now enumerated ; all which prove to us, with a cogency as great as that of a physical demonstration, that she comes not of earth, that she holds not of earth, that she is no servant of man, else he who made could have destroyed her.

How different, again I say, how different are all religions that ever were, from this lofty and unchangeable Catholic Church ! They depend on time and place for their existence, they live in periods or in regions. They are children of the soil, indigenous plants, which readily flourish under a certain temperature, in a certain aspect, in moist or in dry, and die if they are transplanted. Their *habitat* is one article of their scientific description. Thus the Greek schism, Nestorianism, the heresy of Calvin, and Methodism, each has its geographical limits. Protestantism has gained nothing in Europe since its first outbreak Some accident gives rise to these religious manifestations ; some sickly season, the burning sun, the vapour-laden marsh, breeds a pestilence, and there it remains, hanging in the air over its birthplace perhaps for centuries; then some change takes place in the earth or in the heavens, and it suddenly is no more. Sometimes, however, it is true, such scourges of God have a course upon earth, and affect a Catholic range. They issue as from some poisonous lake or pit in Ethiopia or in India, and march forth with resistless power to fulfil their mission of evil, and walk to and fro over the face of the world. Such was the Arabian imposture of which Mahomet was the framer; and you will ask, perhaps, whether it has not done that, which I have said the Catholic Church alone can do, and proved thereby that it had in it an internal principle, which, depending not on man, could subdue him in any time or place? No, my brethren; look narrowly, and you will see the marked distinction which exists between the religion of Mahomet and the Church of Christ. For Mahometanism has done little more than the Anglican communion is doing at present. That communion is found in many parts of the world; its primate has a jurisdiction even greater than the Nestorian patriarch of old; it has establishments in Malta, in Jerusalem, in India, in China, in Australia, in South Africa, and in Canada, whereas Mahometanism is only an indigenous religion, and that in certain portions of two continents, with little power or wish to propagate its faith.

However, at least in Anglicanism, you will say, there is that note of Catholicity which in Mahometanism is not. Oh, my brethren, be not beguiled by words; will any thinking man say for a moment, whatever this objection be worth, that the Established Religion *is* superior to time and place? well, if not, why set about proving that it is? rather, does not its essence lie in its recognition by the State? is not its establishment its very *form?* what would it be, would it last ten years, if abandoned to itself? It is its establishment which erects it into a unity and individuality; can you contemplate it, though you stimulate your imagination to the task, as abstracted from its churches, palaces, colleges, parsonages, revenues, civil precedence, and national position? Strip it of this world, and you have performed a mortal operation upon it, for it has ceased to be. Take its bishops out of the legislature, tear its formularies from the Statute Book, open its universities to Dissenters, allow its clergy to become laymen again, legalise its private prayer-meetings, and what would be its definition? You know that, did not the State compel it to be one, it would split at once into three several bodies, each bearing within it the elements of further divisions. Even the small party of Non-jurors, a century and a half since, when released from the civil power, split into two. It has then no internal consistency, or individuality, or soul, to give it the capacity of propagation. Methodism represents some sort of an idea, Congregationalism an idea; the Established Religion has in it no idea beyond establishment. Its extension has been, for the most part, passive not active; it is carried forward into other places by State policy, and it moves because the State moves; it is an appendage, whether weapon or decoration, of the sovereign power; it is the religion, not even of a race, but of the ruling portion of a race. The Anglo-Saxon has done in this day what the Saracen did in a former. He does grudgingly for expedience, what the other did heartily from fanaticism. This is the chief difference between the two; the Saracen, in his commencement, converted the heretical East with the sword; but at least in India the extension of his faith was by immigration, as the Anglo-Saxon's may be now; he grew into other nations by commerce and colonisation; but, when he encountered the Catholic of the West, he made as little impression upon Spain, as the Protestant Anglo-Saxon makes on Ireland.

There is but one form of Christianity, my brethren, possessed of that real internal unity which is the primary condition of independence. Whether you look to Russia, England, or Germany, this note of divinity is wanting. In this country, especially, there is nothing broader than class religions; the established form itself is but the religion of a class. There is one persuasion for the rich, and another for the poor; men are born in this or that sect; the enthusiastic go here, and the sober-minded and rational go there. They make money, and rise in the world, and then they profess to belong to the Establishment. This body lives in the world's smile, that in its frown; the one would perish of cold in the world's winter, and the other would melt away in the summer. Not one of them undertakes human nature: none compasses the whole man; none places all men on a level; none addresses the intellect and the heart, fear and love, the active and the contemplative. It is considered, and justly, as an evidence for Christianity, that the ablest men have been Christians ; not that all sagacious or profound minds have taken up its profession, but that it has gained victories among them, such and so many, as to show that it is not the meie fact of ability or learning which is the reason why all are not converted. Such, too, is the characteristic of Catholicity ; not the highest in rank, not the meanest, not the most refined, not the rudest, is beyond the influence of the Church ; she includes specimens of every class among her children. She is the solace of the forlorn, the chastener of the prosperous, and the guide of the wayward. She keeps a mother's eye for the innocent, bears with a heavy hand upon the wanton, and has a voice of majesty for the proud. She opens the mind of the ignorant, and she prostrates the intellect of even the most gifted. These are not words ; she has done it, she does it still, she undertakes to do it. All she asks is an open field, and freedom to act. She asks no patronage from the civil power : in former times and places she indeed has asked it ; and, as Protestantism also, has availed herself of the civil sword. It is true she did so, because in certain ages it has been the acknowledged mode of acting, the most expeditious, and open at the time to no objection, and because, where she has done so, the people clamoured for it and did it in advance of her ; but her history shows that she needed it not, for she has extended and flourished without it. She is ready for any service which occurs ; she will take the world as it comes ; nothing but force can repress her. See, my brethren, what she is doing in this country now ; for three centuries the civil power has trodden down the goodly plant of grace, and kept its foot upon it ; at length circumstances have removed that tyranny, and lo ! the fair form of the Ancient Church rises up at once, as fresh and as vigorous as if she had never intermitted her growth. She is the same as she was three centuries ago, ere the present religions of the country existed ; you know her to be the same ; it is the charge brought against her that she does not change; time and place affect her not, because she has her source where there is neither place nor time, because she comes from the throne of the Illimitable, Eternal God.

With these feelings, my brethren, can we fear that we shall not have work enough in a vast city like this, which has such need of us ? He on whom we repose is "yesterday, and to-day, and the same for ever". If He did His wonders in the days of old, He does His wonders now ; if in former days the feeble and unworthy were made His instruments of good, so are they now. While we trust in Him, while we are true to His Church, we know that He intends to use us ; how, we know not ; who are to be the objects of His mercy, we know not ; we know not to whom we are sent ; but we know that tens of thousands cry out for us, and that of a surety we shall be sent to His chosen. " The word which shall issue from His mouth shall not return unto Him void, but shall do His pleasure, and shall prosper in the things whereto He hath sent it." None so innocent, none so sinful, none so dull, none so wise, but are objects for the grace of the Catholic Church.

If we do not prevail with the educated, we shall prevail with the rude ; if we fail with the old, we shall gain the young ; if we persuade not the serious and respectable, we shall succeed with the thoughtless ; if we come short of those who are near the Church, we shall reach even to those who are far distant from it. God's arm is not shortened ; He has not sent us here for nothing ; unless (which He Himself forbid !) we come to nothing by reason of our own disobedience.

True, there is one class of persons to whom we might seem to be sent more than to others, to whom we could naturally address ourselves, and on whose attention we have a sort of claim. How can I fitly bring these remarks to an end without referring to them ? There are those, I say, who, like ourselves, were in times past gradually led on step by step, till with us they stood on the threshold of the Church. They felt with us that the Catholic religion was different from anything else in the world ; and though it is difficult to say what more they felt in common (for no two persons exactly felt alike), yet they felt they had something to learn, their course was not clear to them, and they wished to find out God's will. Now, what might have been expected of such persons, what was natural in them, when they heard that their own friends, with whom they had sympathised so fully, had gone forward, under a sense of duty, to join the Catholic Church ? Surely it was natural—I will not say that they should at once follow them (for they had authority also on the side of remaining)—but, at least, it was natural that they should weigh the matter well, and listen with interest to what their friends might have to tell them. Did they do this in fact? alas, some of them did just the contrary : they said: " Since our common doctrines and principles have led you forward, for that very reason we will go backward ; the more we have hitherto agreed with you, the less can we now be influenced by you. Because you have gone, therefore we make up our minds once for all to remain. You are a temptation to us, because your arguments are strong. You are a warning to us, because you must not be our example. We do not wish to hear more, lest we hear too much. You were straightforward when on our side, therefore you must be sophistical now that you have left it. You were right in making converts then, therefore you are wrong in making converts now. You have spoiled a promising cause, and you deserve from us no mercy."

Thus they speak; let them say it before the judgment-seat of Christ! Take it at the best advantage, my brethren, and what is the argument based upon but this—that all investigation must be wrong which results in a change of religion? The process is condemned by its issue ; it is a mere absurdity to give up the religion of our birth, the home of our affections, the seat of our influence, the well-spring of our maintenance. It was an absurdity in St. Paul to become a Christian ; it was an absurdity in him to weep over his brethren who could not listen to him. I understand now, as I have not understood before, why it was that the Jews hugged themselves in their Judaism, and were proof against persuasion.

In vain the Apostles insisted, " Your religion leads to ours, and ours is a fact before your eyes ; why wait for what is already present, as if it were still to come? do you consider your Church perfect? do you profess to have attained? why not turn at least your thoughts towards Christianity?"   "No," said they ; "we will live, we will die, where we were born ; the religion of our ancestors, the religion of our nation, is the only truth ; it must be safe not to move.   We will not un- church ourselves, we will not descend from our preten- sions ; we will shut our hearts to conviction, and will stake eternity on our position."   Oh, great argument, not for Jews only, but for Mahometans, for Hindoos! great argument for heathen of all lands, for all who prefer this world to another, who prefer a temporary peace to truth, present ease to forgiveness of sins, the smile of friends to the favour of Christ! but weak argument, strong delusion, in the clear ray of heaven, and in the eye of Him who comes to judge the world with fire.

O my dear brethren, if any be here present to whom these remarks may more or less apply, do us not the injustice to think that we aim at your conversion for any party purpose of our own.   What should we gain from your joining us but an additional charge and responsibility?   But who can bear to think that pious, religious hearts, on which the grace of God has been so singularly shed, who so befit conversion, who are intended for heaven, should be falling back into the world out of which they have been called, and losing a prize which was once within their reach.

17

Who that knows you, can get himself to believe that you will always disappoint the yearning hopes of those whom once you loved so much, and helped forward so effectually! *Dies venit, Dies Tua,* the day shall come, though it may tarry, and we will in patience wait for it. Still the truth must be spoken —we do not need you, but you need us; it is not we who shall be baffled if we cannot gain you, but you who will come short, if you be not gained. Remain, then, in the barrenness of your affections, and the decay of your zeal, and the perplexity of your reason, if you will not be converted. Alas! there is work enough to do, less troublesome, less anxious, than the care of your souls. There are thousands of sinners to be reconciled, of the young to be watched over, of the devout to be consoled. God needs not worshippers; He needs not objects for His mercy; He can do without you; He offers His benefits, and passes on; He delays not; He offers once, not twice and thrice; He goes on to others; He turns to the Gentiles; He turns to open sinners; He refuses the well-conducted for the outcast; " He hath filled the hungry with good things, and the rich He hath sent empty away ".

For me, my brethren, it is not likely that you will hear me again; these may be my first and last words to you, for this is not my home. *Si justificare me voluero, os meum condemnabit me,* " If I wish to justify myself, my mouth shall condemn me; if I shall show forth my innocence, it shall prove me perverse "; yet, though full of imperfections, full of miseries, I trust that I may say in my measure after the Apostle, " I have lived in all good conscience before God unto this day. Our glory is this, the testimony of our conscience, that in simplicity of heart and sincerity of God, and not in carnal wisdom, but in the grace of God, we have lived in this world, and more abundantly towards you." I have followed His guidance, and He has not disappointed me ; I have put myself into His hands, and He has given me what I sought ; and as He has been with me hitherto, so may He, and His Blessed Mother, and all good Angels and Saints, be with me unto the end.

DISCOURSE XIII.

MYSTERIES OF NATURE AND OF GRACE.

I AM going to assert what some persons, my brethren, those especially whom it most concerns, will nor hesitate to call a great paradox; but which, nevertheless, I consider to be most true, and likely to approve itself to you more and more, the oftener you turn your thoughts to the subject, and likely to be confirmed in the religious history of this country as time proceeds. It is this: that it is quite as difficult, and quite as easy, to believe that there is a God in heaven, as to believe that the Catholic Church is His oracle and minister on earth. I do not mean to say that it is really difficult to believe in God (God Himself forbid!) no; but that belief in God and belief in His Church stand on the same kind of foundation; that the proof of the one truth is like the proof of the other truth, and that the objections which may be made to the one are like the objections which may be made to the other; and that, as right reason and sound judgment overrule objections to the being of a God, so do they supersede and set aside objections to the Divine mission of the Church. And I consider that, when once

(260)

a man has a real hold of the great doctrine that there is a God, in its true meaning and bearings, then (provided there be no disturbing cause, no peculiarities in his circumstances, involuntary ignorance, or the like), he will be led on without an effort, as by a natural continuation of that belief, to believe also in the Catholic Church as God's Messenger or Prophet, dismissing as worthless the objections which are adducible against the latter truth, as he dismisses objections adducible against the former. And I consider, on the other hand, that when a man does not believe in the Church, then (the same accidental impediments being put aside as before), there is nothing in reason to keep him from doubting the being of a God.

The state of the case is this ;— every one spontaneously embraces the doctrine of the existence of God, as a first principle, and a necessary assumption. It is not so much proved to him, as borne in upon his mind irresistibly, as a truth which it does not occur to him, nor is possible for him, to doubt ; so various and so abundant is the witness for it contained in the experience and the conscience of every one. He cannot unravel the process, or put his finger on the independent arguments, which conspire together to create in him the certainty which he feels ; but certain of it he is, and he has neither the temptation nor the wish to doubt it, and he could, should need arise, at least point to the books or the persons from whence he could obtain the various formal proofs on which the being of a God rests, and the irrefragable demonstration thence resulting against the freethinker and the sceptic. At the same time he certainly would find, if he was in a condition to pursue the subject himself, that unbelievers had the advantage of him so far as this,—that there were a number of objections to the doctrine which he could not satisfy, questions which he could not solve, mysteries which he could neither conceive nor explain ; he would perceive that the body of proof itself might be more perfect and complete than it is ; he would not find indeed anything to invalidate that proof, but many things which might embarrass him in discussion, or afford a plausible, though not a real, excuse for doubting about it.

The case is pretty much the same as regards the great moral law of God. We take it for granted, and rightly ; what could we do, where should we be, without it ? how could we conduct ourselves, if there were no difference between right and wrong, and if one action were as acceptable to our Creator as another ? Impossible ! if anything is true and Divine, the rule of conscience is such, and it is frightful to suppose the contrary. Still, in spite of this, there is quite rooms for objectors to insinuate doubts about its authority or its enunciations ; and where an inquirer is cold and fastidious, or careless, or wishes an excuse for disobedience, it is easy for him to perplex and disorder his reason, till he begins to question whether what he has all his life thought to be sins; are really such, and whether conscientiousness is not in fact a superstition.

And in like manner as regards the Catholic Church ; she bears upon her the tokens of divinity, which come home to any mind at once, which has not been pos·

sessed by prejudice, and educated in suspicion. It is not so much a process of inquiry as an instantaneous recognition, on which the mind believes. Moreover, it is possible to analyse the arguments and draw up in form the great proof, on which her claims rest ; but, on the other hand, it is quite possible also for opponents to bring forward certain imposing objections, which, though they do not really interfere with those claims, still are specious in themselves, and are sufficient to arrest and entangle the mind, and to keep it back from a fair examination of the proof, and of the vast array of arguments of which it consists. I am alluding to such objections as the following ;— How can Almighty God be Three and yet One ; how can Christ be God and yet man ; how can He be at once in the Blessed Sacrament under the form of Bread and Wine, and yet in heaven ; how is the doctrine of eternal punishment consistent with the Infinite Mercy of God ;—or, again, how is it that, if the Catholic Church be from God, the gift of belonging to her is not, and has not been, granted to all men ; how is it that so many apparently good men are external to her ; why does she pay such honour to the Blessed Virgin and all Saints ; how is it that, since the Bible also is from God, it admits of being quoted in opposition to her teaching ; in a word, how is it, if she is from God, that everything which she does and says, is not perfectly intelligible to man, intelligible, not only to man in general, but to the reason and judgment and taste of every individual of the species, taken one by one?

Now, whatever my anxiety may be about the next generation, I trust I need at present have none in insisting, before a congregation however mixed, on the mysteries or difficulties which attach to the doctrine of God's existence, and which must be of necessity acquiesced in by every one who believes it. I trust, and am sure, that as yet it is safe even to put before one who is not a Catholic some points which he is obliged to accept, whether he will or no, when he confesses that there is a God. I am going to do so, not wantonly, but with a definite object, by way of showing him, that he is not called on to believe anything in the Catholic Church more strange or inexplicable than he already admits when he believes in a God ; so that, if God exists in spite of the difficulties attending the doctrine, so the Church may be of Divine origin, though that truth also has its difficulties ;—nay, I might even say, the Church is Divine, *because* of those difficulties ; for the difficulties which exist in the doctrine that there is a Divine Being, do but give countenance and protection to parallel difficulties in the doctrine that there is a Catholic Church. If there be mysteriousness in her teaching, this does but show that she proceeds from Him, who is Himself Mystery, in the most simple and elementary ideas which we have of Him, whom we cannot contemplate at all except as One who is absolutely greater than our reason, and utterly strange to our imagination.

First then, consider that Almighty God had no beginning, and that this is necessary from the nature of the case, and inevitable. For if (to suppose what is absurd) the maker of the visible world was himself made by some other maker, and that maker again by another, you must anyhow come at last to a first Maker who had no maker, that is, who had no beginning. If you will not admit this, you will be forced to say that the world was not made at all, or made itself, and itself had no beginning, which is more wonderful still ; for it is much easier to conceive that a Spirit, such as God is, existed from eternity, than that this material world was eternal. Unless then we are resolved to doubt that we live in a world of beings at all, unless we doubt our own existence, if we do but grant that there is something or other now existing, it follows at once, that there must be something or other which has always existed, and never had a beginning. This then is certain from the necessity of the case ; but can there be a more overwhelming mystery than it is ? To say that a being had no beginning seems a contradiction in terms ; it is a mystery as great, or rather greater, than any in the Catholic Faith. For instance, it is the teaching of the Church that the Father is God, the Son God, and the Holy Ghost God, yet that there is but one God ; this is simply incomprehensible to us, but at least, so far as this, it involves no self-contradiction, because God is not Three and One in the same sense, but He is Three in one sense and One in another ; on the contrary, to say that any being has no beginning, is like a statement which means nothing, and is an absurdity. And so again, Protestants think that the Catholic doctrine of the Real Presence cannot be true, because, if so (as they argue), our Lord's Body is in two places at once, in Heaven and upon the Altar, and this they say is an impossibility. Now, Catholics do not see that it is impossible at all, that our Lord should be in Heaven yet on the Altar ; they do not indeed see *how* it can be both, but they do not see *why* it should not be ; there are many things which exist, though we do not know *how* ;—do we know *how* anything exists?—there are many truths which are not less truths because we cannot picture them to ourselves or conceive them ; but at any rate, the Catholic doctrine concerning the Real Presence is not more mysterious than how Almighty God can exist, yet never have come into existence. We do not know what is meant by saying that Almighty God will have no end, but still there is nothing here to distress or confuse our reason, but it distorts our mental sight and makes our head giddy to have to say (what nevertheless we cannot help saying), that He had no beginning. Reason brings it home clearly to us, yet reason again starts at it ; reason starts back from its own discovery, yet is obliged to endure it. It discovers, it shrinks, it submits ; such is the state of the case, but, I say, they who are obliged to bow their neck to this mystery, need not be so sensitive about the mysteries of the Catholic Church.

Then think of this again, which, though not so baffling to the reason, still is most bewildering to the imagination ;—that, if the Almighty had no beginning He must have lived a whole eternity by Himself. What an awful thought! for us, our happiness lies in looking up to some object, or pursuing some end ; we, poor mortal men, cannot understand a prolonged rest, except as a sort of sloth and self-forgetfulness ; we are wearied if we meditate for one short hour ; what then is meant when it is said, that He, the Great God, passed infinite ages by Himself ? What was the end of His being ? He was His own end ; how incomprehensible ! And since He lived a whole eternity by Himself, He might, had He so willed, never have created anything ; and then from eternity to eternity there would have been none but He, none to witness Him, none to contemplate Him, none to adore and praise Him. How oppressive to think of! that there should have been no space, no time, no succession, no variation, no progression, no scope, no termination. One Infinite Being from first to last, and nothing else! And why He ? Which is the less painful to our imagination, the idea of only one Being in existence, or of nothing at all ? O my brethren, here is mystery without mitigation, without relief! how severe and frightful! The mysteries of Revelation, the Catholic dogmas, inconceivable as they are, are most gracious, most loving, laden with mercy and consolation to us, not only sublime, but touching and winning ;—such is the doctrine that God became man. Incomprehensible it is, and we can but adore, when we hear that the Almighty Being, of whom I have been speaking, " who inhabiteth eternity," has taken flesh and blood of a Virgin's veins, lain in a Virgin's womb, been suckled at a Virgin's breast, been obedient to human parents, worked at a humble trade, been despised by His own, been buffeted and scourged by His creatures, been nailed hand and foot to a Cross, and has died a male-factor's death; and that now, under the form of Bread, He should lie upon our Altars, and suffer Himself to be hidden in a small tabernacle!

Most incomprehensible, but still, while the thought overwhelms our imagination, it also overpowers our heart; it is the most subduing, affecting, piercing thought which can be pictured to us. It thrills through us, and draws our tears, and abases us, and melts us into love and affection, when we dwell upon it. O most tender and compassionate Lord! You see, He puts out of our sight that mysteriousness of His, which is only awful and terrible; He insists not on His past eternity; He would not scare and trouble His poor children, when at length He speaks to them; no, He does but surround Himself with His own infinite bountifulness and compassion; He bids His Church tell us only of His mysterious conde-scension. Still our reason, prying, curious reason, searches out for us those prior and more austere mysteries, which are attached to His Being, and He suffers us to find them out. He suffers us, for He knows that that same reason, though it recoils from them, must put up with them; He knows that they will be felt by it to be clear, inevitable truths, appalling as they are. He suffers it to discover them, in order that, both by the parallel and by the contrast between what reason infers and what the Church reveals, we may be drawn on from the awful discoveries of the one to the gracious announcements of the other; and in order, too, that the rejection of Revelation may be its own punishment, and that they who stumble at the Catholic mysteries may be dashed back upon the adamantine rocks which base the throne of the Everlasting, and may wrestle with the stern conclusions of reason, since they refuse the bright consolations of faith.

And now another difficulty, which reason discovers, yet cannot explain. Since the world exists, and did not *ever* exist, there was a time when the Almighty changed that state of things, which had been from all eternity, for another state. It was wonderful that He should be by Himself for an eternity; moreover, it had been wonderful, had He never changed it; but it is wonderful, too, that He did change it. It is wonderful that, being for an eternity alone, He should ever pass from that solitary state, and surround Himself with millions upon millions of living beings. A state which had been from eternity might well be considered unchangeable; yet it ceased, and another superseded it. What end could the All-blessed have had in beginning to create, and in determining to pass a second eternity so differently from the first? This mystery, my brethren, will tend to reconcile us, I think, to the difficulty of a question sometimes put to us by unbelievers, viz., if the Catholic Religion is from God, why was it set up so late in the world's day? Why did some thousands of years pass before Christ came and His gifts were poured upon the race of man? But, surely, it is not so strange that the Judge of men should have changed his dealings towards them " in the midst of the years," as that He should have changed the history of the heavens in the midst of eternity. If creation had a beginning at a certain date, why should not redemption ? And if we be forced to believe, whether we will or no, that there was once an innovation upon the course of things on high, and that the universe arose out of nothing, and if, even when the earth was created, still it remained " empty and void, and darkness was upon the face of the deep," what so great marvel is it, that there was a fixed period in God's inscrutable counsels, during which there was " a bond fastened upon all people," and a " web drawn over them," and then a date, at which the bond of thraldom was broken, and the web of error was unravelled ?

Well, let us suppose the innovation decreed in the eternal purpose of the Most High, and that creation is to be ; of whom, my brethren, shall it consist ? Doubtless of beings who can praise and bless Him, who can admire His perfections, and obey His will, who will be least unworthy to minister about His Throne, and to keep Him company. Look around, and say how far facts bear out this anticipation. There is but one race of intelligent beings, as far as we have experience by nature, and a thousand races which cannot love or worship Him who made them. Millions upon millions enjoy their brief span of life, but man alone can look up to heaven ; and what is man, many though he be, what is he in the presence of so innumerable a multitude ? Consider the abundance of beasts that range the earth, of birds under the firmament of heaven, of fish in the depths of the ocean, and, above all, the exuberant varieties of insects, which baffle our enumeration by their minuteness, and our powers of conception by their profusion. Doubtless they all show forth the glory of the Creator, as do the elements, "fire, hail, snow, and ice, stormy winds, which fulfil His word". Yet not one of them has a soul, not one of them knows who made it, or that it is made, not one can render Him any proper service, not one can love Him. Indeed how far does the whole world come short in all respects of what it might be! It is not even possessed of created excellence in fulness. It is stamped with imperfection; everything indeed is good in its kind, for God could create nothing otherwise, but how much more fully might He have poured His glory and infused His grace into it, how much more beautiful and Divine a world might he have made, than that which, after an eternal silence, He summoned into being! Let reason answer, I repeat— Why is it that He did not surround himself with spiritual intelligences, and animate every material atom with a soul? Why made He not the very footstool of his Throne and the pavement of His Temple of an angelic nature, of beings who could praise and bless Him, while they did Him menial service? Set man's wit and man's imagination to the work of devising a world, and you would see, my brethren, what a far more splendid design he would submit for it, than met the good pleasure of the Omnipo-

272 Mysteries of Nature and of Grace.

tent and All-wise. Ambitious architect he would have been, if called to build the palace of the Lord of All, in which every single part would have been the best conceivable, the colours all the brightest, the materials the most costly, and the lineaments the most perfect. Pass from man's private fancies and ideas, and fastidious criticisms on the vast subject; come to facts which are before our eyes, and report what meets them. We see a universe, material for the most part and corruptible, fashioned indeed by laws of infinite skill, and betokening an All-wise Hand, but lifeless and senseless; huge globes, hurled into space, and moving mechanically; subtle influences, penetrating into the most hidden corners and pores of the world, as quick and keen as thought, yet as helpless as the clay from which thought has departed. And next, life without sense; myriads of trees and plants, "the grass of the field," beautiful to the eye, but perishable and worthless in the sight of heaven. And, then, when at length we discover sense as well as life, what, I repeat, do we see but a greater mystery still? We behold the spectacle of brute nature; of impulses, feelings, propensities, passions, which in us are ruled or repressed by a superintending reason, but from which, when ungovernable, we shrink, as fearful and hateful, because in us they would be sin. Millions of irrational creatures surround us, and it would seem as though the Creator had left part of His work in its original chaos, so monstrous are these beings, which move and feel and act without reflection and without principle. To matter He has given laws ; He has divided the moist and the dry, the heavy and the rare, the light and the dark ; He has " placed the sand as a boundary for the sea, a perpetual precept which it shall not pass ". He has tamed the elements, and made them servants of the universal good ; but the brute beasts pass to and fro in their wildness and their isolation, no yoke on their neck or " bit in their lips," the enemies of all they meet, yet without the capacity of self-love. They live on each other's flesh by an original necessity of their being ; their eyes, their teeth, their claws, their muscles, their voice, their walk, their structure within, all speak of violence and blood. They seem made to inflict pain ; they rush on their prey with fierceness, and devour it with greediness. There is scarce a passion or a feeling which is sin in man, but is found brute and irresponsible in them. Rage, wanton cruelty, hatred, sullenness, jealousy, revenge, cunning, malice, envy, lust, vain-glory, gluttony, each has its representative ; and say, O theistical philosopher of this world, who wouldest fain walk by reason only, and scornest the Catholic faith, is it not marvellous, or explain it, if thou canst, that the All-wise and All-good should have poured over the face of His fair creation these rude and inchoate existences, to look like sinners, though they be not and these too created before man, perhaps for an untold period, and dividing the earth with him since, and the actual lords of a great portion of it even now ?

The crowning work of God is man ; he is the flower

and perfection of creation, and made to serve and worship his Creator ; look at him then, O Sages, who scoff at the revealed word, scrutinise him, and say in sincerity, is he a fit offering to present to the great God ? I must not speak of sin ; you will not acknowledge the term, or will explain it away ; yet consider man as he is found in the world, and,—owning as you must own, that the many do not act by rule or principle and that few give any honour to their Maker—seeing as you see, that enmities, frauds, cruelties, oppressions injuries, excesses are almost the constituents of human life—knowing too the wonderful capabilities of man, yet their necessary frustration in so brief an existence,—can you venture to say that the Church's yoke is heavy, when you yourselves, viewing the Universe from end to end, are compelled, by the force of reason, to submit your reason to the confession that God has created nothing perfect, a world of order which is dead and corruptible, a world of immortal spirits which is in rebellion ?

I come then to this conclusion ;—if I must submit my reason to mysteries, it is not much matter whether it is a mystery more or a mystery less, when faith anyhow is the very essence of all religion, when the main difficulty to an inquirer is firmly to hold that there is a Living God, in spite of the darkness which surrounds Him, the Creator, Witness, and Judge of men. When once the mind is broken in, as it must be, to the belief of a Power above it, when once it understands, that it is not itself the measure of all things in heaven and earth, it will have little difficulty in going forward. I do not say it will, or can, go on to other truths, without conviction; I do not say it ought to believe the Catholic faith without grounds and motives; but I say that, when once it believes in God, the great obstacle to faith has been taken away,—a proud, self-sufficient spirit. When once a man really, with the eyes of his soul and by the power of Divine grace, recognises his Creator, he has passed a line; that has happened to him which cannot happen twice; he has bent his stiff neck, and triumphed over himself. If he believes that God has no beginning, why not believe that He is Three yet One? if he owns that God created space, why not own also that He can cause a body to subsist without dependence on place? if he is obliged to grant that God created all things out of nothing, why doubt His power to change the substance of bread into the Body of His Son? It is as strange that, after an eternal rest, He should begin to create, as that, when He had once created, He should take on Himself a created nature; it is as strange that man should be allowed to fall so low, as we see before our eyes in so many dreadful instances, as that Angels and Saints should be exalted even to religious honours; it is as strange that such large families in the animal world should be created without souls and subject to vanity, as that one creature, the Blessed Mother of God, should be exalted over all the rest; as strange, that the book of nature should sometimes seem to vary from the rule of conscience or the conclusions of reason, as that the Church's Scriptures should admit of being interpreted in opposition to her Tradition. And if it shocks a religious mind to doubt of the being of the All-wise and All-good God, on the ground of the mysteries in Nature, why may it not shrink also from using the revealed mysteries as an argument against Revelation ?

And now, my dear brethren, who are as yet external to the Church, if I have brought you as far as this, I really do not see why I have not brought you on to make your submission to her. Can you deliberately sit down amid the bewildering mysteries of creation, when a refuge is held out to you, in which reason is rewarded for its faith by the fulfilment of its hopes ? Nature does not exempt you from the trial of believing, but it gives you nothing in return ; it does but disappoint you. You must submit your reason anyhow ; you are not in better circumstances if you turn from the Church ; you merely do not secure what you have already sought in nature in vain. The simple question to be decided is one of fact, has a revelation been given ? You lessen, not increase your difficulties by receiving it. It comes to you recommended and urged upon you by the most favourable anticipations of reason. The very difficulties of nature make it likely that a revelation should be made ; the very mysteries of creation call for some act on the part of the Creator, by which those mysteries shall be alleviated to you or compensated. One of the greatest of the perplexities of nature is this very one, that the Creator should have left you to yourselves. You know there is a God, yet you know your own ignorance of Him, of His will, of your duties, of your prospects. A revelation would be the greatest of possible boons which could be vouchsafed to you. After all, you do not know, you only conclude that there is a God; you see Him not, you do but hear of Him. He acts under a veil; He is on the point of manifesting Himself to you at every turn, yet He does not. He has impressed on your hearts anticipations of His majesty; in every part of creation has He left traces of His presence and given glimpses of His glory; you come up to the spot, He has been there, but He is gone. He has taught you His law, unequivocally indeed, but by deduction and by suggestion, not by direct command. He has always addressed you circuitously, by your inward sense, by the received opinion, by the events of life, by vague traditions, by dim histories; but as if of set purpose, and by an evident law, He never actually appears to your longing eyes or your weary heart, He never confronts you with Himself. What can be meant by all this? a spiritual being abandoned by its Creator! there must doubtless be some awful and all-wise reason for it; still a sore trial it is; so sore, surely, that you must gladly hail the news of His interference to remove or diminish it.

The news then of a revelation, far from suspicious, is borne in upon our hearts by the strongest presumptions of reason in its behalf. It is hard to believe that it has not been given, as indeed the conduct of mankind has ever shown. You cannot help expecting it from the hands of the All-merciful, unworthy as you feel yourselves of it. It is not that you can claim it, but that He inspires hope of it; it is not you that are worthy of the gift, but it is the gift which is worthy of your Creator. It is so urgently probable, that

little evidence is required for it, even though but little
were given. Evidence that God has spoken you
must have, else were you a prey to impostures; but its
extreme likelihood allows you, were it necessary, to
dispense with all proof that is not barely sufficient
for your purpose. The very fact, I say, that there is
a Creator, and a hidden one, powerfully bears you on
and sets you down at the very threshold of revelation,
and leaves you there looking up earnestly for Divine
tokens that a revelation has been made.

Do you go with me as far as this, that a revelation
is probable? well then, a second remark, and I have
done. It is this,—the teaching of the Church manifestly is that revelation. Why should it not be?
This mark has she upon her at very first sight, that
she is unlike every other profession of religion. Were
she God's Prophet or Messenger, she would be distinctive in her characteristics, isolated, and special;
and so she is. She is one, not only in herself, but
in contrast to everything else: she has no relationship with any other body. And hence too, you see
the question lies between the Church and no Divine
messenger at all; there is no revelation given us,
unless she is the organ of it, for where else is there a
Prophet to be found? The anticipation, which I
have been urging, has failed, the probability has
been falsified, if she be not that Prophet of God.
Not that this conclusion is an absurdity, for you cannot
take it for granted that your hope of a revelation will
be fulfilled; but in whatever degree it is probable that
it will be fulfilled, in that degree it is probable that

the Church, and nothing else, is the means of fulfilling it. Nothing else; for you cannot believe in your
heart that this or that Sect, that this or that Establishment is, in its teaching and its commands, the
oracle of the Most High. I know you cannot say in
your heart, "I believe this or that, because the
English Establishment or the Scotch declares that it
is true". Nor could you, I am sure, trust the Russian
hierarchy, or the Nestorian, or the Eutychian, as
speaking from God; at the utmost you might, if you
were learned in these matters, look on them as venerable depositories of historical matter, and witnesses
of past ages. You would exercise your judgment and
criticism on what they said, and would never think
of taking their word as decisive; they are in no sense
Prophets, Oracles, Judges, of supernatural truth; and
the contrast between them and the Catholic Church
is a preliminary evidence in her favour.

A Prophet is one who comes from God, who speaks
with authority, who is ever one and the same, who is
precise and decisive in his statements, who is equal to
successive difficulties, and can smite and overthrow
error. Such has the Catholic Church shown herself
in her history, such is she at this day. She alone has
had the Divine spell of controlling the reason of man,
and of eliciting faith in her word from high and low,
educated and ignorant, restless and dull-minded.
Even those who are alien to her, and whom she does
not move to obedience, she moves to respect and
admiration. The most profound thinkers and the
most sagacious politicians predict her future triumphs

while they marvel at her past. Her enemies are frightened at the sight of her, and have no better mode of warfare against her than that of blackening her with slanders, or of driving her into the wilderness. To see her is to recognise her; her look and bearing is the evidence of her royal lineage. True, her tokens might be clearer than they are; I grant it; she might have been set up in Adam, and not in Peter; she might have embraced the whole family of man; she might have been the instrument of inwardly converting all hearts; she might have had no scandals within or misfortunes without; she might in short have been, I repeat, a heaven on earth; but, I repeat, does she not show as glorious in our sight as a creature, as her God does as the Creator? If He does not display the highest possible tokens of His presence in nature, why should His Messenger display such in grace? You believe the Scriptures; does she not in her character and conduct show as Divine as Jacob does, or as Samuel, or as David, or as Jeremias, or in a far higher measure? Has she not notes far more than sufficient for the purpose of convincing you? She takes her rise from the very coming of Christ, and receives her charter, as also her very form and mission, from His mouth. "Blessed art thou, Simon Barjona, for flesh and blood hath not revealed it unto thee, but My Father who is in heaven. And I say unto thee, that thou art Peter, and upon this rock I will build My Church, and the gates of hell shall not prevail against it. And I will give to thee the keys of the kingdom of heaven; and whatsoever thou shalt bind upon earth, shall be bound also in heaven, and whatsoever thou shalt loose on earth, shall be loosed also in heaven."

Coming to you then from the very time of the Apostles, spreading out into all lands, triumphing over a thousand revolutions, exhibiting so awful a unity, glorying in so mysterious a vitality, so majestic, so imperturbable, so bold, so saintly, so sublime, so beautiful, O ye sons of men, can ye doubt that she is the Divine Messenger for whom you seek? Oh, long sought after, tardily found, desire of the eyes, joy of the heart, the truth after many shadows, the fulness after many foretastes, the home after many storms, come to her, poor wanderers, for she it is, and she alone, who can unfold the meaning of your being and the secret of your destiny. She alone can open to you the gate of heaven, and put you on your way. "Arise, shine, O Jerusalem; for thy light is come, and the glory of the Lord is risen upon thee; for, behold, darkness shall cover the earth, and a mist the people, but the Lord shall arise upon thee, and His glory shall be seen upon thee." "Open ye the gates, that the just nation, that keepeth the truth, may enter in. The old error is passed away; Thou wilt keep peace—peace, because we have hoped in Thee. Lord, Thou wilt give peace to us, for Thou hast wrought all our works for us. O Lord, our God, other lords besides Thee have had dominion over us, but in Thee only make we mention of Thy Name. The dying, they shall not live; the giants, they shall not rise again; therefore Thou hast visited and broken them, and hast destroyed all their memory."

O my brethren, turn away from the Catholic Church, and to whom will you go? it is your only chance of peace and assurance in this turbulent, changing world. There is nothing between it and scepticism, when men exert their reason freely. Private creeds, fancy religions, may be showy and imposing to the many in their day; national religions may lie huge and lifeless, and cumber the ground for centuries, and distract the attention or confuse the judgment of the learned; but on the long run it will be found that either the Catholic Religion is verily and indeed the coming in of the unseen world into this, or that there is nothing positive, nothing dogmatic, nothing real, in any of our notions as to whence we come and whither we are going. Unlearn Catholicism, and you open the way to your becoming Protestant, Unitarian, Deist, Pantheist, Sceptic, in a dreadful, but inevitable succession; only not inevitable by some accident of your position, of your education, and of your cast of mind; only not inevitable, if you dismiss the subject of religion from your view, deny yourself your reason, devote your thoughts to moral duties, or dissipate them in engagements of the world. Go, then, and do your duty to your neighbour, be just, be kindly-tempered, be hospitable, set a good example, uphold religion as good for society, pursue your business, or your profession, or your pleasure, eat and drink, read the news, visit your friends, build and furnish, plant and sow, buy and sell, plead and debate, work for the world, settle your children, go home and die, but eschew religious inquiry, if you will not have faith, nor fancy that you can have faith, if you will not join the Church.

Else avoid, I say, inquiry; for it will but lead you thither, where there is no light, no peace, no hope; it will lead you to the deep pit, where the sun, and the moon, and the stars, and the beauteous heavens are not, but chilliness, and barrenness, and perpetual desolation. O perverse children of men, who refuse truth when offered you, because it is not truer! O restless hearts and fastidious intellects, who seek a gospel more salutary than the Redeemer's, and a creation more perfect than the Creator's! God, forsooth, is not great enough for you; you have those high aspirations and those philosophical notions, inspired by the original tempter, which are content with nothing that is, which determine that the Most High is too little for your worship, and His attributes too narrow for your love.

But enough—while we thus speak of the Evil One and his victims, let us not forget to look to ourselves. God forbid that, while we preach to others, we ourselves should become castaways!

DISCOURSE XIV.

THE Eternal Word, the Only-begotten Son of the Father, put off His glory, and came down upon earth, to raise us to heaven. Though He was God, He became man; though He was Lord of all, He became as a servant; "though He was rich, yet for our sakes He became poor, that we, through His poverty, might be rich". He came from heaven in so humble an exterior, that the self-satisfied Pharisees despised Him, and treated Him as a madman or an impostor. When He spoke of His father Abraham, and implied His knowledge of him, who was in truth but the creature of His hands, they said in derision, "Thou art not yet fifty years old, and hast Thou seen Abraham?" He made answer, "Amen, amen, I say unto you, Before Abraham was made, I am." He had seen Abraham, who lived two thousand years before; yet in truth He was not two thousand years old, more than He was fifty. He was not two thousand years old, because He had no years; He was the Ancient of Days, who never had beginning, and who never will have an end; who is above and beyond time ; who is ever young, and ever is beginning, yet never has not been, and is as old as He is young, and was as old and as young when Abraham lived as when He came on earth in our flesh to atone for our sins. And hence He says, " Before Abraham was, I *am*," and not " I *was* "; because with Him there is no past or future. It cannot be properly said of Him, that He was, or that He will be, but that He is ; He is always ; always the same, not older because He has lived two thousand years in addition, not younger because He has not lived them.

My brethren, if we could get ourselves to enter into this high and sacred thought, if we really comtemplated the Almighty in Himself, then we should understand better what His incarnation is to us, and what it is in Him. I do not mean, if we worthily contemplated Him as He is ; but, even if we contemplated Him in such a way as is really possible to us, if we did but fix our thoughts on Him, and make use of the reason which He has given us, we should understand enough of His greatness to feel the awfulness of His voluntary self-abasement. Attend, then, while I recall to your mind the doctrines which reason and revelation combine to teach you about the Most High, and, next, when you have fixed your mind upon His infinity, then go on to view, in the light of that infinity, the meaning of His incarnation.

Now first consider that reason teaches you there must be a God ; else how was this all-wonderful universe made ? It could not make itself ; man could not make it, he is but a part of it ; each man has a beginning, there must have been a first man, and who made him? To the thought of God then we are forced from the nature of the case; we must admit the idea of an Almighty Creator, and that Creator must have been from everlasting. He must have had no beginning, else how came He to be? Else, we should be in our original difficulty, and must begin our argument over again. The Creator, I say, had no beginning; for, if He was brought into being by another before Him, then how came that other to be? And so we shall proceed in an unprofitable series or catalogue of creators, which is as difficult to conceive as an endless line of men. Besides, if it was not the Creator Himself who was from everlasting, then there would be one being who was from everlasting, and another who was Creator; which is all one with saying there are two Gods. It is least trial then to our reason, it is simplest and most natural, to pronounce, that the Creator of the world had no beginning;—and if so, He is self-existing; and if so, He can undergo no change. What is self-existing and everlasting has no growth or decay; It is what It ever was, and ever shall be the same. As It originated in nothing else, nothing else can interfere with It or affect It. Besides, everything that is has originated in It; everything therefore is dependent on It, and It is independently of everything.

Contemplate then the Supreme Being, the Being of beings, even so far as I have yet described Him; fix the idea of Him in your minds. He is one; He has no rival; He has no equal; He is unlike anything else ; He is sovereign ; He can do what He will. He is unchangeable from first to last ; He is all-perfect ; He is infinite in His power and in His wisdom, or He could not have made this immense world which we see by day and by night.

Next, this follows from what I have said ;—that, since He is from everlasting, and has created all things from a certain beginning, He has lived in an eternity before He began to create anything. What a wonderful thought is this ! there was a state of things in which God was by Himself, and nothing else but He. There was no earth, no sky, no sun, no stars, no space, no time, no beings of any kind ; no men, no Angels, no Seraphim. His throne was without ministers ; He was not waited on by any ; all was silence, all was repose, there was nothing but God ; and this state continued, not for a while only, but for a measureless duration ; it was a state which had ever been ; it was the rule of things, and creation has been an innovation upon it. Creation is, comparatively speaking, but of yesterday ; it has lasted a poor six thousand years, say sixty thousand, if you will, or six million, or six million million ; what is this to eternity ? nothing at all ; not so much as a drop compared to the whole ocean, or a grain of sand to the whole earth. I say, through a whole eternity God was by Himself, with no other being but Himself ; with nothing external to Himself, not working, but at rest, not speaking, not receiving homage from any, not glorified in creatures, but blessed in Himself and by Himself, and wanting nothing.

What an idea this gives us of the Almighty! He is above us, my brethren, we feel He is; how little can we understand Him! We fall in even with men upon earth, whose ways are so different from our own, that we cannot understand them; we marvel at them; they pursue courses so unlike ours, they take recreations so peculiar to themselves, that we despair of finding anything in common between them and us; we cannot make conversation when we are with them. Thus stirring and ambitious men wonder at those who live among books; sinners wonder at those who attend the Sacraments and mortify their passions; thrifty persons wonder at those who are lavish of their money; men who love society wonder at those who live in solitude and are happy in it. We cannot enter even into our fellows; we call them strange and incomprehensible; but what are they, compared with the all-marvellousness of the Everlasting God? He alone indeed is incomprehensible, who has not only lived an eternity without beginning, but who has lived through a whole eternity by Himself, and has not wearied of the solitude. Which of us, or how few of us, could live a week in comfort by ourselves? You have heard, my brethren, of solitary confinement as a punishment assigned to criminals, and at length it becomes more severe than any other punishment: it is said at length to drive men mad. We cannot live without objects, without aims, without employments, without companions. We cannot live simply in ourselves; the mind preys upon itself, if left to itself. This is the case with us mortal men; now raise your minds to God. Oh, the vast contrast! He lived a whole eternity in that state, of which a few poor years to us is madness. He lived a whole eternity without change of any kind. Day and night, sleep and meal-time, at least are changes, unavoidable changes, in the life of the most solitary upon earth. A prison, if it has nothing else to relieve its dreariness and its hopelessness, has at least this, that the poor prisoner sleeps ; he sleeps, and suspends his misery ; he sleeps and recruits his power of bearing it ; but the Eternal is the Sleepless, He pauses not, He suspends not His powers, He is never tired of Himself; He is never wearied of His own infinity. He was from eternity ever in action, though ever at rest ; ever surely in rest and peace profound and ineffable, yet with a living, present mind, self-possessed, and all-conscious, comprehending Himself and sustaining the comprehension. He rested ever, but He rested in Himself ; His own resource, His own end, His own contemplation, His own blessedness.

Yes, so it was ; and if it is incomprehensible that He should have existed solitary through an eternity, is it not incomprehensible too, that He should have ever given up that solitariness, and have willed to surround Himself with creatures? Why was He not content to be as He had been? Why did He bring into existence those who could not add to His blessedness and were not secure of their own ? Why did He give them that gift which we see they possess, of doing right or wrong as they please, and of working out their ruin as well as their salvation? Why did He create a world like that which is before our eyes, which at best so dimly shows forth His glory, and at worst is a scene of sin and sorrow ? He might have made a far more excellent world than this ; He might have excluded sin ; but, oh, wonderful mystery, He has surrounded Himself with the cries of fallen souls, and has created and opened the great pit. He has willed, after an eternity of peace, to allow of everlasting anarchy, of pride, and blasphemy, and guilt and hatred of Himself, and the worm that dieth not. Thus He is simply incomprehensible to us, mortal men. Well might the ancient heathen shrink from answering, when a king, his patron, asked him what God was ! He begged for a day to consider his reply ; at the end of it, for two more ; and, when the two were ended, for four besides ; for in truth he found that meditation, instead of bringing him towards the solution of the problem, did but drive him back ; the more he questioned, the vaster grew the theme, and where he drew one conclusion, thence issued forth a hundred fresh difficulties to confound his reason. For in truth the being and attributes of God are a subject, not for reason simply, but for faith also ; and we must accept His own word about Himself.

And now proceed to another thought, my brethren, which I have partly implied and partly expressed already. If the Almighty Creator be such as I have described Him, He in no wise depends on His creatures. They sin, they perish, they are saved, they praise Him eternally ; but, though He loves all the creatures of His hand, though He visits all of them without ex-

ception with influences of His grace, so numerous and
so urgent, that not till the disclosures of the last day
shall we rightly conceive of them ; though He deigns
to be glorified in His Saints, though He is their all in
all, their continued life, and power, and blessedness,
still they are nothing to Him. They do not increase
His happiness if they are saved, or diminish it if they
are lost. I do not mean that He is at a distance from
them ; He does not so live in Himself as to abandon His
creation to the operation of laws which He has stamped
upon it. No ; He is everywhere a vigilant and active
Providence ; He is in every one of His creatures, and
in every one of their actions ; if He were not in them,
they would fall back into nothing. He is everywhere
on earth, and sees every crime committed, whether
under the sun or in the gloom of night ; He is even
the sustaining power of those who sin ; He is most
close to every, the most polluted soul ; He is in the
midst of the eternal prison ; but what I mean to say
is, that nothing touches Him, though He touches all
things. The sun's rays penetrate into the most hideous
recesses, yet keep their brightness and their perfection ;
and so the Almighty witnesses and suffers evil, yet
is not touched or tried by the creature's wilfulness,
pride, uncleanness, or unbelief. The lusts of earth
and the blasphemies of hell neither sully His purity
nor impair His majesty. If the whole world were to
plunge wilfully into the eternal gulf, the loss would be
theirs, not His. In the dread contest between good
and evil, whether the Church conquers at once, or is
oppressed for the time, and labours, whether she is

in persecution, or in triumph, or in peace, whether His enemies hold out or are routed, when the innocent sin, when the just are falling, when good Angels weep, when souls are hardened, He is one and the same. He is in His blessedness still, and not even the surface is ruffled of His everlasting rest. He neither hopes nor fears, nor desires, nor sorrows, nor repents. All around Him seems full of agitation and confusion, but in His eternal decrees and infallible foreknowledge there is nothing contingent, nothing uncertain, nothing which is not part of one vast plan, as fixed in its issue, and as unchangeable, as His own Essence.

Such is the great God, so all-sufficient, so all-blessed, so separate from creatures, so inscrutable, so unapproachable. Who can see Him? who can fathom Him? who can move Him? who can change Him? who can even speak of Him? He is all-holy, all-patient, all-peaceful, and all-true. He says and He does; He delays and He executes; He warns and He punishes; He punishes, He rewards, He forbears, He pardons, according to an eternal decree, without imperfection, without vacillation, without inconsistency.

And now that I have set before you, my brethren, in human language, some of the attributes of the Adorable God, perhaps you are tempted to complain that, instead of winning you to the All-glorious and All-good, I have but repelled you from Him. You are tempted to exclaim,—He is so far above us that the thought of Him does but frighten me; I cannot believe that He cares for me. I believe firmly that He is infinite perfection ; and I love that perfection, not so much indeed as I could wish, still in my measure I love it for its own sake, and I wish to love it above all things, and I well understand that there is no creature but must love it in his measure, unless he has fallen from grace. But there are two feelings, which, alas, I have a difficulty in entertaining ; I believe and I love, but without fervour, without keen-ness, because my heart is not kindled by hope, nor subdued and melted with gratitude. Hope and grati-tude I wish to have, and have not ; I know that He is loving towards all His works, but how am I to believe that He gives to me personally a thought, and cares for me for my own sake? I am beneath His love ; He looks on me as an atom in a vast universe. He acts by general laws, and if He is kind to me it is, not for my sake, but because it is according to His nature to be kind. And hence it is that I am drawn over to sinful man with an intenser affection than to my glorious Maker. Kings and great men upon earth, when they appear in public, are not content with a mere display of their splendour, they show themselves as well as their glories ; they look around them ; they notice individuals; they have a kind eye, or a cour-teous gesture, or an open hand, for all who come near them. They scatter among the crowd the largess of their smiles and of their words. And then men go home, and tell their friends, and treasure up to their latest day, how that so great a personage took notice of them, or of a child of theirs, or accepted a present at their hand, or gave expression to some sentiment, without point in itself, but precious as addressed to them. Thus does my fellow-man engage and win me; but there is a gulf between me and my great God. I shall fall back on myself, and grovel in my nothingness, till He looks down from heaven, till He calls me, till He takes interest in me. It is a want in my nature to have one who can weep with me, and rejoice with me, and in a way minister to me; and this would be presumption in me, and worse, to hope to find in the Infinite and Eternal God.

This is what you may be tempted to say, my brethren, not without impatience, while you contemplate the Almighty God, as conscience portrays Him, and as reason concludes about Him, and as creation witnesses of Him; and I have dwelt on it, in order, by way of contrast, to set before you, as I proposed when I began, how your complaint is answered in the great mystery of the Incarnation. Never suppose that you are left by God; never suppose that He does not know you, your minds and your powers, better than you do yourselves. Ought you not to trust Him, that, if your complaint be true, He has thought of it before you? "Before they call, I will attend," says He, "and while they speak, I will hear." Add this to your general notion of His incomprehensibility, viz., that though He is infinite, He can bow Himself to the finite; have faith in the mystery of His condescension; confess that, though He "inhabiteth eternity," He "dwelleth with a contrite and humble spirit," and "looketh down upon the lowly". Give up this fretfulness, quit these self-consuming thoughts, go out of yourselves, lift up your eyes, look around, and see if you can discern nothing more hopeful, more gracious in this wide world, than these perplexities over which you have been brooding. No, my brethren, we are so constituted by our Maker, as to be able to love Him ardently, and He has given us means of doing so. He has not founded our worship of Him in hope, nor made self-interest the measure of our veneration. And we have eyes to see much more than the difficulties of His Essence; and the great consolatory disclosures of Him, which Nature begins, Revelation brings to perfection. Lift up your eyes, I say, and look out even upon the material world, and there you will see one attribute above others on its very face which will reverse your sad meditations on Him who made it. He has traced out many of His attributes upon it, His immensity, His wisdom, His power, His loving-kindness, and His skill; but more than all, its very face is illuminated with the glory and beauty of His eternal excellence. This is that attribute in which all His attributes coalesce, which is the perfection, or (as I may say) the flower and bloom of their combination. As among men, youth, and health, and vigour, have their finish in that grace of outline, and lustre of complexion, and eloquence of expression, which we call beauty, so in the Almighty God, though we cannot comprehend His holy attributes, and shrink from their unfathomable profound, yet we can, as creatures, recognise and rejoice in the brightness, harmony, and serenity, which is their resulting excellence. This is that quality which, by the law of our nature, is ever able to draw us off ourselves in admiration, which moves our affections, which wins from us a disinterested homage ; and it is shed in profusion, in token of its Creator, over the visible world.

Leave, then, the prison of your own reasonings, leave the town, the work of man, the haunt of sin ; go forth, my brethren, far from the tents of Cedar and the slime of Babylon : with the patriarch go forth to meditate in the field, and from the splendours of the work imagine the unimaginable glory of the Architect. Mount some bold eminence, and look back, when the sun is high and full upon the earth, when mountains, cliffs, and sea rise up before you like a brilliant pageant, with outlines noble and graceful, and tints and shadows soft, clear, and harmonious, giving depth, and unity to the whole; and then go through the forest, or fruitful field, or along meadow and stream, and listen to the distant country sounds, and drink in the fragrant air which is poured around you in spring or summer ; or go among the gardens, and delight your senses with the grace and splendour, and the various sweetness of the flowers you find there ; then think of the almost mysterious influence upon the mind of particular scents, or the emotion which some gentle, peaceful strain excites in us, or how soul and body are rapt and carried away captive by the concord of musical sounds, when the ear is open to their power ; and then, when you have ranged through sights, and sounds, and odours, and your heart kindles, and your voice is full of praise and worship, reflect—

not that they tell you nothing of their Maker,—but that they are the poorest and dimmest glimmerings of His glory, and the very refuse of His exuberant riches, and but the dusky smoke which precedes the flame, compared with Him who made them. Such is the Creator in His Eternal Uncreated Beauty, that, were it given to us to behold it, we should die of very rapture at the sight. Moses, unable to forget the token of it he had once seen in the Bush, asked to see it fully, and on this very account was refused. " He said, Show me Thy glory ; and He said, Thou canst not see My Face ; for man shall not see Me and live." When saints have been favoured with glimpses of it, it has thrown them into ecstasy, broken their poor frames of dust and ashes, and pierced them through with such keen distress, that they have cried out to God, in the very midst of their transports, that He would hold His hand, and, in tenderness to them, check the abundance of His consolations. What saints partake in fact, we enjoy in thought and imagination ; and even that mere reflection of God's glory is sufficient to sweep away the gloomy, envious thoughts of Him, which circle round us, and to lead us to forget ourselves in the contemplation of the All-beautiful. He is so bright, so majestic, so serene, so harmonious, so pure ; He so surpasses, as being its archetype and fulness, all that is graceful, gentle, sweet, and fair on earth ; His voice is so touching, and His smile so winning while so awful, that we need nothing more than to gaze and listen, and be happy. Say not this is not enough for love and joy ; even in sights of this earth, the pomp and ceremonial of royalty is sufficient for the beholder ; he needs nothing more than to be allowed to see ; and were we but admitted to the courts of heaven, the sight of Him, ever transporting, ever new, though He addressed us not, would be our meat and drink to all eternity.

And if He has so constituted us, that, in spite of the abyss which lies between Him and us, in spite of the mystery of His attributes and the feebleness of our reason, the very vision of Him dispels all doubt, allures our shrinking souls, and is our everlasting joy, what shall we say, my brethren, when we are told that He has also condescended to take possession of us and to rule us by means of hope and gratitude, those "cords of Adam," by which one man is bound to another ? You say that God and man never can be one, that man cannot bear the sight and touch of his Creator, nor the Creator condescend to the feebleness of the creature ; but blush and be confounded to hear, O peevish, restless hearts, that He has come down from His high throne and humbled Himself to the creature, in order that the creature might be inspired and strengthened to rise to Him. It was not enough to give man grace ; it was little to impart to him a celestial light, and a sanctity such as Angels had received ; little to create Adam in original justice, with a heavenly nature superadded to his own, with an intellect which could know God and a soul which could love Him ; He purposed even in man's first state of innocence a higher mercy, which in the fulness of time was to be accomplished in his behalf. It became the

Wisdom of God, who is the eternally glorious and beautiful, to impress these attributes upon men by His very presence and personal indwelling in their flesh, that, as He was by nature the Only-begotten Image of the Father, so He might also become "the First-born of every creature". It became Him who is higher than the highest, to act as if even humility, if this dare be said, was in the number of His attributes, by taking Adam's nature upon Himself, and manifesting Himself to men and Angels in it. It became Him, of whom are all things, and who is in all things, not to create new natures, which had not been before, inconstant spirit and corruptible matter, without taking them to Himself and absorbing them into a personal union with God. And see, my brethren, when you complain that we men are cut off from God, see that He has done more for you than He has done for those "who are greater in strength and power". The Angels surpass us in their original nature ; they are immortal spirits, and we are subject to death ; they have been visited by larger measures of God's grace, and they serve in His heaven, and are blessed by the vision of His face ; yet "nowhere doth He take hold of the Angels" ; He turned aside from the eldest-born of creation, He chose the younger. He chose him in whom an immortal spirit was united to a frail and perishable body. He turned aside to him whom an irritable, wayward, dim-sighted, and passionate nature rendered less worthy of His love ; to him He turned ; He made "the first last, and the last first " ; " He raised the needy from the earth, and lifted the poor out of the mire," and bade Angels bow down in adoration to a material form, for it was His own.

Well, my brethren, your God has taken on Him your nature, and now prepare yourself to see in human flesh that glory and that beauty on which the Angels gaze. Since you are to see Emmanuel, since " the brilliancy of the Eternal Light and the unspotted mirror of God's majesty, and the Image of His goodness," is to walk the earth, since the Son of the Highest is to be born of woman, since the manifold attributes of the Infinite are to be poured out before your eyes through material channels and the operations of a human soul, since He, whose contemplation did but trouble you in Nature, is coming to take you captive by a manifestation, which is both intelligible to you and a pledge that He loves you one by one, raise high your expectations, for surely they cannot suffer disappointment. Doubtless, you will say, He will take a form such as " eye hath not seen, nor ear heard of " before. It will be a body framed in the heavens, and only committed to the custody of Mary ; a form of light and glory, worthy of Him, who is " blessed for evermore," and comes to bless us with His presence. Pomp and pride of men He may indeed despise ; we do not look for Him in kings' courts, or in the array of war, or in the philosophic school ; but doubtless He will choose some calm and holy spot, and men will go out thither and find their Incarnate God. He will be tenant of some paradise, like Adam or Elias, or He will dwell in the mystic garden of the Canticles, where nature ministers its best and purest to its Creator. "The fig-tree will put forth her green figs, the vines in flower yield their sweet smell;" "spikenard and saffron" will be there; "the sweet cane and cinnamon, myrrh and aloes, with all the chief perfumes;" "the glory of Libanus, the beauty of Carmel," before "the glory of the Lord and the beauty of our God". There will He show Himself at stated times, with Angels for His choristers and saints for His doorkeepers, to the poor and needy, to the humble and devout, to those who have kept their innocence undefiled, or have purged their sins away by long penance and masterful contrition.

Such would be the conjecture of man, at fault when he speculated on the height of God, and now again at fault when he tries to sound the depth. He thinks that a royal glory is the note of His presence upon earth; lift up your eyes, my brethren, and answer whether he has guessed aright. Oh, incomprehensible in eternity and in time! solitary in heaven, and solitary upon earth! "Who is this, that cometh from Edom, with dyed garments from Bozra? Why is Thy apparel red, and Thy garments like theirs that tread in the wine press?" It is because the Maker of man, the Wisdom of God, has come, not in strength, but in weakness. He has come, not to assert a claim, but to pay a debt. Instead of wealth, He has come poor; instead of honour, He has come in ignominy; instead of blessedness, He has come to suffer. He has been delivered over from His birth to pain and contempt; His delicate frame is worn down by cold and heat, by hunger and sleeplessness; His hands are rough and bruised with a mechanic's toil; His eyes are dimmed with weeping; His Name is cast out as evil. He is flung amid the throng of men; He wanders from place to place; He is the companion of sinners. He is followed by a mixed multitude, who care more for meat and drink than for His teaching, or by a city's populace which deserts Him in the day of trial. And at length " the Brightness of God's Glory and the Image of His Substance" is fettered, haled to and fro, buffeted, spit upon, mocked, cursed, scourged, and tortured. " He hath no beauty nor comeliness; He is despised and the most abject of men, a Man of sorrows and acquainted with infirmity; " nay, He is a "leper, and smitten of God, and afflicted". And so His clothes are torn off, and He is lifted up upon the bitter Cross, and there He hangs, a spectacle for profane, impure, and savage eyes, and a mockery for the evil spirit whom He had cast down into hell.

Oh, wayward man! discontented first that thy God is far from thee, discontented again when He has drawn near,—complaining first that He is high, complaining next that He is low!—unhumbled being, when wilt thou cease to make thyself thine own centre, and learn that God is infinite in all He does, infinite when He reigns in heaven, infinite when He serves on earth, exacting our homage in the midst of His Angels, and winning homage from us in the midst of sinners? Adorable He is in His eternal rest, adorable in the glory of His court, adorable in the beauty of His works, most adorable of all, most royal, most persuasive in His deformity. Think you not, my brethren, that to Mary, when she held Him in her maternal arms, when she gazed on the pale countenance and the dislocated limbs of her God, when she traced the wandering lines of blood, when she counted the weals, the bruises, and the wounds, which dishonoured that virginal flesh, think you not that to her eyes it was more beautiful than when she first worshipped it, pure, radiant, and fragrant, on the night of His nativity? *Dilectus meus candidus et rubicundus*, as the Church sings ; " My beloved is white and ruddy ; His whole form doth breathe of love, and doth provoke to love in turn ; His drooping head, His open palms, and His breast all bare. My beloved is white and ruddy, choice out of thousands ; His head is of the finest gold ; His locks are branches of palm-trees, black as a raven. His eyes as doves upon brooks of waters, which are washed with milk, and sit beside the plentiful streams. His cheeks are as beds of aromatical spices set by the perfumers ; His lips are lilies dropping choice myrrh. His hands are turned and golden, full of jacinths ; His throat is most sweet, and He is all lovely. Such is my beloved, and He is my friend, O ye daughters of Jerusalem."

So is it, O dear and gracious Lord, " the day of death is better than the day of birth, and better is the house of mourning than the house of feasting ". Better for me that Thou shouldst come thus abject and dishonourable, than hadst Thou put on a body fair as Adam's when he came out of Thy Hand. Thy glory sullied, Thy beauty marred, those five wounds welling out blood, those temples torn and raw, that broken heart, that crushed and livid frame, they teach me more, than wert Thou Solomon "in the diadem wherewith his mother crowned him in the day of his heart's joy". The gentle and tender expression of that Countenance is no new beauty, or created grace; it is but the manifestation, in a human form, of Attributes which have been from everlasting. Thou canst not change, O Jesus; and, as Thou art still Mystery, so wast Thou always Love. I cannot comprehend Thee more than I did, before I saw Thee on the Cross; but I have gained my lesson. I have before me the proof, that in spite of Thy awful nature, and the clouds and darkness which surround it, Thou canst think of me with a personal affection. Thou hast died, that I might live. "Let us love God," says Thy Apostle, "because He first hath loved us." I can love Thee now from first to last, though from first to last I cannot understand Thee. As I adore Thee, O Lover of souls, in Thy humiliation, so will I admire Thee and embrace Thee in Thy infinite and everlasting power.

DISCOURSE XV.

THE INFINITUDE OF THE DIVINE ATTRIBUTES.

WE all know well, and firmly hold, that our Lord Jesus Christ, the Son of God, died on the Cross in satisfaction for our sins. This truth is the great foundation of all our hopes, and the object of our most earnest faith and most loving worship. And yet, however well we know it, it is a subject which admits of drawing out, and insisting on in detail, in a way which most persons will feel profitable to themselves. I shall now attempt to do this in some measure, and to follow the reflections to which it leads ; though at this season* many words would be out of place.

Christ died for our sins, for the sins of the whole world ; but He need not have died, for the Almighty God might have saved us all, might have saved the whole world, without His dying. He might have pardoned and brought to heaven every individual child of Adam without the incarnation and death of His Son. He might have saved us without any ransom and without any delay. He might have abolished original sin, and restored Adam at once. His word had been enough ; with Him to say is to do. " All things are

---

* Passion-tide.

possible to Thee," was the very reason our Lord gave in His agony for asking that the chalice might pass from Him. As in the beginning He said, "Let light be, and light was"; so might He have spoken again, and sin would have vanished from the soul, and guilt with it. Or He might have employed a mediator less powerful than His own Son; He might have accepted the imperfect satisfaction of some mere man. He wants not for resources; but He willed otherwise. He who ever does the best, saw in His infinite wisdom that it was expedient and fitting to take a ransom. As He has not hindered the reprobate from resisting His grace and rejecting redemption, so He has not pardoned any who are to enter His eternal kingdom, without a true and sufficient satisfaction for their sin. Both in the one case and the other, He has done, not what was possible merely, but what was best. And this is why the coming of the Word was necessary; for if a true satisfaction was to be made, then nothing could accomplish this, short of the incarnation of the All-holy.

You see, then, my brethren, how voluntary was the mission and death of our Lord; if an instance can be imagined of voluntary suffering, it is this. He came to die when He need not have died; He died to satisfy for what might have been pardoned without satisfaction; He paid a price which need not have been asked, nay, which needed to be accepted * when paid. It may be said with truth, that, rigorously speaking, one

---

* Dicendum videtur satisfactionem Christi, licet fuerit rigorosa quoad æqualitatem et condignitatem pretii soluti, non tamen fuisse

being can never, by his own suffering, simply discharge the debt of another's sin.* Accordingly, He
died, not in order to exert a peremptory claim on the
Divine justice, if I may so speak,—as if He were bar-
gaining in the market-place, or pursuing a plea in a
court of law,—but in a more loving, generous, muni-
ficent way, did He shed that blood, which was worth ten
thousand lives of men, worth more than the blood of
all the sons of Adam poured out together, in accordance with His Father's will, who, for wise reasons
unrevealed, exacted it as the condition of their pardon.

Nor was this all ;—one drop of His blood had been
sufficient to satisfy for our sins; He might have
offered His circumcision as an atonement, and it would
have been sufficient ; one moment of His agony of
blood had been sufficient, one stroke of the scourge
might have wrought a sufficient satisfaction. But
neither circumcision, agony, nor scourging was our
redemption, because He did not offer them as such.

rigorosam quoad modum solutionis, sed indiguisse aliquâ *gratiâ
liberâ* Dei. . . . Si aliquis ita peccavit, ut justè puniatur exilio
unius mensis, et velit redimere pecuniâ illud exilium, offeratque
summam æquivalentem, immo excedentem, non dubium quin satisfiat rigori justitiæ vindicativæ, si attendas ad mensuram pœnæ ;
non tamen satisfit, si attendas ad modum ; si enim judex *gratiosè*
non admittat illam compensationem, *jus habet* ex rigore justitiæ
punitivæ ad exigendum exilium, quantumvis alia æqualis et longè
major pœna offeratur.—De Lug. Incarn. iii. 10.

* Qui redemit captivum solvendo pretium, solvit quantum domino
debetur ex justitiâ, solum enim debetur illi pretium ex contractu
et conventione inter ipsum et redemptorem. . . . Nullum est justitiæ debitum cui non satisfiat per solutionem illius pretii. At vero
pro *injuriâ* non solum debetur ex justitiâ satisfactio utcunque, sed
exhibenda ab ipso effensore . . . sicut nec qui abstulit librum,
satisfacit adæquatè reddendo pretium æquivalens.—Ibid. iv. 2.

The price He paid was nothing short of the whole treasure of His blood, poured forth to the last drop from His veins and sacred heart. He shed His whole life for us; He left Himself empty of His all. He left His throne on high; He gave up His home on earth; He parted with His Mother, He gave His strength and His toil, He gave His body and soul, He offered up His passion, His crucifixion, and His death, that man should not be bought for nothing. This is what the apostle intimates in saying that we are "bought with a *great* price"; and the prophet, while he declares that "with the Lord there is mercy, and with Him a *copious*" or "plenteous redemption".

This is what I wished to draw out distinctly, my brethren, for your devout meditation. We might have been pardoned without the humiliation of the Eternal Word; again, we might have been redeemed by one single drop of His blood; but still on earth He came, and a death He died, a death of inconceivable suffering; and all this He did as a free offering to His Father, not as forcing His acceptance of it. From beginning to the end it was in the highest sense a voluntary work; and this is what is so overpowering to the mind in the thought of it. It is as if He delighted in having to suffer; as if He wished to show all creatures, what would otherwise have seemed impossible, that the Creator could practise, in the midst of His heavenly blessedness, the virtues of a creature, self-abasement and humility. It is, as if He wished, all-glorious as He was from all eternity, as a sort of addition (if we may so speak) to His perfections, to submit to a creature's condition in its most afflictive form. It is, if we may use human language, a prodigality of charity, or that heroic love of toil and hardship, which is poorly shadowed out in the romantic defenders of the innocent or the oppressed, whom we read of in history or in fable, who have gone about the earth, nobly exposing themselves to peril for any who asked their aid.

Or, rather, and that is what I wish to insist upon, it suggests to us, as by a specimen, the infinitude of God. We all confess that He is infinite; He has an infinite number of perfections, and He is infinite in each of them. This we shall confess at once; but, we ask, what is infinity? what is meant by saying He is infinite? We seem to wish to be told, as if we had nothing given us to throw light on the question. Why, my brethren, we have much given us; the outward exhibition of infinitude is mystery; and the mysteries of nature and of grace are nothing else than the mode in which His infinitude encounters us and is brought home to our minds. Men confess that He is infinite, yet they start and object, as soon as His infinitude comes in contact with their imagination and acts upon their reason. They cannot bear the fulness, the superabundance, the inexhaustible flowing forth, and "vehement rushing,"* and encompassing flood of the Divine attributes. They restrain and limit them to their own comprehension, they measure them by their own standard, they fashion

* Tanquam advenientis spiritûs vehementis.

them by their own model: and when they discern aught of the unfathomable depth, the immensity, of any single excellence or perfection of the Divine Nature, His love or His justice, or His power, they are at once offended, and turn away, and refuse to believe.

Now this instance of our Lord's humiliation is a case in point. What would be profusion and extravagance in man, is but suitable or necessary, if I may say so, in Him whose resources are illimitable. We read in history accounts of oriental munificence, which sound like fiction, and which would gain, not applause, but contempt in Europe, where wealth is not concentrated, as in the East, upon a few out of a whole people. "Royal munificence" has become a proverb, from the idea that a king's treasures are such, as to make the giving of large presents and bounties, not allowable only, but appropriate in him. He, then, who is infinite, may be only doing what is best, and holiest, and wisest, in doing what to man seems infinitely to exceed the necessity; for He cannot exceed His own powers or resources. Man has limited means and definite duties; it would be waste in him to lavish a thousand pieces of gold on one poor man, when with the same he might have done substantial good to many; but God is as rich, as He is profound and vast, as infinite, after He has done a work of infinite bounty, as before He set about it. "Knowest thou not," He says, or "hast thou not heard? the Lord is the Everlasting God, who has created the ends of the earth; He shall not faint, nor weary; nor is there any searching out of His wisdom." He cannot do a small work ; He cannot act by halves ; He ever does whole works, great works. Had Christ been incarnate for one single soul, who ought to have been surprised? who ought not to have praised and blessed Him for telling us in one instance, and by a specimen, what that love and bounty are which fill the heavens? and in like manner, when in fact He has taken flesh for those, who might have been saved without it, though more suitably to His glorious majesty with it, and moreover has shed His whole blood in satisfaction, when a drop might have sufficed, shall we think such teaching strange and hard to receive, and not rather consider it consistent and merely consistent, with that great truth, which we all start with admitting, that He is infinite? Surely it would be most irrational in us, to admit His infinitude in the general, and to reject the examples of. it in particular; to maintain that He is mystery, yet to deny that His acts can be mysterious.

We must not, then, bring in our economical theories, borrowed from the schools of the day, when we would reason about the Eternal God. The world is ever doing so, when it speaks of religion. It will not allow the miracles of the saints, because it pretends that those wrought by the apostles were sufficient for the purpose which miracles had, or ought forsooth to have, in view. I wonder how the world comes to admit that such multitudes of human beings are born and die in infancy; or that a profusion of seeds is cast over the face of the earth, some of which fall by the way-side, some on the rock, some among thorns, and only a remnant on the good ground. How wasteful was that sower! so thinks the world, but an apostle cries out, "Oh, the depth of the riches of the wisdom and of the knowledge of God! how incomprehensible are His judgments, and how unsearchable His ways!"

The world judges of God's condescension as it judges of His bounty. We know from Scripture that "the teaching of the Cross" was in the beginning "foolishness" to it; grave, thinking men scoffed at it as impossible, that God, who is so high, should humble Himself so low, and that One who died a malefactor's death should be worshipped on the very instrument of His punishment. Voluntary humiliation they did not understand then, nor do they now. They do not indeed express their repugnance to the doctrine so openly now, because what is called public opinion does not allow them; but you see what they really think of Christ, by the tone which they adopt towards those who in their measure follow Him. Those who are partakers of His fulness are called on, according as the gift is given them, whether by His ordinary suggestions or by particular inspiration, to imitate His pattern; they are carried on to the sacrifice of self, and thus they come into collision with the maxims of the world. A voluntary or gratuitous mortification in one shape or another, voluntary chastity, voluntary poverty, voluntary obedience, vows of perfection, all this is the very point of contest between the world and the Church, the world hating it, and the Church counselling it. "Why cannot they stop with me?"

says the world; "why will they give up their station
or position, when it is certain they might be saved
where they are? Here is a lady of birth; she might
be useful at home, she might marry well, she might
be an ornament to society, she might give her countenance to religious objects, and she has perversely
left us all; she has cut off her hair, and put on a coarse
garment, and is washing the feet of the poor. There
is a man of name and ability, who has thrown himself
out of his sphere of influence and secular position, and
he chooses a place where no one knows his worth; and
he is teaching little children their catechism." The
world is touched with pity, and shame, and indignation at the sight, and moralises over persons who act
so unworthily of their birth or education, and are so
cruel towards themselves. And worse still, "here is a
saint, and what must he do but practise eccentricities?"
—as they really would be in others, though in him they
are but the necessary antagonists to the temptations
which otherwise would come on him from "the greatness of the revelations," or are but tokens of the love
with which he embraces the feet of His Redeemer.
And "here again is another, and she submits her flesh
to penances shocking to think of, and wearies herself
out in the search after misery, and all from some notion
that she is assimilating her condition to the voluntary
self-abasement of the Word". Alas, for the world!
which is simply forgetful that God is great in all He
does, great in His sufferings, and that He makes
saints and holy men in their degree partakers of that
greatness.

Here, too, is another instance in point. If there is one Divine attribute rather than another, which forces itself upon the mind from the contemplation of the material world, it is the glory, harmony, and beauty of its Creator. This lies on the surface of the creation, like light on a countenance, and addresses itself to all. To few men indeed is it given to penetrate into the world's system and order so deeply, as to perceive, in addition, the wonderful skill and goodness of the Divine Artificer; but the grace and loveliness which beam from the very face of the visible creation are cognisable by all, rich and poor, learned and ignorant. It is indeed so beautiful, that those same philosophers, who devote themselves to its investigation, come to love it idolatrously, and to think it too perfect for them to allow of its infringement or alteration, or to tolerate even that idea. Not looking up to the Infinite Creator, who could make a thousand fairer worlds, and who has made the fairest portion of this the most perishable— blooming, as it does, to-day, and to-morrow is cast into the oven—loving, I say, the creature more than the Creator, they have taken on them in all ages to dis- believe the possibility of interruptions of physical order, and have denied the miracles of Revelation. They have denied the miracles of apostles and prophets, on the ground of their marring and spoiling what is so perfect and harmonious, as if the visible world were some work of human art, too exquisite to be wantonly dashed on the ground. But He, my brethren, the Eternal Maker of time and space, of matter and sense, as if to pour contempt upon the forward and minute speculations of

His ignorant creatures about His works and His will, in order to a fuller and richer harmony, and a higher and nobler order, confuses the laws of this physical universe and untunes the music of the spheres. Nay, He has done more, He has gone further still ; out of the infinitude of His greatness, He has defaced His own glory, and wounded and deformed His own beauty —not indeed as it is in itself, for He is ever the same, transcendently perfect and unchangeable, but in the contemplation of His creatures,—by the unutterable condescension of His incarnation.

Semetipsum exinanivit, " He made Himself void or empty," as the earth had been " void and empty " at the beginning ; He seemed to be unbinding and letting loose the assemblage of attributes which made Him God, and to be destroying the idea which He Himself had implanted in our minds. The God of miracles did the most awful of signs and wonders, by revoking and contradicting, as it were, all His perfections, though He remained the while one and the same. Omnipotence became an abject ; the Life became a leper ; the first and only Fair came down to us with an " inglorious visage," and an "unsightly form," bleeding and (I may say) ghastly, lifted up in nakedness and stretched out in dislocation before the eyes of sinners. Not content with this, He perpetuates the history of His humiliation ; men of this world, when they fall into trouble, and then recover themselves, hide the memorials of it. They conceal their misfortunes in prospect, as long as they can ; bear them perforce, when they fall into them ; and, when they have overcome them, affect to make light of them. Kings of the earth, when they have rid themselves of their temporary conquerors, and are reinstated on their thrones, put all things back into their former state, and remove from their palaces, council-rooms, and cities, whether statue or picture or inscription or edict, all of which bear witness to the suspension of their power. Soldiers indeed boast of their scars, but it is because their foes were well-matched with them, and their conflicts were necessary, and the marks of what they have suffered is a proof of what they have done ; but He, who *oblatus est, quia voluit,* who " was offered, for He willed it," who exposed Himself to the powers of evil, yet could have saved us without that exposure, who was neither weak in that He was overcome, nor strong in that He overcame, proclaims to the whole world what He has gone through, without the tyrant's shame, without the soldier's pride—He (wonderful it is) has raised up on high, He has planted over the earth, the memorial, that that Evil One whom He cast out of heaven in the beginning, has in the hour of darkness inflicted agony upon Him. For in truth, by consequence of the infinitude of His glory, He is more beautiful in His weakness than in His strength ; His wounds shine like stars of light ; His very Cross becomes an object of worship ; the instruments of His passion, the nails and the thorny crown, are replete with miraculous power. And so He bids the commemoration of His Bloody Sacrifice to be made day by day all over the earth, and He Himself is there

in Person to quicken and sanctify it; He rears His
bitter but saving Cross in every Church and over
every Altar; He shows Himself torn and bleeding
upon the wood at the corners of each street and in
every village market-place; He makes it the symbol
of His religion; He seals our foreheads, our lips, and
our breast with this triumphant sign; with it He
begins and ends our days, and with it He consigns
us to the tomb. And when He comes again, that
Sign of the Son of Man will be seen in heaven; and
when He takes His seat in judgment, the same
glorious marks will be seen by all the world in His
Hands, Feet, and Side, which were dug into them at
the season of His degradation. Thus "hath King
Solomon made himself a litter of the wood of Libanus.
The pillars thereof he made of silver, the seat of gold,
the going up of purple; the midst he covered with
charity for the daughters of Jerusalem. Go forth,
ye daughters of Sion; and see King Solomon in the
diadem, wherewith his mother crowned him in the
day of his espousals, and in the day of his heart's joy."

I must not conclude this train of thought, without
alluding to a sterner subject, on which it seems to
throw some light. There is a class of doctrines
which to the natural man are an especial offence and
difficulty; I mean those connected with the Divine
judgments. Why has the Almighty assigned an
endless punishment to the impenitent sinner? Why
is it that vengeance has its hold on him when he
passes out of this life, and there is no remedy? Why,
again, is it that even the beloved children of God,

those holy souls who leave this life in His grace and in His favour, are not at once admitted to His face ; but, if there be an outstanding debt against them, first enter purgatory and liquidate it? Men of the world shrink from a doctrine like this as impossible, and religious men answer that it is a mystery ; and a mystery it is,—that is, it is but another of those instances which Nature and Revelation bring before us of the Divine Infinitude ; it is but one of the many overpowering manifestations of the Almighty, when He acts, which remind us, which are intended to remind us, that He is infinite, and above and beyond human measure and understanding,—which lead us to bow the head and adore Him, as Moses did, when He passed by, and with him awfully to proclaim His Name, as " the Lord God, who hath dominion, keeping mercy for thousands, and returning the iniquity of the fathers upon the children and children's children to the third and fourth generation ".

Thus the attributes of God, though intelligible to us on their surface,—for from our own sense of mercy and holiness and patience and consistency, we have general notions of the All-merciful and All-holy and All-patient, and of all that is proper to His Essence,— yet, for the very reason that they are infinite, transcend our comprehension, when they are dwelt upon, when they are followed out, and can only be received by faith. They are dimly shadowed out, in this very respect, by the great agents which He has created in the material world. What is so ordinary and familiar to us as the elements, what so simple and level to us, as their presence and operation? yet how their character changes, and how they overmaster us, and triumph over us, when they come upon us in their fulness! The invisible air, how gentle is it, and intimately ours! we breathe it momentarily, nor could we live without it; it fans our cheek, and flows around us, and we move through it without effort, while it obediently recedes at every step we take, and obsequiously pursues us as we go forward. Yet let it come in its power, and that same silent fluid, which was just now the servant of our necessity or caprice, takes us up on its wings with the invisible power of an Angel, and carries us forth into the regions of space, and flings us down headlong upon the earth. Or go to the spring, and draw thence at your pleasure, for your cup or your pitcher, in supply of your wants; you have a ready servant, a domestic ever at hand, in large quantity or in small, to satisfy your thirst, or to purify you from the dust and mire of the world. But go from home, reach the coast; and you will see that same humble element transformed before your eyes. You were equal to it in its condescension, but who shall gaze without astonishment at its vast expanse in the bosom of the ocean? who shall hear without awe the dashing of its mighty billows along the beach? who shall without terror feel it heaving under him, and swelling and mounting up, and yawning wide, till he, its very sport and mockery, is thrown to and fro, hither and thither, at the mere mercy of a power which was just now his companion and almost his slave? Or, again, approach the flame: it warms you, and it enlightens you ; yet approach not too near, presume not, or it will change its nature. That very element which is so beautiful to look at, so brilliant in its character, so graceful in its figure, so soft and lambent in its motion, will be found in its essence to be of a keen, resistless nature ; it tortures, it consumes, it reduces to ashes that of which it was just before the illumination and the life. So it is with the attributes of God; our knowledge of them serves us for our daily welfare ; they give us light and warmth and food and guidance and succour ; but go forth with Moses upon the mount and let the Lord pass by, or with Elias stand in the desert amid the wind, the earthquake, and the fire, and all is mystery and darkness; all is but a whirling of the reason, and a dazzling of the imagination, and an overwhelming of the feelings, reminding us that we are but mortal men and He is God, and that the outlines which Nature draws for us are not His perfect image, nor to be pronounced inconsistent with those further lights and depths with which it is invested by Revelation.

Say not, my brethren, that these thoughts are too austere for this season, when we contemplate the self-sacrificing, self-consuming charity wherewith God our Saviour has visited us. It is for that very reason that I dwell on them; the higher He is, and the more mysterious, so much the more glorious and the more subduing is the history of His humiliation. I own it, my brethren, I love to dwell on Him as the Only-begotten Word ; nor is it any forgetfulness of His sacred humanity to contemplate His Eternal Person.

It is the very idea, that He is God, which gives a meaning to His sufferings; what is to me a man, and nothing more, in agony, or scourged, or crucified? there are many holy martyrs, and their torments were terrible. But here I see One dropping blood, gashed by the thong, and stretched upon the Cross, and He is God. It is no tale of human woe which I am reading here; it is the record of the passion of the great Creator. The Word and Wisdom of the Father, who dwelt in His bosom in bliss ineffable from all eternity, whose very smile has shed radiance and grace over the whole creation, whose traces I see in the starry heavens and on the green earth, this glorious living God, it is He who looks at me so piteously, so tenderly from the Cross. He seems to say,—I cannot move, though I am omnipotent, for sin has bound Me here. I had had it in mind to come on earth among innocent creatures,* more fair and lovely than them all, with a face more

---

* " An ex vi præsentis Decreti, an saltem ex vi alterius, Adamo non peccante, adhuc futura fuisset Incarnatio, Thomistæ, Vasquez, Amicus, utrumque negant, putantes Christum unicè venisse ad nos redimendos. Contra, Scotistæ docent Redemptionem non fuisse unicum et adæquatum Incarnationis motivum, sed etiam ipsam Christi excellentiam et exaltationem naturæ humanæ; atque adeo, Adamo non peccante, Verbum incarnandum fuisse . . . ad exaltandam naturam humanam innocentem.

" Suarez vero docet, motivum incarnationis esse manifestationem divinæ gloriæ perfectissimo modo; . . . idcirco, Adamo peccante, Verbum incarnatum fuit in carne passibili ad satisfaciendum; Adamo vero non peccante, Verbum incarnatum fuisset in carne impassibili ad exaltandam naturam humanam innocentem. . . .

" Dico ex vi præsentis *Decreti*, Adamo non peccante, Verbum fuisse incarnatum. . . . Angelicus censet sententiam nostram probabilem, quamvis probabiliorem putet oppositam."—*Viva Curs. Theolog. de Incar. Disp. iii. Qu. i. p.* 74.

radiant than the Seraphim, and a form as royal as that of Archangels, to be their equal yet their God, to fill them with My grace, to receive their worship, to enjoy their company, and to prepare them for the heaven to which I destined them; but, before I carried My purpose into effect, they sinned, and lost their inheritance; and so I come indeed, but come, not in that brightness in which I went forth to create the morning stars and to fill the sons of God with melody, but in deformity and in shame, in sighs and tears, with blood upon My cheek, and with My limbs laid bare and rent. Gaze on Me, O My children, if you will, for I am helpless; gaze on your Maker, whether in contempt, or in faith and love. Here I wait, upon the Cross, the appointed time, the time of grace and mercy; here I wait till the end of the world, silent and motionless, for the conversion of the sinful and the consolation of the just; here I remain in weakness and shame, though I am so great in heaven, till the end, patiently expecting My full catalogue of souls, who, when time is at length over, shall be the reward of My passion and the triumph of My grace to all eternity.

DISCOURSE XVI.

MENTAL SUFFERINGS OF OUR LORD IN HIS PASSION.

EVERY passage in the history of our Lord and
Saviour is of unfathomable depth, and affords
inexhaustible matter of contemplation.   All that concerns Him is infinite, and what we first discern is but
the surface of that which begins and ends in eternity.
It would be presumptuous for any one short of saints
and doctors to attempt to comment on His words and
deeds, except in the way of meditation; but meditation
and mental prayer are so much a duty in all who wish
to cherish true faith and love towards Him, that it
may be allowed us, my brethren, under the guidance
of holy men who have gone before us, to dwell and
enlarge upon what otherwise would more fitly be
adored than scrutinised.   And certain times of the
year, this especially,* call upon us to consider, as
closely and minutely as we can, even the more sacred
portions of the Gospel history.   I would rather be
thought feeble or officious in my treatment of them,
than wanting to the Season; and so I now proceed
because the religious usage of the Church requires it,

* Passion-tide.

and though any individual preacher may well shrink from it, to direct your thoughts to a subject, especially suitable now, and about which many of us perhaps think very little, the sufferings which our Lord endured in His innocent and sinless soul.

You know, my brethren, that our Lord and Saviour, though He was God, was also perfect man ; and hence He had not only a body, but a soul likewise, such as ours, though pure from all stain of evil. He did not take a body without a soul, God forbid! for that would not have been to become man. How would He have sanctified our nature by taking a nature which was not ours ? Man without a soul is on a level with the beasts of the field ; but our Lord came to save a race capable of praising and obeying Him, possessed of immortality, though that immortality had lost its promised blessedness. Man was created in the image of God, and that image is in his soul; when then his Maker, by an unspeakable condescension, came in his nature, He took on Himself a soul in order to take on Him a body ; He took on Him a soul as the means of His union with a body ; He took on Him in the first place the soul, then the body of man, both at once, but in this order, the soul and the body; He Himself created the soul which He took on Himself, while He took His body from the flesh of the Blessed Virgin, His Mother. Thus He became perfect man with body and soul ; and as He took on Him a body of flesh and nerves, which admitted of wounds and death, and was capable of suffering, so did He take a soul, too, which was susceptible of that suffering, and moreover was susceptible of the pain and sorrow which are proper to a human soul; and, as His atoning passion was undergone in the body, so it was undergone in the soul also.

As the solemn days proceed, we shall be especially called on, my brethren, to consider His sufferings in the body, His seizure, His forced journeyings to and fro, His blows and wounds, His scourging, the crown of thorns, the nails, the Cross. They are all summed up in the Crucifix itself, as it meets our eyes; they are represented all at once on His sacred flesh, as it hangs up before us—and meditation is made easy by the spectacle. It is otherwise with the sufferings of His soul; they cannot be painted for us, nor can they even be duly investigated: they are beyond both sense and thought; and yet they anticipated His bodily sufferings. The agony, a pain of the soul, not of the body, was the first act of His tremendous sacrifice; "My soul is sorrowful even unto death," He said; nay; if He suffered in the body, it really was in the soul, for the body did but convey the infliction on to that which was the true recipient and seat of the suffering.

This it is very much to the purpose to insist upon; I say, it was not the body that suffered, but the soul in the body; it was the soul and not the body which was the seat of the suffering of the Eternal Word. Consider, then, there is no real pain, though there may be apparent suffering, when there is no kind of inward sensibility or spirit to be the seat of it. A tree, for instance, has life, organs, growth, and decay; it may be wounded and injured ; it droops, and is killed; but it does not suffer, because it has no mind or sensible principle within it.   But wherever this gift of an immaterial principle is found, there pain is possible, and greater pain according to the quality of the gift. Had we no spirit of any kind, we should feel as little as a tree feels ; had we no soul, we should not feel pain more acutely than a brute feels it ; but, being men, we feel pain in a way in which none but those who have souls can feel it.

Living beings, I say, feel more or less according to the spirit which is in them ; brutes feel far less than man, because they cannot reflect on what they feel ; they have no advertence or direct consciousness of their sufferings.   This it is that makes pain so trying, viz., that we cannot help thinking of it, while we suffer it.   It is before us, it possesses the mind, it keeps our thoughts fixed upon it.   Whatever draws the mind off the thought of it lessens it; hence friends try to amuse us when we are in pain, for amusement is a diversion.   If the pain is slight, they sometimes succeed with us ; and then we are, so to say, without pain, even while we suffer.   And hence it continually happens that in violent exercise or labour, men meet with blows or cuts, so considerable and so durable in their effect, as to bear witness to the suffering which must have attended their infliction, of which nevertheless they recollect nothing.   And in quarrels and in battles wounds are received which, from the excitement of the moment, are brought home to the consciousness of the combatant, not by the pain at the time of receiving them, but by the loss of blood that follows.

I will show you presently, my brethren, how I mean to apply what I have said to the consideration of our Lord's sufferings ; first I will make another remark. Consider, then, that hardly any one stroke of pain is intolerable ; it is intolerable when it continues. You cry out perhaps that you cannot bear more ; patients feel as if they could stop the surgeon's hand, simply because he continues to pain them. Their feeling is that they have borne *as much* as they can bear ; as if the continuance and not the intenseness was what made it too much for them. What does this mean, but that the memory of the foregoing moments of pain acts upon and (as it were) edges the pain that succeeds ? If the third or fourth or twentieth moment of pain could be taken by itself, if the succession of the moments that preceded it could be forgotten, it would be no more than the first moment, as bearable as the first (taking away the shock which accompanies the first); but what makes it unbearable is, that it *is* the twentieth ; that the first, the second, the third, on to the nineteenth moment of pain, are all concentrated in the twentieth ; so that every additional moment of pain has all the force, the ever-increasing force, of all that has preceded it. Hence, I repeat, it is that brute animals would seem to feel so little pain, because, that is, they have not the power of reflection or of consciousness. They do not know they exist ; they do not contemplate themselves ; they do not look backwards or forwards ; every moment as it succeeds is their all ; they wander over the face of the earth, and see this thing and that, and feel pleasure and pain, but still they take everything as it comes, and then let it go again, as men do in dreams. They have memory, but not the memory of an intellectual being ; they put together nothing, they make nothing properly one and individual to themselves out of the particular sensations which they receive ; nothing is to them a reality, or has a substance, beyond those sensations ; they are but sensible of a number of successive impressions. And hence, as their other feelings, so their feeling of pain is but faint and dull, in spite of their outward manifestations of it. It is the intellectual comprehension of pain, as a whole diffused through successive moments, which gives it its special power and keenness, and it is the soul only, which a brute has not, which is capable of that comprehension.

Now apply this to the sufferings of our Lord ;—do you recollect their offering Him wine mingled with myrrh, when He was on the point of being crucified ? He would not drink of it ; why ? because such a portion would have stupefied His mind, and He was bent on bearing the pain in all its bitterness. You see from this, my brethren, the character of His sufferings ; He would have fain escaped them, had that been His Father's will ; "If it be possible," He said, " let this chalice pass from Me;" but since it was not possible, He says calmly and decidedly to the Apostle, who would have rescued Him from suffering, "The chalice which My Father hath given Me, shall I not drink it?" If He was to suffer, He gave Himself to suffering; He did not come to suffer as little as He could; He did not turn away His face from the suffering; He confronted it, or, as I may say, He breasted it, that every particular portion of it might make its due impression on Him. And as men are superior to brute animals, and are affected by pain more than they, by reason of the mind within them, which gives a substance to pain, such as it cannot have in the instance of brutes; so, in like manner, our Lord felt pain of the body, with an advertence and a consciousness, and therefore with a keenness and intensity, and with a unity of perception, which none of us can possibly fathom or compass, because His soul was so absolutely in His power, so simply free from the influence of distractions, so fully directed *upon* the pain, so utterly surrendered, so simply subjected to the suffering. And thus He may truly be said to have suffered the whole of His passion in every moment of it.

Recollect that our Blessed Lord was in this respect different from us, that, though He was perfect man, yet there was a power in Him greater than His soul, which ruled His soul, for He was God. The soul of other men is subjected to its own wishes, feelings, impulses, passions, perturbations; His soul was subjected simply to His Eternal and Divine Personality. Nothing happened to His soul by chance, or on a sudden; He never was taken by surprise; nothing affected Him without His willing beforehand that it should affect Him. Never did He sorrow, or fear, or desire, or rejoice in spirit, but He first willed to be sorrowful, or afraid, or desirous, or joyful.   When we suffer, it is because outward agents and the uncontrollable emotions of our minds bring suffering upon us. We are brought under the discipline of pain involuntarily, we suffer from it more or less acutely according to accidental circumstances, we find our patience more or less tried by it according to our state of mind, and we do our best to provide alleviations or remedies of it.   We cannot anticipate beforehand how much of it will come upon us, or how far we shall be able to sustain it; nor can we say afterwards why we have felt just what we have felt, or why we did not bear the suffering better.   It was otherwise with our Lord. His Divine Person was not subject, could not be exposed, to the influence of His own human affections and feelings, except so far as He chose.   I repeat, when He chose to fear, He feared; when He chose to be angry, He was angry; when He chose to grieve, He was grieved.   He was not open to emotion, but He opened upon Himself voluntarily the impulse by which He was moved.   Consequently, when He determined to suffer the pain of His vicarious passion, whatever He did, He did, as the Wise Man says, *instanter*, "earnestly," with His might; He did not do it by halves; He did not turn away His mind from the suffering as we do—(how should He, who came to suffer, who could not have suffered but of His own act?) no, He did not say and unsay, do and undo; He said and He did; He said, "Lo, I come to do Thy will, O God; sacrifice and offering Thou wouldest not, but a body hast Thou fitted to Me".   He took a body in order that He might suffer; He became man, that He might suffer as man; and when His hour was come, that hour of Satan and of darkness, the hour when sin was to pour its full malignity upon Him, it followed that He offered Himself wholly, a holocaust, a whole burnt-offering;—as the whole of His body, stretched out upon the Cross, so the whole of His soul, His whole advertence, His whole consciousness, a mind awake, a sense acute, a living co-operation, a present, absolute intention, not a virtual permission, not a heartless submission, this did He present to His tormentors. His passion was an action; He lived most energetically, while He lay languishing, fainting, and dying. Nor did He die, except by an act of the will; for He bowed His head, in command as well as in resignation, and said, " Father, into Thy hands I commend My Spirit;" He gave the word, He surrendered His soul, He did not lose it.

Thus you see, my brethren, had our Lord only suffered in the body, and in it not so much as other men, still as regards the pain, He would have really suffered indefinitely more, because pain is to be measured by the power of realising it. God was the sufferer; God suffered in His human nature; the sufferings belonged to God, and were drunk up, were drained out to the bottom of the chalice, because God drank them; not tasted or sipped, not flavoured, disguised by human medicaments, as man disposes of the cup of anguish. And what I have been saying will further serve to answer an objection, which I shall proceed to notice, and which perhaps exists latently in the minds of many, and leads them to overlook the part which our Lord's soul had in His gracious satisfaction for sin.

Our Lord said, when His agony was commencing, "My soul is sorrowful unto death"; now you may ask, my brethren, whether He had not certain consolations peculiar to Himself, impossible in any other, which diminished or impeded the distress of His soul, and caused Him to feel, not more, but less than an ordinary man. For instance, He had a sense of innocence which no other sufferer could have; even His persecutors, even the false apostle who betrayed Him, the judge who sentenced Him, and the soldiers who conducted the execution, testified His innocence. "I have condemned the innocent blood," said Judas; "I am clear from the blood of this just Person," said Pilate; "Truly this was a just Man," cried the centurion. And if even they, sinners, bore witness to His sinlessness, how much more did His own soul! And we know well that even in our own case, sinners as we are, on the consciousness of innocence or of guilt mainly turns our power of enduring opposition and calumny; how much more, you will say, in the case of our Lord, did the sense of inward sanctity compensate for the suffering and annihilate the shame! Again, you may say that He knew that His sufferings would be short, and that their issue would be joyful, whereas uncertainty of the future is the keenest element of human distress; but He could not have anxiety, for He was not in suspense; nor despondency or despair, for He never was deserted.

And in confirmation you may refer to St. Paul, who expressly tells us that, "for the joy set before Him," our Lord "despised the shame". And certainly there is a marvellous calm and self-possession in all He does: consider His warning to the Apostles, "Watch and pray, lest ye enter into temptation ; the spirit indeed is willing, but the flesh is weak" ; or His words to Judas, "Friend, wherefore art thou come?" and, "Judas, betrayest thou the Son of Man with a kiss ?" or to Peter, "All that take the sword shall perish with the sword" ; or to the man who struck Him, "If I have spoken evil, bear witness of the evil ; but if well, why smitest thou Me?" or to His Mother, "Woman, behold thy Son".

All this is true and much to be insisted on ; but it quite agrees with, or rather illustrates, what I have been observing. My brethren, you have only said (to use a human phrase) that He was always Himself. His mind was its own centre, and was never in the slightest degree thrown off its heavenly and most perfect balance. What He suffered, He suffered because He put Himself under suffering, and that deliberately and calmly. As He said to the leper, "I will, be thou clean"; and to the paralytic, "Thy sins be forgiven thee" ; and to the centurion, "I will come and heal him" ; and of Lazarus, "I go to wake him out of sleep"; so He said, "Now I will begin to suffer," and He did begin. His composure is but the proof how entirely He governed His own mind. He drew back, at the proper moment, the bolts and fastenings, and opened the gates, and the floods fell right upon His soul in all their fulness. That is what St. Mark tells us of Him ; and he is said to have written his Gospels from the very mouth of St. Peter, who was one of three witnesses present at the time. " They came," he says, " to the place which is called Gethsemani ; and He saith to His disciples, Sit you here while I pray. And He taketh with Him Peter and James and John, and He *began to be* frightened and to be very heavy." You see how deliberately He acts ; He comes to a certain spot ; and then, giving the word of command, and withdrawing the support of the Godhead from His soul, distress, terror, and dejection at once rush in upon it. Thus He walks forth into a mental agony with as definite an action as if it were some bodily torture, the fire or the wheel.

This being the case, you will see at once, my brethren, that it is nothing to the purpose to say that He would be supported under His trial by the consciousness of innocence and the anticipation of triumph ; for His trial consisted in the withdrawal, as of other causes of consolation, so of that very consciousness and anticipation. The same act of the will which admitted the influence upon His soul of any distress at all, admitted all distresses at once. It was not the contest between antagonist impulses and views, coming from without, but the operation of an inward resolution. As men of self-command can turn from one thought to another at their will, so much more did He deliberately deny Himself the comfort, and satiate Himself with the woe. In that moment His soul thought not of the future, He thought only of the present burden which was upon Him, and which He had come upon earth to sustain.

And now, my brethren, what was it He had to bear, when He thus opened upon His soul the torrent of this predestinated pain ?   Alas ! He had to bear what is well known to us, what is familiar to us, but what to Him was woe unutterable.   He had to bear that which is so easy a thing to us, so natural, so welcome, that we cannot conceive of it as of a great endurance, but which to Him had the scent and the poison of death—He had, my dear brethren, to bear the weight of sin ; He had to bear your sins ; He had to bear the sins of the whole world.   Sin is an easy thing to us ; we think little of it ; we do not understand how the Creator can think much of it ; we cannot bring our imagination to believe that it deserves retribution, and, when even in this world punishments follow upon it, we explain them away or turn our minds from them.   But consider what sin is in itself ; it is re- bellion against God ; it is a traitor's act who aims at the overthrow and death of His sovereign ; it is that, if I may use a strong expression, which, could the Divine Governor of the world cease to be, would be sufficient to bring it about.   Sin is the mortal enemy of the All-holy, so that He and it cannot be together ; and as the All-holy drives it from His presence into the outer darkness, so, if God could be less than God, it is sin that would have power to make Him less.   And here observe, my brethren, that when once Almighty Love, by taking flesh, entered this created system, and submitted Himself to its laws, then forthwith this

antagonist of good and truth, taking advantage of the
opportunity, flew at that flesh which He had taken,
and fixed on it, and was its death.   The envy of the
Pharisees, the treachery of Judas, and the madness of
the people, were but the instrument or the expression
of the enmity which sin felt towards Eternal Purity
as soon as, in infinite mercy towards men, He put
Himself within its reach.   Sin could not touch His
Divine Majesty ; but it could assail Him in that way
in which He allowed Himself to be assailed, that is,
through the medium of His humanity.   And in the
issue, in the death of God incarnate, you are but
taught, my brethren, what sin is in itself, and what it
was which then was falling, in its hour and in its
strength, upon His human nature, when He allowed
that nature to be so filled with horror and dismay at
the very anticipation.

There, then, in that most awful hour, knelt the
Saviour of the world, putting off the defences of His
divinity, dismissing His reluctant Angels, who in
myriads were ready at His call, and opening His
arms, baring His breast, sinless as He was, to the
assault of His foe,—of a foe whose breath was a
pestilence, and whose embrace was an agony.   There
He knelt, motionless and still, while the vile and
horrible fiend clad His spirit in a robe steeped in all
that is hateful and heinous in human crime, which
clung close round His heart, and filled His conscience,
and found its way into every sense and pore of His
mind, and spread over Him a moral leprosy, till He
almost felt Himself to be that which He never could

be, and which His foe would fain have made Him.
Oh, the horror, when He looked, and did not know
Himself, and felt as a foul and loathsome sinner, from
His vivid perception of that mass of corruption which
poured over His head and ran down even to the skirts
of His garments! Oh, the distraction, when He found
His eyes, and hands, and feet, and lips, and heart, as
if the members of the Evil One, and not of God! Are
these the hands of the Immaculate Lamb of God, once
innocent, but now red with ten thousand barbarous
deeds of blood? are these His lips, not uttering prayer,
and praise, and holy blessings, but as if defiled with
oaths, and blasphemies, and doctrines of devils? or
His eyes, profaned as they are by all the evil visions
and idolatrous fascinations for which men have abandoned their adorable Creator? And His ears, they
ring with sounds of revelry and of strife; and His
heart is frozen with avarice, and cruelty, and unbelief;
and His very memory is laden with every sin which
has been committed since the fall, in all regions of the
earth, with the pride of the old giants, and the lusts
of the five cities, and the obduracy of Egypt, and the
ambition of Babel, and the unthankfulness and scorn
of Israel. Oh, who does not know the misery of a
haunting thought which comes again and again, in
spite of rejection, to annoy, if it cannot seduce? or of
some odious and sickening imagination, in no sense
one's own, but forced upon the mind from without? or
of evil knowledge, gained with or without a man's
fault, but which he would give a great price to be rid
of at once and for ever? And adversaries such as

22

these gather around Thee, Blessed Lord, in millions now; they come in troops more numerous than the locust or the palmer-worm, or the plagues of hail, and flies, and frogs, which were sent against Pharaoh. Of the living and of the dead and of the as yet unborn, of the lost and of the saved, of Thy people and of strangers, of sinners and of saints, all sins are there. Thy dearest are there, Thy saints and Thy chosen are upon Thee; Thy three Apostles, Peter, James, and John; but not as comforters, but as accusers, like the friends of Job, "sprinkling dust towards heaven," and heaping curses on Thy head. All are there but one; one only is not there, one only; for she who had no part in sin, she only could console Thee, and therefore she is not nigh. She will be near Thee on the Cross, she is separated from Thee in the garden. She has been Thy companion and Thy confidant through Thy life, she interchanged with Thee the pure thoughts and holy meditations of thirty years; but her virgin ear may not take in, nor may her immaculate heart conceive, what now is in vision before Thee. None was equal to the weight but God; sometimes before Thy saints Thou hast brought the image of a single sin, as it appears in the light of Thy countenance, or of venial sins, not mortal; and they have told us that the sight did all but kill them, nay, would have killed them, had it not been instantly withdrawn. The Mother of God, for all her sanctity, nay by reason of it, could not have borne even one brood of that innumerable progeny of Satan which now compasses Thee about. It is the long history of a world, and God alone can bear the load of it. Hopes blighted, vows broken, lights quenched, warnings scorned, opportunities lost; the innocent betrayed, the young hardened, the penitent relapsing, the just overcome, the aged failing; the sophistry of misbelief, the wilfulness of passion, the obduracy of pride, the tyranny of habit, the canker of remorse, the wasting fever of care, the anguish of shame, the pining of disappointment, the sickness of despair; such cruel, such pitiable spectacles, such heartrending, revolting, detestable, maddening scenes; nay, the haggard faces, the convulsed lips, the flushed cheek, the dark brow of the willing slaves of evil, they are all before Him now; they are upon Him and in Him. They are with Him instead of that ineffable peace which has inhabited His soul since the moment of His conception. They are upon Him, they are all but His own; He cries to His Father as if He were the criminal, not the victim; His agony takes the form of guilt and compunction. He is doing penance, He is making confession, He is exercising contrition, with a reality and a virtue infinitely greater than that of all saints and penitents together; for He is the One Victim for us all, the sole Satisfaction, the real Penitent, all but the real sinner.

He rises languidly from the earth, and turns around to meet the traitor and his band, now quickly nearing the deep shade. He turns, and lo! there is blood upon His garment and in His footprints. Whence come these first-fruits of the passion of the Lamb? no soldier's scourge has touched His shoulders, nor

the hangman's nails His hands and feet.   My brethren,
He has bled before His time ; He has shed blood ; yes,
and it is His agonising soul which has broken up
His framework of flesh and poured it forth.   His
passion has begun from within.   That tormented
Heart, the seat of tenderness and love, began at
length to labour and to beat with vehemence beyond
its nature ; "the foundations of the great deep were
broken up ;" the red streams rushed forth so copious
and fierce as to overflow the veins, and bursting
through the pores, they stood in a thick dew over His
whole skin ; then forming into drops, they rolled down
full and heavy, and drenched the ground.

"My soul is sorrowful even unto death," He said.
It has been said of that dreadful pestilence which
now is upon us, that it begins with death ; by which
is meant that it has no stage or crisis, that hope is
over when it comes, and that what looks like its
course is but the death agony and the process of dissolution ; and thus our Atoning Sacrifice, in a much
higher sense, began with this passion of woe, and only
did not die, because at His Omnipotent will His Heart
did not break, nor Soul separate from Body, till He
had suffered on the Cross.

No ; He has not yet exhausted that full chalice,
from which at first His natural infirmity shrank.   The
seizure and the arraignment, and the buffeting, and
the prison, and the trial, and the mocking, and the
passing to and fro, and the scourging, and the crown
of thorns, and the slow march to Calvary, and the
crucifixion, these are all to come.   A night and a

day, hour after hour, is slowly to run out before the end comes, and the satisfaction is completed.

And then, when the appointed moment arrived, and He gave the word, as His passion had begun with His soul, with the soul did it end. He did not die of bodily exhaustion, or of bodily pain; at His will His tormented Heart broke, and He commended His Spirit to the Father.

* * * * * *

" O Heart of Jesus, all Love, I offer Thee these humble prayers for myself, and for all those who unite themselves with me in Spirit to adore Thee. O holiest Heart of Jesus most lovely, I intend to renew and to offer to Thee these acts of adoration and these prayers, for myself a wretched sinner, and for all those who are associated with me in Thy adoration, through all moments while I breathe, even to the end of my life. I recommend to Thee, O my Jesus, Holy Church, Thy dear spouse and our true Mother, all just souls and all poor sinners, the afflicted, the dying, and all mankind. Let not Thy Blood be shed for them in vain. Finally, deign to apply it in relief of the souls in Purgatory, of those in particular who have practised in the course of their life this holy devotion of adoring Thee."

DISCOURSE XVII.

THE GLORIES OF MARY FOR THE SAKE OF HER SON.

WE know, my brethren, that in the natural world nothing is superfluous, nothing incomplete, nothing independent; but part answers to part, and all details combine to form one mighty whole. Order and harmony are among the first perfections which we discern in this visible creation; and the more we examine into it, the more widely and minutely they are found to belong to it. "All things are double," says the Wise Man, "one against another; and He hath made nothing defective." It is the very character and definition of "the heavens and the earth," as contrasted with the void or chaos which preceded them, that everything is now subjected to fixed laws; and every motion, and influence, and effect can be accounted for, and, were our knowledge sufficient, could be anticipated. Moreover, it is plain, on the other hand, that it is only in proportion to our observation and our research that this truth becomes apparent; for though a number of things even at first sight are seen to proceed according to an established and beautiful order, yet in other instances the law to which they are conformed is with difficulty discovered ; and the words " chance," and " hazard," and " fortune," have come into use as expressions of our ignorance. Accordingly, you may fancy rash and irreligious minds who are engaged day after day in the business of the world, suddenly looking out into the heavens or upon the earth, and criticising the great Architect, arguing that there are creatures in existence which are rude or defective in their constitution, and asking questions which would but evidence their want of scientific education.

The case is the same as regards the supernatural world. The great truths of Revelation are all connected together and form a whole. Every one can see this in a measure even at a glance, but to understand the full consistency and harmony of Catholic teaching requires study and meditation. Hence, as philosophers of this world bury themselves in museums and laboratories, descend into mines, or wander among woods or on the sea-shore, so the inquirer into heavenly truths dwells in the cell and the oratory, pouring forth his heart in prayer, collecting his thoughts in meditation, dwelling on the idea of Jesus, or of Mary, or of grace, or of eternity, and pondering the words of holy men who have gone before him, till before his mental sight arises the hidden wisdom of the perfect, " which God predestined before the world unto our glory," and which He " reveals unto them by His Spirit ". And, as ignorant men may dispute the beauty and harmony of the visible creation, so men, who for six days in the week are absorbed in worldly toil, who live for wealth, or name, or self-indulgence, or profane knowledge, and do but give their leisure moments to the thought of religion, never raising their souls to God, never asking for His enlightening grace, never chastening their hearts and bodies, never steadily contemplating the objects of faith, but judging hastily and peremptorily according to their private views or the humour of the hour ; such men, I say, in like manner, may easily, or will for certain, be surprised and shocked at portions of revealed truth, as if strange, or harsh, or extreme, or inconsistent, and will in whole or in part reject it.

I am going to apply this remark to the subject of the prerogatives with which the Church invests the Blessed Mother of God. They are startling and difficult to those whose imagination is not accustomed to them, and whose reason has not reflected on them ; but the more carefully and religiously they are dwelt on, the more, I am sure, will they be found essential to the Catholic faith, and integral to the worship of Christ. This simply is the point which I shall insist on—disputable indeed by aliens from the Church, but most clear to her children—that the glories of Mary are for the sake of Jesus ; and that we praise and bless her as the first of creatures, that we may duly confess Him as our sole Creator.

When the Eternal Word decreed to come on earth, He did not purpose, He did not work, by halves ; but He came to be a man like any of us, to take a human soul and body, and to make them His own. He did not come in a mere apparent or accidental form, as Angels appear to men ; nor did He merely overshadow an existing man, as He overshadows His saints, and call Him by the name of God ; but He "was made flesh". He attached to Himself a manhood, and became as really and truly man as He was God, so that henceforth He was both God and man, or, in other words, He was One Person in two natures, divine and human.   This is a mystery so marvellous, so difficult, that faith alone firmly receives it ; the natural man may receive it for a while, may think he receives it, but never really receives it; begins, as soon as he has professed it, secretly to rebel against it, evades it, or revolts from it.   This he has done from the first ; even in the lifetime of the beloved disciple men arose who said that our Lord had no body at all, or a body framed in the heavens, or that He did not suffer, but another suffered in His stead, or that He was but for a time possessed of the human form which was born and which suffered, coming into it at its baptism, and leaving it before its crucifixion, or, again, that He was a mere man.   That " in the beginning was the Word, and the Word was with God, and the Word was God, and the Word was made flesh and dwelt among us," was too hard a thing for the unregenerate reason.

The case is the same at this day ; mere Protestants have seldom any real perception of the doctrine of God and man in one Person.   They speak in a dreamy, shadowy way of Christ's divinity ; but, when their meaning is sifted, you will find them very slow to commit themselves to any statement sufficient to express the Catholic dogma.   They will tell you at once, that the subject is not to be inquired into, for that it is impossible to inquire into it at all without being technical and subtile. Then, when they comment on the Gospels, they will speak of Christ, not simply and consistently as God, but as a being made up of God and man, partly one and partly the other, or between both, or as a man inhabited by a special Divine presence. Sometimes they even go on to deny that He was in heaven the Son of God, saying that He became the Son when He was conceived of the Holy Ghost; and they are shocked, and think it a mark both of reverence and good sense to be shocked, when they hear the Man spoken of simply and plainly as God. They cannot bear to have it said, except as a figure or mode of speaking, that God had a human body, or that God suffered; they think that the "Atonement," and "Sanctification through the Spirit," as they speak, is the sum and substance of the Gospel, and they are shy of any dogmatic expression which goes beyond them. Such, I believe, is the ordinary character of the Protestant notions among us as to the divinity of Christ, whether among members of the Anglican communion, or dissenters from it, excepting a small remnant of them.

Now, if you would witness against these unchristian opinions, if you would bring out distinctly and beyond mistake and evasion, the simple idea of the Catholic Church that God is man, could you do it better than by laying down in St. John's words that "God *became* man"? and again could you express this more emphatically and unequivocally than by declaring that He was *born* a man, or that He had a *Mother?* The world allows that God *is* man; the admission costs it little, for God is everywhere, and (as it may say) is everything; but it shrinks from confessing that God is the Son of Mary. It shrinks, for it is at once confronted with a severe fact, which violates and shatters its own unbelieving view of things; the revealed doctrine forthwith takes its true shape, and receives an historical reality; and the Almighty is introduced into His own world at a certain time and in a definite way. Dreams are broken and shadows depart; the Divine truth is no longer a poetical expression, or a devotional exaggeration, or a mystical economy, or a mythical representation. "Sacrifice and offering," the shadows of the Law, "Thou wouldest not, but a body hast Thou fitted to me. That which was from the beginning, which we have heard, which we have seen with our eyes, which we have diligently looked upon, and our hands have handled," "That which we have seen and have heard, declare we unto you";—such is the record of the Apostle, in opposition to those "spirits" which denied that "Jesus Christ had appeared in the flesh," and which "dissolved" Him by denying either His human nature or His divine. And the confession that Mary is *Deipara,* or the Mother of God, is that safeguard wherewith we seal up and secure the doctrine of the Apostle from all evasion, and that test whereby we detect all the pretences of those bad spirits of "Antichrist which have gone out into the world". It declares that He is God; it implies that He is man; it suggests to us that He is God still, though He has become man, and that He is true man

though He is God.   By witnessing to the *process* of the
union, it secures the reality of the two *subjects* of the
union, of the divinity and of the manhood.   If Mary
is the Mother of God, Christ must be literally Emmanuel, God with us.   And hence it was, that, when
time went on, and the bad spirits and false prophets
grew stronger and bolder, and found a way into the
Catholic body itself, then the Church, guided by God,
could find no more effectual and sure way of expelling
them than that of using this word *Deipara* against
them ; and, on the other hand, when they came up
again from the realms of darkness, and plotted the
utter overthrow of Christian faith in the sixteenth
century, then they could find no more certain expedient
for their hateful purpose than that of reviling and
blaspheming the prerogatives of Mary, for they knew
full well that, if they could once get the world to dishonour the Mother, the dishonour of the Son would
follow close.   The Church and Satan agreed together
in this, that Son and Mother went together ; and the
experience of three centuries has confirmed their testimony, for Catholics who have honoured the Mother,
still worship the Son, while Protestants, who now have
ceased to confess the Son, began then by scoffing at
the Mother.

You see, then, my brethren, in this particular, the
harmonious consistency of the revealed system, and
the bearing of one doctrine upon another ; Mary is
exalted for the sake of Jesus.   It was fitting that she,
as being a creature, though the first of creatures,
should have an office of ministration.   She, as others,

came into the world to do a work, she had a mission
to fulfil ; her grace and her glory are not for her own
sake, but for her Maker's; and to her is committed
the custody of the Incarnation ; this is her appointed
office,—"A Virgin shall conceive, and bear a Son,
and they shall call His Name Emmanuel". As she
was once on earth, and was personally the guardian of
her Divine Child, as she carried Him in her womb,
folded Him in her embrace, and suckled Him at her
breast, so now, and to the latest hour of the Church,
do her glories and the devotion paid her proclaim and
define the right faith concerning Him as God and
man. Every church which is dedicated to her, every
altar which is raised under her invocation, every image
which represents her, every litany in her praise, every
Hail Mary for her continual memory, does but remind
us that there was One who, though He was all-blessed
from all eternity, yet for the sake of sinners, "did not
shrink from the Virgin's womb". Thus she is the
Turris Davidica, as the Church calls her, "the Tower
of David "; the high and strong defence of the King of
the true Israel; and hence the Church also addresses
her in the Antiphon, as having "alone destroyed all
heresies in the whole world ".

And here, my brethren, a fresh thought opens upon
us, which is naturally implied in what has been said
If the *Deipara* is to witness of Emmanuel, she must
be necessarily more than the *Deipara.* For consider ;
a defence must be strong in order to be a defence ; a
tower must be, like that Tower of David, " built with
bulwarks "; " a thousand bucklers hang upon it, all

the armour of valiant men ". It would not have sufficed, in order to bring out and impress on us the idea
that God is man, had His Mother been an ordinary
person. A mother without a home in the Church,
without dignity, without gifts, would have been, as far
as the defence of the Incarnation goes, no mother at
all. She would not have remained in the memory, or
the imagination of men. If she is to witness and remind the world that God became man, she must be on
a high and eminent station for the purpose. She must
be made to fill the mind, in order to suggest the lesson.
When she once attracts our attention, then, and not
till then, she begins to preach Jesus. " Why should
she have such prerogatives," we ask, "unless He be
God? and what must He be by nature, when she is
so high by grace?" This is why she has other prerogatives besides, namely, the gifts of personal purity
and intercessory power, distinct from her maternity ;
she is personally endowed that she may perform her
office well ; she is exalted in herself that she may
minister to Christ.

For this reason, she has been made more glorious
in her person than in her office ; her purity is a higher
gift than her relationship to God. This is what is
implied in Christ's answer to the woman in the crowd,
who cried out, when He was preaching, " Blessed is
the womb that bare Thee, and the breasts which Thou
hast sucked ". He replied by pointing out to His
disciples a higher blessedness ; " Yea, rather, blessed,"
He said, " are they who hear the word of God and
keep it ". You know, my brethren, that Protestants

take these words in disparagement of our Lady's greatness, but they really tell the other way. For consider them; He lays down a principle, that it is more blessed to keep His commandments than to be His Mother; but who, even of Protestants, will say that she did *not* keep His commandments? She kept them surely, and our Lord does but say that such obedience was in a higher line of privilege than her being His Mother; she was more blessed in her detachment from creatures, in her devotion to God, in her virginal purity, in her fulness of grace, than in her maternity. This is the constant teaching of the Holy Fathers: "More blessed was Mary," says St. Augustine, "in receiving Christ's faith, than in conceiving Christ's flesh;" and St. Chrysostom declares, that she would not have been blessed, though she had borne Him in the body, had she not heard the word of God and kept it. This, of course, is an impossible case; for she was made holy, that she might be made His Mother, and the two blessednesses cannot be divided. She who was chosen to supply flesh and blood to the Eternal Word, was first filled with grace in soul and body; still, she had a double blessedness, of office and of qualification for it, and the latter was the greater. And it is on this account that the Angel calls her blessed; "*Full of grace*," he says, "Blessed among women"; and St. Elizabeth also, when she cries out, "Blessed thou that hast *believed*". Nay, she herself bears a like testimony, when the Angel announced to her the high favour which was coming on her. Though all Jewish women in each successive age had been hoping to be Mother of the Christ, so that marriage was honourable among them, childlessness a reproach, she alone had put aside the desire and the thought of so great a dignity. She, who was to bear the Christ, gave no welcome to the great announcement that she was to bear Him ; and why did she thus act towards it ? because she had been inspired, the first of woman-kind, to dedicate her virginity to God, and she did not welcome a privilege which seemed to involve a forfeiture of her vow. How shall this be, she asked, seeing I am to live separate from man ? Nor, till the Angel told her that the conception would be miraculous and from the Holy Ghost, did she put aside her " trouble " of mind, recognise him securely as God's messenger, and bow her head in awe and thankfulness to God's condescension.

Mary then is a specimen, and more than a specimen, in the purity of her soul and body, of what man was before his fall, and what he would have been, had he risen to his full perfection. It had been hard, it had been a victory for the Evil One, had the whole race passed away, nor any one instance in it occurred to show what the Creator had intended it to be in its original state. Adam, you know, was created in the image and after the likeness of God ; his frail and imperfect nature, stamped with a Divine seal, was supported and exalted by an indwelling of Divine grace. Impetuous passion did not exist in him, except as a latent element and a possible evil ; ignorance was dissipated by the clear light of the Spirit; and reason, sovereign over every motion of his soul, was simply subjected to the will of God. Nay, even his body was preserved from every wayward appetite and affection, and was promised immortality instead of dissolution. Thus he was in a supernatural state; and, had he not sinned, year after year would he have advanced in merit and grace, and in God's favour, till he passed from paradise to heaven. But he fell; and his descendants were born in his likeness; and the world grew worse instead of better, and judgment after judgment cut off generations of sinners in vain, and improvement was hopeless; "because man was flesh," and, "the thoughts of his heart were bent upon evil at all times".

However, a remedy had been determined in heaven; a Redeemer was at hand; God was about to do a great work, and He purposed to do it suitably; "where sin abounded, grace was to abound more". Kings of the earth, when they have sons born to them, forthwith scatter some large bounty, or raise some high memorial; they honour the day, or the place, or the heralds of the auspicious event, with some corresponding mark of favour; nor did the coming of Emmanuel innovate on the world's established custom. It was a season of grace and prodigy, and these were to be exhibited in a special manner in the person of His Mother. The course of ages was to be reversed; the tradition of evil was to be broken; a gate of light was to be opened amid the darkness, for the coming of the Just;—a Virgin conceived and bore Him. It was fitting, for His honour and glory, that she, who was the instrument of His bodily presence, should

23

first be a miracle of His grace ; it was fitting that she should triumph, where Eve had failed, and should " bruise the serpent's head " by the spotlessness of her sanctity. In some respects, indeed, the curse was not reversed ; Mary came into a fallen world, and resigned herself to its laws; she, as also the Son she bore, was exposed to pain of soul and body, she was subjected to death ; but she was not put under the power of sin. As grace was infused into Adam from the first moment of his creation, so that he never had experience of his natural poverty, till sin reduced him to it ; so was grace given from the first in still ampler measure to Mary, and she never incurred, in fact, Adam's deprivation. She began where others end, whether in knowledge or in love. She was from the first clothed in sanctity, destined for perseverance, luminous and glorious in God's sight, and incessantly employed in meritorious acts, which continued till her last breath. Hers was emphatically "the path of the just, which, as the shining light, goeth forward and increaseth even to the perfect day"; and sinlessness in thought, word, and deed, in small things as well as great, in venial matters as well as grievous, is surely but the natural and obvious sequel of such a beginning. If Adam might have kept himself from sin in his first state, much more shall we expect immaculate perfection in Mary.

Such is her prerogative of sinless perfection, and it is, as her maternity, for the sake of Emmanuel ; hence she answered the Angel's salutation, *Gratia plena*, with the humble acknowledgment, *Ecce ancilla Domini,*

" Behold the handmaid of the Lord ". And like to this is her third prerogative, which follows both from her maternity and from her purity, and which I will mention as completing the enumeration of her glories. I mean her intercessory power. For, if " God heareth not sinners, but if a man be a worshipper of Him, and do His will, him He heareth " ; if " the continual prayer of a just man availeth much " ; if faithful Abraham was required to pray for Abimelech, " for he was a prophet " ; if patient Job was to " pray for his friends," for he had " spoken right things before God " ; if meek Moses, by lifting up his hands, turned the battle in favour of Israel against Amalec ; why should we wonder at hearing that Mary, the only spotless child of Adam's seed, has a transcendent influence with the God of grace ? And if the Gentiles at Jerusalem sought Philip, because he was an Apostle, when they desired access to Jesus, and Philip spoke to Andrew, as still more closely in our Lord's confidence, and then both came to Him, is it strange that the Mother should have power with the Son, distinct in kind from that of the purest angel and the most triumphant saint ? If we have faith to admit the Incarnation itself, we must admit it in its fulness ; why then should we start at the gracious appointments which arise out of it, or are necessary to it, or are included in it ? If the Creator comes on earth in the form of a servant and a creature, why may not His Mother, on the other hand, rise to be the Queen of heaven, and be clothed with the sun, and have the moon under her feet ?

I am not proving these doctrines to you, my brethren; the evidence of them lies in the declaration of the Church. The Church is the oracle of religious truth, and dispenses what the apostles committed to her in every time and place. We must take her word, then, without proof, because she is sent to us from God to teach us how to please Him ; and that we do so is the test whether we be really Catholics or no. I am not proving then what you already receive, but I am showing you the beauty and the harmony, in one out of many instances, of the Church's teaching ; which are so well adapted, as they are divinely intended, to recommend that teaching to the inquirer and to endear it to her children. One word more, and I have done ; I have shown you how full of meaning are the truths themselves which the Church teaches concerning the Most Blessed Virgin, and now consider how full of meaning also has been the Church's dispensation of them.

You will find, that, in this respect, as in Mary's prerogatives themselves, there is the same careful reference to the glory of Him who gave them to her. You know, when first He went out to preach, she kept apart from Him ; she interfered not with His work ; and, even when He was gone up on high, yet she, a woman, went not out to preach or teach, she seated not herself in the Apostolic chair, she took no part in the priest's office ; she did but humbly seek her Son in the daily Mass of those, who, though her ministers in heaven, were her superiors in the Church on earth. Nor, when she and they had left this lower scene, and she was a Queen upon her Son's right hand, not even

then did she ask of Him to publish her name to the
ends of the world, or to hold her up to the world's gaze,
but she remained waiting for the time, when her own
glory should be necessary for His. He indeed had been
from the very first proclaimed by Holy Church, and
enthroned in His temple, for He was God ; ill had it
beseemed the living Oracle of Truth to have with-
holden from the faithful the very object of their adoration ; but it was otherwise with Mary. It became
her, as a creature, a mother, and a woman, to stand
aside and make way for the Creator, to minister to her
Son, and to win her way into the world's homage by
sweet and gracious persuasion. So when His name
was dishonoured, then it was that she did Him service ;
when Emmanuel was denied, then the Mother of
God (as it were) came forward ; when heretics said
that God was not incarnate, then was the time for
her own honours. And then, when as much as this
had been accomplished, she had done with strife ;
she fought not for herself. No fierce controversy, no
persecuted confessors, no heresiarch, no anathema,
were necessary for her gradual manifestation ; as she
had increased day by day in grace and merit at Nazareth, while the world knew not of her, so has she raised
herself aloft silently, and has grown into her place
in the Church by a tranquil influence and a natural
process. She was as some fair tree, stretching forth
her fruitful branches and her fragrant leaves, and
overshadowing the territory of the saints. And
thus the Antiphon speaks of her : " Let thy dwelling
be in Jacob, and thine inheritance in Israel, and

strike thy roots in My elect". Again, "And so in Sion was I established, and in the holy city I likewise rested, and in Jerusalem was my power. And I *took root* in an honourable people, and in the glorious company of the saints was I *detained*. I was exalted like a cedar in Lebanus, and as a cypress in Mount Sion ; I have stretched out my branches as the terebinth, and my branches are of honour and grace." Thus was she reared without hands, and gained a modest victory, and exerts a gentle sway, which she has not claimed. When dispute arose about her among her children, she hushed it ; when objections were urged against her, she waived her claims and waited ; till now, in this very day, should God so will, she will win at length her most radiant crown, and, without opposing voice, and amid the jubilation of the whole Church, she will be hailed as immaculate in her conception.

Such art thou, Holy Mother, in the creed and in the worship of the Church, the defence of many truths, the grace and smiling light of every devotion. In thee, O Mary, is fulfilled, as we can bear it, an original purpose of the Most High. He once had meant to come on earth in heavenly glory, but we sinned ; and then He could not safely visit us, except with a shrouded radiance and a bedimmed Majesty, for He was God. So He came Himself in weakness, not in power ; and He sent thee, a creature, in His stead, with a creature's comeliness and lustre suited to our state. And now thy very face and form, dear Mother, speak to us of the Eternal ; not like earthly beauty, dangerous to look upon, but like the morning star, which is thy emblem, bright and musical, breathing purity, telling of heaven, and infusing peace. O harbinger of day! O hope of the pilgrim! lead us still as thou hast led ; in the dark night, across the bleak wilderness, guide us on to our Lord Jesus, guide us home.

> Maria, mater gratiæ,
> Dulcis parens clementiæ,
> Tu nos ab hoste protege
> Et mortis horâ suscipe.

DISCOURSE XVIII.

ON THE FITNESS OF THE GLORIES OF MARY.

YOU may recollect, my brethren, our Lord's words when on the day of His resurrection He had joined the two disciples on their way to Emmaus, and found them sad and perplexed in consequence of His death. He said, "*Ought not* Christ to suffer these things, and so enter into His glory?" He appealed to the fitness and congruity which existed between this otherwise surprising event and the other truths which had been revealed concerning the Divine purpose of saving the world. And so, too, St. Paul, in speaking of the same wonderful appointment of God ; " It *became* Him," he says, "for whom are all things, and through whom are all things, who had brought many sons unto glory, to consummate the Author of their salvation by suffering ". Elsewhere, speaking of prophesying, or the exposition of what is latent in Divine truth, he bids his brethren exercise the gift " according to the *analogy* or rule of faith " ; that is, so that the doctrine preached may correspond and fit into what is already received. Thus, you see, it is a great evidence of truth, in the case of revealed teaching, that it is so consistent, that it so hangs together, that one thing springs out of another, that each part requires and is required by the rest.

This great principle, which is exemplified so variously in the structure and history of Catholic doctrine, which will receive more and more illustrations the more carefully and minutely we examine the subject, is brought before us especially at this season, when we are celebrating the Assumption of our Blessed Lady, the Mother of God, into heaven. We receive it on the belief of ages; but, viewed in the light of reason, it is the *fitness* of this termination of her earthly course which so persuasively recommends it to our minds : we feel it " ought " to be; that it " becomes " her Lord and Son thus to provide for one who was so singular and special, both in herself and her relations to Him. We find that it is simply in harmony with the substance and main outlines of the doctrine of the Incarnation, and that without it Catholic teaching would have a character of incompleteness, and would disappoint our pious expectations.

Let us direct our thoughts to this subject to-day, my brethren ; and with a view of helping you to do so, I will first state what the Church has taught and defined from the first ages concerning the Blessed Virgin, and then you will see how naturally the devotion which her children show her, and the praises with which they honour her, follow from it.

Now, as you know, it has been held from the first, and defined from an early age, that Mary is the Mother of God. She is not merely the Mother of our Lord's manhood, or of our Lord's body, but she is to be considered the Mother of the Word Himself, the Word incarnate. God, in the person of the Word, the Second Person of the All-glorious Trinity, humbled Himself to become her Son. *Non horruisti Virginis uterum*, as the Church sings, " Thou didst not disdain the Virgin's womb ". He took the substance of His human flesh from her, and clothed in it He lay within her ; and He bore it about with Him after birth, as a sort of badge and witness that He, though God, was hers. He was nursed and tended by her ; He was suckled by her ; He lay in her arms. As time went on, He ministered to her, and obeyed her. He lived with her for thirty years, in one house, with an uninterrupted intercourse, and with only the saintly Joseph to share it with Him. She was the witness of His growth, of His joys, of His sorrows, of His prayers ; she was blest with His smile, with the touch of His hand, with the whisper of His affection, with the expression of His thoughts and His feelings, for that length of time. Now, my brethren, what ought she to be, what is it *becoming* that she should be, who was so favoured ?

Such a question was once asked by a heathen king, when he would place one of his subjects in a dignity becoming the relation in which the latter stood towards him. That subject had saved the king's life, and what was to be done to him in return ? The king asked, " What should be done to the man whom the king desireth to honour?" And he received the following answer, " The man whom the king wisheth to honour ought to be clad in the king's apparel, and to be mounted on the king's saddle, and to receive the royal diadem on his head ; and let the first among the king's princes and presidents hold his horse, and let him walk through the streets of the city, and say, Thus shall he be honoured, whom the king hath a mind to honour ". So stands the case with Mary ; she gave birth to the Creator, and what recompense shall be made her ? what shall be done to her, who had this relationship to the Most High ? what shall be the fit accompaniment of one whom the Almighty has deigned to make, not His servant, not His friend, not His intimate, but His superior, the source of His second being, the nurse of His helpless infancy, the teacher of His opening years ? I answer, as the king was answered : Nothing is too high for her to whom God owes His human life ; no exuberance of grace, no excess of glory, but is becoming, but is to be expected there, where God has lodged Himself, whence God has issued.   Let her " be clad in the king's apparel," that is, let the fulness of the Godhead so flow into her that she may be a figure of the incommunicable sanctity, and beauty, and glory, of God Himself : that she may be the Mirror of Justice, the Mystical Rose, the Tower of Ivory, the House of Gold, the Morning Star.   Let her " receive the king's diadem upon her head," as the Queen of heaven, the Mother of all living, the Health of the weak, the Refuge of sinners, the Comforter of the afflicted.   And " let the first amongst the king's princes walk before her," let angels and prophets, and apostles, and martyrs, and all saints, kiss the hem of her garment and rejoice under the shadow of her throne.   Thus is it that King Solomon has risen up to meet his mother, and bowed himself unto her, and caused a seat to be set for the king's mother, and she sits on his right hand.

We should be prepared then, my brethren, to believe that the Mother of God is full of grace and glory, from the very fitness of such a dispensation, even though we had not been taught it; and this fitness will appear still more clear and certain when we contemplate the subject more steadily. Consider then, that it has been the ordinary rule of God's dealings with us, that personal sanctity should be the attendant upon high spiritual dignity of place or work. The angels, who, as the word imports, are God's messengers, are also perfect in holiness; "without sanctity, no one shall see God;" no defiled thing can enter the courts of heaven; and the higher its inhabitants are advanced in their ministry about the throne, the holier are they, and the more absorbed in their contemplation of that Holiness upon which they wait. The Seraphim, who immediately surround the Divine Glory, cry day and night, "Holy, Holy, Holy, Lord God of Hosts". So is it also on earth; the prophets have ordinarily not only gifts but graces; they are not only inspired to know and to teach God's will, but inwardly converted to obey it. For surely those only can preach the truth duly who feel it personally; those only transmit it fully from God to man, who have in the transmission made it their own.

I do not say that there are no exceptions to this rule, but they admit of an easy explanation; I do not say that it never pleases Almighty God to convey any in-

timation of His will through bad men ; of course, for
all things can be made to serve Him. By all, even
the wicked, He accomplishes His purposes, and by the
wicked He is glorified. Our Lord's death was brought
about by His enemies, who did His will, while they
thought they were gratifying their own. Caiaphas,
who contrived and effected it, was made use of to predict it. Balaam prophesied good of God's people in
an earlier age, by a Divine compulsion, when he wished
to prophesy evil. This is true; but in such cases
Divine Mercy is plainly overruling the evil, and manifesting His power, without recognising or sanctioning
the instrument. And again, it is true, as He tells us
Himself, that in the last day "Many shall say, Lord,
Lord, have we not prophesied in Thy Name, and in
Thy Name cast out devils, and done many miracles?"
and that He shall answer, "I never knew you". This,
I say, is undeniable; it is undeniable first, that those
who have prophesied in God's Name may *afterwards*
fall from God, and lose their souls. Let a man be ever
so holy now, he may fall away ; and, as present grace
is no pledge of perseverance, much less are present
gifts ; but how does this show that gifts and graces do
not commonly go together? Again, it is undeniable
that those who have had miraculous gifts may nevertheless have *never* been in God's favour, not even when
they exercised them ; as I will explain presently. But
I am now speaking, not of having gifts, but of being
prophets. To be a prophet is something much more
personal than to possess gifts. It is a sacred office, it
implies a mission, and is the high distinction, not of

the enemies of God, but of His friends. Such is the Scripture rule. Who was the first prophet and preacher of justice? Enoch, who walked "by faith," and "pleased God," and was taken from a rebellious world. Who was the second? "Noe," who "condemned the world, and was made heir of the justice which is through faith." Who was the next great prophet? Moses, the lawgiver of the chosen people, who was the "meekest of all men who dwell on the earth". Samuel comes next, who served the Lord from his infancy in the Temple; and then David, who, if he fell into sin, repented, and was "a man after God's heart". And in like manner Job, Elias, Isaias, Jeremias, Daniel, and above them all St. John Baptist, and then again St. Peter, St. Paul, St. John, and the rest, are all especial instances of heroic virtue, and patterns to their brethren. Judas is the exception, but this was by a particular dispensation to enhance our Lord's humiliation and suffering.

Nature itself witnesses to this connexion between sanctity and truth. It anticipates that the fountain from which pure doctrine comes should itself be pure; that the seat of Divine teaching, and the oracle of faith should be the abode of angels; that the consecrated home, in which the word of God is elaborated, and whence it issues forth for the salvation of the many, should be holy, as that word itself is holy. Here you see the difference of the office of a prophet and a mere gift, such as that of miracles. Miracles are the simple and direct work of God; the worker of them is but an instrument or organ. And in consequence he need not be holy, because he has not, strictly speaking, a share in the work. So again the power of administering the Sacraments, which also is supernatural and miraculous, does not imply personal holiness ; nor is there anything surprising in God's giving to a bad man this gift, or the gift of miracles, any more than in His giving him any natural talent or gift, strength or agility of frame, eloquence, or medical skill. It is otherwise with the office of preaching and prophesying, and to this I have been referring ; for the truth first goes into the minds of the speakers, and is apprehended and fashioned there, and then comes out from them as, in one sense, its source and its parent. The Divine word is begotten in them, and the offspring has their features and tells of them. They are not like "the dumb animal, speaking with man's voice," on which Balaam rode, a mere instrument of God's word, but they have "received an unction from the Holy One, and they know all things," and "where the Spirit of the Lord is, there is liberty"; and while they deliver what they have received, they enforce what they feel and know. "We have *known and believed*," says St. John, "the charity which God hath to us."

So has it been all through the history of the Church; Moses does not write as David ; nor Isaias as Jeremias ; nor St. John as St. Paul. And so of the great doctors of the Church, St. Athanasius, St. Augustine, St. Ambrose, St. Leo, St. Thomas, each has his own manner, each speaks his own words, though he speaks the while the words of God. They speak from themselves, they speak in their own persons, they speak from the heart, from their own experience, with their own arguments, with their own deductions, with their own modes of expression. Now can you fancy, my brethren, such hearts, such feelings to be unholy? how could it be so, without defiling, and thereby nullifying, the word of God? If one drop of corruption makes the purest water worthless, as the slightest savour of bitterness spoils the most delicate viands, how can it be that the word of truth and holiness can proceed profitably from impure lips and an earthly heart? No; as is the tree, so is the fruit; "beware of false prophets," says our Lord; and then He adds, "from their fruits ye shall know them. Do men gather grapes of thorns, or figs of thistles?" Is it not so, my brethren? which of you would go to ask counsel of another, however learned, however gifted, however aged, if you thought him unholy? nay, though you feel and are sure, as far as absolution goes, that a bad priest could give it as really as a holy priest, yet for advice, for comfort, for instruction, you would not go to one whom you did not respect. "Out of the abundance of the heart, the mouth speaketh;" "a good man out of the good treasure of his heart bringeth forth good, and an evil man out of the evil treasure bringeth forth evil".

So then is it in the case of the soul; but, as regards the Blessed Mary, a further thought suggests itself. She has no chance place in the Divine Dispensation; the Word of God did not merely come to her and go from her; He did not pass through her, as He visits us in Holy Communion. It was no heavenly body which the Eternal Son assumed, fashioned by the angels, and brought down to this lower world : no ; He imbibed, He absorbed into His Divine Person, her blood and the substance of her flesh ; by becoming man of her, He received her lineaments and features, as the appropriate character in which He was to manifest Himself to mankind. The child is like the parent, and we may well suppose that by His likeness to her was manifested her relationship to Him. Her sanctity comes, not only of her being His mother, but also of His being her son. " If the first fruit be holy," says St. Paul, " the mass also is holy ; if the mass be holy, so are the branches." And hence the titles which we are accustomed to give her. He is the Wisdom of God, she therefore is the Seat of Wisdom ; His Presence is Heaven, she therefore is the Gate of Heaven ; He is infinite Mercy, she then is the Mother of Mercy. She is the Mother of " fair love and fear, and knowledge and holy hope " ; is it wonderful then that she has left behind her in the Church below " an odour like cinnamon and balm, and sweetness like to choice myrrh " ?

Such, then, is the truth ever cherished in the deep heart of the Church, and witnessed by the keen apprehension of her children, that no limits but those proper to a creature can be assigned to the sanctity of Mary. Therefore, did Abraham believe that a son should be born to him of his aged wife ? then Mary's faith must be held as greater when she accepted Gabriel's message. Did Judith consecrate her widowhood to God to the surprise

24

of her people? much more did Mary, from her first youth, devote her virginity. Did Samuel, when a child, inhabit the Temple, secluded from the world? Mary too was by her parents lodged in the same holy precincts, even at the age when children first can choose between good and evil. Was Solomon on his birth called " dear to the Lord "? and shall not the destined Mother of God be dear to Him from the moment she was born? But further still; St. John Baptist was sanctified by the Spirit before his birth; shall Mary be only equal to him? is it not fitting that her privilege should surpass his? is it wonderful, if grace, which anticipated his birth by three months, should in her case run up to the very first moment of her being, outstrip the imputation of sin, and be beforehand with the usurpation of Satan? Mary must surpass all the saints; the very fact that certain privileges are known to have been theirs persuades us, almost from the necessity of the case, that she had the same and higher. Her conception was immaculate, in order that she might surpass all saints in the date as well as the fulness of her sanctification.

But in a festive season, my dear brethren, I must not weary you with argument, when we should offer specially to the Blessed Virgin the homage of our love and loyalty; yet, let me finish as I have begun;—I will be brief, but bear with me if I view her bright Assumption, as I have viewed her immaculate purity, rather as a point of doctrine than as a theme for devotion.

It was surely fitting then, it was becoming, that she

should be taken up into heaven and not lie in the grave till Christ's second coming, who had passed a life of sanctity and of miracle such as hers. All the works of God are in a beautiful harmony; they are carried on to the end as they begin. This is the difficulty which men of the world find in believing miracles at all; they think these break the order and consistency of God's visible word, not knowing that they do but subserve a higher order of things, and introduce a supernatural perfection. But at least, my brethren, when one miracle is wrought, it may be expected to draw others after it for the completion of what is begun. Miracles must be wrought for some great end; and if the course of things fell back again into a natural order before its termination, how could we but feel a disappointment? and if we were told that this certainly was to be, how could we but judge the information improbable and difficult to believe? Now this applies to the history of our Lady. I say, it would be a greater miracle if, her life being what it was, her death was like that of other men, than if it were such as to correspond to her life. Who can conceive, my brethren, that God should so repay the debt, which He condescended to owe to His Mother, for the elements of His human body, as to allow the flesh and blood from which it was taken to moulder in the grave? Do the sons of men thus deal with their mothers? do they not nourish and sustain them in their feebleness, and keep them in life while they are able? Or who can conceive that that virginal frame, which never sinned, was to undergo the death of a sinner? Why should she share the curse of Adam, who had no share in his fall ? " Dust thou art, and into dust thou shalt return," was the sentence upon sin ; she then, who was not a sinner, fitly never saw corruption. She died, then, as we hold, because even our Lord and Saviour died ; she died, as she suffered, because she was in this world, because she was in a state of things in which suffering and death are the rule. She lived under their external sway ; and, as she obeyed Cæsar by coming for enrolment to Bethlehem, so did she, when God willed it, yield to the tyranny of death, and was dissolved into soul and body, as well as others. But though she died as well as others, she died not as others die ; for, through the merits of her Son, by whom she was what she was, by the grace of Christ which in her had anticipated sin, which had filled her with light, which had purified her flesh from all defilement, she was also saved from disease and malady, and all that weakens and decays the bodily frame. Original sin had not been found in her, by the wear of her senses, and the waste of her frame, and the decrepitude of years, propagáting death. She died, but her death was a mere fàct, not an effect ; and, when it was over, it ceased to be. She died that she might live, she died as a matter of form or (as I may call it) an observance, in order to fulfil, what is called, the debt of nature,—not primarily for herself or because of sin, but to submit herself to her condition, to glorify God, to do what her Son did ; not however as her Son and Saviour, with any suffering for any special end ; not with a martyr's death, for

her martyrdom had been in living ; not as an atonement, for man could not make it, and One had made
it, and made it for all ; but in order to finish her
course, and to receive her crown.

And therefore she died in private. It became Him,
who died for the world, to die in the world's sight ; it
became the Great Sacrifice to be lifted up on high, as
a light that could not be hid. But she, the lily of
Eden, who had always dwelt out of the sight of man,
fittingly did she die in the garden's shade, and amid
the sweet flowers in which she had lived. Her departure made no noise in the world. The Church went
about her common duties, preaching, converting, suffering ; there were persecutions, there was fleeing from
place to place, there were martyrs, there were triumphs;
at length the rumour spread abroad that the Mother
of God was no longer upon earth. Pilgrims went to
and fro ; they sought for her relics, but they found
them not ; did she die at Ephesus ? or did she die at
Jerusalem ? reports varied ; but her tomb could not
be pointed out, or if it was found, it was open ; and
instead of her pure and fragrant body, there was a
growth of lilies from the earth which she had touched.
So inquirers went home marvelling, and waiting
for further light. And then it was said, how that
when her dissolution was at hand, and her soul was
to pass in triumph before the judgment-seat of her
Son, the apostles were suddenly gathered together in
the place, even in the Holy City, to bear part in the
joyful ceremonial ; how that they buried her with
fitting rites ; how that the third day, when they came

to the tomb, they found it empty, and angelic choirs with their glad voices were heard singing day and night the glories of their risen Queen. But, however we feel towards the details of this history (nor is there anything in it which will be unwelcome or difficult to piety), so much cannot be doubted, from the consent of the whole Catholic world and the revelations made to holy souls, that, as is befitting, she is, soul and body, with her Son and God in heaven, and that we are enabled to celebrate, not only her death, but her Assumption.

And now, my dear brethren, what is befitting in us, if all that I have been telling you is befitting in Mary? If the Mother of Emmanuel ought to be the first of creatures in sanctity and in beauty; if it became her to be free from all sin from the very first, and from the moment she received her first grace to begin to merit more; and if such as was her beginning, such was her end, her conception immaculate and her death an assumption; if she died, but revived, and is exalted on high; what is befitting in the children of such a Mother, but an imitation, in their measure, of her devotion, her meekness, her simplicity, her modesty, and her sweetness? Her glories are not only for the sake of her Son, they are for our sakes also. Let us copy her faith, who received God's message by the angel without a doubt; her patience, who endured St. Joseph's surprise without a word; her obedience, who went up to Bethlehem in the winter and bore our Lord in a stable; her meditative spirit, who pondered in her heart what she saw and heard about Him : her fortitude, whose heart the sword went through ; her self-surrender, who gave Him up during His ministry and consented to His death.

Above all, let us imitate her purity, who, rather than relinquish her virginity, was willing to lose Him for a Son. O my dear children, young men and young women, what need have you of the intercession of the Virgin-mother, of her help, of her pattern, in this respect ! What shall bring you forward in the narrow way, if you live in the world, but the thought and patronage of Mary ? What shall seal your senses, what shall tranquillise your heart, when sights and sounds of danger are around you, but Mary ? What shall give you patience and endurance, when you are wearied out with the length of the conflict with evil, with the unceasing necessity of precautions, with the irksomeness of observing them, with the tediousness of their repetition, with the strain upon your mind, with your forlorn and cheerless condition, but a loving communion with her ! She will comfort you in your discouragements, solace you in your fatigues, raise you after your falls, reward you for your successes. She will show you her Son, your God and your all. When your spirit within you is excited, or relaxed, or depressed, when it loses its balance, when it is restless and wayward, when it is sick of what it has, and hankers after what it has not, when your eye is solicited with evil and your mortal frame trembles under the shadow of the tempter, what will bring you to yourselves, to peace and to health, but the cool breath of the Immaculate and the fragrance of the Rose of Sharon? It is the boast of the Catholic Religion, that it has the gift of making the young heart chaste; and why is this, but that it gives us Jesus Christ for our food, and Mary for our nursing Mother? Fulfil this boast in yourselves; prove to the world that you are following no false teaching, vindicate the glory of your Mother Mary, whom the world blasphemes, in the very face of the world, by the simplicity of your own deportment, and the sanctity of your words and deeds. Go to her for the royal heart of innocence. She is the beautiful gift of God, which outshines the fascinations of a bad world, and which no one ever sought in sincerity and was disappointed. She is the personal type and representative image of that spiritual life and renovation in grace, "without which no one shall see God". "Her spirit is sweeter than honey, and her heritage than the honeycomb. They that eat her shall yet be hungry, and they that drink her shall still thirst. Whoso hearkeneth to her shall not be confounded, and they that work by her shall not sin."

THE END.

EDITOR'S NOTES

(Scripture references are to the Douai-Rheims version which Newman used after 1845.

The Patrology Collection – a collection of Greek and Latin Christian writers – assembled by J. P. Migne from 1844 onwards and known as Patrologia Graeca and Patrologia Latina, is referred to as PG and PL.)

Dedication:

in your Lordship's district: Nicholas Wiseman was bishop of the Midland district from 1840 until 1847 when he moved to London. He was made Cardinal and first Archbishop of Westminster in 1850.

to the service of St. Philip: Newman wrote to T. F. Knox on 20 August 1846, 'Dr W (iseman) wishes us to join some body such as the Oratorians ... the name of St. Philip Neri is great, and there is no one whole personage I would sooner be under.' *Letters and Diaries* XI, p. 226.

a controversial paper: 'The Anglican Claim of Apostolical Succession', *Dublin Review* vii, August 1839, pp. 139–180. See *Apologia*, p. 116ff. Newman writes to Frederic Rogers on 22 September 1839, 'Since I wrote to you, I have had the first real hit from Romanism which has happened to me.' *Letters and Diaries* VII, p. 154.

DISCOURSE 1

p. 1. *Alcester Street*: The establishment began on 2 February 1849. Newman notes in his diary, 'Chapel opened: F. Ambrose (St. John) cele- brated, I preached.' *Letters and Diaries* XIII, p. 22. This probably became the basis of the first discourse.

p. 2. *it is a laborious, energetic, indefatigable world*: Newman frequently alludes to the frenetic pace of industrial England. 'Dissipation of mind, which these amusements create, is itself indeed miserable enough: but far worse than this dissipation is the concentration of mind upon some wordly object, which admits of being constantly pursued, – and such is the pursuit of gain. Nor is it a slight aggravation of the evil, that anxiety is almost sure to attend it.' *Parochial and Plain Sermons* II, p. 353. Henry Mayhew wrote in 1849 in *The Morning Chronicle* about sweated labour. Dickens would later write of Coketown in *Hard Times* 'You saw nothing in Coketown but what was severely workful.' (I, p. 5).

p. 3. *so pleasant is the excitement*: Newman contrasts the effort bestowed on earthly pleasures compared with heavenly delights: 'How will the soul feel when stripped of its present attire, which the world bestows, it stands naked and shuddering before the pure, tranquil and severe majesty of the Lord its God? ... What are to be the pleasures of the soul in another life? Can they be the same as they are here? They cannot.' *Parochial and Plain Sermons* VII, p. 234.

p. 4. *For religion itself ... is ... a hidden thing*: Tract 87 says 'The Church realizes the kingdom of God albeit in secret.' The theme forms part of Newman's treatment of the communion of saints which came to the fore in his later sermons. See in this respect the sermons: 'The Church and the World', *Sermons on Subjects of the Day* 8 'The Invisible World' and 'Christ Hidden from the World', *Parochial and Plain Sermons Sermons* IV, pp. 14 and 18.

p. 5. *sin, judgment, heaven and hell*: The doctrine of the Four Last Things deals with death, judgement, hell and heaven.

p. 5. *like children sitting*: Matt. 11:16–18; 25–26.

p. 6. *in a district, so destitute*: Birmingham was at the heart of the Industrial Revolution. It was constantly wreathed in smoke and attracted many immigrants, particularly the Irish, as a result of the famine. These were to provide the basis for the Alcester Street congregation. Newman wrote to J. D. Dalgairns on 9 November 1845, 'London is a centre – Oxford is a centre – Brummagem is no centre', *Letters and Diaries* XI, p. 30.

p. 6. *The world forms its views of things for itself*: This theme is treated in 'The World our Enemy', *Parochial and Plain Sermons* VII, p. 3.

p. 6. *little does it trouble itself*: Newman preached 'How will the soul feel when stripped of its present attire, which the world bestows, it stands naked and shuddering before the pure, tranquil and severe majesty of the Lord its God? What are to be the pleasures of the soul in another life? Can they be the same as they are here? They cannot.' *Parochial and Plain Sermons* VII, p. 24.

p. 6. *is not solicitous*: Matt. 6:34.

p. 7. *all mortification and self-discipline*: Newman had come up against all these arguments before, especially over Littlemore where he was accused of starting 'a monastery'. Mrs John Ruskin writing from Venice cannot hide her horror about 'miracles, the gift of the Spirit, Penance and crucifying the flesh.' *Effie in Venice: Unpublished Letters of Mrs John Ruskin written from Venice between 1849–1852*, London, John Murray, 1963, p. 330.

p. 7. *fated to perdition*: Catholic faith rejects predestination to glory or to damnation. The Council of Trent states 'Those who fall away by sin from the grace of justification which they had received, can again be justified when at God's prompting they have made the effort through the sacrament of penance to recover, by the merit of Christ, the grace which was lost' (Session 6, Chapter 14).

p. 10. *engaging manners*: Newman puts this into his literary character Jucundus in *Callista* 'He was a good-natured man, self-indulgent, positive, and warmly attached to the reigning paganism' (*Callista*, p. 21).

p. 11. *in came the devil, and took possession*: The allusion is to the parable in Matt. 12:44.

p. 12. *Cain*: I John 3:12; *Eliseus* 2; Kings 2:23–25.

p. 13. *Posuisti saeculum nostrum in illuminatione vultus Tui*: Ps. 89:9. The complete text reads 'Posuisti iniquitates nostras in conspectu tuo, saeculum nostrum in illuminatione vultus tui.' Newman left out the 'iniquities before your eyes'.

p. 14. *a whited sepulchre*: Matt. 11:44.

p. 14. *without faith, and without hope*: Eph. 2:12.

p. 14. *his old enemy*: Satan, who brushes aside the guardian angel.

p. 15. *"lamented by a large circle of friends"*: Newman is quoting the standard obituaries, with a large dose of irony.

p. 15. *he is lifting up his eyes*: Dives the rich man in the parable (Luke 16:23).

p. 16. *"As soon as they are born"*: Ps. 58:4.

p. 16. *Such as is the tree*: The reference is to Matt. 12:33 'Either make the tree good and its fruit good: or make the tree evil, and its fruit evil. For by the fruit the tree is known.'

p. 17. *Presence of the Word Incarnate*: Newman wrote to Henry Wilberforce when he first came to Maryvale, with its own chapel 'It is such an incomprehensive blessing to have Christ in bodily presence in one's house within one's walls.' *Letters and Diaries* XI, p. 129.

p. 18. *what have we done, that we should be distrusted?*: This will surface again in Charles Kingsley's remarks (which occasioned the *Apologia* in 1864) 'Truth, for its own sake, had never been a virtue with the Roman clergy.' *MacMillan's Magazine*, January, 1864, p, 217.

p. 18. *"Freely ye have received"*: Matt. 10:8.

p. 18. *a napkin*: a reference to the parable of the talents (Matt. 25:18).

p. 19. *"I am come to send fire.."*: Luke 12:49.

p. 19. *"I send thee to the Gentiles"*: Acts 26:17–19.

p. 19. *". . . the charity of Christ constrained him"*: See 2 Cor. 5:14.

p. 19. *"made all things to all"*: 1 Cor. 9:22.

p. 19. *". . . bore all for the elect's sake"*: 2 Tim. 2:10.

DISCOURSE 2
p. 22. Some of this discourse is based on St. Alphonsus' homily for the first Sunday in Lent in *Sermons for all the Sundays of the Year* (James Duffy, Dublin, 1843). Newman remarks to F. W. Faber in *Letters and Diaries* XIII, p. 341: 'In the said Sermon I have but made easy-going Catholics in danger of hell. But the best joke is that the Sermon (the only one in the Volume) is taken from St. Alfonso's for the 1st Sunday in Lent, on "The number of sins beyond which God pardons no more" – with text "Thou shalt not tempt the Lord thy god."'

p. 23. *The last Sacraments:* These are penance, the sacrament of the sick and viaticum.

p. 24. *"fiery serpents"*: Num. 21:6 and see 1 Cor. 10:9.

p. 24. *"Thou shalt not tempt the Lord"*: Matt. 4:5–8.

p. 25. "I cannot give up sin now": Augustine in his *Confessions* (Book 8, Chapter 11) says 'Do you think you can live without them?' (i.e. his vices).

p. 27. *"Thou hast sealed up my sins as in a bag"*: Job 31:33.

p. 28. *"Fill ye up the measure of your fathers"*: i.e. complete what they started (Matt. 23:32).

p. 28. *"the iniquities of the Amorrhites . . ."*: They were defeated in the reign of King Sihon, and their land divided up among the tribes (Gen. 15:16).

p. 29. *"God hath numbered thy kingdom"*: Dan. 4:28.

p. 29. *"What shall I do.."*: Luke 12:17ff.

p. 30. *"Is not this great Babylon ..?"*: Dan. 4:27ff.

p. 31. *"if the inhabitants of Tyre and Sidon"*: Matt. 11:21ff.

p. 32. *The last Sacraments*: See note on page 23.

p. 33. *The Bethsamites looked upon the ark of the Lord*: In fact they looked *into* the ark (1 Sam. 6:19).

p. 33. *Oza touched it with his hand*: 2 Sam. 6:6.

p. 33. *The man of God from Juda*: 1 Kings 13.

p. 33. *Ananias and Sapphira:* Acts 5:1ff.

p. 33. *We do not know what sin is*: Newman comments in 'Self-Denial The Test of Religious Earnestness: 'Men are satisfied to have numberless secret faults. They do not think about them, either as sins or as obstacles to strength of faith, and live on as if they had nothing to learn.' *Parochial and Plain Sermons* I, p. 43.

p. 34. *showed what he thought of sin by dying for it*: Newman had originally written '... what he thought of sin by resolving to become man'. He supported the theological argument of Blessed John Duns Scotus, the Scottish Franciscan (1274–1308) as he explained in a letter to F.W. Faber on 9 December 1849 – *Letters and Diaries* XIII p. 335 – that Christ would have become incarnate without sin, as our Saviour, but since humanity had sinned, He came also in order to redeem, 'to make satisfaction'. See also note on p. 307 and compare with *Pastoral and Plain Sermons* VI, 'The

Incarnate Son, a Sufferer and Sacrifice', p. 79.

p. 35. *They are not in the labour of men*: Job 21:8–14.

p. 35. *"See ye all these things"*: Matt. 24:2.

p. 35. *"He beheld the city"*: Luke 19:41–43.

p. 37. *some poor measure of contrition*: At least imperfect (i.e. because of the fear of eternal punishment) is required for the absolution of sins.

p. 38. *when the judge speaks*: Matt. 18:34.

p. 39. *Demas*: Col. 4:14; *Judas*: Acts 15:22; *Nicholas*: Acts 6:5; *Philetus*: 2 Tim. 2:17; *Alexander*: 2 Tim. 4:14; *Diotrephes*: A disciple who loved pre-eminence (3 John 1:9).

p. 40. *"the saying of a very sensible man"*: Jucundus says to Agellius, to persuade him to renounce his faith "Now be a sensible fellow, as you are when you choose ... You must give in" (*Callista* pp. 242–3).

p. 40. *O vanity of vanities*: Eccles. 1:2.

p. 42. *pit's mouth*: The Offertory Prayer for Requiems (before the reforms of Vatican II) prayed 'O Lord Jesus Christ, King of Glory, deliver the souls of all the faithful departed from the pains of hell and from the deep pit.'

p. 42. *five dear Wounds*: A Roman Catholic devotion to the wounds Jesus received during his Passion (celebrated in some countries on the fourth Friday of Lent).

p. 42. *"God, have mercy on us, and bless us"*: Ps. 67:1.

DISCOURSE 3

p. 43. *Immaculate Mother*: Newman's devotion to Mary Immaculate led him to ask Pius IX that his congregation might celebrate a feast under that name instead of the Assumption. He was to dedicate the church of the Birmingham Oratory under that title in 1851, three years before the definition of the dogma. See his remarks to W. G. Ward in *Letters and Diaries* XIII, p. 82.

p. 43. *Sun of justice*. Mal. 3:20.

p. 44. *in the garb of men*: see Gen. 18:2; Heb. 13:2.

p. 44. *those blessed realms*: Richard Baxter (1615–1691) the Shropshire clergyman who later became a chaplain to Charles II begins his hymn 'Ye holy angels bright,/ Who wait at God's right hand,/ Or through the realms of light/ Fly at your Lord's command' (An edition of his complete works – in 23 volumes – was published in 1830).

p. 45. *'Ye men of Galilee'*: Acts 1:11.

p. 45. *"the world, the flesh, and the devil"*: The Catechism of Christian Doctrine (Question 348) asks 'Which are the enemies we must fight against all the days of our life?' The answer is 'The devil, the world and the flesh.'

p. 45. *"O men why do ye this?"*: Acts 14:15.

p. 45. *"We preach not ourselves"*: 2 Cor. 4:5–8.

p. 46. *".. an angel of Satan"*: 2 Cor. 12:7.

p. 46. *"The finest wheat-flour"*: Valid matter for the Eucharist is bread made from wheat and wine made from the juice of grapes (Code of Canon Law Canon 924).

p. 47. *girdle of celibacy ... maniple of sorrow*: This refers to the prayers used in vesting: 'Gird me, O Lord, with the cincture of purity and extinguish in my body every carnal vestige so that the virtue of continence and chastity will live in me always.' And for the maniple 'May I merit, O Lord to carry this maniple of tears and suffering that, one day, I may with great joy receive the reward of my labour.'

p. 47. *"Every high Priest"*: Heb. 5:1–4.

p. 47. *"Suscipe, Sancte Pater"*: The *oblatio* in the Roman Canon of the Mass (before the reforms of Vatican II).

p. 47. *"condole with those who are in ignorance"*: Heb. 5:2.

p. 48. *"was tempted in all things"* Heb. 4:15.

p. 48. *Doctors*: Eminent teachers of Christian faith, given the title 'Doctors of the Church'. In the eighth century the Latin Church recognised St. Ambrose, St. Jerome, St. Augustine and St. Gregory the Great. The Eastern Churches venerated St. Basil, St. Gregory of Nazianzus and St. John Chrystostom. The Latin Church has since added over twenty.

p. 49. *Grace has vanquished nature*: St. Augustine says 'God has not only given us the ability and his help in exercising it, but he also works in us 'to will and to do' not because we do not will, or because we do not do, but because without his help we neither will nor do anything good. *The Grace of Christ and Original Sin*, PL 44. 373.

p. 49. *"Tota pulchra es Maria.."*: First antiphon at Vespers on 8 December, the feast of the Immaculate Conception.

p. 50. *children of wrath*: Eph. 2:3.

p. 51. *kept his baptismal robe unsullied*: St. Philip Neri (1515–1595), the founder of the Oratorians, told several people, including Baronius who was then his confessor that God had 'kept him in virginity from his youth' Ponnelle & Bordet, *St. Philip Neri and The Roman Society of his Times*, London, Sheed & Ward, 1937, p. 69; 'perhaps he never committed a mortal sin', *Catholic Sermons*, p. 74.

p. 51. *a much higher state*: As a development of the pauline comment 'Where sin increased, grace abounded all the more (Rom. 5:20), Catholic teaching says that the sinner, through grace, can attain a higher state than before the Fall of Adam.'

p. 52. *A publican became an Apostle*: i.e. St. Matthew. Mark 2:14ff.

p. 52. *the learned Pharisee*: Nicodemus, John 3:1ff.

p. 53. *St. Augustine*: Augustine, first Archbishop of Canterbury, sent by St. Gregory in 597, died 604.

p. 54. *a far-spread sect*: The Manichees (owing its origin to Mani who first preached in Persia in 242) held that there were two principles at work in creation, Good and Evil. St. Augustine was a follower for twelve years. See *Confessions* Book 5, Chapter 13 and Book 6, Chapter 11.

p. 55. *A great Saint*: St. Ambrose of Milan (339–397). He baptised Augustine in 386. Newman visited his church in Milan in September 1846.

p. 55. O, sin was so sweet: Augustine says in his *Confessions* 'I was bound by this need of the flesh, and dragged with me the chain of its poisonous delights.' Book 6, Chapter 12.

p. 57. *"his flesh was restored to him"*: 2 Kings 5:14.

p. 57. *St. Agnes*: Died *c.* 350 in Rome, aged 13.

p. 57. *Aloysius*: St. Aloysius Gonzaga (1568–91) died as a result of nursing plague victims.

p. 57. *St. Agatha*: Virgin and martyr, died in Catania in the third century.

p. 57. *St Juliana*: Probably martyred in Naples in the fourth century.

p. 57. *St. Rose*: St. Rose of Lima (1586–1617) was the first canonised saint of America.

p. 57. *St. Casimir*: (1458–1484), prince of Poland, renowned for his asceticism, died of a lung disease.

p. 57. *St. Stanislas*: St. Stanislas Koska (1550–1568), son of a Polish senator, died shortly after joining the Jesuit noviciate.

p. 58. minsters of reconciliation: 2 Cor. 5:18.

p. 60. *instruct you in the spirit of meekmess*: Gal. 6:1.

p. 60. *Come then unto us*: See Matt. 11:28.

p. 61. *"come, listen, all ye that fear God"*: Ps. 66:16.

p. 61. *the glorious liberty of the sons of God*: Rom. 8:21.

p. 61. *after they have preached to others*: See 1 Cor. 9.27: Newman preached in 1838 'Beware, lest by objections you provoke God to take from you His aid, His preventing and enlightening grace.' *Parochial and Plain Sermons* VI, p. 149.

DISCOURSE 4
p. 64. *original guilt*: This refers to the tradition that John the Baptist was freed from sin in the womb, see Luke 1:41.

p. 64. *St. Gregory*: St. Gregory the Great (540–604).

p. 64. *St. Bernard*: (1090–1153), Abbot of Clairvaux 1115–1153.

p. 64. *St. Aloysius*: (1568–1591), St. Aloysius Gonzaga, Jesuit.

p. 64. *except perhaps the prophet Jeremias*: This is a reference to Jer. 1:5

'Before I found you in the womb I knew you.'

p. 65. *"Greatly to be honoured is blessed John"*: This is a translation of the first responsory from the old breviary reading for the feast of St. John.

p. 66. *professed his readiness to drink Christ's chalice*: Matt. 20:23.

p. 66. *plunged into the hot oil*: According to the traditional account of John's passion at the Latin Gate in Rome. He survived miraculously and was subsequently exiled to Patmos.

p. 66. *"a voice crying"*: Matt. 3:3.

p. 66. *"in the Spirit on the Lord's Day"*: Rev. 1:10.

p. 67. *The great St. Antony*: Antony (251-356), the Egyptian abbot, the pioneer of desert monasticism.

p. 67. *St. Cecilia*: The early Christian martyr who convinced her husband to respect her virginity by promising that he would see her guardian angel. He then saw the angel offering Cecilia and himself floral crowns.

p. 67. *St. Peter Celestine*: Peter Morone, Celestine V (1210–1296), the hermit chosen to be pope.

p. 67. *St. Rose of Viterbo*: 1234–1252.

p. 67. *St. Catherine of Siena*: (1347–1380), the Dominican tertiary and author of *The Dialogue*.

p. 67. *"seat of wisdom . . . ark of the covenant"*: Titles of Mary in the Litany of Loreto. See Newman's comments in *Meditations and Devotions*, p. 47.

p. 68. *out of the very stones*: Matt. 3:9.

p. 69. *His own Mother Mary*: In the person of St. John (John 19:27).

p. 69. *"by the cords of Adam"*: Hos. 11:4.

p. 69. *"instruments of iniquity"*: Rom. 7:18. Newman seems to have modified the Douai text which reads "Being then made free from sin, you are become the servants of justice."

p. 69. *"Thou hast seduced me, O Lord"*: Jer. 20:7.

p. 70. *"bringing into captivity the whole intellect"*: A variation of 2 Cor. 10:5 'bringing into captivity every understanding unto the obedience of Christ.'

p. 70. *"the vision of Angels"*: The reference is to Jacob's vision at Bethel (Gen. 28:12).

p. 70. *"How dear are Thy tabernacles"*: Ps. 84:11–12.

p. 70. *"It is not enough to be drawn by the will"*: Newman expresses the sense of the passage from Augustine's homilies on St. John "I say it is not enough to be drawn by the will; thou art drawn even by delight. What is it to be drawn by delight? 'Delight thyself in the Lord, and He shall give thee the desires of thy heart.' There is a pleasure of the heart to which that bread of heaven is sweet." Homily 26,4 on St. John PL 35, 1608.

p. 70. *"if the poet saith"*: George Herbert (1593–1633) among others 'Hearken unto a Verser, who may chance, /Rhyme thee to good, and make a bait of pleasure.' *The Church Porch.*

p. 71. *The sons of men shall hope*: Ps. 36:8–10.

p. 71. *"He, whom the Father draweth"*: John 6:44.

p. 71. *"Thou art Christ"*. Matt. 16:16.

p. 71. *it is the very triumph of His grace*: Augustine says '(Grace) goes before us so that we may be cured; it will follow so that we may be glorified; it goes before so that we may live faithfully: it will follow so that we may live forever with him, for "without him we can do nothing"' 35, 36 P L 44, p. 266.

p. 72. *the flame of charity*: A reference to the words in the Prayer to the Holy Spirit 'Kindle in them the fire of Thy love ...' also 'With love our hearts inflame' from the Hymn 'Veni Creator Spiritus'.

p. 72. *"the first-fruits"*: Rev. 7:13ff.

p. 73. *"Simon, son of John"*: John 21:16ff.

p. 73. *"they knew not that it was Jesus"*: John 21:4.

p. 73. *"the clean of heart shall see God"*: Matt. 5:8.

p. 73. *"Lord, if it be Thou"*: Matt. 14:28.

p. 74. *"And the Lord turned"*: Luke 22:61.

p. 74. *"Do you too wish to go away?"*: John 6:67ff.

p. 74. *"for the charity of Christ constraineth us"*: 2 Cor.. 5:13ff.

p. 74. "*With Christ I am nailed to the cross*": Gal. 2:19.

p. 74. *"I am the least of the Apostles"*: 1 Cor. 15:9.

p. 75. *"Whether we live"*: Phil. 1:20.

p. 75. *"strong as death"*: Song 6:6.

p. 75. *"I have fought the good fight"*: 2 Tim. 4:7.

p. 75. *"the woman who was a sinner"*: Luke 7:39.

p. 75. *"rejoicing in her youth"*: Eccles. 11:9.

p. 76. *"compass sea and land"*: Matt. 23:15.

p. 76. *"the brightness of the Eternal Light"*: Heb. 1:3.

p. 77. seven bad spirits: Mark 16:9.

p. 77. *Destruction is thine own, O Israel*: Jer. 3:23ff.

p. 78. *"Many sins are forgiven her"*: Luke 7:47.

p. 78. *St. Ignatius Loyola*: (1491–1556), the founder of the Jesuits, who turned to God after being wounded at the siege of Pamplona.

p. 78. *the best part*: Luke 10:42.

p. 79. *"Tell me where"*: John 20:15.

p. 79. *what is contrition without love?*: Perfect contrition proceeds from the motive of love of God rather than fear of punishment.

p. 80. *Author and Finisher of faith*: Heb. 12:2.

p. 80. *"poured over your hearts by the Holy Ghost"*: Rom. 5:5.

p. 81. *Alas! how will you present yourselves?*: Rom. 14:10; 2 Cor. 5:10.

p. 81. *to be at once remanded from Thee*: Newman returns to the theme in *The Dream of Gerontius* 'I go before my Judge ... Take me away, and in the lowest deep/ There let me be', *Verses on Various Occasions*, p. 362.

p. 81. Yea, though I be now descending thither. On this and the 'willing plunge' see *Sermon Notes of Cardinal Newman*, p. 270.

p. 82. *a land desert*: Deut. 8:15.

p. 82. *Confiteor*: The first words of the *I Confess* penitential prayer which began the Mass before the Vatican II reforms.

p. 82. *"bring me out of prison"*: Gen. 40:14ff.

p. 82. *"God shall wipe away every tear"*: Rev. 21:4.

DISCOURSE 5

p. 83. *It is called conscience*: Newman has Callista say to the aristocrat, Polemo "I feel that God within my heart. I feel myself in His presence ... It carries with it its proof of its divine origin ... I believe in what is more than a mere 'something'. *Callista*, p. 314. This will be further developed in *An Essay in aid of A Grammar of Assent*, pp. 117–8.

p. 84. *the Light, which lightens*: John. 1:9.

p. 84. *our Eternal Home*: Newman evokes Eccles. 12:5 which forms part of the Anglican funeral service.

p. 86. *It is like those ashes*: The sixth plague (Exod. 9:8ff).

p. 87. *the light of the invisible world*: See sermon of the same title *Parochial and Plain Sermons* IV, p. 13.

p. 87. *"in the land of wretchedness and gloom"*: Job 10:21–22.

p. 88. *"walk in the light of their fire"*: Dan. 3:24.

p. 89. *They measure happiness by wealth*: Newman preached in 1835 on The Danger of Riches 'The danger of possessing riches is the carnal security to which they lead; that of 'desiring' and pursuing them, is, that an object of this world is thus set before us as the aim and end of life.' *Parochial and Plain Sermons* II, p. 349.

p. 90. *Never could notoriety*: Notice the repetition of the word *notoriety* used in connection with news now being rapidly disseminated. Newman was to write in 1850 about the 'wonderful' knowledge 'Just as in England, the whole community, whatever the moral state of the individuals *knows* about railroads and electric telegraph; and about the Court and men in power, and proceedings in Parliament; and about religious affairs, and about foreign affairs, and about all that is going on around and beyond them,' (*Certain Difficulties Felt by Anglicans in Catholic Teaching* I, p. 276) and he preached at the same time on the Mission of St. Philip 'to some minds notoriety itself is a gratification and a snare' (*Sermons Preached on Various Occasions* p. 242). See also *Catholic Sermons*, p. 38.

p. 90. *news of the hour*: *The Times* with its eight-feed rotary press installed in 1849 could produce 9,600 copies in an hour. The *News of the World* started publication in 1843.

p. 91. *great experimentalist*: Possibly Michael Faraday (1791–1867), Professor of Chemistry at the Royal Institution who was then conducting experiments in electricity.

p. 92. *"These are Thy gods, O Israel"*: Exod. 32:4.

p. 92. *Jesus, the Sun of Justice*: Mal. 3:20.

p. 92. *Morning Star*: Title of Mary in the Litany of Loreto. See Newman in *Meditations and Devotions*, p. 111.

p. 93. *"His face did shine"*: Matt. 17:2ff.

p. 93. *"to the city of the Living God"*: Heb. 12:22–24.

p. 94. *they praise what they do not imitate*: Newman makes a pertinent observation about Roman Catholics keeping an allegiance even though they cannot remain faithful to all of the demands of their faith. This was often argued against his co-religionists.

p. 95. *a child of wrath*: Eph. 2:3.

p. 95. *"bids fair to be a Saint"*: This was said of St. Philip Neri (Pippo buono).

p. 96. *"the wicked one toucheth him not"*: 1 John 5:18.

p. 96. *such things are accidents*: Unless there is a deliberate act of the will, the grace of God abides, in spite of such imperfections.

p. 96. *".. a living, holy, acceptable sacrifice"*: A translation of the words in the Canon of the Mass (before the Vatican II reforms) 'Be pleased, O God, to bless this offering, to accept it fully, to make it perfect and worthy to please You.'

p. 97. *witness of the world unseen*: In 1836 Newman preached 'There are in every age a certain number of souls in the world, known to God, unknown to us ... God is neither 'without witness' nor without fruit, even in a heathen country.' *Parochial and Plain Sermons* IV, pp. 153–4.

p. 98. *to be tried as in a furnace*: See Wisd. 3:6.

p. 98. *crown reserved for him*: Jas. 1:12.

p. 99. *St. Benedict*: He received the monastic habit from a monk called Romanus *c.* AD 500 and retired for three years to a cave at Subiaco on Monte Calvo.

p. 99. *St. Thomas*: St. Thomas Aquinas (1225–74) was given the title of Angelic Doctor, because of the sublimity of his theology. He was declared Doctor of the Church in 1567 by Pope Pius V.

p. 99. *"Even from a youth"*: This is Newman's translation of parts of the Office of Doctors of the Church in the old breviary.

p. 99. *bit off his tongue ... out*: Newman is quoting the *Depositio Martyrum* which relates the second-century death of seven brothers. The account was based upon the death of the seven Maccabees in 2 Macc. 7, and is probably spurious.

p. 100. *what God can do, and what man can be*: Newman returns to this theme in his *Essay in Aid of a Grammar of Assent* when he writes that 'the sovereign Thought in which (the martyrs) had lived was their adequate support and consolation in their death: *Essay in aid of a Grammar of Assent*, p. 478.

p. 101. *redemption of Christian slaves*: St. John of Maltha founded the Trinitarian Order for ransoming Christian captives in 1198.

p. 101. *such as turning the cheek*: Matt. 5:39–40.

p. 102. *it leads to decency and order*: Newman comments in the *Lectures* of 1851 'No wonder, then, that Protestantism, being the religion of our literature, has become the Tradition of civil intercourse and political life; no wonder that its assumptions are among the elements unchangeable as the moods of logic, or the idioms of language, or the injunctions of good taste, or the proprieties of good manners.' *Present Position of Catholics*, p. 72.

p. 102. *It is powerless to resist the world*: In *Arians of the Fourth Century* Newman makes the point 'Certain it is, that the true faith never could come into contact with the heathen philosophies, without exercising its right to arbitrate between them, to protest against their vicious or erroneous dogmas, and to extend its countenance to whatever bore an exalted or a practical character.' p. 101.

p. 103. *There is but one real Antagonist*: i.e. Satan, Rev. 12:9.

DISCOURSE 6

p. 105. *the first act of reason*: The Code of Canon Law states that 'with the completion of the seventh year one is presumed to have the use of reason' (97 §2).

p. 105. *the great Babylon*: Isa. 21:9; Rev. 14:8.

p. 105. *Every man is doing his own will*: Newman draws loosely on the parable in Luke 12:19ff.

p. 106. *This is the end of man*: A refrain which Newman loads with irony.

p. 106. *medicines for the credulous*: James Graham (1745–1794) – the so-called Emperor of Quacks – sold in his Grand Temple of Health in London electrical aether, elixirs of life, nervous aetherials and imperial pills (See Williams Guy, *The Age of Agony*, London, Constable, 1975, pp. 188ff).

p. 107. *wars and rumours of wars*: The reference is to Matthew 24:6. 1848 saw revolutions in Paris, Vienna and Berlin. The Roman Republic was proclaimed at the end of February. The Chartist movement reached its height in June 1848 when Wellington mobilised troops to guard London.

p. 107. *old statesmen going off the scene*: Sir Robert Peel (1788–1850) had resigned in 1846 after the debate over the repeal of the Corn Laws. The Duke of Wellington (1769–1852) who had been minister without portfolio in his government also retired from public life, and Lord Melbourne (b. 1779) died in 1848. All were former Prime Ministers.

p. 109. *"Lo, I come to do Thy will"*: Ps. 40:7; Heb. 10:7.

p. 109. *".. the Lord God hath opened Mine ear"*: Isa. 50:5.

p. 109. *".. the will of Him that sent Me"*: John 4:34.

p. 109. *"Not My will but Thine"*: Matt. 26:39.

p. 109. *"Christ pleased not Himself"*: Rom. 15:3.

p. 109. *"though He was God's Son"*: Heb. 4:15.

p. 110. *two journeys:* to visit Elizabeth and for the birth of Jesus in a stable.

p. 110. *He had not where to lay His head*: Matt. 8:20.

p. 111. *to call her coldly* "woman": At the marriage feast of Cana (John 2:4).

p. 111. *as Levi, His type*: The tribe of Levi has no portion or inheritance with his brothers (Deut. 10:9).

p. 111. *"I know you not"*: In fact "Who is my mother and who are my brethren?' Matt. 12:49.

p. 111. *"He that loveth mother more than Me"*: Matt. 10:37.

p. 112. *as a scene in a theatre*: 'For I think that God hath set forth us apostles, the last, as it were men appointed to death: we are made a spectacle (spectaculum=stage show) to the world, and to angels, and to men' (1 Cor. 4:9).

p. 113. *a sort of science of their sensuality*: The use of alliteration provides a neat summary of the parable in Luke 16:19ff. Newman comments in *The Idea of a University* 'the very refinement of intellectualism which began by repelling sensuality, ends by excusing it' (p. 202).

p. 115. *Catholic and Methodist*: Newman comments to E. L. Badeley on 23 August 1844 'Every form of heresy is tolerated, but there is an instinctive irritation, or shudder at anything too Catholic' *Correspondence of John Henry Newman with John Keble and Others 1839–1845,* London, 1917, p. 327. This is the theme of much of *Present Position of Catholics*. See the introduction to the Millennium Edition p. xlff. In a clear allusion to Methodism and other dissenters, Newman queries '… whether the Protestant Establishment is as indulgent and as wise as might be desired in its treatment of such persons, inasmuch as it provides no occupation for them, does not understand how to turn them to account, lets them run to waste, tempts them to dissent, loses them, is weakened by the loss, and then denounces them.' *Historical Sketches* II, p. 98.

p. 115. *frivolous publications*: *Reynolds Miscellany* (gossip journal) began publication in 1847.

p. 115. *to have read the latest novel*: Since Newman was an avid reader of Anthony Trollope, he was probably thinking of *The Kellys and the O'Kellys* published in 1848.

p. 115. *to have heard the singer*: Jenny Lind sang at the London premiere of Verdi's *I Masnadieri* conducted by the composer on 22 July 1847.

p. 115. *seen the actor of the day*: William Charles Macready (1793–1873) was famous for his Lear and Hamlet.

p. 116. *"the brightness of the Eternal Light"*: Heb. 1:3.

p. 116. *brutes by the law of their nature*: Aristotle in *The Nichomachean Ethics* (I, 5) says men of this kind are evidently quite slavish in their tastes, preferring a life suitable to beasts.

p. 119. *the prerogative of the Mother of God*: i.e. her immaculate conception.

p. 120. *"through many tribulations"*: Acts 14:21.

p. 121. *Mortal sins are the children of venial (sins)*: Although they do not deprive us of the grace and loving presence of God, they do predispose us gradually towards mortal or grave sin. See note on p. 128.

p. 121. *under your vine and under your fig-tree*: The symbol of established peace and contentment (1 Kings 5:5).

p. 121. *"I have glorified Thee on earth"*: John 17:4.6.

p. 121. *"I have fought the good fight"*: 2 Tim. 4:7ff.

p. 123. *the ships of Tarshish*: They brought with them gold, silver, ivory, apes and peacocks (1 Kings 10:22), but Psalm 48:7 sees them broken to pieces.

p. 123. *O my Lord and Saviour*: A Newman prayer based on the reception of the last sacraments and the prayer of commendation which proceeds them.

DISCOURSE 7

p. 124. *It is true indeed that we merit*: This expresses the teaching of the Council of Trent 'Thus, to those who work well right to the end and keep their trust in God, eternal life should be held out, both as a grace promised in his mercy through Jesus Christ to the children of God, and as a reward to be faithfully bestowed, on the promise of God himself, for their good works and merits' (Session 6, Chapter 16).

p. 125. *grace brings us into that state of grace*: Trent says that 'Those who had been turned away from God by sins are disposed by God's grace inciting and helping them, to turn towards their own justification by giving free assent to and co-operating with this same grace' (Session 6, Chapter 5).

p. 125. *"..hidden things"*: Deut. 29:28.

p. 126. *He is the Alpha and Omega*: Rev. 21:6.

p. 127. *His grace begins the work*: See note on page 125.

p. 127. *"Holy Father, keep in Thy name"*: John 17:11.15.

p. 127. *"He who had begun"*: Phil. 1:6.

p. 127. *"God who had called His brethren"*: 1 Pet. 5:10.

p. 127. *"perfect his walking"*: Newman slightly adapts 'Perfect thou my goings in thy paths that my footsteps be not moved' Ps. 17:5.

p. 127. *"I will put My fear in their hearts"*: Jer. 32:40.

p. 128. *a special prerogative*: To be conceived without sin – see note on p. 119.

p. 128. *these lesser or venial sins*: Contrast what Newman says on p. 121.

p. 131. he is taken away *à facie malitiae*: Newman is combining Hos. 10:15 and Wisd. 4:10ff.

p. 132. *I am wealthy*: The Church of Laodicea (Rev. 3:17).

p. 132. *an Eastern king*: The sage is Solon and the rich King is Croesus, as told by Herodotus *Histories* I, p. 32.

p. 133. *"if he thinketh he standeth"*: 1 Cor. 10:12.

p. 133. *"chastise his body"*: 1 Cor. 9:27.

p. 133. *a man of strife and toil*: 1 Chron. 28:3.

p. 134. *"Ask what I shall give thee"*: Chron. 1:7–12.

p. 136. *"Thou shalt not build a house"*: 1 Chron. 28:3ff.

p. 136. *"Thou provest hearts"*: 1 Chron. 29:17ff.

p. 137. *"They who sow in tears"*: Ps. 126:5.

p. 137. *"like the flowers of the field"*: Matt. 6:30.

p. 137. *"King Solomon loved"*: 1 Kings 11:4ff.

p. 137. *Astarte*: Semitic goddess of fertility; *Moloch*: an Ammonite deity appeased by the sacrifice of children.

p. 138. *"incline their hearts"*: 1 Kings 8:58.

p. 138. *they are always full of their sin*: See Rom. 7:18ff.

p. 138. *"Now I begin to be Christ's disciple"*: Letter to the Romans Ch. 5. P G 5, p. 700.

p. 138. *the great Basil*: In Letter 136 he says 'It is the scourge of the Lord which goes on increasing my pain according to my deserts.' *Historical Sketches* II, p. 14.

p. 138. *St. Gregory*: Having relinquished high imperial office as Prefect of Rome, St. Gregory had devoted himself to the monastic life and was reluctant to leave it.

p. 139. *says his biographer*: Pietro Jacopo Bacci, *Vita di S. Filippo Neri Fiorentino, fondatore della Congregazione dell'Oratorio*, Rome, 1622. Translated into English in 1847.

p. 139. *When a penitent of his*: Costanza del Drago, quoted from Bacci.

p. 141. *When Hazael came*: 2 Kings 8:9.

p. 142. *"wax fat and kick"*: An elaborated version of Deut. 31:20.

p. 142. *"like a crooked bow!"*: Ps. 78:57.

p. 143. *"be sober"*: 1 Pet. 5:8.

p. 144. *when the evil one is making his last effort*: A possible reference to the death of St. Martin of Tours (d. 397) who said "You will find nothing of yours in me, you living death".

DISCOURSE 8
p. 145. *"I am the Door"*: John 10:9.27–28.

p. 145. *"I have manifested Thy Name"*: John 17:6–7.11.

p. 146. *"Fear not, little flock"*: Luke 12:32.

p. 146. *"I thank Thee, Father"*: Luke 10.21.

p. 146. *"How narrow is the gate"*: Matt. 7:14.

p. 146. *"Ye were once darkness"*: Eph. 5:8.

p. 146. *"Greater is He"*: 1 John 4:4.6.

p. 147. *private judgment*: Newman wrote in Tract 83 'The Latitudinarian doctrine is this: that every man's view of Revealed Religion is acceptable to God, if he acts up to it; that no one view is in itself better than another, or at least that we cannot tell which is the better. All that we have to do then is to act consistently with what we hold and to value others if they act consistently with what they hold; that to be consistent constitutes sincerity.' *Discussions and Arguments*, p. 12.

p. 147. "that they shall be saved": Hugues de Lamennais (1782–1854) looked forward to a kingdom in which everyone would be saved (see his *Paroles d'un Croyant*, 1834, p. 27).

p. 147. *"There is no such place as hell"*: Queen Victoria maintained that the 'doctrines of hell and the devil were unutterably horrible and revolting'. Elizabeth Longford, *Queen Victoria*, London, Collins, 1985, p. 343.

p. 148. *natural man*: Newman preached in 'The Religion of the Day' 'It cannot be denied that, pleasant as religious observances are declared in Scripture to be holy, yet to men in general they are said to be difficult and distasteful; to all men *naturally* impossible . . .' *Parochial and Plain Sermons* I, p. 318.

p. 149. *"the corruption of concupiscence"*: See 1 John 2:16.

p. 150. *the existence of miracles*: In his Preface to Fleury's *Ecclesiastical History* which he wrote in 1842–3, Newman comments 'We have been accustomed to believe that Christianity is little more than a creed or doctrine, introduced into the world once for all, and then left to itself, after the manner of human institutions, and under the same ordinary governance with them, stored indeed with hopes and fears for the future, and containing certain general promises of aid for this life, but unattended by any special Divine Presence or any immediately supernatural gift.' *Essays on Miracles*, p. 184.

p. 150. *the source of the hatred*: In 1850 Newman comments 'Now here at once the Church and the world part company; for the world, too, as is necessary, has its scale of offences as well as the church; but, referring them to a contrary object, it classifies them on quite a contrary principle; so that what is heinous in the world is often regarded patiently by the Church, and what is horrible and ruinous in the judgment of the Church may fail to exclude a man from the best society of the world. And, this being so, when the world contemplates the training of the Church and its results, it cannot, from the nature of the case, if for no other reason, avoid thinking very contemptuously of fruits, which are so different from those which it makes the standard and token of moral excellence in its own code of right and wrong.' *Certain Difficulties Felt by Anglicans in Catholic Teaching* I, pp. 245–6.

p. 150. *the proud spirit*: i.e. Satan.

p. 152. *"do many things willingly"*: 2 Cor. 9:17.

p. 154. *we cannot take what we see*: Newman preached in 'Secret Faults' 'Men are satisfied to have numberless secret faults. They do not think about them, either as sins or as obstacles to strength of faith, and live on as if they had nothing to learn.' *Parochial and Plain Sermons* I, p. 43.

p. 156. *it is* but *poetry, not religion*: In a lecture at St. Chad's school in Birmingham in 1849, Newman maintained that 'poetry always delighted, for poetry was the science of the beautiful. The poet's province was the colour objects: others coloured objects too, but the poet coloured them with loveliness.' *Sayings of Cardinal Newman*, p. 2.

p. 158. *"If Balac"*: Num. 24:13; 23:10.

p. 158. *"I will show thee"*: Mic. 6:8.

p. 160. *the number of Catholics*: Such was the belief of many including Bishop Thomas Newton, author of *Dissertations on the Prophecies, which have been remarkably fulfilled, and are at this time fulfilling in the world* (1758). Newman comments in 1840 '... who will say that this is the man, not merely to unchurch, but to smite, to ban, to wither the whole of Christendom for many centuries, and the greater part of it even in his own day.' *Essays Critical and Historical* II, p. 139.

p. 160. *"Many are called"*: Matt. 22:14.

p. 160. *"a remnant is saved"*: Rom. 1:5.

p. 161. *he appeared to a holy religious*: According to Bacci, this was a Capuchin who was shown in a vision that St. Philip was leading many of his followers who had died, into heaven.

p. 161. *the Fathers of the Oratory*: The Congregation founded by St. Philip Neri in 1556.

p. 161. *the dark lake of purgatory*: This is taken from the expression 'de profundo lacu' in the Offertory Prayer of the Mass for the faithful departed (before the Vatican II reforms). See note to page 42.

p. 162. *four times a year*: A reference to the Ember Days or Quarter Days when an indulgence, or pardon for the temporal punishment due to sin, could be gained.

p. 164. *"what reward have ye?"*: Matt. 5:46.

p. 166. *"If ye be of the word"*: John 15:19.

p. 167. *"a friend of the world"*: Jas. 4:4.

p. 167. *Does it not slander the profession of celibacy?*: Carlton says to Reding 'It was said in the beginning, "Increase and multiply"; therefore celibacy is unnatural.' *Loss and Gain*, p. 195.

p. 168. *"I know My sheep"*: John 10:27.

p. 168. *"Show me"*: Song of Songs 1: 7–8.

p. 168. *"on us sinners"*: *Nobis quoque peccatoribus* ... from the Roman Canon (Eucharistic Prayer I).

DISCOURSE 9

p. 169. *in a state of exhaustion*: Newman neatly expresses the effects of 'wounded nature' as a result of original sin.

p. 169. *one of the defects*: The others include lack of infused knowledge, concupiscence and physical mortality.

p. 170. *"Blessed art Thou"*: Matt. 16:17.

p. 170. *"I thank thee"*: Luke 10:21–22.

p. 170. *"The animal or natural man"*: 1 Cor. 2:14.

p. 170. *"No one can say the Lord Jesus"*: 1 Cor. 12:3. See note to p. 149.

p. 170. *"Ye have an unction"*: 1 John 2:20. A favourite text of Newman which occurs frequently in these discourses along with 'cords of Adam'.

p. 170. *"taught of the Lord"*: Isa. 54:13.

p. 170. *"No more shall man teach his neighbour"*: Jer. 31:34.

p. 173. *a new planet*: Neptune, the eighth planet from the sun was discovered by Johann Galle and Heinrich D'Arrest in Berlin in 1846, based on observations of the disturbance of other planetary orbits by Le Verrier and Adams in 1845.

p. 175. *not from faith but from poetical feeling*: Newman earlier commented on the relation which feelings bore to true religious principles 'They are sometimes natural, sometimes suitable; but they are not religion itself. They come and go. They are not to be counted on, or encouraged.' *Parochial and Plain Sermons* I, p. 185.

p. 176. *works on the Evidences of religion*: William Paley published his *Evidences of Christianity* in 1794. Newman comments on them in his *University Sermons* p. 65ff; 197ff and in his *Sermon Notes* pp. 83 and 177.

p. 177. *heretics of modern times*: Cornelius Jansen (1585–1638) was condemned in 1653 for saying justified humanity did not possess the grace to keep the commandments of God; Pasquier Quesnel (1634–1719) was condemned in 1713 for holding among other things that without the grace of God humanity is bound to give way to evil. Newman notes in his *Lectures* of 1850 'What circle of names can be produced, comparable in their times for the combination of ability and virtue, of depth of thought, of controversial dexterity, of poetical talent, of extensive learning, and of religious reputation, with those of Launoy, Pascal, Nicole, Arnaud, Racine, Tillemont, Quesnel, and their co-religionists, admirable in every point, but in their deficiency in the primary grace of a creature, humility?" *Certain Difficulties Felt by Anglicans in Catholic Teaching* I, p. 322.

p. 178. *"in whom we live and move and are"*: Acts 17:28.

p. 178. *grace gives certainty*: Newman returns to the theme in his discussion of the illative sense '(We) are bound in conscience to seek truth and to look for certainty by modes of proof, which, when reduced to the shape of formal propositions, fail to satisfy the severe requisitions of science.' *Essay in aid of a Grammar of Assent*, p. 412.

p. 179. *faith and reliance in the Church Established*: Newman wrote to the Editor of *The Globe* on 28 June 1862, when questions again surfaced that he wished to return to the Church of England 'I should be a consummate fool (to use a mild term) if in my old age I left "the land flowing with milk and honey" for the city of confusion and the house of bondage.' *Letters and Diaries* XX, p. 216. See also p. 231.

p. 179. *they attribute it to mere restlessness*: Newman speaks from experience. Unable to accept that conversion to Rome was a matter of considered and reasoned judgement, many Anglicans resorted to psychological arguments. In the judgement of Geoffrey Faber 'the struggle between intellect and feeling for priority of place necessitate submission to a paramount arbitrator, such as (Newman) could only discover in the Roman system.' *Oxford Apostles: A Character Study of the Oxford Movement*, Faber, London, 1933, p. 403.

p. 181 *No one is a Martyr for a conclusion*: In his account of the early centuries of Christian persecution, Newman concluded 'It is no dreary matter of antiquarianism; we do not contemplate it in conclusions drawn from dumb documents and dead events, but by faith exercised in ever-living objects, and by the appropriation and use of ever-recurring gifts.' *Essay in aid of a Grammar of Assent*, p. 488.

p. 182. *a branch of the Catholic Church*: This is the theology of the *Via Media* to which Newman himself had once subscribed.

p. 182. *"can a woman forget her babe?"*: Isa. 49:15.

p. 186. *how narrow-minded is this world*: Newman preached in 'The Religion of the Day' 'Religion is pleasant and easy; benevolence is the chief virtue; intolerance, bigotry, excess of zeal, are the first of sins. Austerity is an absurdity; – even firmness is looked on with an unfriendly, suspicious eye.' *Parochial and Plain Sermons* I, p. 312.

p. 186. *"Behold what manner of love"*: 1 John 3:1.

p. 189. *to be on the Mount with Christ*: i.e. the mount of transfiguration; for the quarrels see Mark 9:14ff.

p. 190. *"Through our Lord Jesus Christ let us have through faith access into this grace"*: Rom. 5:2.

p. 190. *And hope confoundeth not*: Rom. 5:5.

p. 190. *"Ye have an unction form the Holy One"*: 1 John 2:20. 27.

p. 190. *"Te maris et terrae . . ."*: Horace, *Carmina* XXVIII. I., pp. 1–6.

DISCOURSE 10

p. 192. *numbers, too, hear very little about Catholicism*: Newman says in his *Lectures* of 1851, 'Tame facts, elaborate inductions, subtle presumptions, will not avail with the many; something which will cut a dash, something guady and staring, something inflammatory, is the rhetoric in request; he must make up his mind then to resign the populace to the action of the Catholic Church, or he must slander her to her greater confusion.' *Present Position of Catholics*, p. 225.

p. 193. *should not be so far attracted by what they see*: In his *Lectures* of 1850 Newman argues that the holiness of the saints in the Church in the midst of poverty and lack of industrial development is an argument for the strength of her claims. *Certain Difficulties felt by Anglicans in Catholic Teaching* I, Lecture 8.

p. 193. *"that great sight"*: Exod. 3:3.

p. 193. *"Come and see"*: John 1:46.

p. 193. *Seeing they see not*: Isa. 6:9; Matt. 13:13.

p. 193. *"He who cometh to Me"*. John 6:35.

p. 194. *they do not believe in anything at all*: Newman preached in 'Inward Witness to the Truth of the Gospel', 'Are not the principles of unbelief certain to dissolve society?' *Parochial and Plain Sermons* VIII, p. 112.

p. 194. *it is assenting to a doctrine as true*: In his *Sermon Notes* for 1850 Newman argues 'Now all acceptable religion is *because God has revealed this or that*. We are all apt to reason, and there is nothing wrong in reason, so that we do not oppose faith; but the great thing is to make an act of faith, whatever we do; to say, I believe this or that or the other on God's word – even in those things which we might know by nature.' *Sermon Notes*, p. 324.

p. 197. *they were an infallible authority*: Newman states in his *Essay on the Development of Christian Doctrine* 'As creation argues continual governance, so are Apostles harbingers of Popes.' p. 86.

p. 198. *"We give thanks to God"*: 1 Thess. 2:13.

p. 198. *"He that heareth you"*: Luke 10:16.

p. 198. *"Men of Israel"*: Acts 2:22, 36.

p. 198. *"We ought to obey God"*: Acts 5:29, 32.

p. 198. *"He commanded us to preach"*: Acts 10:42.

p. 198. *"Believe, and thou shalt be saved"*: v.g. Acts 8:37.

p. 199. *"the word of hearing"*: Rom. 10:8.

p. 199. *"How shall they believe Him?"*: Rom. 10:14.17.

p. 200. *who would be better content with the writer's absence*: Newman's side swipe at liberal exegetes which he takes with a measure of humour.

p. 202. "attain to unity of faith": Eph. 4:13.

p. 202. *"that we be* not *as children"*. Eph. 4:14.

p. 202. *They call it priestcraft*: Newman is not alone in his detestation of the word. Dr. George Hicks mentions those who 'call the divine institution of priesthood by the spiteful name of priestcraft.' *Several Letters between Dr George Hicks and a Popish Priest*, London, 1705.

p. 204. *"See your vocation"*: 1 Cor. 1:26–27.

p. 204. *"the foolishness of preaching"*: 1 Cor. 1:21.

p. 204. *"I thank Thee Father"*: Matt. 11:25.

p. 205. *"lying wonders"*: Newman in his 1851 *Lectures* says 'Observe then, we affirm that the Supreme Being has wrought miracles on earth ever since the time of the Apostles: Protestants deny it.' *Present Position of Catholics*, p. 301.

p. 205. *Esau's and Saul's rejection*: See Gen. 27:28 and 1 Sam. 13:14.

p. 205. *"God is true, and every man a liar"*: Saying based on Psalm 116:11, 'Ego dixi in excessu meo: omnis homo mendax.'

p. 207. *and will bargain for private judgment*: The whole argument of the *Development of Doctrine* hinges on the necessity of a living infallible apostolic authority which precisely imposes itself on human judgement – see note to page 198.

p. 208. *"Whithersoever thou shalt go"*. Ruth 1:16.

p. 209. *"Without faith it is impossible to please God"*: Heb. 11:6.

p. 209. *"by faith we stand"*: 2 Cor. 1:24.

p. 209. *"by faith we walk"*: 2 Cor. 5:7.

p. 209. *"by faith we overcome the world"*: 1 John 5:4.

p. 209. *"He that believeth and is baptised"*: Mark 16:16.

p. 209. *"He that believeth in the Son"*: John 3:18.

p. 209. *"If you believe not"*: John 8:24.

p. 209. *"Ye believe not, because ye are not of My sheep"*: John 10:26.

p. 209. *"All things are possible"*: Matt. 19:26.

p. 209. *"He could not do any miracle"*: Matt. 13:58.

p. 209. *"purify our hearts"*: Jas. 4:8.

p. 211. *Let them stake their eternal prospects on kings and nobles*: Newman takes this to its ultimate conclusion in his *Lectures* of 1851 when he says 'The British Bible, as I may call it, distinctly ascribes an absolute sinlessness to the King of Great Britain and Ireland.' *Present Position of Catholics*, p. 30.

p. 213. *acts of faith, hope, love*: These acts of faith, hope, charity and contrition are fundamental Catholic devotional prayers.

p. 213. *"Who art thou, O great mountain"*: Zech. 4:7.

p. 213. *"He shall strengthen your feet"*: Ps. 18:33–34.

p. 213. *"There is no God like the God of the righteous"*: Deut. 33:26–27.

p. 213. *"The young shall faint"*: Isa. 40:30–31.

DISCOURSE 11

p. 214. *that, once a Catholic, he never, never can doubt again*: Newman would distinguish between a corrosive mistrust and difficulty in believing 'If by "unclouded certainty" is meant the absence of all involuntary misgivings, or a sense of imperfection or incompleteness in the argumentative grounds of religion, a certitude so circumstanced is *not* (according to Catholic teaching) "necessary for a Christian's faith and hope". Nor can real "doubt" be anything short of a deliberate withholding of assent to the Church's teaching.' *The Via Media* I, p. 85, n. 4.

p. 214. *must give up altogether the search after truth*: Newman returns to this theme in his *Apologia* 'I am defending myself here from a plausible charge brought against Catholics ... that I also believe in the existence of a power on earth, which at its own will imposes upon men any new set of *credenda*, when it pleases, by a claim to infallibility; in consequence, that my own thoughts are not my own property; that I cannot tell that to-morrow I may not have to give up what I hold to-day, and that the necessary effect of such a condition of mind must be a degrading bondage.' p. 246.

p. 216. *if it is once true, it never can be false*: In 1870 Newman will say 'If by certitude about a thing is to be understood the knowledge of its truth, let it be considered that what is once true is always true, and cannot fail, whereas what is once known need not always be known, and is capable of failing. It follows, that if I am certain of a thing, I believe it will remain what I now hold it to be, even though my mind should have the bad fortune to let it drop.' *Essay in aid of a Grammar of Assent*, p. 197.

p. 217. *They begin in self-will*: See Newman's comments on Quesnel etc. to p. 177.

p. 219. *who will take my part?*: Newman always placed great weight on loyalty and concluded the *Apologia* by saying 'I gather up and bear in memory those familiary affectionate companions and counsellors ... who were my thorough friends, and showed me true attachment in times long past; and also those many younger men, whether I knew them or not, who have never been disloyal to me by word or deed.' *Apologia*, p. 283.

p. 221. *"the cords of Adam"*: Hos. 11:4.

p. 221. *Blessed Mary her advocate*: Title used in the *Hail, Holy Queen* prayer.

p. 221. *is secretly desirous of retracing his steps*: See note to p. 180.

p. 222. *how much of hypocrisy*: The nub of Kingsley's argument, see note to p. 18.

p. 223. *"O My people"*: The Good Friday *Reproaches* sung during the veneration of the Cross.

p. 227. *"He that despiseth"*. 1 Thess. 4:8.

p. 227. *"We are of God"*. 1 John 4:6.

p. 228. *"The spirit of Elias"*. 2 Kings 2:15.

p. 228. *"there are with thy servants fifty strong men"*. 2 Kings 2:16ff.

p. 229. *"Thou shalt not go with them"*: Num. 22:12, 20.

p. 230. *not on faith in it, but on attachment to it*: This was Newman's own drama, worked out at Littlemore which he describes in the *Apologia*, 'There is a divine life among us, clearly manifested, in spite of all our disorders, which is as great a note of the Church, as any can be. Why should we seek our Lord's presence elsewhere, when He vouchsafes it to us where we are?' p. 193.

p. 231. *the remembrance of past years*: from *The Pillar of the Cloud*, 'I loved the garish day, and, spite of fears,/ Pride ruled my will: remember not past years' *Verses on Various Occasions*, p. 152.

p. 232. *He who has begun a good work in you*: A probable reference to the prayer *Actiones nostras* which says 'Go before us, O Lord, we beseech Thee, in all our doings with Thy gracious inspiration, and further us with Thy continual help, that every prayer and work of ours may begin from Thee, and by Thee be duly ended.'

p. 233. *"If all prophesy"*. 1 Cor. 14:24–26.

p. 233. *some men are converted merely by entering a Catholic Church*: Newman makes this happen to his hero, Charles Reding, when he enters the Passionist Church 'Charles's feelings were indescribable, but all pleasurable. His heart beat, not with fear or anxiety, but with the thrill of delight with which he realised that he was beneath the shadow of a Catholic community.' *Loss and Gain*, p. 428.

p. 235. *"Wisdom preacheth abroad"*: Prov. 1:20–32.

p. 237. *"O Lord, my God"*: Ps. 116:16–18.

DISCOURSE 12
p. 238. *In this huge city*: The population of London in 1841 was 2,207,653, the greatest in the world at that time. It was to be passed by New York by the end of the century.

p. 238. *"Cry aloud, spare not!"*: Isa. 58:1.

p. 239. *present din of turmoil*: Compare Dickens description of Coketown 'where there was a rattling and a trembling all day long, and where the piston of the steam engine worked monotonously up and down.' *Hard Times* I, p. 5.

p. 239. *Look to the rock*: Isa. 51:1.

p. 239. *Magni nominis umbra*: This is from Lucan, *Pharsalia* I, p. 135 'the shadow of a great name' (applied to the degenerate son or descendant of an illustrious figure).

p. 240. *power is truth*: Newman preached on 'Religion A Weariness to the Natural Man'. The transactions of worldly business, speculations in trade, ambitious hopes, the pursuit of knowledge, the public occurences of the day, these find a way directly to the heart; they rouse, they influence.' *Parochial and Plain Sermons* VII, pp. 18–19.

p. 240. *Porta manes et Stella maris*: from the hymn *Alma Redemptoris Mater* 'You remain the gate and the star of the sea'.

p. 240. *vacant spaces of the great City*: i.e. Rome.

p. 241. *"massive iron hammers"*: The cyclops forging a thunderbolt for King Zeus wanted but one ray which they were beating out with their iron hammers. Apollonius Rhodius, *The Argonautica* I, p. 733.

p. 242. *St. Gregory Nazianzen*: (329–389), Newman writes of his rise and fall 'It is plain that the gentle and humble-minded Gregory was unequal to the government of the Church and province of Constantinople, which were as unworthy, as they were impatient of him.' *Historical Sketches* II, p. 83.

p. 242. *Arian city of Constantinople*: i.e. it had succumbed to the heretical teachings of Arius (256–336).

p. 242. *Donatists in Africa*: The rigourists who believed in re-baptising those who had compromised their faith, which flourished in North Africa in the fourth century.

p. 242. *a third heresy in Egypt*: Monophysitism, a fifth-century heresy which taught that there was only one nature in Christ led by Dioscurus and then Timothy the Cat.

p. 242. *a fourth in Gaul*: Adoptionism which held the double sonship of Christ, one natural, the other adoptive.

p. 243. *the six Jesuit Fathers*: Peter Favre, Diego Laynez, Alfonso Salmeron, Nicholas Bobadilla, Simon Rodriguez, Francis Xavier on 15 August 1534.

p. 243. *"made merry and sent their gifts"*: Rev. 1:10.

p. 243. *into India in the East*: Francis Xavier journeyed to Japan and Isaac Jogues and John de Brebeuf to North America.

p. 243. *the Carthaginian conqueror*: i.e. Hannibal in the second Punic War.

p. 244. upon our banners: As battle honours are put on the standards of army regiments.

p. 244. *The great philosopher of antiquity*: Aristotle. The phrase is from *Nicomachean Ethics* II, p. xi, p. 2.

p. 245. *Society of Friends*: They had a significant presence in Birmingham and were the owners of Cadbury's chocolate factory in Bournville.

p. 245. *Caesarem vehis et fortunam Caesaris*: Newman adapts 'Caesarem portas et fortunas eius' which was a remark made by Caesar to his pilot in the middle of a storm, as reported in Plutarch's *Lives*.

p. 245. *We began our work*: i.e. as members of the Oratory on the feast of the chair (cathedra) of St. Peter, 22 February 1847. Newman writes to Mrs Bowden on 23 February 'It is no secret we are to be Oratorians.' *Letters and Diaries* XII, p. 46.

p. 247. *that Revelation was ever in progress in the Jewish period*: Newman preached frequently on Christianity, the continuation and fulfilment of the Jewish dispensation. See MS Sermons 117, 133, 135, 138, 139, 143, 149, 176, 201, 441, 578, 593, 594.

p. 248. *like the armed bands*: King Ahaziah sent them to Elijah.

p. 248. *"heaping coals of fire"*: Rom. 12:20–21.

p. 250. *the Nestorian patriarch*: Nestorius, who as Patriarch of Constantinople in 428 maintained that Mary was Mother of Christ but not Mother of God.

p. 251. *open its universities to Dissenters*: Admission to a degree at Oxford entailed subscription to The Thirty-Nine Articles of Religion; at Cambridge one either had to declare oneself a member of the Church of England or subscribe to the three articles of the Canons of 1604. Religious tests were finally removed in 1871.

p. 251. *Non-jurors*: those who refused to take the oath of allegiance to William and Mary in 1688, headed by William Sancroft, Archbishop of Canterbury.

p. 251. some sort of an idea: For Newman's treatment of ideas, see his *Essay on Development*, pp. 33ff.

p. 252. *as the Protestant Anglo-Saxon makes on Ireland*: In *The Rambler* Newman will write in 1859 'There is a visitor who rouses memories as dark as the look of a Cardinal are inspiring and consolatory. That visitor is the Saxon.' *Historical Sketches* III, p. 257.

p. 254. *as she was three centuries ago*: i.e. since before the Act of Supremacy in 1536, the start of the Reformation in England.

p. 254. *"yesterday, and to-day, and the same for ever"*: Heb. 13:8.

p. 254. *"The word which shall issue from His mouth"*: Isa. 55:11.

p. 255. *God's arm is not shortened.* Isa. 59:1.

p. 256. *it was an absurdity in him to weep*: Paul says 'I have great sorrow and unceasing anguish in my heart. For I could wish that I myself were accursed for the sake of my brethren, my kinsmen by race.' Rom. 9:2–4.

p. 257. *who comes to judge the world with fire*: See 1 Cor. 3:13.

p. 258. *Dies venit, Dies Tua*: a reference to Hab. 2:3.

p. 258. *"He hath filled the hungry"*: Luke 1:53.

p. 258. *"If I wish to justify myself"*: Job 9:20.

p. 258. *"I have lived in all good conscience"*: 2 Cor. 1:12.

p. 259. *"I have followed His guidance"*: Newman expresses it in the *Apologia* as 'I have not sinned against light.' p. 35.

DISCOURSE 13

p. 260. *that it is . . . quite as easy, to believe*: In 1870 Newman says that arguing from first principles the mind can be led 'by an infallible succession from the rejection of atheism to theism, and from theism to Christianity, and from Christianity to Evangelical Religion, and from these to Catholicity.' *Essay in aid of a Grammar of Assent*, Note II, p. 463 '. . . *she bears upon her the tokens of divinity.*' The traditional *notes* of the Church are her unity, sanctity, Catholicity and apostolicity which it is argued could not have lasted so long and so amazingly and with such evidence of goodness without God being the ultimate cause.

p. 265. a contradiction in terms: The vicious circle argument is dealt with by Thomas Aquinas in his *Compendium of Theology* 3 and in his *Summa Contra Gentiles* I, p. 13.

p. 267. *"who inhabiteth eternity"*: Isa. 57:15.

p. 269. *the adamantine rocks*: See Milton, *Paradise Lost* II, p. 646.

p. 270. *"in the midst of the years"*: Hab. 3:2.

p. 270. *"empty and void"*: Gen. 1:2.

p. 270. *"a bond fastened upon all people"*: Isa. 25:7. Newman is translating literally from the *Vulgate*.

p. 271. *"fire, hail snow and ice"*. Ps. 148:7.

p. 272. *the most hidden corners and pores of the world*: The expression is used also by the poet Shelley 'I pass through the pores of the ocean and shores;/ I change, but I cannot die' *The Cloud*.

p. 272. *"the grass of the field"*: Matt. 6:30.

p. 273. *"placed the sand as a boundary"*: Jer. 5:22.

p. 273. *"bit in their lips"*. See Ps. 32:9.

p. 273. *enemies of all they meet*: London Zoo, opened in 1845 in Regents Park, boasted a man-eating hyena.

p. 279. *or the Nestorian*: See note to p. 250.

p. 279. *or the Eutychian*: The fifth-century heresy took its name from a Constantinopolitan archimandrite, who maintained that in Christ there was only one nature – hence the other name *monophysites* – the divine. Newman deals with this in *Certain Difficulties felt by Anglicans in Catholic Teaching I*, p. 346.

p. 279. *most sagacious politicians*: Macaulay in his Essay in *The Edinburgh Review* (1843, vol. 3) on Leopold von Ranke's History of the Popes wrote 'She (the Roman Catholic Church) may still exist in undiminished vigour when some traveller from New Zealand shall, in the midst of a vast solitude, take his stand on a broken arch of London Bridge to sketch the ruins of St. Paul's.'

p. 280. *"Simon Barjona"*: Matt. 16:17–20. Newman uses his own version of Simon's name which in the *Douai* and *Vulgate* versions has Bar-jona.

p. 281. *Arise, shine, O Jerusalem*: Isa. 60:1–3.

p. 281. *"Open ye the gates"*: Isa. 26:2–4; 12–15.

p. 282. *nothing between it and scepticism*: Newman had the personal reminder of his friend Joseph Blanco White (1775–1841) who had relapsed from Catholicism to unbelief. See also *Lectures on the Present Position of Catholics in England*, pp. 142–160.

p. 282. *Unitarian*: Of special relevance in Birmingham, where there were several chapels, and James Martineau (1805–1900) was held in high regard. Joseph Blanco White (q.v. supra) and Francis Newman had both become Unitarians before lapsing into unbelief.

p. 283. *deep pit*: See note to page 42.

p. 283. *should become castaways*: St. Paul's prayer 1 Cor. 9:27.

DISCOURSE 14

p. 284. *"though He was rich"*: 2 Cor. 8–9.

p. 284. *"Thou art not yet fifty years old"*: John 8:57–59.

p. 284. *the Ancient of Days*: Dan. 7:9.

p. 285. *man could not make it.*: See note to page 265.

p. 287. *a poor six thousand years*: Archbishop Ussher (1581–1646) fixed the time of creation in the year 4004 BC on Sunday 23 October at 9a.m. Newman clearly did not share his chronology and was acquainted with geological evidence which gave a far longer timescale. He was later to write to Canon Walker 'Mr Darwin's theory *need* not then be atheistical, be it true or not.' *Letters and Diaries* XXIV, p. 77.

p. 288. *mortify their passions*: See note to page 7.

p. 290. *the great pit*: Rev. 9:2ff.

p. 290. *the worm that dieth not*: Isa. 66:24; Mark 9:44.

p. 290. *when a king, his patron asked him what God was!*: Hiero, King of Syracuse asked the poet Simonides this question. He requested a delay and every time he met, he doubled the time he needed to give a reply. When the King finally asked why this was necessary, Simonides replied 'The longer I think on the subject, the farther I am from making it out.' Stories about Simonides/Hieron are found in Athenaeus and Aelian and a minor work of Plato.

p. 294. *"Before they call, I will attend"*: Isa. 57:15.

p. 294. *"inhabiteth eternity"*: Isa. 57:15.

p. 294. *"a contrite and humble spirit"*: See Ps. 51:17.

p. 294. *"looketh down upon the lowly"*: Ps. 138:6.

p. 296. *the tents of Cedar*: Num. 24:6.

p. 297. *"Show me Thy glory"*: Exod. 33:18.

p. 298. *"cords of Adam"*: Hos. 11:4.

p. 298. *to create Adam in original justice*: See note to p. 170.

p. 298. *He purposed even in man's first state*: Newman again stresses the Scotist perspective, revising what he said in the 1849 edition 'He (the Son) revealed to our first father in his state of innocence a higher purpose which in the fulness of time was to be accomplished in his descendants.' See also p. 307.

p. 299. *"the First-born of every creature"*: Col. 1:15.

p. 299. *"greater in strength and power"*: 2 Pet. 2:11.

p. 299. *"take hold of the Angels"*: Heb. 2:16.

p. 299. *"the first last"*: Matt. 19:30.

p. 299. *He raised the needy*: Ps. 113:7.

p. 300. *"the brilliancy of the Eternal Light"*: Heb. 1:3.

p. 300. *"eye hath not seen"*: 1 Cor. 2:9.

p. 300. *"blessed for evermore"*: Ps. 89:52.

p. 301. *The fig-tree will put forth her green figs*: Song of Songs 2:13.

p. 301. *"spikenard and saffron"*: Song of Songs 4:14–15.

p. 301. *"the glory of the Lord"*: Isa 35:2.

p. 301. *"Who is This, that cometh from Edom?"*: Isa. 63:1.

p. 302. *"the Brightness of God's Glory"*: Heb. 1:3.

p. 302. *"He hath no beauty nor comeliness"*: Isa. 53:2.

p. 302. *"a leper, and smitten of God"*: Isa. 53:4.

p. 303. *"My beloved is white and ruddy"*: Song of Songs 5:10.

p. 303. *"the day of death"*: Eccles. 7:1.

p. 304. *"in the diadem"*: an adaptation of Isa. 62:3.

p. 304. *"Let us love God"*: 1 John 4:19.

DISCOURSE 15

p. 305. *in satisfaction for our sins*: See Council of Trent Session 14, Chapter 8.

p. 305. *He might have saved us*: Newman again uses the Scotist argument, or, in this case, the position of Athanasius who states 'Without His coming among us at all, God was able just to speak and undo the curse.' *Contra Arianos* II, p. 68.

p. 306. *All things are possible*: Mark 14:36.

p. 306. *"Let light be"*: Gen. 1:3.

p. 306. *fitting to take a ransom*: Newman makes clear that he did not accept vindictive satisfaction because 'One being can never, by his own suffering, simply discharge the debt of another's sin.' It was a question of the love which offered to the Father that perfect praise and apology on behalf of and in union with that humanity of which he was the first among many brethren.

p. 306. *which needs to be accepted*: In his footnote Newman quotes de Lugo that Christ's satisfaction was strict in regards to the price demanded but not strict insofar as the way in which the satisfaction was paid.

p. 307. *simply discharge the debt*: Newman quotes de Lugo who argues that when satisfying an injury, you cannot simply repay the price but also must consider the person injured.

p. 307. *De. Lug*: Cardinal Juan de Lugo (1583–1660). His treatise on the Incarnation was used in this context by Newman – judging by the underlining of texts in his copy of *Disputationes de Mysterio Incarnationis* (Second Edition, Venice, 1751) in the Birmingham archives.

p. 308. *"bought with a great price"*: 1 Cor. 6:20.

p. 308. *"with the Lord there is mercy"*: Ps. 130:7.

p. 309. *"vehement rushing"*: The description of the Descent of the Holy Spirit on Pentecost Sunday: Acts. 2:2.

p. 310. *"Royal munificence"*: Newman may have been thinking of Herodotus, but Orientalism had begun to exert a fascination since Pitton de Tournefort's *Relation d'un voyage du Levant* (1727) followed by the researches of Sir William Jones and Anquetil Duperron.

p. 310. *"Knowest thou not"*: Isa. 40:28.

p. 312. *"How wasteful was that sower!"*: A reference to the parable in Matt. 13:1–9.

p. 312. *"Oh, the depth of the riches"*: Rom. 11:33.

p. 312. *"the teaching of the Cross"*: 1 Cor. 1:18.

p. 312. *A voluntary or gratuitous mortification"*: See note to page 7.

p. 312. *voluntary chastity . . .*: The three vows of religious life.

p. 313. *"what must he do but practise eccentricities"*: Newman is almost certainly thinking of St. Philip Neri who delighted to play the fool and make others look similarly ridiculous as he did when he made Tarugi carry his little dog, Capriccio, in procession – so pride was completely overcome.

p. 313. *"the greatness of the revelations"*: 2 Cor. 12:7.

p. 313. *she submits her flesh to penances*: Newman is probably thinking of St. Rose of Lima (1568–1617).

p. 314. *blooming, as it does, to-day*: Matt. 6:30.

p. 314. *the creature more than the Creator*: Rom. 1:25.

p. 315. "*He made Himself void or empty*": Newman translates Phil. 2:7 'semetipsum exinanivit' literally.

p. 315. "*inglorious visage*": Isa. 52:14ff.

p. 316. "*was offered, for He willed it*": Isa. 53:7.

p. 317. *Sign of the Son of Man*. Matt. 26:64.

p. 317. "*King Solomon made himself a litter*": Song of Songs 3:9–11.

p. 318. *first enter purgatory*: For the development of Newman's views on life after death see 'A Blessed and Ever Enduring Fellowship', Tolhurst, J., *Catholic Recusant* Vol 22.3, 1995, pp. 424–457.

p. 318. "*the Lord God, who hath dominion*": Exod. 20:5–6.

p. 320. *or with Elias stand in the desert*: I Kings 19:11ff.

p. 321. *The Word and Wisdom of the Father*: John 1:18.

p. 321. FOOTNOTE Newman quotes from De Lugo's Treatise *De Incarnatione* on the debate between Scotists and Thomists concerning whether Christ would have become incarnate even if Adam had not sinned. He admits that St. Thomas Aquinas stated that Christ could have become incarnate even if Adam had not sinned, but that the contrary theological position was more probable. This establishes that a Scotist perspective is allowable, even though most theologians at that time inclined to the Thomist position.

DISCOURSE 16

p. 324. *not only a body, but a soul*: Apollinaris, Bishop of Laodicea (d. 390) denied that Jesus had a human soul.

p. 324. *How would He have sanctified our nature?*: See Heb. 2:14.

p. 325. *It is otherwise with the sufferings of His soul*: Newman anticipating modern psychology, shows that because of his divinity, Jesus suffered *more* in his mind, not less.

p. 325. "*My soul is sorrowful*": Matt. 26:38.

p. 328. "*If it be possible*": Matt. 26:39.

p. 328. *"The chalice which my Father hath given me"*: John 18:11.

p. 329. *so absolutely in His own power*: See note to page 325.

p. 330. *He did, as the Wise Man says,* instanter: 'Whatsoever thy hand is able to do, do it earnestly' (Eccles. 9:10).

p. 330. *"Lo, I come to do Thy will"*: Ps. 40:7–9; Heb. 10:5–8.

p. 331. *"I commend My Spirit"*: Luke 23:46.

p. 332. *"My soul is sorrowful unto death"*: Matt. 26:38.

p. 332. *"I have condemned the innocent blood"*: Matt. 27:4.

p. 332. *"I am clear from the blood of this just Person"*: Matt. 27:24. Newman translated the Latin literally.

p. 332. *"Truly this was a just Man"*: Luke 23:47.

p. 333. *"for the joy set before Him"*: Heb. 12:2.

p. 333. *"Watch and pray"*: Matt. 26:41.

p. 333. *"Friend, wherefore art thou come?"*: Matt. 26:50.

p. 333. *"Judas, betrayest thou the Son of Man with a kiss?"*: Luke 22:48.

p. 333. *"All that take the sword"*: Matt. 26:52.

p. 333. *"If I have spoken evil"*: John 18:23.

p. 333. *"Woman, behold thy Son"*: John 19:26.

p. 333. *"I will, be thou clean"*: Luke 5:13.

p. 333. *"Thy sins be forgiven thee"*: Matt. 9:5.

p. 333. *"I will come and heal him"*: Matt. 8:7.

p. 333. *"I go to wake him out of sleep"*: John 11:11.

p. 333. *"Now I will begin to suffer"*: A rendering of Matt: 26:37.

p. 334. *"the place which is called Gethsemani"*: Mark 14:32.

p. 334. *".. and He began to be frightened .."*: Mark 14:33.

p. 335. *"Sin is an easy thing to us"*: Newman preached in 1832 on 'Contest between Faith and Sight'; ... they think they possess real wisdom ... yet in their hearts they learn to believe that sin is a matter of course, not a serious evil, a failing in which all have share, indulgently to be spoken of, or rather, in the case of each individual, to be taken for granted, and passed over in silence. *Sermons preached before the University of Oxford,* p. 126.

p. 336. *in that most awful hour.*: In the garden of Gethsemane.

p. 337. *with the pride of the old giants*: Goliath and his descendants (1 Chron. 20:8).

p. 337. *the five cities*: Sodom, Gomorrah, Adama, Zeboim and Bela (Gen. 14:8).

p. 338. the palmer-worm: a reference to Amos 4:9. The palmer-worm is a moth larva, *dichomeris ligulella.*

p. 338. *"sprinkling dust towards heaven"*: Job 2:12.

p. 340. *"the foundations of the great deep"*: The beginning of the flood (Gen. 7:11).

p. 340. *"My soul is sorrowful"*: Matt. 26:38.

DISCOURSE 17
p. 342. *"All things are double"*: Sir. 42:25.

p. 343. *or wander among woods or on the sea-shore*: Newman is perhaps recalling Gilbert White (1720–93) whose *Natural History and Antiquities of Selborne* was first published in 1788. He had also attended lectures given by Sir Charles Lyell (1797–1875) the geologist when he was an undergraduate.

p. 343. *"which God predestined before the world"*: Eph. 1:4.

p. 344. *"we praise and bless her"*: Newman disposes of the objection that honour to Mary takes away from worship of Jesus.

p. 345. *who said that our Lord had no body at all*: The Docetists, who, having a contempt for matter, held that Jesus came only in an etherial way, but was not physically present.

p. 345. *"in the beginning was the Word"*: John 1:1.

p. 345. *was made flesh*: John 1:14.

p. 345. *They speak in a dreamy, shadowy way*: This was Newman's objection to Dr R. D. Hampden in 1836 'You surely do deny that "the truths of the Trinity and Incarnation are revealed".' *Letters and Diaries* V, p. 236 and note. He also deals with the matter in Tract 73 'On the Introduction of Rationalistic Principles into Religion' *Essays Critical and Historical* I, p. 30ff.

p. 346. *saying that He became the Son*: The heresy of Adoptionism promulgated originally by Paul of Samosata in the third century. See *Arians of the Fourth Century*, pp. 3, 34.

p. 347. *"Sacrifice and offering"*: Heb. 10:5.

p. 347. *"That which we have seen and have heard"*: 1 John 1:3.

p. 347. *"in opposition to those spirits"*: 1 John 4:2.

p. 347. *Deipara*: God bearer, Latin translation of the Greek term *Theotokos* used at the Council of Ephesus in 431 against Nestorius.

p. 349. *"A Virgin shall conceive"*: Isa. 7:14.

p. 349. *"did not shrink from the Virgin's womb"*: from the *Te Deum*.

p. 349. *"Tower of David"*: a title in the Litany of Loreto. See Newman's comment in *Meditations and Devotions*, p. 99.

p. 349. *"having alone destroyed all heresies"*: A prayer in the *Raccolta* (no. 210) which begins 'O powerful Virgin, who alone hast destroyed all heresies throughout the world.'

p. 349. *"built with bulwarks"*: Song of Songs 4:4.

p. 350. *"Blessed is the womb"*: Luke 11:27ff.

p. 351. *"More blessed was Mary"*: *De Sancta Virginitate* I, 3 PL 40, p. 390.

p. 351. *and St Chrysostom declares*: *Homily on Matthew 44* PG 57, p. 458.

See *Certain Difficulties Felt by Anglicans in Catholic Teaching* II, p. 131, where Newman quotes the whole passage.

p. 351. *Full of grace*: Luke 1:28.

p. 351. *"Blessed art thou"*: Luke 1:45.

p. 353. *"because man was flesh"*: Newman roughly translates 'multa malitia hominum' (Gen. 6:5).

p. 353. *"where sin abounded"*: Rom. 5:20.

p. 354. *"bruise the serpent's head"*: Gen. 3:15.

p. 354. *"the path of the just"*: Prov. 4:18.

p. 355. *"Behold the handmaid of the Lord"*: Luke 1:38.

p. 355. *"if God heareth not sinners"*: John 9:31.

p. 355. *"the continual prayer of a just man"*: Jas. 5:16.

p. 355. *"if faithful Abraham"*: Gen. 20:7, 17.

p. 355. *"if patient Job"*: Job 42:8.

p. 355. *"if meek Moses"*: Exod. 17:11.

p. 355. *"if the Gentiles at Jerusalem"*: John 12:21.

p. 355. *clothed with the sun*: See Rev. 12:1.

p. 357. *the living Oracle of Truth*: compare 'the lively oracles' Acts 7:38 (King James Version).

p. 357. *"Let thy dwelling be in Jacob"*: Sir. 24:8ff. Newman subsequently quotes verses 9–16.

p. 358. *the morning star*: a title of Mary in the Litany of Loreto. See Newman's comments in *Meditations and Devotions*, p. 111.

p. 359. *"Maria, mater gratiae"*: from hymns in honour of the Blessed Virgin Mary in the *Liber Usualis* 'Mary, mother of grace/ Sweet mother of mercy/ Protect us from the enemy /And receive us at the hour of death.'

DISCOURSE 18

p. 360. *"Ought not Christ to suffer these things?"*: Luke 24:26.

p. 360. *"for whom are all things"*: Heb. 2:10.

p. 360. *the analogy of faith*: The coherence of the truths of faith and the understanding of individual doctrines within the whole context of Christian doctrine.

p. 361. *we feel it ought to be*: 'Potuit, decuit, ergo fecit' is a gloss on the words of Eadmer (1064–1124) the chaplain to St. Anselm who wrote 'potuit plane. Si igitur voluit, fecit' – 'He surely could have; if therefore he willed it, he did it'. Tract on the Immaculate Conception PL 159, p. 305.

p. 361. *not merely the Mother of our Lord's manhood*: The heresy of Nestorius. See note to p. 347.

p. 362. *"Thou didst not disdain the Virgin's womb"*: from the *Te Deum*.

p. 362. *Such a question was once asked*: King Ahasuerus asked the question of Haman, the son of Hammedatha who answered, thinking that he would be rewarded. Instead the honour went to Mordecai. Esth. 6:6ff (according to the Vulgate numbering – the text does not occur in modern versions).

p. 363. *Mirror of Justice*: titles of Mary in the Litany of Loreto.

p. 364. *and caused a seal to be set*: The image is that of Ps. 45:9.

p. 364. *"Holy, Holy, Holy"*: Isa. 6:3.

p. 365. *Caiaphas*: John 11:51.

p. 365. *"Many shall say Lord, Lord"*: Matt. 7:22.

p. 366. *Enoch*: Heb. 11:5.

p. 366. *"Noe"*: Heb. 11:7.

p. 366. *Moses*. Num. 12:3.

p. 366. *David*: 1 Sam. 13:14.

p. 366. *Miracles are the simple and direct work of God*: Newman wrote in his article on miracles in 1825, 'We take it, therefore for granted, that real

Miracles, i.e., interruptions in the course of nature, cannot reasonably be referred to any power but divine.' *Essay on Miracles*, p. 53.

p. 367. *"the dumb animal"*: 2 Pet. 2:16, referring to the passage in Num. 23:28.

p. 367. *an unction from the Holy One*: 1 John 2:27.

p. 367. *"where the Spirit of the Lord is"*: 2 Cor. 3:17.

p. 367. *"We have known"*: 1 John 4:16.

p. 368. *"beware of false prophets"*: Matt. 7:15.

p. 368. *"Out of the abundance of the heart"*: Both this and the succeeding are from Luke 6:45.

p. 368. *it was no heavenly body*: The Docetists, a heterodox group in the early centuries of Christianity who taught that since matter was flawed, Jesus did not have a real body, but an ethereal one. See note to p. 345.

p. 369. *"the first fruit"*: Matt. 12:33.

p. 369. *"the Mother of fair love and fear"*: Sir. 24:24.

p. 369. *"an odour like cinnamon and balm"*: Sir. 24:20.

p. 370. *"Was Solomon on his birth"*: 2 Sam. 12:24.

p. 370. *St. John Baptist*: See note to page 64.

p. 370. *It was surely fitting then*: Newman repeats the argument on p. 362.

p. 372. *"Dust thou art"*: Gen. 3:19.

p. 372. "she died, as she suffered": St. Alphonsus of Liguori (1696–1787) says 'The death (or dormition) of the Queen of Heaven proved that she was a truly human participant in the common lot of all mankind.' *Glories of Mary* 2, 7.

p. 372. *the tyranny of death*: See in particular Heb. 2:15.

p. 372. *Original sin had not been found in her*: Newman sees the Assumption of Mary as the logical development of the Immaculate Conception.

p. 373. *did she die at Ephesus?*: There is the house of St. John at Ephesus, which is thought to be the place of her death but there is also the Church of the Dormition on Mount Sion which gave rise to another tradition.

p. 374. *if she died, but revived*: Newman floats the argument whether Mary's death was momentary – which is still the subject of debate among theologians.

p. 376. *the Rose of Sharon*: Song of Songs 2:1.

p. 376. *"without which no one shall see God"*: Heb. 12:14.

p. 376. *"Her spirit is sweeter than honey"*: Sir. 24: 19–22.

APPENDIX 1

Distribution of Discourses

The Salvation of the Hearer (1) 2 February 1849

LENT 1849

Neglect of Divine Calls (2) 1st of Lent
God's Will The End of Life (6)

Faith and Private Judgment (10)
Faith and Doubt (11)

PASSIONTIDE 1849

The mystery of Divine Condescension (14)
The Infinitude of the Divine Attributes (15)
Mental Sufferings of Our Lord (16)

Prospects (12) May 31
Men, not Angels (3)----------

Perseverance in Grace (7)
Nature and Grace (8)
Illuminating Grace (9)
Mysteries of Nature and Grace (13)(July)

Purity and Love (4)
Saintliness (5) (July)

On the Fitness of Mary (18)
The Glories of Mary (17)

APPENDIX 2

Textual Variants

Discourses was published in seven editions, the first in 1849 and the last, by Longmans, Green & Co. in 1891. This list contains the *main* variants contained in the first edition, and the corrections made in the seventh. The reading to the left of the square bracket belongs to the seventh edition.

Page Line

frontispiece   – described by Newman in a letter to F. W. Faber on 7 December 1849 'Hated the idea of Mary sitting on the moon "as on the sharp side of a sickle"' *Letters and Diaries* XIII, p. 330.

34   4   what he thought of sin] by resolving to become man

53   21   and became the first Archbishop of Canterbury, but of ... two centuries before him] Augustine I say

63   3   cannot be pure] in some object we must fix our affections, we must find pleasure; and we cannot find pleasure in two objects, as we cannot serve two masters, which are contrary to each other. Much less can a Saint be deficient either in purity or in love for the

63   3   Purity prepares the soul for love, and love confirms the soul in purity] The flame of love

| 90 | 5 | or again, though he may be ignorant or diseased, or feeble-minded, though he have the character of being a tyrant or a profligate] yet, if he be rich |

| 120 | 11 | in spiritual matters ?] Is it your mission only |

| 125 | 9 | is the gift of God] All this is perfectly consistent with our free will, because Holy Church teaches |

| 125 | 20 | divines have devised] various explanations of it, which have severally been received by some, |

| 128 | 20 | or forfeit its perseverance in grace] and are permitted |

| 144 | 30 | and love everlasting] ... Jesus, Joseph, and Mary, I offer you my heart and my soul ! Jesu, Joseph and Mary, assist me in my last agony ! Jesu, Joseph, and Mary, let me breathe out my soul with you in peace !* |

| 151 | 8 | And in explaining this very grave matter, I wish, lest I should be misunderstood, first to say distinctly, that I am merely comparing and contrasting nature and grace one with another in their several characters, and by no means presuming to apply what I shall say of them to actual individuals, or to judge what persons, living or dead, are specimens of the one or of the other. This being my object, I repeat that, contrary to what might be thought] they may easily be mistaken for each other |

| 152 | 19 | One man has no temptation] to hoard; another has no temptation to gluttony and drunkenness; another has no temptation to ill humour; another has no temptation to be ambitious and overbearing. |

*This devotional prayer owed its dissemination to the Confraternity of the *Bona Mors* (=to help people to make a good death) founded by the Jesuits, in Rome in 1648.

152	21	to great advantage] it may be meek, amiable, kind, benevolent, generous, honest, upright and temperate
153	30	and may be surprised, when they grow up, to find how unworthy he is of their respect or affection] as the uneducated, who have seen
162	15	Do you really mean that for an excuse ?] Well, have you improved
179	6	in the Church Established] except he were in a state of gross ignorance,
201	6	as found in Scripture] he would have had no wish at all to be a Scripture Christian
215	4	let us say, for instance, the divinity of our Lord, or the existence of God,] we ought always to reserve to ourselves
227	20	spirit of error] There is a remarkable instance in the Old Testament also, which teaches us at once the incongruity of doubt in those who make a religious profession, and the conduct of the Church in regard to them.
250	23	whereas Mahometanism is only an indigenous religion, and that in certain portions of two continents, with little power or wish to propagate its faith] However, at least in Anglicanism
279	9	or the Nestorian, or the] Jacobite*
283	18	too narrow for your love.] Satan fell by pride; and what was said of old as if of him, may surely now, by way of warning, be applied to all who copy him:

*The monophysite bishops of Syria and Egypt set up an independent Church which followed the teachings of Eutyches, called *Jacobite* after their founder Jocus Baradai, Bishop of Edessa.

– "Beause thy heart is lifted up, and thou hast said, I am God, and sit in the chair of God in the heart of the sea, whereas thou art a man and not God, and hast set thy heart as if it were the heart of God, therefore ... I will bring thee to nothing, and thou shalt not be, and if thou be sought for, thou shalt not be found any more for ever.

283   19   ... But enough – while we thus speak of the Evil One and his victims, let us not forget to look to ourselves. God forbid that, while we preach to others, we ourselves should become castaways!]

298   29   love him;] He (the Son) revealed to our first father in His state of innocence a higher purpose which in the fulness of time was to be accomplished in his descendants.

321   19   FOOTNOTES to De Lugo]

368   28   the Word of God did not merely] come and go; He did not merely pass through her, as He may pass through

369   21   like to choice myrrh'?] Can we set bounds to the holiness of her who was the Mother of the Holiest?

370   22   fullness of her sanctification] But though the grace bestowed upon her was so marvelously great, do not therefore suppose, my brethren, that it excluded her cooperation; she, as we, was on her trial; she, as we, increased in grace; she, as we, merited the increase. Here is another thought leading to the conclusion which I have been drawing. She was not like some inanimate work of the Creator, made beautiful and glorious by the law of its being; she ended, not began, with her full perfection. She had a first grace and a second grace, and she gained the second from the use of the first. She was altogether a moral agent, as others; she

advanced on, as all Saints do, from strength to
strength, from height to height, so that at five years
old she had merited what she had not merited at
her birth, and at thirteen what she had not merited
at five. Well, my brethren, of what was she thought
worthy, when she was thirteen? what did it seem
fitting to confer on that poor child, at an age when
most children have not begun to think of God or
of themselves, or to use the grace He gives them at
all; at an age, when many a Saint, as he is in the
event, is still in the heavy slumber of sin, and is
meriting, not good, but evil at the hands of his just
Judge? It befitteth the sanctity with which she was
by that time beautified, that she should be then
raised even to the dignity of Mother of God. There
is doubtless no measure between human nature and
God's rewards; He allows us to merit what we
cannot claim except from His allowance. He
promises us heaven for our good deeds here, and
under the covenant of that promise we are justly
said to merit it, though heaven is an infinite good
and we are but finite creatures. When, then, I say
that Mary merited to be the Mother of God, I am
speaking of what it was natural and becoming that
God, being God, should grant to the more than
angelical perfection which she by His grace had
obtained. I do not say that she could simply claim,
any more than she did contemplate, the reward
which she received; but allowing this, still consider
how heroical, how transcendental, must have been
that saintliness, for which this prerogative was
God's return. Enoch was taken away[1] from among
the wicked, and we therefore say, Behold a just
man who was too good for the world. Noe was
saved, and saved others, from the flood; and we say
therefore that he earned it by his justice.[2] How
great was Abraham's faith, since it gained him the

[1] Enoch was taken away: Gen. 5:24; Heb. 11:5.
[2] Noe … earned it by his justice: Heb. 11:7.

title of the friend of God![3] How great was the zeal of the Levites,[4] since they merited thereby to be the sacerdotal tribe! How great the love of David, since, for his sake, the kingdom was not taken away from his son when that son fell into idolatry! How great was the innocence of Daniel,[6] since he had it revealed to him in this life that he should persevere to the end! What then the faith, the zeal, the love, the innocence of Mary, since it prepared her after so brief a period to be the Mother of God!

Hence you see, my brethren, that our Lady's glories do not rest simply on her maternity; that prerogative is rather the crown of them: unless she had been 'full of grace', as the Angel speaks, unless she had been predestinated to be the Queen of Saints, unless she had merited more than all men and Angels together, she would not have fitly been exalted to her unspeakable dignity. The feast of the Annunciation, when Gabriel came to her, the Christmas Feast, when Christ was born, is the centre, not the range of her glories; it is the noon of her day, the measure of her beginning and her ending. It recalls our thoughts to suggest to us how pure had been her first rising, and it anticipates for us how transcendent were to be the glories of her setting.

In this Millennium Edition, footnote references have been added to the text from p. 370.

[3] Abraham … the friend of God: 2 Sam. 12:24.

[4] How great was the zeal of the Levites: Exod. 32:26.

[5] How great was the love of David: I Kings 9:5.

[6] How great was the innocence of Daniel: Dan. 12:12–13.